CW00675019

ASQUITH AS WAR LEADER

ASQUITH AS WAR LEADER

GEORGE H. CASSAR

THE HAMBLEDON PRESS
LONDON AND RIO GRANDE

Published by the Hambledon Press 1994

102 Gloucester Avenue, London NW1 8HX (U.K.)
P.O. Box 162, Rio Grande, Ohio 45674 (U.S.A)

ISBN 1 85285 117 1

A description of this book is available from
the British Library and from the Library of Congress

Typeset, printed on acid-free paper and bound in Great
Britain by Cambridge University Press

Contents

Illustrations

(Between pp. 76 and 77)

Illustrations in Text

Maps

Acknowledgements

The author and publisher are grateful to the following for permission to reproduce illustrations: Milton Gendel, pl. 3; The Imperial War Museum, pls 1, 6, 7, 8, 9, 11, 12; The National Portrait Gallery, pls 2, 13, 14.

Preface

This study is not a biography of Herbert Henry Asquith, a monumental task I leave to other pens. Rather it covers the period of his war administration from August 1914 to December 1916. Against a background of cabinet in-fighting and political intrigues, it seeks to examine and analyze Asquith's role in bringing Britain into the war, in shaping strategy and war aims as well as in mobilizing the nation's resources for total war.

When the war broke out in 1914, Asquith was at the pinnacle of his prestige, widely admired as a man of courage and resourcefulness. But he did not remain in power long enough to see final victory consummated. As the gruelling months of the war stretched into years, the accumulation of frustrations and disasters proved fatal to Asquith and he left office on 6 December 1916, with his reputation in ruins. He was widely regarded to have failed in the face of a great challenge and to have clung to office long after his deficiencies were apparent. Since then the general perception of Asquith has not changed significantly.

This investigation departs from the traditional assessment of Asquith and presents a more balanced view of his achievements and failures. That Asquith had serious defects as war leader cannot be denied. Often overlooked, however, is the fact that he faced problems of a size and complexity unforeseen by anyone before the war. Forced to improvise, in the absence of a plan to control the home front, hesitations and mistakes were inevitable. Yet when the overall record is examined thoroughly, Asquith's accomplishments are substantial and impressive. If as war leader he will certainly never rank with Pitt the Elder or Churchill, his reputation should rest safely beyond mediocrity.

It has been said that it is difficult for a person of ordinary attainments to write about a versatile statesman without developing sympathy for his

attitudes and feelings. I have resisted that temptation, though not owing
to any great virtues on my part. Intellectually arrogant and outwardly
cold, Asquith's personality does not easily lend itself to lavish praise or
romantic adulation. Although I have found him to be a fascinating
subject, I have no partisan interest in his career. I have done my best to
present all the evidence, whether or not the truth is to his advantage.
Readers should have no doubt as to where I stand. I believe it is incumbent
on an academic historian to explain or analyze his subject's doings and not
merely chronicle events with an occasional comment. I do not pretend to
have written the last word on Asquith, for there is no such thing as
definitive history.

This book is based on a wide array of departmental records, private
papers and secondary works. The most important archival sources are
Asquith's own papers – shopworn but still indispensable; the cabinet
records; and Asquith's letters to Sylvia Henley, which have only recently
come to light and can be consulted at the Bodleian Library. In addition,
the papers of Asquith's principal colleagues and antagonists were helpful
in shaping this work. It has also been been possible to make reference to the
unpublished diary of Violet Asquith (later Lady Bonham Carter).
Asquith's letters to Venetia Stanley, brilliantly edited by Michael and
Eleanor Brock and published in 1982, are by far the most useful source in
print. Asquith wrote to her once or twice a day until mid May 1915 when
she announced plans to marry Edwin Montagu. The letters are extremely
informative, providing an insight into his daily movements, opinions and
reaction to events. A compulsive letter writer, Asquith then found a new
confidante in Sylvia Henley, Venetia Stanley's sister. Between May 1915
and December 1916 he wrote well over a hundred letters to her. As with
Venetia Stanley, he kept few secrets fom Sylvia Henley.

This study contains a considerable amount of new material, plus some
novelty of interpretation and emphasis. Particular attention was paid to
episodes during Asquith's wartime administration which previous writers
have either ignored or, at best, treated allusively. It is hoped that this
revisionist treatment of Asquith will round out the picture and add to the
understanding of both the man himself and British policy during the first
half of the war.

G. H. C.

Acknowledgements

Work on this book has stretched over five years and it is a pleasure to acknowledge the numerous debts I have incurred. My research could not have been completed without the support of Eastern Michigan University which awarded me two Faculty Research Grants. Another grant to spend part of a summer at Bulmershe College in Reading provided a most agreeable base from which to carry on my work at Oxford. I should like to express my appreciation to the Trustees and to the then Principal, Mr Brian G. Palmer.

As with my preceding studies on the Great War, I am grateful to Her Majesty The Queen for granting me access to the papers of King George V. For guidance in identifying the relevant material and for much forebearance in attending to my requests, I am indebted to Oliver Everett, Librarian, and to the staff of the Royal Archives. Lord Bonham Carter graciously allowed me to see portions of his mother's as yet unpublished diary. Dr Cameron Hazlehurst kindly gave me permission to reproduce excerpts from the Pease (Lord Gainford) papers which he is currently editing. I would also like to thank the staffs of the following institutions for their unfailing courtesy and help: the Bodleian Library, Oxford; the British Library, London; the British Library of Political and Economic Science, London; Cambridge University Library; Churchill College, Cambridge; the County Record Office, Chichester; the House of Lords Record Office, London; the Imperial War Museum; the India Office Library, London; the Liddell Hart Centre for Military Archives, King's College, London; Liverpool Central Library; the National Library of Scotland, Edinburgh; the Public Record Office, London; the Scottish Record Office, Edinburgh; Trinity College Library, Cambridge; the University of Birmingham Library; the University of Buckingham Library, Buckingham; the University of Newcastle upon Tyne Library.

The following individuals, institutions and publishers have kindly given me permission to quote from material to which they own the copyright: Lady Addison; the Beaverbrook Trustees; Lord Bonham Carter; the British Library; the Clerk of the Records, House of Lords; the Earl of Derby; Lord Gainford; Lord Kitchener; Lord Reading; Viscount Simon; the Master and Fellows of Trinity College, Cambridge; the Trustees of the Curzon papers and Lord Scarsdale; the Trustees of the National Library of Scotland; the University of Birmingham; the University of Buckingham, Buckingham. Correspondence in the Royal Archives is cited with the gracious permission of Her Majesty the Queen. Crown copyright material is reproduced by permission of the Controller of Her Majesty's Stationary Office. I also acknowledge my indebtedness to Oxford University Press in respect of quotations from *H. H. Asquith: Letters to Venetia Stanley*, edited by Michael and Eleanor Brock. Although every effort has been made to contact owners of all copyright material, some have proved elusive. I trust that anyone whose copyright has been inadvertently infringed will accept my sincere apologies.

So many people have assisted me at various stages of my work that I am bound to overlook some of them. I must begin by thanking Dr Keith Neilson who set aside his own research to read the entire manuscript. His extensive comments saved me from some embarrassing mistakes and prodded me to rethink some of my conclusions. Dr Richard Goff likewise read the original draft and his advice was instrumental in the re-organization of the early chapters. I received helpful suggestions and criticisms from Dr Roger Long who scrutinized portions of the manuscript. I am indebted to my former department chairman, Dr Ira Wheatley, not only for his invaluable editorial advice but also for his unfailing encouragement. Mr Paul Mackaill graciously helped me to track down several elusive documents at the Public Record Office. Dr Michael Brock gave me the benefit of his considerable knowledge of Asquith, in addition to supplying me with extracts from Lady Bonham Carter's diary. As usual I imposed terribly on my friend, Dr Robert Ward, who drew the maps with the assistance of Miss Kazumi Segawa. Special thanks are also due to Miss Nancy Snyder and the history secretarial staff at Eastern Michigan University for help in a number of ways. Others who assisted me with my research were: Dr Fred Anderson, Dr Hank Abbott, Dr Donald Briggs, Dr Robert Citino, Dr Margaret Crouch, Mr David DeSilvio, Dr Sidney Gendin, Dr Louis Gimelli, Mr John Grigg, Dr Robin Higham, Dr Michael Homel, Professor Michael Howard, Dr Michael Reed, Mr James Roberts, Mrs Mary Meilinger, Mr J. F. Russell, Dr Janice Terry, Dr Jiu-Hwa Upshur. Finally I should like to thank my wife for proofreading the manuscript with scrupulous care as well as for her patience while this work was in progress.

The responsibility for the interpretations and any remaining errors, needless to say, rests with me alone.

By the Same Author

The French and the Dardanelles: A Study of Failure in the Conduct of War (London: Allen and Unwin, 1971)

Kitchener: Architect of Victory (London: Kimber, 1977)

The Tragedy of Sir John French (Cranbury, NJ: Associated University Presses, 1985)

Beyond Courage: The Canadians at the Second Battle of Ypres (Ottawa: Oberon, 1985)

A Survey of Western Civilization, co-authored with Richard Goff, Anthony Esler, James Holoka and James Waltz (New York: McGraw-Hill, 1994). Second edition.

World History, co-authored with Jiu-Hwa Upshur, Janice Terry, James Holoka and Richard Goff (St Paul, MN: West, 1991). Second edition will come out in 1995.

To the memory of my brother
Stephen Cassar
(1949–1985)

Abbreviations

BEF	British Expeditionary Force
CGS	Chief of the General Staff
CIGS	Chief of the Imperial General Staff
C-in-C	Commander-in-Chief
CID	Committee of Imperial Defence
FM	Field Marshal
FO	Foreign Office
GHQ	General Headquarters
GOC	General Officer Commanding
GQG	Grand Quartier-Général
GHQ	General Headquarters
K	Kitchener
PM	Prime Minister
PRO	Public Record Office – the location of the Cabinet (CAB) Records, Foreign Office (FO) Records, Ministry of Munitions (MUN) Records and War Office (WO) Records
S of S	Secretary of State
WO	War Office

Chapter 1

Asquith before the July Crisis of 1914

Herbert Henry Asquith was born in Morley, near Leeds, on 12 September 1852, the second son of a Nonconformist wool spinner and weaver.[1] When he was only eight his father died, following a cricket accident,and in 1863 he and his elder brother went to live with an uncle in London. There young Herbert attended the City of London School and at the age of seventeen was awarded a classical scholarship to the prestigious Balliol College, Oxford, the first student from his relatively unknown academic institution to have achieved such an honour. Without taxing himself unduly at Oxford, he collected all the major academic honours, winning a first in Greats, the highly-prized Craven Sholarship and a fellowship of his college. Asquith's future as a don was assured but he declined to pursue an academic career. Instead he had his heart set on becoming a lawyer which, for a young man without wealth or social position, promised security and status. Accordingly, at the end of 1875 he left Oxford for London to study under Charles Bowen, one of the most distinguished nineteenth-century legal minds.

While still a struggling barrister, Asquith married the daughter of a Manchester physician named Helen Melland, whom he had met when he was eighteen and she only fifteen. The couple moved into a spacious, early nineteenth-century house in Hampstead and settled down to a happy, placid life which was soon enlivened by the arrival of their first child, Raymond, in 1878 and a second son, Herbert, three years later. A third son, Arthur, was born in 1883 and he was followed by Helen Violet (better known as Violet) in 1887 and, lastly, Cyril in 1890. All the children were gifted in their own way, especially Raymond, whose academic record at Oxford surpassed even that of his father. During these early years at the bar, Asquith supplemented his fairly erratic earnings by marking Oxford and Cambridge Certificate examination papers, giving lectures to law students and contributing articles to the *Economist* and the *Spectator*.

By the time Asquith reached his early thirties his career prospects had improved considerably and he was able to earn a good living entirely from his professional work. It now was practicable for him to entertain political ambitions. He had become interested in Liberal politics, essentially through his friendship with R. B. Haldane, a portly Scotsman and fellow barrister, and in 1886 he became a Member of Parliament for East Fife.

In 1891 Asquith suffered a shattering personal loss. His wife was taken ill and died while they were on holiday on the Isle of Arran, leaving him with five children. A gentle and kind woman, Helen Asquith had few interests besides her family and preferred the quiet home life. Her death occurred at a time when Asquith aspired to move into wider social circles and represented a significant and symbolic break with the past. Emotionally drained but free to change his life's pattern and indulge his social proclivities, he left Hampstead and settled the children in a comfortable house near Dorking, leaving them in the care of a series of housekeepers, nannies and nursery maids.

Now a widower, Asquith began to court Margaret Tennant, whom he married in 1894 to the astonishment and dismay of his more sober colleagues. Margaret, or Margot as she was called, came from a rich upper middle-class family and had practically nothing in common with Asquith's first wife. She was a fashion leader, well read and outgoing, who enjoyed being the centre of attention, and a witty conversationalist who sought the the company of the great and famous. She preferred the drama of high events and could never adapt herself to play the role of a soothing confidante or quiet supporting wife. Margot was passionate in her loyalties and animosities and her unrestrained candour, at times amounting to rudeness, lost her as many friends as she made. Highly ambitious for Asquith, she brought him into the centre of a more glittering social world and encouraged his tendency to live beyond his means. Since she preferred her husband's middle name, Herbert became Henry to his family and friends. Of the five children Margot carried, only two survived infancy – Elizabeth born in 1897 and Anthony in 1902.

Asquith's rapid rise in the political ranks had begun before his marriage to Margot. In 1892, with only six years of parliamentary experience, he was appointed Home Secretary in the last Gladstone cabinet. He continued in the post during Rosebery's administration and won a deserved reputation as a gifted administrator and parliamentary debater. But his term ended in 1895 when the Liberal Party, which was hopelessly in disarray, suffered a humiliating defeat in the general election. Asquith, returned as Member for East Fife, found himself in Opposition.

Asquith remained out of office for eleven years, during which there were times when the Liberal Party, leaderless and further divided by the Boer War, seemed condemned to perpetual political exile. Deprived of his ministerial salary, and with seven children to raise and a lavish and expensive life-style to maintain, Asquith broke with established custom and returned to the Bar, where his practice brought him a substantial income. His legal work and the distractions caused by his new wife frequently kept him from the House of Commons. Some of his friends feared he was tiring of politics.

Ironically it was the Conservatives who reenergized Asquith and helped reunite the Liberal Party when they embarked on reforming measures which antagonized powerful and articulate sections of the public. The most controversial of these was the campaign for tariff reform. Asquith made numerous speeches around the country challenging the government's protectionist stand with reams of facts, not the least being convincing evidence that it would lead to an increase in the price of food. Confronted with the loss of public confidence, the Conservative government resigned early in December 1905. The Liberals went to the voters with a programme that included bold social change and returned to power with a massive majority. Asquith became Chancellor of the Exchequer under Sir Henry Campbell-Bannerman. Charting a new direction, the heirs of Gladstone broke with some of the fundamental principles of nineteenth-century Liberal ideology.

A cautious and able financier, Asquith trimmed armament expenditures, reallocating the savings to reduce the national debt and to promote social welfare. He introduced three budgets during his term of office, the last one after he became Prime Minister. His second budget differentiated between earned and unearned income and his third established provisions for old age pensions. A leading exponent of free trade, Asquith withstood great pressure for imperial preference during a conference with dominion Prime Ministers in 1907.

In February 1908 Campbell-Bannerman suffered a second heart attack which shattered his health and forced his resignation two months later. Asquith had no rivals in the Liberal Party and his appointment as Prime Minister was a foregone conclusion. Fifty-five years of age when he moved to 10 Downing Street, he held on to his office for eight years and eight months during which he presided over the transformation of British society. Asquith's real strength as Prime Minister was not in providing dynamic leadership but in his tactful and effective coordination of day-to-day business.

Although lukewarm about state intervention, Asquith continued and extended the policy of social reform begun by his predecessor. A parliamentary committee's investigation of poverty in Britain led to several important pieces of legislation. One act set up labour exchanges to assist able-bodied workers find jobs suited to their skill. Another fixed minimum wages in the 'sweated' industries. These measures were followed by the controversial Lloyd George budget of 1909 which sought to raise additional revenue almost exclusively from the wealthy classes. The budget cleared the House of Commons after a bruising debate but was easily rejected by the Tory-dominated Lords.

In theory the Lords could veto any bill but it had generally been accepted for more than 200 years that finance was a special function of the Commons. That the Lords had in recent months thrown out a number of Liberal reform measures made their veto of the budget all the more intolerable. Asquith at once put the issue before the electorate, only to see his party lose its clear majority. To stay in office he had to rely on the Labour and Irish Nationalist MPs.

As soon as the Lloyd George budget was enacted, Asquith took over the conduct of the constitutional struggle, determined to reduce the Lords to second-class status. After a second general election (which did not materially alter the relative strength of the parties in the Commons), he announced that the King had agreed to create enough new pro-reform peers to overcome the opposition. Under this threat, the Lords capitulated. The resulting Parliament Bill of 1911 provided that measures passed by the Commons in three successive sessions within a two-year period, even if rejected by the Lords, would become law.

Asquith was now free to turn again to the question of social reform. The crowning achievement of the period came with the National Insurance Act of 1911 which provided unemployment benefits and health care. Although after 1912 the pace of reform slowed down, the Liberal Party had taken giant steps along the road to the welfare state.

Asquith was far too immersed in his domestic programme to devote much time to external affairs. Foreign policy was largely controlled by Sir Edward Grey, who frequently consulted Asquith and decided with him what items should be brought before the cabinet. Asquith read the important telegrams and if he had suggestions to make did so but without trying to influence policy. Asquith was not one to override expert knowledge.

Believing in continuity of foreign policy, Grey had accepted the Entente with France and supported France against Germany. During the

Moroccan Crisis in 1906 he authorized the British general staff to enter into confidential discussions with its French counterpart to arrange common action in the event of Britain joining France in a continental war.[2] Grey withheld these developments from the cabinet to avoid criticism by the more radical ministers. He also kept Asquith in the dark, at least until June 1908.[3]

Asquith never felt comfortable with the military exchanges which he feared might encourage France to base its war plans on the assumption that Britain aid was certain. Britain's role in Europe was to promote peace, not to become entangled in disputes between potentially warring powers. Still Asquith was no pacifist or anti-imperialist and understood that vital national interests had to be defended. Despite a natural preference for France, he was by no means anti-German and, in fact, would have welcomed improved relations with Berlin. But he recognized that a rapprochment with Germany was impossible as long as the Kaiser was bent on rivalling British sea-power.

Asquith had come to understand that if he broke off the joint staff talks he would antagonize the French and disrupt the Entente Cordiale. Partly because the military talks were already in progess, and partly because of his faith in Grey, he allowed the *pourparlers* to continue, providing they were pursued prudently and with a full understanding on both sides of the absence of any military obligation. At no time did the Prime Minister consider the staff discussions as committing Britain to assist France in any circumstances.[4] Rather they were intended to concert Britain's military preparations with those of France if the two powers were together involved in a war with Germany.

Asquith, following the example of his predecessor, did not bring the issue of joint planning to the cabinet's attention. Only a handful of ministers were notified. Asquith knew his colleagues intimately and, like Grey, was aware that the military talks would be fiercely opposed by a large section of the cabinet. Not yet secure in his position, he was eager to avoid a Liberal split over what seemed a hypothetical issue.[5]

It was perhaps unrealistic of Asquith to think that the cabinet could be excluded indefinitely from the most important secret in defence planning. The day of reckoning came during the Agadir Crisis in 1911. The radical ministers were furious both at not being consulted and at the news of the military conversations which they suspected had committed the government to a policy of intervention. Asquith took great pains to explain the non-binding nature of the talks and ultimately agreed that future staff contacts with a foreign power would not be held without the prior sanction of the cabinet.[6]

The confrontation ended in a stalemate and it was left to a future crisis to force a decision. Asquith was able to deflate the opposition but at the expense of his expert's efforts to develop a national policy. The joint-planning process continued until the outbreak of war in 1914 but, as always, with the provision that any decision to intervene in a Franco-German conflict or to send the British Expeditionary Force (BEF) to the Continent was subject to the approval of the cabinet of the day.

Given the Prime Minister's determination to avoid military pledges, British defence authorities were compelled to emphasise the role of the navy, instead of the army, in planning for a future war against Germany. They perceived that the land campaigns would essentially be fought, on the Entente's side, by the Russians and the French. Britain's main contribution to the war effort would consist of providing its allies with money and supplies, keeping its own sea lanes open and subjecting its enemies to a blockade which would help ensure their eventual defeat. This concept of a strategy of limited liability was unrealistic but was not discarded until after the European war broke out in 1914.[7]

The failure to define a coherent national strategy could have been averted if there had existed a central authority to oversee and implement defence policy. The Committee of Imperial Defence (CID) had been established in 1903 as the cabinet's advisory and consultative body on matters relating to home and imperial defence. Presided over by the Prime Minister, its purpose was not to formulate strategy but to ascertain facts and supply technical information.[8] Although the CID's terms of reference severely circumscribed its power and influence, it did carry out much useful work.

Asquith was generally lax about defence issues during the early years of his administration. He never allowed the CID to develop into an agency powerful enough to influence strategic planning. He regarded it with indifference and only on occasions set it to work on central issues. Even when he did so, he failed to impose its findings on the War Office and Admiralty. At meetings, which he called only infrequently, he seldom used his authority to bring matters to a head. Asquith never initiated, responding only when proposals were placed before him. Even then he gave no lead and refused to be pushed into adopting measures before the necessity for them was apparent.

After the Agadir Crisis, Asquith adopted a more positive attitude and accelerated the pace of defensive preparations. By August 1914 his administration had, mainly through the agency of the CID, taken far-reaching steps to strengthen the nation's security. Two invasion inquiries, one in 1908 and the other in 1914, confirmed the Admiralty's claim that it could protect Britain from an outside attack.[9] The army, though small, was ready to fight in a continental war.[10] Every detail had been worked out to transport the troops to their assigned place in the French line. The modernization of the navy was complete and numerically it enjoyed a significant preponderence over any rival.[11] A national air force was established in 1912.[12] Imperial conferences and discussions fostered unity and coordination in military affairs between Britain and the dominions.[13] A War Book was prepared, setting out in minute detail the action to be taken by every department the moment war threatened.[14] Finally a war risk insurance scheme was adopted and arrangements were made for the state to take control of the railways on the outbreak of war.[15]

These measures were certainly adequate for a brief and limited war but they fell far short for the kind of conflict that developed in the closing weeks of 1914. What was missing when the nation found itself compelled to wage a modern war? Despite a decade of international tension and excitement, the authorities had taken no steps to build a continental-size army or an ordnance industry sufficient to meet the requirements of such a force. They neglected to set up a permanent central planning staff to coordinate the work of the naval and military departments. A reasoned strategy was lacking, as was a structure of supreme command to oversee operations in the opening days. On top of this, there were no arrangements to convert the nation's industries to war purposes. Nothing had been done to regulate manpower so as to prevent skilled men, who would be more valuable in industry or transport, from enlisting in the services. Indeed there was no mechanism to study, let alone deal with, the nature of the national effort required in total war.

Given the near unanimous belief of the experts that any future war would be brief, Asquith can scarcely be held accountable for many of the deficiencies that arose. There were certain problems, however, which could have been foreseen and dealt with through better planning and greater allocation of financial resources. Matters relating to national security were not a high priority for Asquith and his colleagues. The Liberal cabinet was largely composed of men unequivocally committed to the ideas of social reform and welfare spending. It viewed defence costs in peacetime as a necessary evil, to be kept as low as possible consistent with a reasonable margin of safety. Generally the military policy of the Asquith government between 1908 and 1914 was defensive and non-provocative.[16]

On the domestic scene, the years immediately before 1914 were extremely troublesome for Asquith. Controversy was caused by the suffragettes' sensational campaign to gain voting rights for women, the militancy of industrial strikers and the disestablishment of the Anglican

Church in Wales. But the greatest challenge to Asquith and his government came from Ireland.[17]

The only way Asquith had assured himself of the support of the Irish Nationalists during Lloyd George's budget fight was to accept their demand for a free Ireland. To that end his government drafted a Home Rule Bill in 1912. The Lords rejected it, but they could only delay it for two years. In 1914 the bill would become law, as the Commons would have passed it in three successive sessions.

The issue was complicated by a division among the Irish themselves. The inhabitants of Ulster in Northern Ireland were predominately Protestant and their region industrial in contrast to the rural, Catholic south. They objected vehemently to inclusion in an autonomous Ireland in which they would be a minority. John Redmond, who led the Irish Nationalists, was equally determined to accept nothing less than a united, self-governing Ireland. Asquith, needing the votes of the Irish Nationalists to stay in power, was reluctant to make any changes in the bill for Ulster's sake.

As the Home Rule Bill passed through the various stages of its transition to the statute book, the situation in Ireland steadily deteriorated. Ulster loyalists found a champion in Sir Edward Carson, a brilliant lawyer who proposed to organize a provisional government in case Home Rule became law. Ulstermen began to arm and drill. The Conservative Party, traditionally opposed to Home Rule and intent on exploiting the crisis to bring down the Liberal regime, encouraged them to armed rebellion. Bonar Law, who had replaced Balfour as the Tory leader, told Carson that he would support any action the latter deemed necessary, whether constitutional or not. In the south Nationalists recruited volunteers to answer the private army in Ulster. Violence flared out. In March 1914 Asquith, before moving the third reading of the Home Rule Bill, included a provision that would allow the Ulster counties to opt out of Home Rule for a period of six years. The measure failed to mollify Carson and was seen as too great a concession by Redmond. Then, in March 1914, the government decided on a show of force, only to be embarrassed when sixty officers of the Third Cavalry Brigade, stationed at the Curragh, announced they would resign their commissions unless given a written assurance that they would not be ordered to march against the Protestant loyalists. The incident at the Curragh was settled by negotiation after the Secretary for War, Jack Seely, unwisely acceded to the officers' demands. The agreement restricted the government's freedom of action in Ireland and was quickly repudiated. In these circumstances, Seely resigned and Asquith personally assumed control of the War Office.[18]

The question of Home Rule, which had bedevilled successive British governments for half a century, appeared to be passing beyond the ability of Asquith and his colleagues to resolve. The problem, inherently difficult, was exacerbated by the irresponsibility of the Unionists and by the weakness and inaction of the Liberal cabinet. Asquith, in fact, was at his worst. Until forced by events or by the extremism of his opponents, he avoided irrevocable commitments and was content simply to pursue a 'wait and see' attitude. He might have been able to check resistance in the early stages by firmness and by making clear that the best he could do was to deliver Ireland without Ulster. The absence of the will to act encouraged both sides to play for higher stakes.

As the threat of civil war hung over Ireland, inter-party discussions continued throughout the summer. Asquith hoped to narrow the differences separating the two sides and in July he believed he had succeeded. At his request the King summoned a formal conference at Buckingham Palace. It opened on 21 July and broke up three days later over irreconcilable differences.[19] At this point events in Ireland were eclipsed by the spectre of a general European war.

COOL STUFF.

The Tabloid. "YOU CAN MAKE IT AS HOT FOR ME AS YOU LIKE, I SHALL *NOT* DISSOLVE."

[The above is prospective. No sensible person desires a dissolution during the present crisis abroad.]

Chapter 2

The Advent of War

The period of relative diplomatic tranquility following the Second Balkan War ended suddenly on 28 June 1914 when a young Bosnian fanatic assassinated the Archduke Franz Ferdinand, heir apparent to the Hapsburg throne, in Sarajevo. The gravity of the latest crisis in the Balkans was not immediately apparent to Grey, still less to Asquith. In a letter to Venetia Stanley, a beautiful young lady with whom he was in love, Asquith mentions the incident only in passing and it is clear that he did not see it as leading to any war involving Britain.[1] There was no reason why he should. Recent years had witnessed a number of conflicts in the Balkans, none of which required the direct intervention of any of the great powers. Asquith counted on the medium of diplomacy to resolve a crisis should one develop. Europe, however, had run out of diplomatic miracles and on 24 July Vienna fired off a harsh ultimatum to Belgrade. Grey conveyed the news to the cabinet which met in mid afternoon that day. The cabinet discussed the Austrian action and its possible consequences. Asquith's letter to Venetia Stanley, written after the meeting, revealed the following:

> Austria has sent a bullying and humiliating ultimatum to Servia, who cannot possibly comply with it, and demanded an answer within 48 hours – failing which she will march. This means, almost inevitably, that Russia will come on the scene in defence of Servia & in defiance of Austria; & if so, it is difficult both for Germany and France to refrain from lending a hand to one side or the other. So that we are within measurable, or imaginable, distance of a real Armageddon.[2]

Asquith's attention in recent weeks had been riveted on the Ulster crisis and to a lesser extent on the next general election, scheduled for the summer of 1915, which he hoped the Liberals would be able to win on a record of peace abroad and reform at home. The evidence suggests that he

did not know until 24 July that anything really dangerous was afoot in
Europe. Once informed he backed Grey's efforts to restrain Austria
through Germany in order to prevent, or at least minimize, the conflict.[3]
The cabinet was not, at this stage, unduly alarmed at the prospect of
Europe in disarray. Asquith and his ministers fully expected to remain
aloof from any European war. 'Happily', Asquith observed, 'there seems
to be no reason why we should be anything more than spectators.'[4] Grey
remained optimistic that a peaceful solution could yet be found. He
wanted to organize a conference at which the powers with no direct
interest in the dispute – Great Britain, France, Germany and Italy –
might seek to come between Austria and Russia.[5] The cabinet endorsed
the proposal.

Serbia's reply on 25 July to the Austrian ultimatum was unexpectedly
conciliatory and produced the impression in many quarters that there was
no longer sufficient cause for war. Asquith, however, suspected that
Vienna would not be satisfied. He expressed his sentiments to Venetia
Stanley:

> The news this morning is that Servia has capitulated on the main points, but it is very
> doubtful if any reservations will be accepted by Austria, who is resolved upon a
> complete & final humiliation. The curious thing is that on many, if not most, of the
> points Austria has a good & Servia a very bad case. But the Austrians are quite the
> stupidest people in Europe ... and there is a brutality about their mode of procedure
> which will make most people think that it is a case of a big power wantonly bullying a
> little one. Anyhow it is the most dangerous situation of the last 40 years ...[6]

Except on occasions, Asquith continued to take a detached view of the
impending hostilities on the Continent. It was not that he was unconcerned, only that Irish affairs absorbed practically all his time and
energy. Initially he welcomed the menacing developments in Europe as
possibly having 'the good effect of throwing into the background the lurid
picture of "civil war" in Ulster'.[7]

During the final days of peace Ireland still competed for attention. On
26 July British troops marching through Dublin were subjected to a shower
of stones and bottles by an angry crowd of Nationalist supporters. The
soldiers turned and opened fire on them, killing three and injuring thirty-
eight.[8] The incident drew Ireland closer to civil war and reinforced
Asquith's belief that the Balkan crisis would eventually come to his rescue.
Curiously enough, his hunch paid off. With the prospects of peace
unrelievedly grim, Bonar Law suggested on 30 July that, in the interest of
preserving national unity, the government ought to postpone the second
reading of the Home Rule Amending Bill.[9] Asquith gratefully accepted.
Ulster ceased to occupy centre stage at last.

A history of the events leading to Britain's entry in the Great War would be incomplete without reference to the looming presence of Ireland. It remains open to question whether Asquith's obsession with Ulster was an obstacle to his playing a more active and constructive role in shaping British policy during the period that preceded Russia's mobilization. On the other hand, it would be grotesque to suggest that he helped rig up a war to escape from the uncertainty of his domestic difficulties. As already mentioned, Asquith anticipated that a continental war might alleviate his Irish troubles. There is, however, a sharp difference between deliberately contriving to subsume a lesser crisis into a greater one and perceiving unwilled events abroad as having a salutary effect on current domestic problems. Facing the likelihood of a civil war, Asquith can hardly be reproached if he found a diversion across the Channel tantalizingly convenient.

The cabinet session on the afternoon of 27 July was devoted almost exclusively to a discussion of foreign policy.[10] Asquith could not tell for sure, any more than his colleagues, in which direction events would flow if negotiations failed and Austria attacked Serbia. The main issue centred around whether Britain would fight to protect France against a German invasion. The British had a mandate to uphold Belgian neutrality but they were under no formal obligation to assist France, much less Russia. A number of ministers, Morley and Burns being the most vocal, warned they would resign if a decision was taken to intervene in any European war. There was as yet no hint that the cabinet was likely to adopt such a course. Nevertheless, on Churchill's initiative, it approved of the Admiralty's order to postpone the dispersal of the First and Second Fleets after a trial mobilization. It further agreed to consider Britain's precise commitments to Belgium at the next meeting.[11]

In the evening word arrived from Berlin that the Kaiser's government had rejected the idea of a four-power conference, claiming that it would be rigged against Austria.[12] It seemed to Asquith that the Germans were interested less in finding a formula to preserve the peace than in allowing Austria a free hand. He regarded Austria as determined to crush Serbia and he expected little result from the Austro-Russian talks which had finally gotten under way. His fears were quickly confirmed. On 28 July Austria declared war on Serbia and the dialogue between Vienna and St Petersburg collapsed.

From the outset Grey had relied on a working partnership with Germany, as in the Balkan Crisis of 1912–13, to resolve the dispute. He was outraged when he discovered that the Germans had deceived him and had in fact done little, if anything, to bring Austria to the bargaining table.

Once Grey realized that general war could not be averted, he favoured active British participation on the side of France in order to uphold the balance of power and make possible the destruction of German militarism. His decision was not influenced by the expected German invasion of Belgium. It was believed unlikely that the Belgians would fight to defend their neutrality or appeal to the British for help. By contrast the French could be counted on to put up a fight. Therefore, when the cabinet could not be persuaded to stand by France, Grey capitalized on the Belgian issue because of its potential impact on British public opinion. The defence of Belgian neutrality, which until 1 August had occupied a secondary place in cabinet deliberations, became the moral and legal pretext for war.

Asquith enjoyed a long-standing friendship with his Foreign Secretary, in whom he had absolute faith. He knew that Grey would leave no stone unturned to preserve the peace and, throughout the crisis, was content to leave the direction of foreign policy in his hands. The Irish question was such a pressing issue that he had no time to exercise indirect executive authority as was his habit. Interestingly enough, he failed to realize at first that there was a divergence of views between him and Grey over what constituted Britain's interests. That was not apparent because Grey, not the most communicative of men, made no effort to move ahead of either cabinet or public opinion or to force the issue in any way. The assertion by some historians that Grey and Asquith were of one mind at the start of the crisis and contrived to bring a united cabinet into the war is not borne out by the facts.

Asquith had never abandoned hope of establishing a friendly bilateral relationship between Britain and Germany. Between 1912 and 1914 Anglo-German relations had in fact improved, as Germany came to recognize that it could not surpass or match British naval power. The two countries had cooperated in limiting the scope of the Balkan wars in 1912–13 and this growing cordiality made Asquith more optimistic about the chances of an Anglo-German entente.

Asquith was much less inclined than Grey to come to the rescue of France, since he did not share his Foreign Secretary's assumption about the nature of the German threat. The Prime Minister appreciated that the conversations between the military staffs of Britain and France had established the nature and sphere of British action, should the two countries become involved in a war against Germany. Nothing was committed to paper but, even if a pledge existed in unwritten form, there was no suggestion that Britain was bound to fight alongside France in all circumstances. It was quite fully recognized on both sides of the Channel that Britain would not automatically intervene in any Franco-German conflict. If the French declared war on Germany, either to regain Alsace and Lorraine or to support Russia as a result of a conflict breaking out in East Europe, there was scant likelihood they would receive British assistance. All along the British assumed that, when the time came, they would be free to intervene or stand aside as they chose. Asquith could not see how the equilibrium in Europe would be appreciably changed by a German victory. Britain had remained neutral in the Franco-Prussian War of 1870. Why could it not do so now?

Nor was the Prime Minister partial towards the ultra-conservative regime in Brussels that was thought to be pro-German. If war erupted, he expected Germany to violate Belgian neutrality, at least to some extent, in order to attack France. As one of the guarantors of the Treaty of London (1839), Great Britain had the right to intervene if Belgian independence was threatened. Asquith had no illusions about the sanctity of international agreements, well aware that when the moment was at hand signatory powers acted in accordance with their own interests. He recognized that the treaty of 1839 would be used as a *casus belli* only if Britain found it expedient to help Belgium against an invader.

Asquith had greater reasons than most men to dread war. He had four sons of military age. His impulse to stay out of the impending continental conflict was understandable but based on wishful thinking, not practical politics. A practitioner of *Realpolitik* would have instantly identified the nation's security with the European balance of power, the preservation of France and the prevention of German hegemony. Asquith was too shrewd and pragmatic to allow emotion to prevail for any length of time. Between 30 July and 2 August he moved reluctantly but inexorably towards a recognition that intervention was inevitable.

Tuesday, 28 July was a hectic day for the Prime Minister. London was in a high state of excitement. It was widely assumed that the current conflict would escalate to include most, if not all, of the major powers. Cloistered in his office, Asquith received a succession of high-level political and military officials and discussed with them the latest international developments and problems of defence. One such visitor was Winston Churchill, First Lord of the Admiralty. Churchill wanted the First Fleet, then anchored off the Isle of Wight in the English Channel, to proceed to its war station at Scapa Flow in Scottish waters. There, he felt, it would be secure against any sudden German attack and at the same time it would serve notice that Britain was prepared, if necessary, to fight. Churchill later recalled: 'He looked at me with a hard stare and gave a sort of a grunt. I did not require anything else.'[13]

Like the First Lord, Captain Maurice Hankey, Secretary of the

Committee of Imperial Defence (CID), worried lest the country be caught off guard. He went to 10 Downing Street and urged Asquith to put into effect the precautionary stage of the War Book. Asquith was reluctant to act on Hankey's suggestion, persuaded that it could be interpreted as provocative and so apt to prejudice whatever chances remained of averting general war.[14]

That night Asquith dined with a small party of friends, then played a rubber or two of bridge. After his guests left he went over to see Grey, who was staying with Lord Haldane at 28 Queen Anne's Gate, and sat and talked with them until 1 a.m. Grey regarded the international situation as very grave but not hopeless. The three men tossed about various proposals as they tried to 'discover bridges and outlets'. Writing to Venetia Stanley, Asquith complained of the conflicting pressures on his government:

> It is one of the ironies of the case that we, being the only power who has made so much as a constructive suggestion in the direction of peace, are blamed by both Germany & Russia for causing the outbreak of war. Germany says: 'If you say you will be neutral, France & Russia wouldn't dare to fight'; and Russia says: 'If you boldly declare that you will side with us, Germany and Austria will at once draw in their horns'. Neither of course is true.[15]

The cabinet on 29 July considered the implications of a European war on British interests and obligations. Asquith had no doubt that the Germans would invade France via Belgium on the outbreak of hostilities.[16] He assumed that, with the French unable or unwilling to live up to their responsibilities in the face of German aggression against their homeland, any Belgian appeal for help would be addressed solely to London.

Asquith's prediction that the German army's invasion route lay through Belgium met a mixed reaction. The majority in the cabinet either disagreed or were unsure. On the other hand, a few well-informed ministers, perhaps four or five, concurred with Asquith. They knew that he was not engaged in wild speculation but that he reflected the considered and unanimous opinion of British military experts. If there was an issue on which unanimity existed in the cabinet it was an aversion to entanglements in a European conflict. With Asquith guiding the discussion, the cabinet decided to follow the precedent set by the Gladstone government in 1870. In so doing it acknowledged that the responsibility to uphold the treaty of 1839 rested with all the signatory powers collectively, not on any single one individually.[17] In case Belgian neutrality was violated, this interpretation left the Asquith government free to act, as the nation's interests dictated. A general discussion of the European crisis followed. Churchill thought that if Europe's monarchs assembled together they might avert the impending calamity. Asquith was less optimistic, observing that the animosity and differences between the Austrian and Russian emperors would be an insurmountable obstacle.[18]

Grey's immediate concern was to contain the Austro-Serbian conflict, which meant keeping the French, Russians and Germans from intervening. He wanted to continue to exert a moderating influence simultaneously on Vienna and St Petersburg. Another tactic he employed was to refuse to make pledges in advance or to state categorically how Britain would react to a European war. Grey claimed that uncertainty about London's intentions would strengthen his hand in negotiations with the quarrelling parties. To do otherwise would encourage France and Russia to be more intransigent while destroying his credibility with Germany and Austria. Asquith seconded Grey, convinced that 'the worst thing we could do would be to announce to the world … that in *no circumstances* would we intervene'.[19] There was general concurrence with that approach.[20] At Churchill's strong urging, the cabinet also decided to inaugurate defensive preparations as laid down in the War Book.[21]

No one in the cabinet had the slightest idea of how to set in motion the precautionary stage of the War Book. After the ministers dispersed Asquith asked his private secretary to contact Hankey. Located at the United Service Club, Hankey hurried to 10 Downing Street. He explained that constitutionally it was up to the Secretary of State for War to inform the Army Council which in turn would, through its secretary, communicate with the departments concerned.

This confusion resulted from the absence of a permanent civilian head at the War Office. Currently the Prime Minister was holding down the War Office, which he had assumed on a temporary basis the previous March when Jack Seely resigned for mishandling the Curragh Incident. Asquith, as chairman of the CID, was acquainted with the broad outline of the War Book but he lacked familiarity with the specific steps to implement its operation. After he took over the seals of the War Office, he had been unable to form strong links with the officials and General Staff because his duties as Prime Minister rarely permitted him to leave 10 Downing Street. Thus he knew little of the details of the carefully concerted war arrangements and the part assigned to the War Office in the overall scheme. As Asquith was being briefed on what the precautionary measures entailed, he learned, much to his dismay, that the Special Service Section of the Territorial Force had been automatically mobilized for certain guard duties. Such a move, he feared, might stir up anti-British feelings in Germany and extinguish the last glimmer of hope for a peaceful settlement. Asquith contacted the War Office at once in an attempt to

cancel the order, only to find out it was too late.[22] The British War Book
was unfolding at its own predetermined pace. To Venetia Stanley, Asquith
wrote somewhat fatuously: 'Rather interesting because it enables one to
realize what are the first steps in an actual war.'[23]

During the interval before the next cabinet session, Berlin made a
clumsy bid to keep Britain from intervening should the conflict on the
Continent expand. The Germans promised that if Britain remained
neutral they would, in the event of a victorious war, respect the territorial
integrity of France. But they would not extend this pledge to cover French
colonies or guarantee Belgian neutrality.[24] Their telegram amounted to an
admission that Germany intended to strike at France, probably through
Belgium. Grey was angry at the naivety and cynicism expressed in the
German proposals, which he dismissed outright. Before noon on Thursday,
30 July, he showed Asquith the dispatch conveying his answer. Because of
the time factor, they decided jointly to send it at once without waiting for
the approval of the cabinet which they considered certain.[25] As expected,
the cabinet quickly endorsed Grey's rebuff to Berlin when it convened at
11 a.m. on 31 July. News of the Russian mobilization did not prompt any
change in British policy. Asquith, among others, expressed concern about
the likely fate of Belgium but none of them suggested that a violation of its
neutrality would be sufficient grounds for a *casus belli*.[26]

After the cabinet adjourned Asquith joined Churchill and Lord
Kitchener, who was on annual leave from his post in Egypt, for lunch at
Admiralty House. He listened attentively to what the latter said. The
element in the current European dispute that most troubled Kitchener
was the likelihood of a German attack on France. He did not have a high
regard for France's military establishment and doubted that the French
could repel the Germans without British help. Kitchener, Asquith reported
to his young female friend, 'is very strong that if we don't back up France
when she is in real danger, we shall never be regarded or exercise real
power again'.[27] Churchill interjected periodically to express his views but
Asquith, apart from an occasional nod, contributed little to the discussion.

Asquith was far less circumspect in a conversation that day with Dr
Randall Davidson, the Archbishop of Canterbury. He explained that
Britain was the only power with diplomatic weight, insofar as it had no
binding commitments or outstanding quarrels with any of the potential
belligerents. By keeping Europe in suspense about Britain's intentions,
Grey hoped to deter both sides from adopting extreme measures. The
Prime Minister was convinced that all the powers, Germany in particular,
were averse to war but that they were trapped by treaty obligations. He
thought that the Serbs had behaved badly and deserved a 'thorough

thrashing' but he feared that Russia would not allow Serbia to be humiliated. He anticipated that the next few days would determine whether the conflict could be localized. Asquith begged the archbishop to use his influence to head off anti-war demonstrations, lest they mislead Europe into believing that British public opinion was committed irretrievably to neutrality.[28]

Asquith's distress mounted as Britain's ability to influence events diminished. Late on the evening of 31 July he had an opportunity to assist the mediation process actively. Sir William Tyrrell, Grey's private secretary, came to 10 Downing Street with a message from the Kaiser offering to restrain Austria if Britain could persuade Russia to delay mobilization. Asquith sat down with Tyrrell and his own secretaries and drafted a direct personal plea from George V to his cousin, the Tsar. He then called a taxi and, along with Tyrrell, drove to Buckingham Palace, arriving at 1.30 a.m. Asquith has left an account of what followed:

> The poor King was hauled out of his bed, and one of my strangest experiences ... was sitting with him – he in a brown dressing gown over his night shirt and with copious signs of having been aroused from his first 'beauty sleep' – while I read the message & the proposed answer.[29]

The appeal came too late. At noon on 1 August Germany's ultimatum to Russia ran out and both braced themselves for a collision. As soon as Germany and Russia unsheathed their swords, war between Germany and France became inescapable. If German troops swept through Belgium and into France could Britain remain neutral? For centuries it had been a cardinal principle of British policy that no great power should control the Channel ports or dominate the Continent. Moreover, there existed arrangements with the French. Quite apart from the informal military conversations, a naval agreement had been concluded in 1912. By its terms the Royal Navy pledged to protect the northern French coast while French warships were patrolling the Mediterranean.[30] Would Britain stand aside and allow a German fleet to enter the English Channel to shell unprotected French ports?

One thing was certain at this time. The country was overwhelmingly opposed to intervention. By Asquith's own estimate 'a good three-quarters of our party in the H. of Commons are for absolute non-interference at any price'.[31] Liberals were traditionally protagonists of peace. Their interests centred on social issues and they were inclined towards isolationism. The Radicals – the left wing of the party – in particular disliked being associated with the repressive Tsarist regime and, if the choice had been theirs, would have accepted Germany's military hegemony, partly because it would have led to the predominance of Germany's social and cultural values in Europe.

The Prime Minister's ingenuity was tested when the cabinet met on the morning of 1 August. Unfortunately the records for this important meeting are incomplete. Asquith communicated the results to the King in person not, as was his habit, in writing. Moreover Pease, an ever-faithful diarist, was away in the north of England. His second-hand account is sketchy at best. The cabinet had been united in supporting Grey's diplomacy throughout July and it was only when it came to a decision as to whether Britain should participate in the war that divisions occurred. At the meeting Grey tried to move his colleagues toward defining the conditions under which Britain would become involved. He was joined by the First Lord, whose request for authorization to call out the fleet reserves and make final preparations for war was rejected. According to Asquith, 'Winston occupied at least half the time' in the course of which he was 'very bellicose'.[32]

Morley and Simon demanded that an immediate statement be issued that in no circumstances would Britain be drawn into the European conflict. Grey threatened to resign if any such declaration was adopted. Asquith tactfully avoided bringing the matter to a vote. The neutralists, however, gained an important victory when their motion to prevent the dispatch of the British Expeditionary Force was carried with no dissension and practically no discussion.[33]

Asquith was reluctant to support involvement and, even at this late hour, clung to the slim hope that diplomacy would find a way out of the nightmare. He knew that any premature declaration on his part, either for or against war, would break up the government and split his party. His immediate concern was to prevent a rupture at all costs. Consequently, he steered a careful course, allowing decisions to be made only in circumstances where general agreement was assured. He could no more than anyone else assess all the forces at work or foresee the outcome of the crisis. He simply used all his experiences and authority to keep his options open, hoping that events would somehow clarify the issue one way or the other. The proceedings that day had been tense, sometimes acrimonious, but the ministers parted in 'fairly amicable mood' and consented to convene again at 11 a.m. the following day, on Sunday – an unprecedented event.[34]

Evening brought the news that Germany had declared war on Russia. Asquith was in conclave with Grey, Haldane and Crewe at 10 Downing Street when Churchill barged in and declared his intention to mobilize the fleet at once. Asquith, who felt bound by the cabinet's standing decision, said nothing but Churchill gathered from his expression that he approved. The First Lord walked back to the Admiralty and issued the order.[35]

Asquith was having breakfast on Sunday morning, 2 August, when Prince Lichnowsky, the German Ambassador, called unexpectedly and requested an interview. Agitated and with tears in his eyes, Lichnowsky made an emotional plea to win him over to neutrality. He implored the Prime Minister to recognize that Germany, with its army forced to fight on two fronts, was far more likely to be annihilated than France. Asquith replied that Britain had no wish to intervene and would not do so unless there was a violation of Belgian territory or the German navy attacked the northern coast of France.[36]

Shortly before 11 a.m. Asquith received a note from the Conservative leaders, Bonar Law and Lord Lansdowne, offering the unconditional support of their party for any measures the government might be obliged to take in resisting German aggression.[37] The Conservatives wanted the government to aid France even if Belgian neutrality remained inviolate. They were troubled by a rumour that Grey, on the basis of faulty information, had misrepresented the attitude of the Opposition to justify British inaction on French appeals for help.[38] The Bonar Law – Lansdowne note on 2 August was clearly intended as a statement of Conservative policy. It never implied, as has sometimes been suggested, a willingness to cooperate with the Liberals in a coalition government. In fact relations between the two parties were so bad that it would have been difficult for either side to work harmoniously with the other.

Asquith read the Conservative statement in the morning cabinet session and laid it aside without comment.[39] Did it, as the Conservatives maintained in 1914, enable Asquith to use the threat of coalition to overcome recalcitrant colleagues? Four years later Asquith, in reaction to an article in the *National Review*, categorically denied that the Conservative pledge had any influence on the decisions then being contemplated.[40] As will be evident, my own reconstruction favours the recent popular interpretation – that it was the march of external events, not Tory pressure, that tipped the scales in the cabinet in favour of war.[41]

Sunday, 2 August, was the turning-point in the cabinet debate over whether Britain should enter the war. There were two meetings that day, one from 11 a.m. to 2 p.m. and the other from 6.30 p.m. to 8 p.m. Grey opened the deliberations at 11 a.m. by claiming that Britain had 'both moral obligations of honour and substantial obligations of policy in taking sides with France'. (For Grey honour and interest went hand-in-hand.)[42] Grey's proposal was unacceptable to all but a few of his colleagues and, in the uproar that ensued, the ministry was brought to the brink of dissolution.

The ministers were essentially divided into three camps. The peace party included Morley, Burns, Beauchamp, Simon and Hobhouse. They were determined that Britain, unless attacked, should remain neutral in all circumstances. Allied with the neutralists but slightly less pacific were Lloyd George and Harcourt. At the other extreme Grey, Churchill and Haldane were solid for intervention, convinced that the nation's security demanded that it support its Entente partners and uphold the balance of power. Between the two committed factions stood a large number of waverers whose chief spokesmen were Samuel, Crewe and McKenna. All would fight if Germany threatened Britain's security but would not do so simply to defend France.[43]

Asquith's own position was irrational. He told his colleagues that if their intransigence caused Grey to resign he would leave as well. Historians have assumed that Asquith's warning meant that he stood firmly with his Foreign Secretary over the nation's duty to honour its unwritten pledge to France. In fact he did so on the basis of friendship rather than conviction. It is true that Asquith's opinion had shifted during the last twenty-four hours but differences remained between them. The Prime Minister held a much narrower view of what constituted British interests. He realized that Britain not only had a long-standing friendship with France, but stood to benefit if the latter remained a great power. This did not mean that Britain was obliged to aid France either on land or sea. He saw only two instances requiring British intervention: if there was a flagrant attempt to destroy the balance of power such as an invasion of Belgium; or if the German navy used the Channel to wage war against the French.[44] By limiting the conditions for involvement, Asquith hoped to avoid Armageddon. In doing so, he occupied a place that was nearer to the waverers than to Grey.

While the cabinet balked at going as far as Grey had urged, it could hardly ignore the balance of power concept which underlay his thinking. Samuel, attempting to reconcile the two extreme groups, advanced a formula that made British intervention contingent on German use of the Channel as a hostile base. His proposal was accepted by nearly everyone, including Lloyd George and Harcourt. Burns, however, indicated he would resign. He refused to be a party to a resolution which he considered to be provocative and tantamount to a declaration of war against Germany. Asquith, with some difficulty, persuaded him to return for the evening meeting, reasoning that circumstances might have changed by then.[45] The shift in the cabinet's mood was the first significant breach in the neutralists' case, but it did not commit Britain to war. In fact, Germany offered not to conduct naval operations in the Channel if the British government would refrain from intervening.[46]

After the cabinet rose, Asquith invited Pease to remain for lunch. The Prime Minister was racked with anxiety. He held little hope that Burns would stay on and feared that other resignations would follow. Turning to Pease he said: 'Jack, we have turned many awkward corners but I don't see how we are to get around this.' At lunch they were joined by Montagu, Bonham Carter, Birrell, Margot and several of the Asquith children. There was a forced atmosphere of cheerfulness. The conversation centred on Dryden.[47] Asquith enjoyed such small informal gatherings which eased the tensions in his mind and recharged his batteries for the next round.

By mid afternoon Asquith was back at his office and drafting a reply to the Conservative leaders. In it he revealed that the government intended to give France only limited support; he was rather vague on the question of intervention if Belgium were invaded. Government action, he went on to say, would be determined by the following considerations:

(1) Our long standing and intimate friendship with France.
(2) It is a British interest that France should not be crushed as a great power.
(3) Both the fact that France has concentrated practically their whole naval power in the Mediterranean, and our own interests, require that we should not allow Germany to use the North Sea or the Channel with her fleet for hostile operations against the coast or shipping of France.
(4) Our treaty obligations (whatever their proper construction) in regard to the neutrality and the independence of Belgium.

Asquith did not believe that (1) and (2) imposed upon the country the obligation to actively assist either by land or sea. He noted that the government opposed the immediate dispatch of the Expeditionary Force to France on the grounds that it would serve no useful purpose. As for (3), Grey had been instructed to tell Cambon (the French Ambassador) that Britain would not tolerate German naval activity in the Channel or against the French coast. Regarding (4), Asquith accepted Gladstone's interpretation of the treaty of 1839 as correctly defining Britain's obligations. He concluded: 'It is right, therefore, before deciding whether any and what action on our part is necessary to know what are the circumstances and conditions of any German interference with Belgian territory.'[48]

The memo was, to say the least, confusing, and it seemed to the Tory chieftains that the Prime Minister was looking for excuses to avoid committing the country to war. They arranged to see him the next morning. Unknown to them, Asquith had not tried to represent his own position but that of the cabinet. In a letter to Venetia Stanley, written at the same time, the Prime Minister was more specific about Belgium: 'We have obligations to Belgium to prevent her being utilized and absorbed by Germany.'[49] There is no doubt that he himself regarded German interference with Belgian independence as a justifiable *casus belli*.

The question of Belgian neutrality loomed larger as the day wore on. Even the neutralists could not ignore that Britain had pledged to defend Belgium against attack. For them, and for others as well, there was uncertainty over what a violation of neutrality really amounted to. Some, like Lloyd George, insisted that they would not be a party to intervention if it were simply a case of German troops marching through the southernmost tip of Belgium.[50]

To further the search for unity a number of small conferences, at which the membership varied, were held in the private homes of ministers preceding and following the cabinet debates on 2 August. As in the morning cabinet session, Samuel played a pivotal role in the informal gatherings. He devised a second formula, making British intervention dependent on a major infringement of Belgian territory, and secured the assent of all the ministers present save for one or two.[51]

Asquith did not attend any of the sessions held outside the cabinet that day. There was nothing secretive about them and from several sources (Pease, Samuel and possibly Crewe) he was kept abreast of the fluctuation of opinion. Of particular interest to him was the attitude of Lloyd George. Occupying an eminent place in the Liberal Party and in the government, the little Welshman had been closely associated throughout his political career with the more pacifist elements in the country. If he took it upon himself to organize and direct the thinking of the dissenters, there was no telling how many he could take with him out of the government. There were, however, grounds for optimism. While Lloyd George had sought to avoid or limit British involvement in a European war, no evidence existed that he had adopted an extreme position. 'What is Lloyd George going to do?' Asquith asked Samuel, who had called in to report what had transpired at the unofficial gatherings. Samuel replied that, as Lloyd George's contributions to the discussions had been somewhat muted, he could not be certain but thought that 'the Belgian issue might decide the matter for almost all the Cabinet'.[52]

When the ministers resumed their deliberations in the cabinet at 6.30 p.m., they knew that German troops had crossed into Luxembourg and it was obvious that an invasion of Belgium was only a few hours away. This development solidified ministerial consensus. In response to Grey's appeal for a strong stand, the cabinet agreed that a 'substantial violation' of Belgian neutrality would be unacceptable. The resolution displeased several members of the peace party. Burns remained adamant about resigning and, while Asquith pleaded with him to reconsider, Morley interrupted to say that he feared he too must go.[53]

At the end of a long day of frenetic activity, Asquith dined with Crewe and several other guests. Afterwards he retired with Crewe to another room. A record of what was said has not been preserved. They were probably discussing the day's events and it may be, judging from what occurred next, that they had all but concluded that Britain could not achieve its objectives without total commitment to the Entente. While they were talking, Grey and Haldane suddenly appeared. Grey was scheduled to make a speech before the House of Commons the following afternoon and he was uncertain of how the Prime Minister would react to a minor infringement of Belgian neutrality. He wanted Asquith to declare himself unequivocally for intervention, regardless of what Germany did in Belgium. Along with Haldane, he pleaded the interventionists' case. Britain had to act to uphold the balance of power, otherwise it would eventually find itself isolated and overwhelmed by a German-dominated Europe. Asquith had heard the same argument before. This time he agreed with it. Apparently so did Crewe.[54]

Haldane then observed that since the Prime Minister would be fully occupied on 3 August he would be happy to go to the War Office and implement the necessary preparations for general mobilization. Asquith approved of the suggestion and wrote out a note authorizing Haldane to mobilize the army.[55] This occurred an hour or two before a dispatch arrived announcing that Germany had presented an ultimatum to Brussels, demanding free passage for its armies across Belgian territory.[56]

At 10.30 a.m. on 3 August Asquith received Bonar Law and Lansdowne at 10 Downing Street. He had much on his mind and, with the cabinet due to meet in three-quarters of an hour, he was anxious not to prolong the conversation. The Opposition leaders asserted that honour and interest alike dictated that Britain take immediate action to prevent the destruction of France. They were certain that, sooner or later, Britain would be drawn into the war and urged Asquith not to dishonour the nation by waiting until events themselves forced the government's hand. Asquith made it clear that he stood with Grey and Churchill and that the note of the previous day did not represent his true sentiments. But he was unwilling to issue a declaration such as called for by the Tory leaders. He indicated that Belgium had until 7 o'clock that morning to meet

Germany's demands. 'Is that not reason for acting at once?' his political adversaries inquired. Asquith replied that the government did not know whether the information was correct but in any case it had agreed, for political and military reasons, to keep the Expeditionary Force at home. Bonar Law and Lansdowne went away with the impression that Asquith was playing for time, waiting until the Germans invaded Belgium when he could carry an undivided cabinet into the struggle.[57]

The cabinet meeting opened at 11.15 a.m. with a discussion of the principal points and form of Grey's statement to the Commons set for 3 o'clock that afternoon. The Prime Minister followed with an announcement that he had received the resignations of Burns, Morley and Simon. As he paused, Beauchamp leaned over the table and asked to be included as well. 'That is four out of our number', said the Prime Minister, 'and others have found it difficult to remain.'[58] Such signs of division, he continued, left him three options. The first, which he would have adopted in normal circumstances, was to submit his resignation. But he could not persuade himself that the other party was led by, or even contained, men competent to direct the nation's affairs at a time of crisis. The second was to enter into an alliance with the Opposition. This too he dismissed on the grounds that he found it no less objectionable to serve beside Conservatives than hand over to them sole power. His remaining course was to fill the vacancies with members of his own party.[59] By effectively eliminating the first two possibilities, Asquith served notice of his determination to continue in office and to uphold Grey's policy. The cabinet adjourned without taking any formal decisions.[60]

More than offsetting the defections was Lloyd George's shift towards intervention. All along he had resisted pressure from zealous radicals that he resign, for he abhorred the idea of surrendering his position as Asquith's chief lieutenant and returning to the backbenches. He found a face-saving formula to remain as Britain's treaty obligations to Belgium enabled him to cloak his final choice in moral terms.[61] Other wavering ministers, reluctant to throw away their careers and jeopardize the viability of the government, followed the line of least resistance and, like Lloyd George, clutched belatedly to the Belgian pledge.

Once the centre of interest moved from eastern Europe and France to the threat to Belgium, opinion in the press and country swung sharply in favour of intervention. Huge pro-war crowds jubilantly thronged Whitehall and Parliament Square. The multitude was so dense that no car could drive through it. As Asquith and his party started to walk towards the House of Commons they were surrounded by large cheering crowds waving Union Jacks. Slowly they made their way across behind a phalanx of heaving, shoving policemen. The Commons was so crowded that chairs had to be placed in the aisles, a sight that Asquith had never seen before in his twenty-eight years as a parliamentarian. Asquith reached his seat as Grey was glancing at his notes and making last-minute changes.

A hush fell over the chamber when Grey rose to give his address. His one hour speech, delivered with evident emotion but calmly and free of rhetorical flourishes, warned that Britain's interest and honour would suffer if it allowed Germany to trample on Belgian neutrality and did not come to the aid of France.[62] Grey's words had an electrifying effect. The wild cheers and resounding applause confirmed that he had carried nearly all his listeners. Pledges of support came instantly from Bonar Law and John Redmond, both of whom spoke on behalf of their parties. Asquith was generally pleased with his Foreign Secretary's speech, describing it as 'almost conversational in tone & with some of his usual ragged ends; but extraordinarily well reasoned & tactful & really *cogent*'.[63]

Unlike the wild jubilation in the Commons, the atmosphere was subdued when the ministers gathered at 6 p.m. The last danger to cabinet unity had been removed in mid afternoon by the news that the Belgians intended to oppose the German army's advance through their territory.[64] Addressing a telegram to the British Sovereign, King Albert of Belgium pleaded for 'diplomatic intervention' to safeguard the neutrality of his country.[65] Asquith made reference to the telegram in the cabinet but did not comment on it. In truth anything that he might have said would have been superfluous. It was understood by everyone that any diplomatic initiative at this stage would be brushed aside by the Kaiser's government. Only by waging war could Britain effectively defend Belgium. Henceforth there was no more dissension, no need to resort to legal technicalities or moral obligations to France to justify intervention.

Asquith invited his colleagues to consider a reply to Germany's demand for the right to move troops through Belgium. There was now less pressure to act hurriedly. The time-limit set by Berlin had expired early in the morning and everyone assumed that German forces had already crossed the Belgian frontier. Some ministers expressed fears that the government's demands might provoke Germany into launching a surprise attack against Britain. The upshot was that the cabinet decided to postpone its response until the following day. The delay would enable further progress to be made in putting the nation on a war footing.[66]

The Prime Minister and his wife held a small dinner-party in the evening. Jack Pease, who was present, described what occurred:

He [Asquith] was much as usual. After dinner we played bridge. When the ladies had gone, he told me privately that he believed in a German rapprochement ... He had believed in Germany's friendship and had played up to it, but in the case of this war, they had not only precipitated but intended it, and were not working for peace, or anxious for it.[67]

Throughout the day Asquith had bent his efforts to pull together his fraying ministry. He contacted each of the four 'peccant' ministers to induce them to stay on. He appealed to their sense of duty, invoked old friendships and recalled past political battles in which they had stood together. In the case of the rising and ambitious Simon, Asquith hinted that if he remained he would soon be promoted. By Tuesday morning, 4 August, Asquith had won over Simon and Beauchamp, but Morley and Burns proved unyielding.[68] At no time did Asquith show the slightest trace of bitterness over the resignations of his two close associates, regarding their decision as a matter of conscience. He continued to see them socially and to invite them occasionally for lunch or dinner.

The cabinet session on the morning of 4 August heard the news that German troops had entered Belgium and intended, if necessary, to force a passage in order to attack France. That simplified matters. Grey was authorized to seek assurances from Berlin that the Germans would withdraw their demands on Belgium and respect its neutrality.[69] The ultimatum was due to expire at midnight German time, or 11 p.m. Greenwich Mean Time. It was unrealistic to think that Germany would recall its armies. But the cabinet was reluctant to openly commit the country to the horrors of a European war and preferred to back into it, to act as if it was responding to events over which it had no control. The hours went by with no reply from Berlin.

In the afternoon Asquith went across to the House of Commons. He read out Germany's ultimatum to Belgium and his government's response to it. There was a great wave of cheering as Asquith concluded his speech and walked slowly to the Bar. There he turned and, facing the Speaker, handed over a royal proclamation calling out the army reserves.[70]

Asquith was drained and in low spirits when he left the Commons. He viewed the onset of war with sadness and despair. He knew that a large part of the nation's manhood would be sent to fight and that thousands would die. He went for a drive as he often did when he wanted solitude to think things out.[71] If, as seems possible, his mind flashed back to the events following the assassination of the Austrian Archduke, he may have thought over the main points which had converted him from an isolationist to an interventionist.

At the outset Asquith was determined to remain neutral: a war in the

Balkans was of no concern to Britain. Throughout July his government acted not as a member of one of the opposing power blocs but rather as a mediator between the two. Until the last possible moment it had refused either to give guarantees to France or to threaten Germany. By keeping its freedom of action, the Asquith government could say to both parties that Great Britain's attitude would depend on the way they behaved. Asquith shared Grey's view that the most practical way to defuse the crisis was to persuade Germany to restrain Austria. He desired a rapprochement with Germany and believed that the feeling was reciprocal. He was convinced that Germany wanted peace and that the warmonger in this case was Austria. Asquith clung to the misconception that German leaders possessed a wide range of options and that they alone could decide the question of war and peace. He felt deceived when advised that Austria was in fact being pushed by Germany. His attitude hardened but, until the evening of 2 August, he remained associated with those who sought to limit Britain's continental commitments. Judging the issue according to the criterion of British interests, as he saw them, he needed to be satisfied that the current crisis required intervention. It was Grey and Haldane who finally convinced him that Germany's designs had left Britain with no alternative but to assist France and preserve the balance of power.

By the time Asquith returned to 10 Downing Street he had no doubts that both he and Grey had acted properly and that the decisions they had steered the cabinet into adopting had been correct. In his mind the real villains were the Germans, who had the ability but not the desire to prevent the dispute from escalating.

In the evening Asquith sat in the cabinet room waiting, without hope, for a positive response from Berlin. He was with Grey, Crewe and Haldane; other ministers drifted in as the night wore on. They were joined, as the last minutes of peace ticked away, by Margot. All showed in their faces the strain of the last few days. They spoke in hushed tones in between puffs on their cigarettes and occasionally stole glances at the clock. The windows at 10 Downing Street had been opened to the warm night air and noises could be heard from the immense and ever-growing crowd around Whitehall and the Mall. Suddenly, above the murmur of voices, the deep chimes of Big Ben boomed out the first stroke of the hour (11 p.m.). Great Britain was at war. The crowd cheered and broke out in a chorus of 'God Save the King'. By contrast gloom hung heavily in the cabinet room. Asquith starred blankly, 'with darkened face and dropped jowl', while Grey sat with his head between his hands.[72]

The British had not fought against a European power since the end of the Crimean War in 1856. Now, for the first time since the defeat of

Napoleon at Waterloo, they faced an enemy powerful enough to threaten their island kingdom. Asquith had endured many trials in the past. He had no doubts that he could deal with what lay ahead.

Chapter 3

Coming to Grips with the War

The transition from peace to war rescued Asquith from the brink of political disaster and lifted him to the pinnacle of his reputation. The press, both Liberal and Conservative, praised him effusively for the way he had handled the crisis, for his admirable answers and statements in the Commons, and for his speech justifying British intervention. He was regarded as a man of commanding ability and high integrity, adept at resolving differences and capable of decisive action. The editor of the Liberal *Nation*, H. W. Massingham, occasionally a harsh critic of Asquith in the pre-war period, wrote: 'If you want a tonic ... have a look at the Prime Minister. Unquestionably Mr Asquith is carrying his burden with great courage; with a steady, massive, self-reliant, and unswerving confidence which is in itself a moral asset of no slight value.'[1] This statement was typical of the high esteem felt for Asquith during the early months of the conflict.

By August 1914 Asquith had been Prime Minister for six and a half years. He was a month away from his sixty-second birthday. He enjoyed being Prime Minister and, in his view, there was no one better suited for the post. In appearance he resembled the Dickensian character of Micawber. He was of medium height with broad shoulders, unathletic, and heavier than he ought have been. His heavy, jowled face was dominated by a broad forehead from which his wavy white hair was swept back. He had wide-set prominent eyes, a large nose and full mouth, and his pale complexion had acquired a reddish hue in later life.[2] He moved slowly and ponderously and if he needed to look behind him turned his whole body and not just his head. Photographs of Asquith at this time show him unfashionably dressed and appearing rather shaggy. His clothes look baggy and carelessly worn and his hair has been allowed to grow too long. A recent biographer wrote that as he advanced in middle age 'he assumed that look of a dignified, benevolent slovenliness, which was how he was to be best remembered'.[3]

Asquith was a pragmatist and showed no interest in abstract ideas. He clung only to concepts that could be given practical effect.[4] He had a prodigious memory and his incisive mind enabled him to grasp an intricate problem and master the details with less effort than most men. He had a barrister's talent for analysis and deduction, forming judgments only after he had carefully researched his subject, sorted the facts, weighed the evidence and consulted the experts.[5] He lacked a sense of adventure and was attracted more by established practice than by innovation.[6] As long as cabinet business preceded along lines which he set, he was content to regulate input and, if necessary, to arbitrate between members. Churchill later recalled that Asquith presided at cabinet meetings with the air of a great magistrate, saying little during the discussion and merely summing up after all views had been presented.[7] Asquith did not regard it as part of his duty to resolve issues under discussion or suggest new directions in policy.[8] He relied on others in the cabinet to provide the dynamism and creative spark.[9]

The war did not bring any change in Asquith's leadership style. He was imperturbable and allowed nothing to fluster or excite him.[10] Patience, which he regarded as the first requisite of statesmanship, was a constant weapon in his armoury. In handling contentious issues he preferred to bide his time, to keep the conflicting parties talking and to allow them to blow off steam and cool down, while he kept the atmosphere as dispassionate as possible and men's mind open until a favourable opportunity for compromise emerged. This forbearance and skill as a mediator had preserved the unity of the government and the party in peacetime during a period of political strife. They were less efficacious in a war in which events moved quickly.

As a parliamentarian Asquith was unsurpassed in his day. His unique ascendancy over the House of Commons was based as much on his integrity and intellect as on his debating skills. A master of the English language, he used words with precision and economy, never using two where one would do.[11] His oratory was cool and restrained, persuasive but without the sparkle to rouse his audience.[12] Asquith's appeal was to reason, never to emotion. He took only a few minutes to prepare his speeches, which he usually delivered without benefit of notes.[13] One one occasion he appeared at a public gathering to defend the government's Licensing Bill.[14] He spoke eloquently for an hour, reinforcing his case with reams of facts and statistics. At the end, an admiring woman spectator came up to the platform and inquired whether she might have his notes as a souvenir.

He obliged and handed her a scrap of paper on which three words were scrawled: 'Too many pubs'.

Asquith adhered to high standards of political behaviour and was even judged by soldiers, who habitually distrust politicians, as a man of frankness and integrity.[15] He was above political chicanery and intrigue and paid no attention to reports of plots against him. Although somewhat of an intellectual snob, he was unable to harbour grudges or feel resentment on personal grounds. If on rare occasions he expressed anger towards an individual it was invariably over an issue of policy.[16]

Asquith's lack of charisma, his impersonal and unemotional approach to public affairs, was a barrier to his becoming a really popular figure – not that he aspired to be one. On the contrary, the thought of courting the press was something that never entered his mind. He never drew attention to his own achievements and, in fact, had an aversion to any form of self-advertisement.[17] It is hard to find a Prime Minister in recent memory, indeed in this century, with less appreciation than Asquith of the need to conciliate the press. Although it is debatable that he paid no heed to the press, as some of his apologists have maintained, it is safe to say that he was indifferent to what journalists wrote about him. He intensely disliked interviews and rarely agreed to sit through one. He made no effort to answer his press critics, let alone try to influence them in his favour.[18] There was an element of arrogance behind his reticence. People could believe what they chose, but he would not stoop to play up to the press. The Prime Minister, according to a journalist who knew him well, would 'as soon have thought of consulting his footman about policy as of making terms with the Northcliffs and Beaverbrooks of the Press'.[19] Asquith's neglect of the press made him particularly vulnerable to criticism when the tide of war took an unfavourable turn.

Asquith's public and private life did not undergo any significant change during the first nine months of the conflict. Parliamentary business occupied much less of his time but he had to deal with a new range of problems. His day was crowded with cabinet and committee meetings, conferences of one kind or another and ceaseless interviews with colleagues and foreign dignitaries. From Monday to Friday his work day began after breakfast and ended between 7 and 8 p.m. When the House of Commons was not sitting it was his custom to retreat to his club, the Athenaeum, late in the afternoon, read a novel or write letters, and after a cup of tea emerge refreshed and ready to return to his duties. There were occasionally informal parties, or 'scratch parties' as he called them, followed by a game of bridge. Because Asquith could not absent himself from Downing Street for more than a few days at a time, long holidays, such as he had enjoyed before the war, became impossible.[20] On weekends he tried to get away to Walmer Castle, near Deal in Kent, which had been placed at his disposal by Lord Beauchamp, Lord Warden of the Cinque Ports.[21]

Asquith did not live and breathe politics in all his waking hours. At the end of the day or on weekends he would cast aside the cares of his office and seek diversion at the theatre, at bridge, on the golf links and in literary pursuits, preferably in the company of attractive and clever women. During the war his fast-paced social life, combined with his ability to maintain an air of unruffled benignity and calm in the midst of crises, were misrepresented again and again as lethargy and indolence. As Lord Beaverbrook and others observed, Asquith's mental acuity enabled him to get through an immense amount of work, leaving him ample time to devote to personal interests.[22]

The Prime Minister's bibulous evenings fostered the same impression of irresponsibility. Fond of the good life, rich foods and cigars, he was also self-indulgent in his consumption of alcohol (especially whisky and brandy) which increased with his growing responsibilites. His detractors charged that he was seldom sober and mockingly referred to him as 'Squiff'. Apart from comments attributed to critics or rivals, there is sufficient evidence from well-informed Liberal and impartial sources to dispel any doubts about Asquith's drinking.[23] During the committee stage of the Parliament Bill in April 1911 Asquith was so drunk that he was barely able to speak and only the traditional discretion of the House averted a scandal.[24] Incidents of this kind were invariably embellished as they were circulated and lent credence to his reputation for insobriety. But if at times his consumption of alcohol left him a little unsteady, he always remained alert and in full command of what he intended to say.[25]

Less well known, but potentially more damaging to his political career, was his romantic attachment to Venetia Stanley, daughter of Lord Sheffield, a prominent Liberal. Venetia, who was a close friend of Asquith's daughter, Violet, and as such a constant visitor to Downing Street, was an intelligent, mature and alluring young women in her mid twenties.[26] What for Asquith began as a flirtatious affair blossomed into a grand passion. Were they lovers? More than one contemporary believed they were having an affair.[27] Our other source of information is Asquith's voluminous correspondence with Venetia, all, or nearly all, of which she preserved. In a number of letters there are tantalizing hints of a possible liaison and several are couched in slightly coy terms with oblique references to some mutual secret. But all the evidence is circumstantial and on reviewing it I am inclined to accept the Brocks' conclusion that Asquith did not consummate his love.[28]

Asquith suffered from loneliness and felt a compulsive need to unburden himself to a female confidante outside of marriage. Before Venetia there had been a number of women with whom he had carried on an extensive correspondence, sometimes concurrently, and after her there were to be a succession of others, among them her older sister, Sylvia Henley. Asquith usually knew where to draw the line between friendship and love but with Venetia he was unable to exert such control. His love for her dominated his thoughts and, as his problems mounted, his emotional dependence on her increased in equal measure. He wrote to her once, often twice and occasionally three times a day, and usually did so during debates in the Commons or at cabinet meetings. In these letters Asquith did not confine himself merely to passionate declarations and tender endearments. He analyzed political events and expressed his opinion of the men with whom he had to deal, besides flattering Venetia by revealing state secrets and soliciting her advice on appointments or other governmental matters. He saw her frequently as well. He invited her for lunch or met her at her home on Mansfield Street, and regularly took her out for a drive on Friday afternoons. When parliament was in recess Asquith occasionally spent weekends at one of Lord Sheffield's country houses, enjoying more of Venetia's company during long walks or while supervising her reading and quizzing her on the classics. Their relationship developed practically unnoticed, disguised as it was by Venetia's existing friendship with Violet, and by Asquith's well-known reputation for enjoying feminine company.

Asquith was not the first, and certainly not the last, Prime Minister who required an emotional outlet which he could not obtain from marriage and family. The Brocks claim that Asquith profited from his early association with Venetia (their correspondence began in mid 1912), observing that it improved his morale and helped reduce his dependence on alcohol.[29] That is undoubtedly true but by 1914 his feelings for her had become too intense and the affair was interfering increasingly with his work. Moreover, since Asquith confided everything to Venetia he put the nation's security at risk. Serious damage might have followed if his young friend had been indiscreet, or had even one of his letters fallen into the wrong hands. The fact that nothing happened does not exculpate Asquith. He could not guarantee that there would be no leaks and by imparting classified information he was violating the Official Secrets Act which his own government had passed in 1911.

The picture of Asquith that emerges is that of a man who on the one hand was reserved, serious, solitary and exclusive, and on the other passionate, frivolous and somewhat irresponsible. The contrasting elements in his personality reflected the age in which he lived and make him a representative figure. As as a political analyst once said about Disraeli, one may justly say of Asquith: 'A great premier must add the vivacity of an idle man to the assiduity of a very laborious one'. [30]

Asquith presided over one of the most talented cabinets in British history. Over the years he had manipulated and tamed a collection of strong-willed, ambitious and unruly men.[31] He had developed intimate friendships with Haldane and Grey and his relationships with the others were relaxed and friendly. Although at times there were tensions and rivalries among some of his ministers, the atmosphere in the cabinet was, on the whole, reasonably harmonious and there was nothing like the factionalism, jealously and animosity which was to have such a destructive effect in the next administration. Asquith was readily accessible to his ministers, listened to their advice or complaints, and conceded to them wide discretion in managing their departments. What set him apart from most Prime Ministers was his unfailing loyalty and generosity. He was as quick to shield his colleagues from the criticisms resulting from their own misjudgments as he was to disguise his personal intervention in the government's accomplishment, assigning the credit to others. These were virtues which earned him the respect and gratitude of his associates, but they were hardly calculated to raise his standing with the public.[32]

For the amusement of Venetia Stanley, Asquith drew up a list on 26 February 1915 in which he ranked the members of his cabinet. He placed Crewe at the very top, followed by Grey and McKenna. Below them and on an equal footing were Lloyd George, Churchill and Kitchener. The most striking feature of the list was the classification of Haldane. A close associate of Asquith before the war, his judgment was rated only as about average (ninth among cabinet ministers).[33]

Asquith had a tendency, as in Crewe's case, to overvalue the aptitude of men stamped in his own mold. A politician who served with Crewe described him as a 'replica of the P. M. with more charm and less ability'.[34] Secretary of State for India since 1910, Crewe was respected for his industry, high sense of honour, quiet sagacity and unerring ability to pinpoint the strongest and weakest links in an argument. As a peer with no public following he was no threat to Asquith. This may also explain why Asquith consulted him more frequently than anyone else.[35]

Grey's primacy in determining foreign policy in August 1914 was unquestioned as he approached his ninth year in office. A tall, reticent and punctilious Northumbrian squire, he exhibited at the Foreign Office a judicious understanding of European affairs and a suppleness and tact in diplomacy. He had little influence in the cabinet on matters outside his field, for it was recognized that he had no boldness or imagination. He had his share of critics, within his own party as well as outside, but no one doubted his sincerity, integrity, courage and steadfastness. Although he was a conscientious public servant, he was not overly ambitious and his enthusiasm was reserved for weekend fishing and bird-watching. During the war he went into semi-obscurity, haunted by his failure to preserve the peace and weakened by diplomatic setbacks and failing eyesight.[36]

Reginald McKenna, the Home Secretary, was born in London in 1853 into an Irish Catholic family. He rose through Trinity College, Cambridge, where he rowed bow in the winning university crew of 1887. Called to the bar that same year, he built up a prosperous practice before entering the House of Commons at the age of thirty-two as the Member for North Monmouthshire. When Asquith summoned him to the Admiralty in 1908 he had already given ample proof of his good sense, energy, business acumen and administrative talent. For all his abilities, McKenna always remained a source of puzzlement and irritation to outsiders or those who knew him only casually. His self-assertiveness and pedagogic manner, together with his cold, businesslike approach to questions about which his audience felt passionately, brought him no following in the country and made him more respected than liked in his own party.[37]

The Chancellor of the Exchequer, Lloyd George, was essentially an opportunist with no fixed principles except a burning desire to succeed Asquith one day. 'He knows no meaning in the words *truth* or *gratitude*', wrote a cabinet minister in 1912.[38] From his humble origins in Wales he had clawed his way up the ladder through sheer determination. He was a natural orator, skilful in parliamentary debate and on the platform able to crush a heckler or move an audience to tears. His nimble mind, air of confident omniscience and outspokenness masked, to all but close associates, both his lack of formal education and limited basic knowledge. One astute political observer wrote that Lloyd George, for all his abilities, didn't have 'a clue about geography … didn't know distances … didn't know logistics' and when 'it came to having an idea he might have one which sounded brilliant, but the practical application was absolutely fatal'.[39] Asquith, who rarely missed an opportunity to poke fun at Lloyd George, told Venetia Stanley that he had once found him 'searching for Gallipoli on a map of Spain'.[40] Always at the centre of controversy, Lloyd George's prestige was shaken in 1912 when he was implicated in the notorious Marconi Scandal.[41] His career almost certainly would have ended had not the Prime Minister come to his rescue. The war effaced the memory of his sordid involvement. He was eager to play a leading part in the struggle and, from the outset, his views were influential in shaping cabinet policy.[42]

The First Lord of the Admiralty, Winston Churchill, like his father Lord Randolph in his day, was the *enfant terrible* of British politics. Following experience in the army and in military journalism, he went to Westminster in 1900 as the young Unionist MP for Oldham, but his enthusiasm for free trade and social reform caused him to break with his party and join the Liberals. Thereafter his political ascent was nothing short of dazzling and, although only thirty-nine when the war broke out, he was one of the three most powerful men in the country. He had many admirable qualities but his political conduct evoked suspicion and resentment, not only because he had shifted party allegiance. Churchill, as was true for most of his career, made no concessions to convention and followed his own star. He was egocentric and unabashedly ambitious, too engrossed in his own affairs and his own opinions to have much heed for others. It was Churchill's impetuosity, penchant for adventure and manifest enjoyment of drama that often led him into unnecessary difficulties and raised questions about his judgment and stability.[43]

The most notable change in the cabinet in August 1914 was the appointment of Lord Kitchener as Secretary of State for War. Kitchener was the empire's most illustrious serving soldier. The sixty-four-year-old Field Marshal gained national prominence when he annihilated the dervishes in the epic battle of Omdurman in 1898, reconquered the Sudan and avenged 'Chinese' Gordon. Increasingly he became an object of public adulation. Succeeding Lord Roberts in South Africa in November 1900, he ended Boer guerrilla resistance. As commander-in-chief of the British army in India (1902–9), Kitchener made many radical reforms in military administration. His actions brought him into conflict with the formidable Viceroy, Lord Curzon, over whom he emerged as clear winner after a battle of wits and intrigue that ranks as one of the most celebrated episodes in imperial history. His most recent service had been in Egypt where, as Agent and Consul-General, he initiated sweeping land reforms, constructed irrigation works and advanced cotton-growing interests. His fame as a soldier and administrator, aided by his personal appearance – tall, broad-shouldered, erect, stern with a large bushy moustache – lent him an aura of divine infallibility. He became in the public eye the embodiment of Britain's might and will to win.[44]

Asquith's decision to invite Kitchener to join the cabinet had been forced on him by the sheer weight of political and press opinion. Kitchener had been home on leave and was set to return to Egypt, as war seemed imminent. He reached Dover on the morning of 3 August and had actually boarded the cross-Channel steamer when he was summoned back to London and asked to hold himself available for consultation.[45] Asquith's object was to have Kitchener present at the forthcoming Council of War, not to offer him the seals of office.[46]

Asquith did not need to be reminded, as he often was, that in an emergency he would be unable to hold the War Office in conjunction with his other duties. Initially he had given serious thought to recalling Jack Seely to the War Office. In a conversation with Pease on 2 August, he touched on the subject but, alas, did not elaborate.[47] Whether or not he had already made a decision cannot be determined. In any case events moved too quickly and, at Haldane's suggestion, he accepted a makeshift arrangement. While remaining Lord Chancellor, Haldane would deputize for Asquith at the War Office and set in motion the military machine he had created and understood better than anyone else.[48] Haldane undoubtedly hoped that this might be the prelude to a permanent arrangement, eager as he was to return to his old department.[49]

Haldane's claims were undermined by the Northcliffe press which maintained that his pro-German sympathies would make him unacceptable as a war leader to the French. The agitation against Haldane was coupled with the demand that Kitchener should be installed in the vacant post. A similar cry was taken up by other newspapers, including the Liberal mouthpiece, the *Westminister Gazette*. The Unionists too joined in the chorus, convinced as they were of Liberal incapacity to prosecute the war with the necessary vigour. In response to the wishes of party leaders, Balfour agreed to sound out Asquith about the possibility of bringing Kitchener into the War Office. Before doing so he sent Churchill a note, requesting that he apply pressure from his end.[50]

Early on 3 August Balfour went over to 10 Downing Street where he received a sympathetic hearing but little else. Asquith was non-committal. That same morning Churchill saw the Prime Minister. He pointed out that, if war came, there would be a continuous flow of interdepartmental work between the Admiralty and the War Office which would require immediate transaction by the service ministers. Since the overall burdens of government would leave the Prime Minister little time to devote to the War Office, would he consider installing Kitchener there as his successor? Churchill was encouraged by his chief's reaction. It seemed to him that Asquith was coming around to his way of thinking.[51]

By 5 August, with the nation already committed to war, the clamour on Kitchener's behalf was overwhelming and came from every quarter. Asquith worried about the large gaps in the Field Marshal's qualifications for the office. His long service abroad, combined with the narrow limitations of army life, had left him with little true understanding of domestic politics and of the plans and inner workings of the War Office. By experience and temperament he was an autocrat, unaccustomed to discussion or compromise. All accounts represented him as notoriously hard to work with.

Asquith remained undecided even after he had interviewed Kitchener. Details of the meeting are lacking. What is known is that Kitchener expressed a desire to return to Egypt. He did not feel that he could serve any useful purpose by remaining in England without defined responsibilities.[52]

As Asquith contemplated his next move, he recognized the obvious benefits of attaching Kitchener's magical name to the war effort. The Field Marshal would provide an instant tonic to public confidence and bring to the government a mystique that none of his ministers, or for that matter anyone else, remotely possessed. He would also bring to the ministry expert military advice as well as a conservative factor that would almost assuredly restrain, if not mute, right-wing criticism. When everything is taken into account, it is hard to see how Asquith could have avoided summoning Kitchener to the War Office. Even Haldane became resigned to the inevitable and recommended his appointment.[53]

Asquith held a Council of War in the cabinet room at 10 Downing Street on 5 August to determine how the war would be fought. Among those present were the heads of the War Office, Admiralty and Foreign Office, along with Britain's leading soldiers. The gathering had a final opportunity to ratify the pre-war General Staff plans or revert to a maritime strategy. It has often been claimed that the absence of any other plan was the decisive factor in the decision to commit the BEF to the Continent. Logically the Council of War could not have acted otherwise, regardless of what the Asquith government had decreed in the past. Britain had gone to war to defend Belgium. Its goals could only be accomplished by relying on the French who alone possessed a large enough army. To do anything less than to send the BEF would have been an empty gesture.[54]

Owing to an invasion scare that brewed up overnight, Kitchener favoured retaining two divisions at home temporarily. The Prime Minister backed Kitchener less because he feared a sudden German invasion than because he wanted troops on hand to deal with civil disturbances in the event of the economy collapsing. He conveyed Kitchener's views, as well as his own, to the cabinet which met in the morning to consider the recommendations of the Council of War. The cabinet agreed, with much less demur than Asquith had expected, to sanction the dispatch of an Expeditionary Force of four divisions to France.[55] Most of the ministers continued to think in terms of a restricted role for the striking force.[56] They might not have acquiesced so readily had they appreciated how dramatically the continental commitment would grow.

The cabinet made another important decision that morning. On 5 August 1914 a subcommittee of the CID, under the chairmanship of Admiral Sir Henry Jackson, recommended that the struggle be carried to Germany's colonies in Africa and the Pacific. The cabinet ministers approved the subcommittee's proposal with some gusto, prompting Asquith to remark that they 'looked more like a gang of Elizabethan buccaneers than a meek collection of black-coated Liberal Ministers'.[57] Asquith's interest in German overseas possessions did not really stem from a desire to add more territory to the British Empire. They were seen as a bargaining chip at the peace conference. More important their seizure would prevent the Germans from employing them as bases for attacks against British territories and as signal stations for their commerce raiders.[58]

After the meeting, Asquith called in Kitchener and offered him the post of Secretary for War. Kitchener accepted reluctantly and only because it was presented to him as a duty. 'It is a hazardous experiment,' Asquith told Venetia Stanley, 'but the best in the circumstances, I think.'[59]

Kitchener assumed a place in the cabinet hierarchy that was second only to Asquith, a status that was symbolized by his sitting on the right hand of the Prime Minister at meetings. Initially the civilian ministers willingly deferred military matters to Kitchener. They were not only awed by his reputation but also bewildered and dazed by the war.

Asquith never saw Kitchener as an infallible demi-god. He quickly identified some of the Field Marshal's shortcomings but his early impressions of him were quite favourable. At times he found him slow to grasp a new point and unnecessarily inflexible in cabinet discussions. Asquith thought that the Field Marshal was too obsessive about security leaks and that he was wrong to withhold classified information from his fellow ministers. But he did not press him for details or encourage others to do so. He did not wish to add to Kitchener's immense labours. He trusted Kitchener's professional judgment and marvelled at the manner in which he had quickly pulled things together at the War Office. 'My ... opinion of K's capacity increases daily,' Asquith wrote to Venetia Stanley. 'I think he is a really fine soldier, and he keeps his head & temper, and above all his equability wonderfully, considering how all three are tried.'[60]

Asquith was in the chair when the Council of War reconvened on the afternoon of 6 August. Discussion centred on the staging area for the BEF. Sir John French, the designated commander of the BEF, favoured the standing arrangements which called for British forces to assemble at

Maubeuge behind the left wing of the French army. Kitchener, who foretold the pattern of the coming German offensive west of the Meuse, argued that Amiens, about sixty-five miles further back, would be a safer place to concentrate. As in the earlier meeting when this point was debated, a decision was deferred until the French General Staff could be consulted.[61]

Asquith had the last word when an impasse developed between Kitchener and the Anglo-French General Staffs. An exasperated Kitchener took Sir John French with him to 10 Downing Street and laid both cases before the Prime Minister. Kitchener was convinced that his military instinct and logic were correct but he could not speak authoritatively on a plan about which he had no detailed knowledge. Quite naturally Asquith could not overturn a plan devised by experts who had devoted years of close study to local and strategic conditions.[62]

Sir John called on the Prime Minister to take leave before crossing to France. He confirmed French impressions that the principal German manoeuvre would not take place in Belgium. According to French theory, the Germans could not deploy enough troops to extend their right wing north of the Sambre-Meuse line without weakening their centre and left. It was supposed that if the Germans tried to debouch into France from central Belgium they would make themselves highly vulnerable to French attacks planned for the Ardennes and Lorraine. Asquith was pleased to see French looking so composed and optimistic and he harboured no doubts that he had been right in choosing him to command the BEF.[63]

The British army undoubtedly included men more competent than French but, in all fairness to Asquith, any other choice would have presented great difficulties. French's exploits during the Boer War had earned him acclaim as a courageous and resourceful cavalry commander and a popular reputation almost equal to that of Kitchener. Some soldiers who had worked closely with him, however, took note of his volatile disposition and inadequate training and wondered if he was really cut out to hold such a post in wartime.[64]

Before the opposing armies clashed in the west, agreement had been reached on the broad outlines of the nation's long-term objectives. The Royal Navy, in addition to hunting down the German fleet and protecting British shipping from enemy cruisers, would impose a blockade of the German coast in order to disrupt its trade and strangle its economy.[65] At the War Office Kitchener, dissenting from the conventional view, predicted that the war might last as long as three years. He asserted that before the war could be won Britain would have to put millions of men in the field, an unprecedented idea for a nation which cherished its traditional role as the principal seapower and paymaster of a coalition. By permitting Kitchener to transform Britain into a 'nation in arms', the cabinet acknowledged the supersession of its strategy of limited liability.[66]

From the start of the war, Kitchener understood that Britain was fighting as a junior military partner of a coalition. He was against adopting a single military policy until Britain had secured a greater measure of control over the alliance. In the interim he favoured an independent strategy that kept Britain secure against invasion, lent support to Russia and concentrated resources in France.

Asquith's faith in his team, and in the plans they had evolved for winning the war, helped to cushion the impact of early setbacks on sea and land. In the opening days of the war the German cruisers *Goeben* and *Breslau* eluded numerous British and French battleships in the Mediterranean and sought refuge in Constantinople, where their presence helped drive Turkey into the war on the side of the Central Powers at the end of October. Another cruiser, the *Emden*, wreaked havoc on British shipping in the Indian Ocean. On 22 September a German submarine managed to torpedo three British cruisers in broad daylight in the North Sea. Early in November grim news reached London that a German squadron had sunk two British cruisers near the Coronel, off Chile. These events made headlines, but they did not play a crucial part in the naval war.

Brought up to believe that the Royal Navy was the best in the world, Britons were first shocked and then angered by the episodes at seas. Asquith, like his colleagues, was equally dismayed. The loss of battleships, especially dreadnoughts, was unsettling. There always lurked the foreboding prospect that some day the German navy would be in a position to emerge from its home base and fight on nearly even terms. Asquith knew that in a single day the Royal Navy could lose the war.

Asquith had only a hazy notion of the changing character of naval warfare. He did not fully appreciate that battle cruisers on patrol or attacking defended positions were vulnerable to the hidden dangers of mines and submarines. He failed to reconcile himself to the concept of acceptable risk. Generally his attitude regarding the Royal Navy stood close to that of the uninformed man on the street. It seemed to him that the Royal Navy ought to be doing more than simply absorbing losses. He did not grasp that it could assert its supremacy without destroying the enemy's fleet. Because he expected resounding victories, it was easy for him to sometimes overlook the less spectacular but vital work of the Royal Navy. It was one of the paradoxes of the war, Asquith lamented to Lloyd George on 4 November 1914, that the Germans 'are so much better than we are on the sea'.[67] On the same day the cabinet barely stopped short of censuring the navy.[68] Asquith did not hold Churchill personally responsible for the navy's misfortunes but admonished him it was time he 'bagged something & broke some crockery'.[69]

Churchill's shaky position at the Admiralty led him to sacrifice his First Sea Lord, Prince Louis of Battenberg, who, because of his German origins, had been the target of a scurrilous press campaign. Churchill made up his mind to bring back Admiral John ('Jacky') Fisher, who was still remarkably fit and active for a man of seventy-four. Churchill visited Asquith on 27 October and indicated that he wished to make changes. 'Our poor blue-eyed German will have to go',[70] Asquith told Venetia Stanley. George V, in contrast, disapproved of Fisher as Battenberg's successor.

On 28 October Lord Stamfordham, the Private Secretary to George V, went to Downing Street and explained the King's opposition to Fisher: 'His Majesty knows the Navy and considers ... the proposed appointment would give a shock to the Navy which no one could wish in the middle of a great war.' Fisher, Stamfordham continued, had grown old and, although he wrote and talked much, his opinions changed from day to day. Asquith loyally defended Churchill's choice, saying there was no alternative. Stamfordham pointed out that Fisher's selection would place the King in a painful position, for the navy would feel that he should not have sanctioned it. Asquith replied that if Fisher was rejected he would find himself in equally disconcerting circumstances, for Churchill would resign. Given Churchill's intimate knowledge of the navy he could not be dispensed with or replaced.[71]

Asquith was summoned to Buckingham Palace the next day to discuss the impasse. The King gave an exhaustive recital of Fisher's 'crimes and defects' and was convinced that he would not get along with Churchill. On the last point Asquith had misgivings of his own but, as Churchill would have no one else, 'stuck to his guns'. The King, having done all he felt he could do, gave his reluctant consent, expressing the hope that his apprehension would prove groundless.[72] The King's instincts about Fisher were right on the mark, as both Asquith and Churchill were soon to discover.

The mishaps on the seas reinforced Kitchener's fears about an imminent invasion. Early on in the war he became convinced that a lull in the fighting on the Western Front would permit the Germans to detach perhaps as many as a quarter of a million men for an invasion while the German fleet kept the Royal Navy occupied elsewhere. Asquith thought that the Germans were hardly likely to risk the loss of men and ships in attempting so wild a venture but, as a prudent measure, asked Hankey to review home defence arrangements.[73] Hankey's findings formed the basis of a discussion on 7 October 1914 at a special meeting of the CID. There was a consensus that at present Germany could not spare sufficient troops for either an invasion or a raid.[74] After the third week in November, when an anticipated German invasion did not materialize, the issue ceased to occupy the cabinet's attention.[75]

The early defeats at sea never amounted to anything more than embarrassments and in no way threatened British naval supremacy. At the height of the public outcry the tide of the naval war started to change. Before the year ended the surface of the high seas was virtually swept clear of the enemy's warships. By eliminating threats to its shipping, Britain was assured of uninterrupted access to overseas resources as well as being able to transfer troops and supplies wherever they were needed.

On land the BEF had its first encounter with the Germans on 23 August near the Belgian mining town of Mons. Here the British fought off a vastly superior force with superb fire control and marksmanship but in the evening French, realizing that his position could be turned by a flanking movement, began a general strategic retreat.[76] As if Sir John's forced retirement was not bad enough, the British government also received word (prematurely as it turned out) that the Belgian town of Namur, a supposedly impregnable fortress and the gateway to France, had fallen in a single day. The mood in the cabinet was sombre.

Asquith was less dispirited than his colleagues at the bad tidings from the Front and, as always, kept an unruffled composure. He opposed any sudden or rash expedient that would jeopardize the chances of recovery. He remembered French's parting words that 'we must be prepared for a reverse or two at the first'.[77] If he had not yet accepted Kitchener's estimate of a three-year war, at least he recognized that the fighting would last longer than originally forecast. The ridiculous optimism of the press angered him with their stories of Belgian victories and of Germans starving and committing suicide. He anticipated that before the war ended the nation would suffer heavy losses and, as early reports of casualties exceeded his worst fears, his anguish mounted as did his concern for his three sons in the front line.[78] During the war he was fond of saying that he was never an optimist about the immediate future but, even if that truly reflected his sentiment at the time, he never doubted the final verdict.

Asquith blamed the French for everything that had gone wrong in the opening battles. He was under the impression that the BEF could have blunted the German invasion if the French had been willing to stand and fight. He poured out his feelings to Venetia Stanley:

> French's troops were in the best of spirits & 'quite ready to take the offensive', but the French resolved on a further retirement, & so our men have had to follow suit & are falling back on their original lines at Cambrai-Cateau. Kitchener is furious with the French who (he says) put their worst troops in the post of danger where they were annihilated by the Prussian Guards. So far the French plan of campaign has been badly bungled.[79]

Asquith was justified in debunking French strategy and planning but not in questioning the resolve of their armies, which suffered casualties between 20 and 23 August amounting to nearly twice the total strength of the BEF.

The distortions in Asquith's account can be traced to the absence of authentic information about the huge and tragic French effort. Kitchener, on whom Asquith relied for battlefield news, had only a sketchy idea of what was happening in France and what little he knew came mostly from Sir John's reports. These contained a summary of events on his own front and occasionally rumours or second-hand information about activities elsewhere, in addition to many unflattering comments about the French. Sir John never forgave Lanrezac, the French commander on his right, for having left him in the lurch at Mons. What began as a loss of confidence in Lanrezac became a distrust in the entire French army.[80] On 30 August the Field Marshal's dispute with the French reached a climax when he dispatched a message to London that he intended to withdraw altogether from the battle-line to rest and refit behind Paris.[81]

Kitchener talked confidentially with Asquith before he read the telegram to the cabinet on the morning of 31 August. He could offer no logical explanation for Sir John's proposed movement but did allude to both the military dangers of leaving a gap in the line and to the disastrous effect it would have on the solidarity of the Entente. There followed a heated debate. Asquith, like Kitchener, was adamant that Sir John must not abandon the French. That view prevailed in the end.[82] Kitchener was authorized to inform French that the cabinet expected him to conform as far as possible 'to the plans of General Joffre for the conduct of the campaign'.[83]

Asquith was very well disposed towards French and refused to jump to the conclusion that he had panicked or that his appointment had been a mistake. Perhaps, he thought, the Field Marshal had a plan which would reveal itself in good time. His hopes were blasted when French's second telegram confirmed his resolve to abandon his position independently of

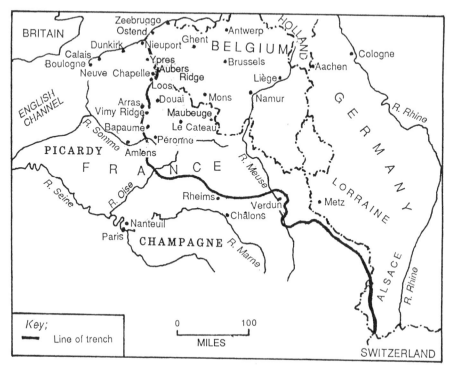

The Western Front at the Close of 1914

his ally, a move Kitchener was certain would open the way for the piece-meal destruction of the Anglo-French armies.[84] The French were of the same mind and President Poincaré made an impassioned appeal to the British government to intercede in the matter. Grey, however, felt that Sir John ought to be free to act as he saw fit.[85]

Since it was too late to summon the cabinet, Asquith held an emergency conference with such ministers as could be contacted on short notice. Besides Asquith and Kitchener, McKenna, Churchill, Pease and Lloyd George were present. Kitchener believed that he could do no more by telegram and that the only way to avert an impending disaster was to see the situation for himself. Asquith feared a collapse of the Anglo-French alliance. He read out Poincaré's moving message, then broke the silence by saying: 'If this is done [the withdrawal of the BEF from the line] the French left will be uncovered, Paris will fall, the French Army will be cut off and we shall never be able to hold our heads up in the world again. Better that the British Army should perish than that this shame should fall on us.'[86] It was unanimously agreed to send Kitchener over without delay to resolve the crisis and if necessary, 'to put the fear of God into them all'.[87]

Asquith's prompt intervention in overruling the commander on the spot rendered inestimable service to the Allied cause. When Kitchener met Sir John in Paris on 1 September and ordered him to remain in the line, it enabled French military leaders to organize a counterattack at the Marne. The BEF played a crucial role in that historic battle, causing the Germans to fall back and wrecking their hopes of a speedy victory in the west.

Since the opening engagement at Mons, Asquith had closely and, at times, anxiously followed the fortunes of the BEF. He held daily conferences with Kitchener, read Sir John's dispatches and interviewed senior generals returning from France.[88] Asquith was not and never claimed to be an authority on strategy. His natural instinct was to regard generals as experts in their own profession and he was most reluctant to support any policy that ran flatly against military opinion. This did not mean that he accepted military judgments in any blind or uncritical spirit. During his meetings with Kitchener he occasionally made suggestions, even though he did not attach great weight to his own views. When, for example, he was told of the proposed counter-offensive at the Marne he thought that it was premature and ought to be delayed another week.[89] Happily the decision did not rest with him. Had General Joffre, the French commander-in-chief, followed Asquith's instincts he would have faced German armies far better placed to repel his attack.

On another occasion the Prime Minister recommended that Smith-Dorrien be appointed to take command of II Corps as successor to General

Grierson, who had died suddenly from an aneurism of the heart.[90] There were good arguments against sending Smith-Dorrien over to France. Sir John had requested General Herbert Plumer for the vacant post. Moreover, his relations with Smith-Dorrien were badly strained – a matter of common knowledge in the army. Yet Kitchener discounted these factors and selected Smith-Dorrien as the replacement. Whether Kitchener deferred to the Prime Minister's wishes, or whether Smith-Dorrien was initially his own choice as well, cannot be determined for sure. Kitchener replied to French in the following terms: 'King and government decide for Smith-Dorrien. Plumer can hardly be spared at present, but will be available later.'[91] It was a sound decision. During the retreat Smith-Dorrien's brilliant generalship probably saved the BEF from destruction.[92]

Among Asquith's major concerns was the deep-seated ill-feeling between Kitchener and French, which he attributed to mere temperamental incompatibility. Asquith admired them both and found it useful, so he said, to have an optimist at the front balanced by a pessimist in the rear. The dispute between the two Field-Marshals grew out of their interview at the British Embassy in Paris. Already ruffled by the summons, French was aghast to see Kitchener wearing the uniform of a Field Marshal which he interpreted as a threat to his authority. He left the meeting in a rage. Thereafter his doubts and insecurities were fed by a persistent rumour that Kitchener was toying with the idea of assuming the post of supreme military commander in addition to his existing office of Secretary of War. This rumour was followed by another – for which there was undeniable proof – that Kitchener, reacting to French hints that the BEF was irresolute, had offered to replace Sir John with General Ian Hamilton. Henry Wilson, Deputy Chief of Staff of the BEF, who was on intimate terms with French leaders, reported the incident to his superior. Shaken and nearly hysterical at what he regarded as an act of treachery, French sent an aide-de-camp to complain to the Prime Minister.[93]

Asquith felt that French's fears were ill-founded. The possibility that he might be replaced by Hamilton, 'whom K. despises and would gladly kick around the Horse Guards Parade',[94] was too ludicrous to even contemplate. Asquith suspected that Wilson had concocted the story to suit his own ends. He asked Churchill (who was a close friend of Sir John's) to write a soothing letter to the Field Marshal and he did likewise.[95] Asquith tried to convince French that the report was baseless, assuring him that the nation was fortunate to have at the head of its army 'a Commander who had never been surpassed in the capital qualities of initiative, tenacity, serenity, and resource'.[96] French wired back: 'I cannot find words which adequately expresses my feeling of profound gratitude and relief on receipt

of your letter. It has put me quite at rest ... Few commanders in the field
have had the good fortune to serve under such a true, loyal and
sympathetic chief as you.'[97] While Sir John was grateful for the vote of
confidence, he knew better than to believe Asquith's assertion that the
story was untrue. He would never again feel secure in his position and his
hatred of Kitchener grew to paranoic proportions.

During the third week in December, Asquith invited both Kitchener
and French to Walmer Castle, his weekend retreat. He hoped to use the
occasion to persuade the Field Marshals to bury the hatchet. He was
unsuccessful. The two soldiers clearly disliked one another and at one point
Asquith was compelled to step between them after their bickering had
erupted into a 'battle royal'.[98]

After calming them down, Asquith left the room for a while. When he
returned discussion centred on a possible successor to General Murray, the
Chief of Staff of the BEF, whose health had broken down under the strain
of war. Normally unassertive on military matters, Asquith intervened
directly this time. French favoured giving the appointment to Wilson
whom he liked and trusted. Asquith would not have Wilson as Chief of
Staff at any price, regarding him as a notorious intriguer and as one of the
principal architects of the Ulster Crisis in March 1914. Kitchener was
equally hostile to Wilson, not the least because he was an outspoken critic
of War Office policies. In the face of such determined opposition French
gave way. Ultimately he accepted their suggestion that he choose Sir
William Robertson as his new Chief of Staff.[99]

The feud between Kitchener and French undoubtedly complicated
Asquith's task but not nearly as much as the sharp differences of opinion
that sometimes occurred in the cabinet. Questions which in time of peace
would have been settled placidly by the give and take of discussion, now
provoked personal strife and friction, and sometimes ended old friendships.
No small part of Asquith's heavily burdened time was devoted to
composing differences and trying to bring harmony out of discord.

The earliest clashes were between Lloyd George and Kitchener. The
little Welshman was the first minister to stand up to the War Secretary
and, as the conflict progressed, undercut him at every opportunity. He
resented Kitchener, partly because he sat next to the Prime Minister and
partly because he was arbitrary and withheld information from the
cabinet. Their most violent quarrel occurred at a cabinet meeting on 28
October over Kitchener's reluctance to create an all-Welsh regiment.
Apart from linguistic difficulties, Kitchener considered that men recruited
from Wales could not be trusted – they were, he told Asquith, 'always wild
& insubordinate & ought to be stiffened by a strong infusion of English or

Scotch [sic]'.[100] The angry exchanges barely stopped short of a shouting-match. Kitchener said he would resign. The Prime Minister cut him off saying, 'that was not practical'.[101] The whole thing, Asquith thought, could have been settled in ten minutes if both parties had exercised a modicum of common sense. Kitchener was much to blame, having spent so much of his life in the Orient that he could not 'acclimatize himself to English conditions'. Before the next cabinet meeting, Asquith asked Churchill to see the War Secretary to 'try and infuse some sense of proportion'.[102] At the same time he collared Lloyd George and 'told him to suspend his feud with Kitchener, who is not ill-disposed but inclined to be slow and rather clumsy'.[103] With Asquith and Churchill working to smooth things over, Kitchener relented and Lloyd George got his Welsh regiment.[104]

Inside the cabinet no one incited greater controversy, resentment and distrust than Churchill. The self-centred First Lord liked to make things happen and there was little that he considered outside the area of his expertise. Asquith was genuinely fond of Churchill and their relationship approached that of father and son. He found the First Lord's conversation stimulating and his manner direct and refreshingly unpretentious. He was amused and fascinated by his young colleague's adventurous and fertile ingenuity, and allowed him freedom to pursue his ideas. Attributing many of Churchill's faults to youth, he fully expected him to succeed to the premiership some day. The first clue that he may have misjudged Churchill was provided by the events surrounding the 'Dunkirk Circus'.

During the third week of September Asquith discovered that Churchill, in response to a request from Joffre, had worked out arrangements with Kitchener to send troops (Oxfordshire Hussars) to Dunkirk in order to deceive the Germans about the strength of the garrison. Asquith, besides being annoyed that he had not been consulted, was highly sceptical of the whole enterprise. He had no faith in the fighting or staying powers of the Hussars and feared few of them would survive an encounter with the Germans.[105] As the days passed, Asquith's anxiety and resentment grew. It seemed to him that Churchill's units – 'Winston's little army' as he described them – were getting themselves involved in a precarious situation. If they advanced as far as Douai, which was their objective, they might have to contend with an estimated 60,000 Germans on their flank.[106] Moreover, he began to lose patience at having to take charge of the Admiralty in the First Lord's absence. Then Churchill complicated matters by not confining his activities in France to his little army. He often skipped over to British Headquarters, initially to see the conflict at close quarters. It was not long before he began to discuss with French schemes for combined operations along the Belgian coast. This brought him into conflict with Kitchener, who complained to Asquith that the First Lord was infringing on his jurisdiction and exacerbating his difficulties with Sir John French. Rather than admit that he might have been wrong, Churchill adopted a belligerent attitude, prompting Asquith to forbid him from crossing over to France again.[107]

Asquith was in Cardiff on a speaking engagement when Churchill got himself involved in another and more serious adventure. On the evening of 2 October 1914 word arrived in London that the Belgian King and his government had decided to abandon Antwerp which was under merciless bombardment. Once Antwerp fell, little could be done to prevent the Germans from sweeping down the Belgian coast to Calais, from whence they could endanger the military position of the Anglo-French army and conceivably launch an invasion of Britain. In the Prime Minister's absence, Grey summoned Churchill and Kitchener to a midnight conference. The small group of ministers agreed that Antwerp could not be abandoned without a further struggle. A brigade of marines was available at once and other detachments from the main army and from Britain itself would follow in the next few days. Churchill, who was on his way to Dunkirk, received permission to go instead to Antwerp to urge the the Belgian authorities not to abandon the city. The next day Asquith, returning to a *fait accompli*, had this to say:

> I have had a long talk with K. ... & we are now both rather anxiously waiting Winston's report. I don't know how fluent he is in French, but if he was able to do himself justice in a foreign tongue, the Belges will have listened to a discourse the like of which they have never heard before. I cannot but think that he will stiffen them up to the sticking point.[108]

As Asquith had predicted, Churchill's presence and activities at Antwerp heartened the dispirited Belgians. He wrote two days later that: 'Winston succeeded in bucking up the Belges who gave up their panicky idea of retreating to Ostend, and are now going to hold Antwerp for as long as they can, trusting upon our coming to their final deliverance.'[109] Exhilarated by the atmosphere of crisis and mindful of the importance of his mission, Churchill was anxious to stay on and coordinate the defences of the city. On 5 October he telegraphed Asquith, offering to resign his post at the Admiralty if given executive command of the British forces. The suggestion astounded Asquith who described it as 'a real bit of tragic-comedy'. Without telling anyone, Asquith replied in the warmest terms, thanking him for his patriotic proposal and appreciating his zeal and enterprise but adding that he could not be spared at the Admiralty.

Privately, he thought Churchill had taken leave of his senses. To Venetia Stanley he painted a ludicrous picture of Churchill, a former lieutenant in the Hussars, requesting to be 'in command of 2 distinguished Major-Generals, not to mention Brigadiers, Colonels etc'. That morning in the cabinet Asquith had not intended to bring up the matter but several members, including Kitchener, pressed him to say when Churchill would be coming home. It was only then that he read Churchill's telegram which was greeted by gales of incredulous laughter.[110]

By 6 August German 17-inch howitzers were pulverizing Antwerp and morale was breaking down. To the Belgian authorities there was no justification for staying any longer and it was best for the army to evacuate the fortress while it still had an escape route. The British naval brigades fell back as well but in the darkness and confusion some 900 men were taken prisoners and two battalions inadvertently crossed the Dutch frontier and were interned. Antwerp surrendered on 10 October. Churchill's intervention had prolonged the defence of the doomed city for an additional five days, giving the Allies just enough time to deploy their forces against the German attempt to break through along the Channel coast.[111]

Asquith paid tribute to Churchill for prolonging the defence of Antwerp, which he recognized was of considerable strategic importance.[112] But he was becoming increasingly troubled by his young colleague's lack of judgment and sense of proportion. Churchill's wild, almost frivolous, telegram requesting a military command had left him bewildered. How could Antwerp be balanced in the scale of events with his responsibilities at the Admiralty, where he was at the head of Britain's greatest fighting service as well as a senior member of the small inner cabinet concerned with the conduct of the war? How could Churchill give up his privileged position at the centre of the nation's affairs in order to command a handful of troops who were not even operating as part of the main army but were struggling on the flank in a forlorn side-show? Nor was it a momentary aberration on Churchill's part. Upon returning to London on the morning of 7 October, he went straight to 10 Downing Street where he implored the Prime Minister not to take a conventional view of his future. Having tasted blood he was beginning, like a tiger, to raven for more and once again asked to be relieved at the Admiralty and given a military command.

Asquith more or less viewed the episode with good humour, describing Churchill as a wonderful creature, possessing 'a curious dash of schoolboy simplicity' and 'a zigzag streak of lightning in the brain' that some called genius.[113] Several days later his delight gave way to anger, after hearing from his son Arthur a first-hand account of the fighting at Antwerp. He made his feelings known to Venetia Stanley:

Strictly between ourselves, I can't tell you what I feel of the *wicked* folly of it all. The Marines of course are splendid troops & can go anywhere & do anything: but nothing can excuse Winston (who knew all the facts) from sending in the two other Naval Brigades. I was assured that all the recruits were being left behind, and that the main body at any rate consisted of seasoned Naval Reserve men. As a matter of fact only about one quarter were Reservists, and the rest were a callow crowd of the rawest tiros, most of whom had never fired off a rifle, while none of them had ever handled an entrenching tool.[114]

If the Antwerp expedition damaged Churchill's reputation in the eyes of the Prime Minister, it also brought out the serious flaws in the structure of supreme command. Since no one had foreseen the scale and nature of the national effort in total war, Asquith had no plans in place in August 1914 to replace conventional peacetime procedures with a wartime organization. There were some in the government who hoped that the CID would be transformed into a centre of strategic control. Asquith rejected the idea, reluctant as he was to circumvent the constitutional practice of collective cabinet responsibility.[115]

A cabinet of twenty-one members was far too large to provide clear direction on the multitude of diverse issues that arose. Until there existed a permanent body charged with looking ahead and making plans to meet probable emergencies, such hasty improvisations as had to be made in prolonging the defence of Antwerp were bound to be repeated. In November Asquith set up a special committee, known as the War Council, to assist the cabinet in the conduct of the war. The War Council was originally composed of eight regular members. With the Prime Minister in the chair, Kitchener, Lloyd George, Grey and Churchill represented the cabinet. Balfour was selected from the Loyal Opposition in view of his long association with the CID and his close friendship with Asquith. Also in attendance, in an advisory capacity, were General Wolfe-Murray (the CIGS) and Admiral Fisher (the First Sea Lord). The subsequent additions of Crewe, Haldane, Harcourt, McKenna and Admiral Sir Arthur Wilson brought the total strength of the War Council to thirteen. Besides the actual members, other individuals might be summoned to attend particular sessions ad hoc. Asquith used the talents of Hankey as secretary. His integrity, discretion, keen and active mind, knowledge of military affairs, capacity for work and flair for dealing with politicians of dissimilar temperments earned him the complete trust of Asquith, who described him as 'the most useful man in Europe ... he has never been wrong'.[116]

In reality Asquith did not bring significant improvement in the higher direction of the war when he established the War Council. He called it only when a crisis demanded a new policy. It therefore had no continuing role in planning. Deprived of executive authority, its discussions were largely duplicated by the cabinet before a final decision was taken, causing delays and hampering secrecy. Finally, Asquith neglected to set up a mechanism to coordinate military and naval planning with the result that the responsible departments framed their plans without much reference to one another. This basic flaw was to have serious repercussions as the war intensified. In summary, the War Council was not an instrument to superintend the day-to-day operation of the war, which remained in the hands of the service ministers in consultation with the Prime Minister. Rather, as Hankey has explained, it 'provided a supplement to the Cabinet for exploring some of the larger questions of policy ... '[117]

Asquith summoned the War Council for the first time on 25 November 1914 to discuss the defence of Egypt, a more pressing concern now that Turkey had joined the Central Powers. Churchill suggested that the Turkish threat to the Suez Canal could be obviated by a combined attack on the Gallipoli Peninsula. Such an expedition, if successful, would give the British control of the Dardanelles and enable them to dictate terms to Constantinople. Asquith did not react except to solicit Kitchener's opinion. Kitchener agreed that it might become necessary to make a diversion on Turkish communications but thought that the moment for it had not yet come.[118]

Apart from Churchill, no one showed any enthusiasm for a major operation in the Mediterranean. A month later, however, sentiment in the cabinet had changed. By then German warships had been driven from the high seas; the Russian 'steamroller', on which many in the West had pinned their hopes, had been brought to a halt while still in Russian Poland; and the Western Front had become stationary along a line of twisted trenches that stretched from Switzerland to Nieuport on the North Sea.[119]

As the implication of these events became evident, the most questioning minds in the cabinet saw the need for an altogether new element in war as a means of achieving victory. One such possibility was to use Britain's strength, particularly sea power, in another and more rewarding theatre of operations.

WANTED, A LEAD.

MR. PUNCH (*to the* PRIME MINISTER). "YOU CAN GET ALL THE WILLING SERVICE YOU NEED, SIR, IF YOU'LL ONLY ORGANISE IT. TELL EACH MAN OF US WHAT IS WANTED OF HIM, AND HE'LL DO IT."

Chapter 4

The Search for a Way Around

On 30 December 1914 Asquith received two memoranda on the future conduct of the war, one from Hankey and the other from Churchill.[1] These were followed, two days later, by yet another from Lloyd George. All three, written quite independently, were looking for alternatives to the interminable war of attrition in France. Asquith was especially impressed by Lloyd George's scheme, which proposed withdrawing most of the British troops from France and using them, together with contingents from Serbia and new Balkan allies, for an offensive against Austria, either from Salonika (Greece) or a port such as Ragusa on the Dalmatian coast.[2]

Asquith had heard enough first-hand accounts of the fighting to sense the ugly realities about conditions on the Western Front. Losses kept piling up and included many young men from the social circle in which both he and his wife moved.[3] He agreed with the main point in the above memos that the war could not be won by conventional frontal attacks in the West.[4] Until new tactics were devised to overcome the system of entrenchment, he saw no point in sending any more men than were needed to hold the line in France. In the interim he favoured a new approach. Asquith was mindful that Kitchener did not have surplus troops at present. But the first divisions of Kitchener's New Army would be ready to take the field in the spring and it seemed appropriate to consider employing them in another theatre where the enemy could be dealt a crippling blow.

Such thinking was anathema to Sir John French, who denied that the German line was impenetrable. It was, he claimed, largely a matter of concentrating sufficient men and ammunition, particularly high explosive shells. Until it was proved that the lines could not be broken, there could be no question of making an effort elsewhere. He warned that to withdraw troops from the Western Front or not to reinforce it might expose the Allies to a crushing and perhaps fatal defeat.[5] French, Asquith noted, made 'a

very able statement of the case against action outside France'.[6] Indeed he
had. Trenches were still in a rudimentary state and in all likelihood a
carefully prepared assault, preceded by a heavy bombardment, would
have broken through. Later on French would be proved wrong but by
then trench defences were very different from those at the start of 1915.

French's memorandum raised the basic issue of where the war was to be
fought. Thus began a controversy, commonly known as 'Westerners v.
Easterners' but perhaps more accurately described as 'Continentalist v.
Peripheral' schools of strategy. This conflict would not be resolved during
1915.

Caught between the two schools, Asquith stood closer to the Continen-
talists. He appreciated that certain British interests might mandate a
diversion of troops to an alternative theatre of war. Yet such an effort,
whatever rewards it might bring, would be counter-productive if it
endangered the safety of the Western Front or so alienated the French as
to reduce their willingness to continue making fearful sacrifices.

Asquith's military outlook was influenced, if not shaped, by Kitchener's
thinking. As a soldier Kitchener recognized that the war could be won only
in France. He was equally convinced that no progress could be made there
until 1916 when the New Armies would be fully trained and the supply of
war material very greatly augmented.[7]

The various plans calling for a redirection of British strategy were
examined by experts and discussed at War Council meetings on 7 and 8
January 1915. All contained more drawbacks than appeared at first sight.
As a result Asquith lost interest in the idea of a subsidiary operation and if
anything appeared to be supporting Sir John's position.

The absence of a consensus on any of the schemes left open other options.
As Asquith was about to bring the War Council meeting to a close on 13
January, Churchill put forward a plan to force the Dardanelles by ships
alone. The members had been sitting all day and they were both weary
and exasperated by the fruitless discussions. In these circumstances
Churchill's proposal was like an answer to a prayer.

Asquith was attracted to the idea. It was assumed that once the ships
knocked out the Turkish forts and sailed up to Constantinople the faction-
ridden and unpopular Turkish regime would be swept away and replaced
by a pro-British group willing to make peace. The capitulation of Turkey
would open a much desired route to Russia from the Mediterranean,
convert the neutral Balkan states to the Allied cause and bring them
together in a united front against Austria-Hungary. Here was a golden
opportunity to shorten the war without the help of a single soldier.
Kitchener gave the project his blessing as well, saying that if the

bombardment proved ineffective the ships could be withdrawn before serious damage was sustained. The upshot was that the War Council gave Churchill its provisional consent to begin preparations along the lines he had laid out.[8]

Fisher remained silent during the meeting but disliked the proposal on the grounds that it threatened his own Borkum project, could not succeed without troops and would weaken British naval strength in the North Sea.[9] On 20 January Asquith learned through Hankey of the growing friction between Churchill and the First Sea Lord. Asquith reported the following to Venetia Stanley:

> Hankey came to me to-day to say ... that Fisher, who is an old friend of his, had come to him in a very unhappy frame of mind. He likes Winston personally, but complains that on purely technical naval matters he is frequently over-ruled ('he out-argues me'!) and he is not by any means at ease about either the present disposition of the fleets, or their future movements. Of course he didn't want Winston, or indeed anybody to know this, but Hankey told him he should pass it on to me. Tho' I think the old man is rather unbalanced, I fear there is some truth in what he says.[10]

The Prime Minister's first intimation that Fisher was specifically opposed to the naval attack came when he received a copy of a dissenting minute Fisher had written to Churchill on 25 January.[11] Before he could follow up on the matter, Churchill was at the door of 10 Downing Street to show Asquith personally his reply to the First Sea Lord. The paper effectively demolished Fisher's arguments. Churchill asserted that the old ships destined to participate in the Dardanelles were of no value to Jellicoe (the naval commander-in-chief); and he drew up a table showing the relative naval strength of Britain and Germany to emphasize the overwhelming superiority of the Grand Fleet.[12]

Churchill added that in a covering note Fisher had requested that his memorandum be published and circulated to the War Council. He in turn had written to suggest that Fisher's memorandum as well as his own be forwarded to Asquith, rather than circulated to the War Council.[13] Much of what passed next in the Prime Minister's room is not known but Churchill ultimately got his way. Asquith, who had no wish to publicize the dissension between the two top officials at the Admiralty, agreed that neither paper should be printed. This was obviously an error in judgment on Asquith's part but it is doubtful that the War Council, even with access to the memoranda in question, would have acted differently in the end. It was a matter of common knowledge that Fisher has misgivings about a purely naval attack on the Dardanelles.

Feeling cheated and furious that his views were being ignored, Fisher protested directly to the Prime Minister early on 28 January. In a note, which was delivered to 10 Downing Street by Hankey, he indicated that he would not be attending the War Council that morning on account of his disagreements with the First Lord. He repeated his argument that, without military assistance, neither the bombardment of the Dardanelles nor that of Zeebrugge – Churchill's scheme to bombard the Belgian port – could be justified, and concluded by expressing his desire to resign:

> I am very reluctant to leave the First Lord. I have a great personal affection and admiration for him, but I see no possibility of a union of ideas, and unity is essential in war, so I refrain from any desire of remaining as a stumbling block.[14]

Fisher also wrote to Churchill in similar terms.[15] When Churchill had read the note he hurried across Horse Guards Parade to 10 Downing Street. Both Churchill and Asquith felt that Fisher was being petulant. Still they wanted him to stay on and considered that his presence at the War Council meeting was indispensable. Hence they arranged to get together with Fisher so that they could thrash out their differences.

Churchill and Fisher entered the Prime Minister's study at 11.10 a.m., twenty minutes before the War Council was due to meet. Acting as arbitrator, Asquith worked out a compromise under which Churchill agreed to drop his latest plan for a bombardment of Zeebrugge, while Fisher withdrew his opposition to the Dardanelles operation.[16] The three men then went downstairs to the cabinet room. The result of their conversation was not communicated to the other members of the War Council.

The War Council discussed a wide range of topics before reaching the subject of the Dardanelles. Asquith then turned the floor over to Churchill. Fisher interrupted to say he had understood the question would not be raised today and that the Prime Minister was well aware of his own views in regard to it. Asquith replied that because of the steps that had already been taken, the question could not be left in abeyance. At that point Fisher rose from the council table and headed for the door but Kitchener intercepted him and persuaded him to return to his seat. The War Council adjourned for lunch and when it reconvened in the evening Asquith found himself presiding over a united body. In the interim Churchill had cajoled Fisher into giving his reluctant consent to the naval enterprise. To the satisfaction of Asquith, Churchill announced that with Fisher's approval the Admiralty had decided 'to undertake the task with which the War Council has charged us so urgently'.[17]

In the post-mortems during and after the war one of the obvious questions was why Fisher's views had carried so little weight with the War Council. Part of the explanation was that the First Sea Lord's arguments were weak and imprecise. Whether in conversation or on paper he never directly challenged the idea of independent naval action on technical grounds. Rather he based his aversion to the plan on fears that it would interfere with his own project and to a certain extent weaken the Grand Fleet. Thus advocates of the Dardanelles campaign were able to claim that Fisher's attitude was in reality the petulance of an old sailor thwarted of his brainchild.[18] Asquith put forward this explanation when he testified before the Dardanelles Commission in 1916:[19]

> Lord Fisher's eyes were always upon the Baltic and he regarded with great suspicion, more than suspicion, great dislike, anything which would diminish the opportunities or impair the force of his projected Baltic operation. So far as I understood, from all the conversations I had with him, it was much more upon that ground than upon any specific objection on what you may call technical naval grounds that he was opposed to it.[20]

If Asquith's testimony can be faulted it was for what he left unsaid. He knew that the upper echelon at the Admiralty, to say nothing of certain authorities like Hankey, had considered the naval plan unfeasible on account of the technical obstacles. Hankey, who had closely inspected the Dardanelles in 1907 while on a visit to Turkey,[21] saw more clearly than anyone else the hazards the fleet would face. Late in January 1915 he told Asquith he doubted the navy could get through without military assistance. A few days later he reported that every naval officer at the Admiralty, from Fisher downwards, had come down strongly against unaided action by the fleet.[22] On 2 February Hankey followed up by sending the Prime Minister a memorandum stating that he had 'been immensely impressed with the cumulative effect of the arguments in favour of military action in the Dardanelles at the earliest possible date'.[23] However, Asquith would not consider marking time until troops were available, satisfied that the navy alone could force the Dardanelles.

It is easy to understand why Asquith disregarded or minimized the technical difficulties involved in a naval operation. The adversaries involved were the Turks, whose fighting capabilities were held in low esteem. Lengthy military preparations, such as would have been required against a first-class military power, were deemed unnecessary.[24]

There was, moreover, a sense of urgency in the air, a crying need to escape from the slugging-match in France and find a new theatre in which decisive results could be obtained. The Dardanelles operation was the only plan, among a number under consideration, that did not require military forces. It had the unanimous support of the War Council, an asset that none of the other schemes remotely enjoyed. The plan was novel and seemed to rule out the danger of serious losses, either in manpower or material. Lying outside the range of enemy guns, the ships would destroy the forts one by one as they proceeded through the Straits. Once the ships entered the Sea of Marmara and a revolution occurred in Constantinople, immense political and military advantages would follow. There was always the comforting thought that, if unforeseen obstacles were encountered in the early stages, the operation could easily be abandoned and explained simply as a demonstration to mask Britain's real intentions in the Mediterranean.

Looking back it is clear that Asquith should have sanctioned the attack on the Dardanelles only if there was an army present to assist the fleet. A small force at the outset probably would have achieved more than the larger one that landed in April. At any rate it was a terrible blunder to plan the operation as a wholly naval effort. The element of surprise was forfeited the moment the fleet began to bombard the Turkish forts. Once it was realized that no progress could be made without ground forces, the damage could not be repaired.

As a rule historians have cast much of the blame – and rightly so – on Churchill for the catastrophe that followed.[25] But Asquith, because of his position, bears ultimate responsibility for the flawed decision of the War Council. Beyond this he was personally culpable as well. He knew what Churchill was like and he alone could have set matters right. He was aware of the forebodings of the experts at the Admiralty and he had other grounds (especially the deep misgivings of Hankey) to doubt the feasibility of the naval operation. He showed poor judgment by concealing relevant information from the War Council and by failing to conduct a fuller investigation. A joint naval and military study would almost certainly have confirmed the conclusion of an earlier one in 1906: that an attack by ships alone was a fundamentally unsound operation.[26] It would have pointed out that, unless the Turkish army was driven from the peninsula, the Straits would be impassable by any vessels other than heavily armed ships. Without supply ships, any battleships that succeeded in breaking through would be forced to return for want of coal and ammunition.

Having casually endorsed a fresh commitment, Asquith and his colleagues were in danger of drifting into yet another. In January ominous reports reached London of an imminent renewal of Austro-German attacks against Serbia. 'I feel strongly that at this moment the point of danger and of importance is Servia', Asquith told the King. 'If she is allowed to be crushed by an Austro-German force, the Allies will have sustained a serious and humiliating blow.'[27]

Concern over the fate of Serbia breathed fresh life into Lloyd George's project. Asquith was not far behind Lloyd George in proclaiming the merits of an expedition to the Balkans. His attitude might have been different if he had been well-informed about the nature of Balkan politics. As it was, his ignorance gave him a distorted impression, causing him to be too optimistic about the chances of creating a coalition of Balkan states. Admittedly such a coalition had been forged in 1912–13 to fight a common enemy but a few months later it fell apart when its members quarrelled over territorial spoils. The Balkan wars had deepened mutual suspicions and rivalries among the Balkan states and left them nursing territorial ambitions at the expense of one another. In particular it was difficult to see how Bulgaria could be brought in as an ally of Serbia, Roumania and Greece, its recent conquerers.[28]

On 15 January Asquith interviewed Charles and Noel Buxton, who were back in London after an unofficial fact-finding mission to the Balkans.[29] As a result of their inquiries the Buxton brothers had identified, or so they believed, the territorial concessions that each Balkan state required before aligning itself with the Entente. They urged that the Allies uphold Bulgaria's claim to territory it had lost in 1913; compensate Serbia with Bosnia, Herzegovina and parts of the Dalmatian coast; give Transylvania to Roumania; and southern Albania, Rhodes and possibly Smyrna to Greece. They were confident that a Balkan confederation could be created without excessive difficulties if the Allies were generous, united and firm in their advocacy of territorial adjustments.[30]

Asquith was impressed by what he heard. He agreed with the Buxtons on the urgent need to make the required concessions to Bulgaria and to rely on Anglo-Russian pressure to overcome Greek and Serbian objections. He thought that one way to circumvent the intense rivalry and hatred between Serbia and Bulgaria was to tell them that they would be fighting not side by side but back to back – the one against Austria and the other against Turkey.[31] Serbia occupied almost all of the cabinet's attention on 20 January. No one challenged Asquith's assertion that its collapse would be a serious setback and would damage, perhaps fatally, Entente chances of drawing in the wavering Balkan states. Lloyd George was adamant that to obtain results British diplomacy, which in the past he had criticized as excessively cautious and timid, must be accompanied by a show of strength in the area. Accordingly he took the lead in pressing for a British expedition to the Balkans. Kitchener remained non-committal but 'promised to examine the situation carefully from a military point of view'.[32]

On 21 January Asquith talked to Kitchener and Lloyd George in his study. The ministers had barely touched on the business at hand when the conversation turned to Serbia. They were in accord that, unless aided, Serbia would be unable to resist successfully an Austro-German onslaught. Lloyd George, with Asquith's support, argued that the mercurial Balkan states were likely to consolidate on the side that took the boldest action. Kitchener did not need to be reminded of the significant military advantages that would accrue from the creation of a Balkan league but he was not as sanguine as Lloyd George and Asquith, both of whom believed that simply committing a British force to the region would be decisive in determining the attitude of Roumania and Greece. He did agree with them, however, that the destruction of Serbia would make it almost impossible to win over the neutral Balkan states. If Kitchener readily conceded that helping Serbia was paramount, he also recognized that it would entail major problems, not the least of which was to find an adequate military force – he calculated that at the very minimum a corps would be needed to have the desired effect. Since the troops would have to be collected from those either already in France or destined to be sent there, he needed to discuss the matter with the French Minister of War, Alexandre Millerand, who was expected in London the following day.

The announcement of Millerand's visit coincided with a report that General Castelnau, reputed to be one of the best French generals, had expressed the opinion that an impasse existed on the Western Front. If so, it reinforced the case for employing the New Armies, or at least some of them, in another theatre of war.[33] Asquith favoured postponing all side-shows, even the Dardanelles operation, in the interest of rendering effective aid to Serbia.[34] He understood, if Lloyd George and Churchill did not always, that Britain's resources were limited. He told Venetia Stanley:

> There are two fatal things in war – one is to push blindly against a stone wall, the other is to scatter & divide your forces in a number of separate & disconnected operations. We are in great danger of committing both blunders ... Happily K. has a good judgment in those matters – never impulsive, sometimes inclined to be over cautious, but with a wide general outlook wh. is of the highest value ...[35]

Asquith notified Grey of the results of his meeting with Kitchener and Lloyd George and concluded by urging him 'to put the strongest possible pressures upon Roumania & Greece to come in without delay, & to promise them if they will form a real Balkan bloc we will send troops of our own to join them & save the situation'.[36] With momentum building in the cabinet for immediate intervention in the Balkans, Asquith held an impromptu meeting with Grey, Lloyd George and Hankey on the morning of 22 January. Kitchener, who was preoccupied with Millerand, was unable to join his colleagues. After a lively discussion, it was agreed that the government ought to send an army corps to the Balkans. Asquith subsequently confided to the King that this action would 'in all probability bring in both Roumania and Greece: in which case a really effective blow will be struck at the heart of the situation'.[37]

Neither Asquith nor Lloyd George had counted on French interference. Millerand, on being sounded by Kitchener, resisted the idea of sending troops to Serbia.[38] Asquith tried his luck with no better results. He left a record of his conversation with the French Minister of War:

> He can't speak a word of English, but was apparently able to follow my French. He ... says that Joffre is anxious that we should pour all our troops during the next month into his theatre, in order that he may be able to organize & carry out a really effective *coup*. Of course I put to him strongly the Balkan situation, and the irreparable disaster which would be involved in the crushing of Servia. He professed to be quite alive to this, but not '*dans ce moment*' etc.[39]

At the start of February Bulgaria accepted a large loan from Germany, leaving no doubt where its sympathies lay. Help for the Serbs seemed more urgent than ever. Asquith received good news from Lloyd George, who had just returned from Paris where he had attended a conference of Allied finance ministers: the Welshman had discovered that Millerand had said nothing to his colleagues about British interest in mounting an expedition in support of Serbia. Lloyd George corrected the omission and lobbied hard for a French commitment of troops to the Balkans. His proposal found a receptive audience.[40] All the leading French politicians, with the notable exception of Millerand, who was under Joffre's domination, were searching for an alternative to the bloody stalemate on the Western Front. This was confirmed by the French Minister of Foreign Affairs, Théophile Delcassé, who followed Lloyd George to London. On 8 February Asquith attended a luncheon party at which Delcassé was the guest of honour. Delcassé thought that if Britain sent a division to Salonika the French could do likewise. Asquith's letter to Venetia Stanley that day contained a summary of the discussion:

> We were all agreed that (1) the Serbian case is urgent (2) we must promise to send them two divisions – one English one French – as soon as may be to Salonica & *force in* the Greeks & Roumanians (3) we must try our damnedest to get the Russians to join if possible with a corps ... Lloyd George thinks he has got Sir John's assent to this [the despatch of a British Division]; but I have told K. to send for him and he is coming over to-night in one of Winston's destroyers.[41]

At the War Council meeting on 9 February, Kitchener insisted that only first-rate troops ought to be sent to Salonika. He proposed using the 29th

Division, the only remaining regular division in Britain, which had previously been destined for France. Asquith observed that by a limited use of British troops 'Greece would be brought into the war', the 'hostile attitude of Bulgaria would be paralyzed' and in 'all probability Roumania would be drawn in'. The political advantages seemed so overwhelming that the War Council instructed Grey to offer the 29th Division to Greece.[42]

Within a week British and French envoys in Athens delivered a joint note to the Venizelos government, promising the cooperation of two Allied divisions. Such limited intervention did little to alleviate Venizelos' anxiety about the Bulgarian menace. He declined to draw his country into the war without the collaboration of Roumania which for the moment, in view of the recent success of the German offensive in Poland, he considered pointless to approach.[43] The Balkan project was then dropped and, in Asquith's words, 'eyes are now fixed on the Dardanelles'.[44]

Chapter 5

Mounting Difficulites

Before the preliminary naval bombardment of the Dardanelles forts began on 19 February, Asquith had come around to the view that an army should be on hand to assist, and exploit the success of, the British fleet. Troops were shown to be available and there was no longer any question of sending them to Greece. On 13 February Asquith surprised Hankey by agreeing that the naval attack should be supported by a military landing. Asquith's own records reveal the following:

> I have been for some time coming to the same opinion [as Hankey], and I think we ought to be able without denuding French to scrape together from Egypt, Malta and elsewhere a sufficiently large contingent. If only these heart-breaking Balkan States could be bribed or goaded into action, the trick would be done with the greatest of ease and with incalculable consequences. It is of much importance that in the course of the next month we should carry through a *decisive* operation somewhere, and this one would do admirably for the purpose.[1]

Asquith was not the only one in the government whose position had shifted. The apprehensions of senior navy officials at the Admiralty had a sobering effect on Churchill and he now took the lead in clamouring for the despatch of troops to the Dardanelles. On 16 February Kitchener consented to send the 29th Division but three days later announced that he was holding it back because of the threat to France resulting from the latest Russian reverses.[2] He proposed to substitute for the 29th Division the 30,000 Australians and New Zealanders stationed in Egypt. Churchill protested vehemently, arguing that new and untried troops should not be employed on so difficult a task without a stiffening of regulars. Asquith was equally concerned. He saw the Dardanelles as the only hope in an otherwise dreary military situation. The Russians were crumbling on the Eastern Front; the Balkans were a wretched lot, bickering, cowering and holding back like the Italians; and, in a recent ten-day stretch in France,

Sir John had lost a hundred officers and 2,600 men with no corresponding gains.[3] Confronted by the persuasive powers of Asquith and Churchill, Kitchener partially relented, saying he would let the division go if its absence threatened to prejudice the success of the operation.[4]

As the War Council debated the fate of the 29th Division, the British fleet under Vice-Admiral Carden opened its bombardment on the outer forts in the Dardanelles.[5] Without any authorization from the cabinet or the Prime Minister, Churchill gave the press a detailed account of the first day's bombardment.[6] There were 'some murmurings' against Churchill but Asquith's only remark to Venetia Stanley was that the Admiralty statement made 'excellent reading after the daily bulletin from the trenches'.[7] Asquith does not initially appear to have understood the significance of the announcement, which committed the British to go through with the naval attack, foreclosing any possible withdrawal. He may have felt that Churchill's motive was to extract the maximum diplomatic advantage from the ships' progress, although it is more likely that the First Lord anticipated a swift Turkish collapse and wanted to ensure that he got the lion's share of the credit. Whatever the case, Churchill's indiscretion set in motion a tragic sequence of events that were to destroy Kitchener's effectiveness in the cabinet and War Council, bring down the Liberal government, set back Allied diplomacy in the Balkans and lead to the vain expenditure of thousands of lives.

The operation had attracted such world-wide attention that, for the sake of British prestige, Kitchener was anxious to avert defeat even if the cost was high. Asquith concurred with Kitchener's statement on 24 February that 'there could be no going back' and that the army 'ought to see the business through', in case the ships were unable to break into the Sea of Marmara.[8] To Asquith and indeed to general sentiment in the War Council, the possibility of an extensive military campaign in the Dardanelles strengthened the case for sending out the 29th Division and, although Kitchener came under greater pressure than ever to do so, he was immovable. As much as Asquith supported Churchill, he was reluctant to overrule Kitchener. He told his confidante prior to the meeting on the 24th:

> We are all agreed (except Kitchener) that the naval adventure in the Dardanelles should be backed up by a strong military force. I say 'except Kitchener', but he quite agrees in principle. Only he is very sticky about sending out there the 29th Division [as he] is rather perturbed by the strategic situation both in the East & West ... One must take a lot of risks in war, & I am strongly of [the] opinion that the chance of forcing the Dardanelles, & occupying Constantinople, & cutting Turkey in half, and arousing on our side the whole Balkan peninsula, presents such a unique opportunity that we ought

to hazard a lot elsewhere rather than forgo it. If he [Kitchener] can be convinced, well
& good; but to discard his advice & overrule his judgment on a military question is to
take a great responsibility.[9]

The tug-of-war between Kitchener and Churchill resumed at the War
Council on 26 February. Kitchener continued to conceive of the
Dardanelles operation as basically a naval concern with the army acting in
an auxiliary capacity. He was certain there would be enough troops on
hand to overcome the few pockets of resistance on the peninsula and to
occupy Constantinople. That being the case, he saw no justification to
send out his last reserve of regular troops as long as the Russian Front
remained fluid.[10] Asquith conceded that Kitchener had offered compelling
arguments. Of the meeting on the 26th he wrote:

> K., I think on the whole rightly, insisted on keeping his 29th Division at home, free to
> go either to the Dardanelles or to France, until we know (as we must in the course of the
> next week) where the necessity is greatest. The Russians are for the moment retiring &
> outmaneuvered: tho' one knows that they have a curious knack of making a good
> recovery. And the difference between sending to the Dardanelles at once 60,000 troops
> (which we can certainly do) & say 90,000 cannot, I think, for the moment at any rate
> be decisive ... We accepted Kitchener's view as right for the immediate situation to
> Winston's immense and unconcealed dudgeon ...[11]

In reading the War Council minutes, one cannot help but detect a note
of desperation in Churchill's arguments. He lost his composure and, in the
words of Asquith, was 'noisy, rhetorical, tactless and temperless'. At the
end of the meeting, Asquith called Churchill to his study. 'Winston was
rather trying', he revealed to Venetia Stanley, '& I felt constrained to talk
to him afterwards a little for his soul's good: a task wh. as you know I do
not relish, & in which I fear I do not excel'.[12]

Events over the next few days served to dissipate Churchill's anger and
alter the mood in the cabinet. The British fleet under Vice-Admiral
Carden was able to enter the mouth of the Dardanelles after the action on
26 February and by 2 March the last of the outer defences had been
silenced. The fall of the outer forts reverberated throughout Europe with
electrifying effect. Bulgaria abruptly broke off its courtship with Germany.
There were reports that Roumania was on the verge of abandoning its
neutrality. Italy made tentative overtures to the Allies about entering the
war against the Central Powers. Most significant of all was an offer from
Venizelos to land three Greek divisions on the Gallipoli Peninsula.

The possibility of dramatic political and military gains stimulated
speculation in Britain about the future disposal of enemy territory. Under
the Pact of London of 5 September 1914, Britain, France and Russia had
pledged not to make a separate treaty or offer peace terms without

previous agreement with both of their partners.[13] Whenever the issue of war aims came up during the Asquith administration, it was usually in connection with insistent demands made by members of the Entente or with efforts to win over new allies. Asquith made it a point to discourage any discussion of Britain's overall objectives either in the cabinet or in parliament. It was not that he was unconcerned with the problem of the peace settlement, only that to formulate a comprehensive programme of war aims would have entailed lengthy negotiations with France and Russia and a risk of serious quarrels.[14] He preferred to wait for definite German peace overtures when Britain, by virtue of its superior strength, would be able to dictate the terms of the treaty.

Asquith never lost sight of the fact that Britain was fighting to protect and maintain what it already possessed and to secure a post-war balance of power which served its interests. He was convinced that Europe would never enjoy peace and security until Germany was crushed and its government prised from the grip of those criminally responsible for the catastrophe, the German military leaders. Neither Asquith nor his colleagues wanted Germany removed from the ranks of the great powers. The common belief was that a chastened Germany, reformed and cleansed of the evil influence of Prussian militarism, would obviate the need for an excessively harsh peace.

From the outset of the war, Asquith sought to legitimize the conflict as a struggle for justice and righteousness. His early speeches singled out the ideals that inspired Britain's entry into the conflict – namely to honour international commitments and protect the integrity of small nations – and centred on the need to liberate Belgium and end the menace of Prussian militarism.[15] After the Marne, his pronouncements became more specific, confident as he was that German aggression had failed and that sooner or later Berlin would be forced to sue for peace. Around the third week in September 1914 Asquith indicated in a note to Grey that any peace settlement must include, quite apart from the additional conditions deemed necessary by Russia and France, Germany's readiness to sign a single treaty with the Entente (rather than making a separate peace with each of its members); to evacuate all occupied territories; to indemnify its opponents; and possibly to surrender its entire war fleet.[16]

During a speech in Dublin several days later Asquith made another pronouncement. Calling for a new world order after the war, he suggested the creation of 'a real European partnership based on the recognition of equal right, and established and enforced by a common will'.[17] Asquith did not initiate the concept of a system of international security to preserve the peace. Nor, it must be admitted, was it among his most cherished war aims.[18] Similarly Asquith gave low priority to the principle of self-determination. It was not until 1916 that he made public mention of subject nationalities and even then limited himself to the cases of the Poles and the Armenians.[19] Asquith was careful never to allow such matters to distract him from his pursuit of what he viewed as larger national interests.

Asquith made his first substantial declaration of Britain's war aims in the cabinet on 1 March 1915. His statement was essentially a composite of what he had said before. He demanded, as a preliminary to a full peace settlement, the restoration of Belgian independence, French security against future aggression, guarantees for the rights of small nations and the destruction of Prussian militarism.[20] There were no further attempts to define detailed objectives until the start of 1916. For the time being, the Asquith government tried to determine British territorial requirements in the Ottoman Empire while taking into account Russian and French claims.

It had been a practice of British policy in the years before the First World War to keep the Ottoman Empire intact, so far as was possible. Britain's relations with Constantinople changed very dramatically after the pro-German faction gained ascendancy in the Turkish cabinet. While still a neutral, Turkey unilaterally abrogated the Capitulations,[21] mistreated British subjects and seized British interests. This so angered Asquith and his colleagues that they resolved to punish Turkey. Just what such punishment would entail became clear on 20 October 1914, when Asquith informed the King that in the future Britain would abandon the formula of upholding the territorial integrity of the Ottoman Empire 'whether in Europe or in Asia'.[22] He repeated the statement during a speech at Guildhall on 9 November.[23] Ten days before, on the eve of hostilities with Turkey, he had told Venetia Stanley:

> Few things would give me greater pleasure than to see the Turkish Empire finally disappear from Europe and Constantinople either become Russian (which I think is its proper destiny) or if that is impossible neutralized and made a free port.[24]

When Asquith rung the death knell of the Ottoman Empire, the Zionist movement in Britain, under the leadership of Dr Chaim Weizmann, a lecturer in Chemistry at Manchester University, was encouraged to believe that an opportunity might arise for the establishment of a Jewish state in Palestine. Weizmann's link with the Asquith administration was Herbert Samuel, President of the Local Government Board and the first practising Jew to sit in a British cabinet.[25] Until Turkey joined the war, Samuel had not taken an active part in Jewish affairs, immersed as he was in furthering his political career. Neither his practical bent, nor his background – his family was connected to the old established Anglo-Jewish community which cherished Jewish loyalties and traditions but had little sympathy with Zionism – suggested that he was likely to espouse the Zionist cause. No one was more surprised than Asquith when he circulated a memorandum in January 1915 under the title 'The Future of Palestine'.

Since the Jews comprised no more than one-sixth of the total population in Palestine, Samuel acknowledged that the creation of an independent Jewish state was not at present viable. The best solution, he concluded, was a British protectorate under which Jewish immigration would be encouraged, so that in due course the Jewish people would reach majority status and be granted self-government. He tried to strengthen his case by pointing out that such an arrangement would be compatible with British interests.[26]

If there were some cabinet ministers favourable to Samuel's formula, none of them wanted to work for it. Asquith's own views are unequivocally expressed in a letter to Venetia Stanley:

> I confess I am not attracted by this proposed addition to our responsibilities. But it is a curious illustration of Dizzy's [Disraeli's] favourite maxim that 'race is everything' to find this almost lyrical outburst proceeding from the well-ordered and methodical brain of H. S.[27]

A revised version of Samuel's note was placed before the cabinet in March 1915.[28] It made as little impression on Asquith as the first one. He described it as a rather 'dithyrambic memorandum', adding with some amusement that the only other partisan of this proposal was Lloyd George, who did not 'care a damn for the Jews' but thought that it would be an outrage to allow the Holy Places to pass into the possession of 'Agnostic Atheistic France'.[29] At no time did Asquith take Zionism seriously. Visiting Palestine in 1924, he wrote that 'the talk of making Palestine into a "Jewish National Home" seems to me as fantastic as it always had done'.[30]

Asquith did not harbour the slightest prejudice against Jews, as evidenced by the inclusion of Samuel in his cabinet and by his close personal and professional association with Edwin Montagu, another Jew. An unimaginative man warily feeling his way to reach common sense solutions, his lack of interest in Zionism is perfectly understandable. As a rule, well-established British Jews shunned Zionism. Most of the recognized spokesmen for Anglo-Jewry, such as Edwin Montagu, who wrote a response to Samuel's memorandum,[31] were eager to prove that Britain was their only home and the centre of their allegiance. An area equal in size to Wales, Palestine was mountainous, desolate, partly waterless and without

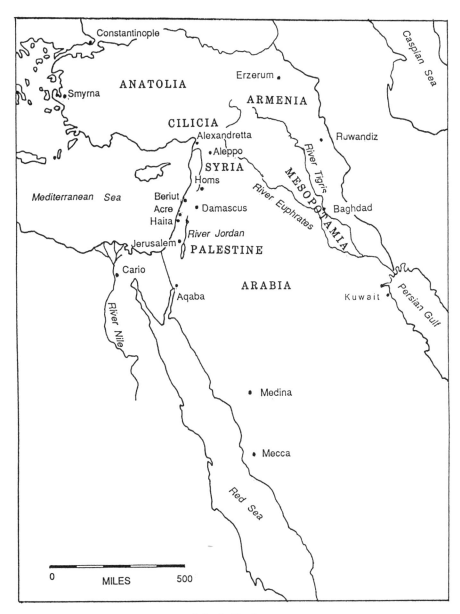

Asiatic Turkey

a single suitable harbour. Kitchener had surveyed Palestine as a young engineer and his bleak description of the region may have helped to colour Asquith's own perspective. His advice to the Prime Minister was to leave 'the Jews and the Holy Places to look after themselves'.[32] To anyone of Asquiths's temperament, the idea of establishing a Jewish minority government in a land dominated by a non-Jewish population was impractical, if not irrational. Then, too, the French were known to have designs on Palestine, a region in which they had special interests. In short, Asquith not only considered Zionism a fantasy but also believed that, for Britain, a protectorate over Palestine would involve a clash with the French as well as new and unnecessary imperial responsibilities. Having taken his final decision on the matter, Asquith turned to consider Russia's demand for reassurance about Constantinople and the Straits.

The Russians, expecting the imminent collapse of the Ottoman Empire and worried that the Straits would fall under the control of another power, adamantly refused to allow the Greeks to participate in the Dardanelles campaign.[33] Although the Foreign Office had implied in November 1914 that the fate of Constantinople and the Straits would be resolved in accordance with St Peterburg's interests, it had refused to consider any settlement with regard to Turkey until after the war. The recent developments, however, drove the Russians to press for a formal recognition of their claims.[34] These included Constantinople, the western shores of the Bosphorus, the Sea of Marmara, southern Thrace up to the Enos-Midia line, part of the Asiatic shore and the islands of Imbros and Tenedos at the mouth of the Straits. In return, the Tsarist government promised to respect French and British demands in other regions of the Ottoman Empire and elsewhere.

Asquith, like Grey, supported a settlement that would leave Russia in post-war possession of both Constantinople and the Straits.[35] He wrote:

> Personally I have always been & am in favour of Russia's claim, subject to proper conditions as to non-fortification of the Straits, and as to free commercial transit. With command of the Sea, we could always block the entrance. It is monstrous that Russia should have only two ports – Archangel and Vladivostok, both of which are ice-bound during the winter.[36]

The Russian *aide-mémoire* was circulated to the cabinet members on 8 March and discussed at their meeting the following day. Neither Kitchener nor Churchill objected to it on strategic grounds. In fact, there was less interest in questioning acceptance of Russian's demands than in formulating British claims in Asiatic Turkey. Asquith brought the cabinet back to the business at hand and it was decided to accept the Russian proposals in principle, subject to 'the creation of a free port at Constantinople and to the free passage of the Straits for the commerce of all nations'. Since the treaty with Russia would mark a radical departure in policy, Asquith thought it desirable to obtain inter-party agreement.[37]

Both Bonar Law and Lansdowne were in attendance when the War Council convened on 10 March to debate the cabinet's decision. Grey emphasized that unless some gesture was made to accommodate the Russians, there was a real danger they would leave the war. Asquith observed that, when consulted, the military and naval authorities had agreed that Russian possession of the Straits would not fundamentally alter the present strategic standing in the Mediterranean. Both Bonar Law and Lansdowne favoured telling the Russians only that they could rely on Britain's good will in settling the Constantinople question at the end of the war. The War Council discounted the views of the Opposition leaders and authorized Grey to accept the Russian terms, provided the war was fought to a successful conclusion and Britain realized its own territorial desiderata.[38]

It is strange that neither Asquith nor any of his ministers perceived the contradiction between the post-war division of Ottoman territory and current military expectation in the Dardanelles. The appearance of Carden's fleet off Constantinople was supposed to trigger a *coup d'état* and bring into office a pro-Entente or neutralist regime that would take Turkey out of the war. But how could the Allies have expected to persuade such a government to surrender vast portions of its empire?

At the meeting of 10 March and at the next one nine days later, the War Council sought to determine Britain's share of the Turkish spoils. Lloyd George felt that Britain's prestige would be enhanced by the acquisition of Palestine. Kitchener argued that Palestine would be of no use whatsoever. Instead he pressed for Mesopotamia, with the Syrian port of Alexandretta as its corridor to the Mediterranean, in order to counter any post-war threat Russia and France might pose to British interests in the Middle East. Fisher and Churchill supported Kitchener. The Admiralty was interested in building a naval base at Alexandretta and in drawing upon the rich oil fields of Mesopotamia. The men in control of the India Office were divided over the value of Alexandretta but favoured the annexation of Mesopotamia on account of its agricultural potential and its large unsettled areas, which could serve as an outlet for the surplus population of India. They appeared inclined towards a formula that would bring in Egypt and Mesopotamia, with Palestine as a geopolitical link between the two.[39]

The expansionist mood in the War Council was disconcerting to

Asquith, whose views in regard to the Ottoman Empire had changed radically since November 1914. Asquith noted 'that, at the moment, Grey & I are the *only* two men who doubt and distrust any such settlement' as the partition of the Ottoman Empire.[40] Asquith disliked the idea of further territorial accessions as it was bound to set Britain on a collision course with its allies and involve it in enormous and unprofitable expenditure. Yet he realized that the British could not remain free agents if Russia took a substantial slice of Turkey and other powers followed suit. As he pointed out: 'If, for one reason or another ... we were to leave other nations to scramble for Turkey without taking anything ourselves, we should not be doing our duty.'[41]

Asquith was circumspect in what he said during the War Council discussions, but he did vent his feelings in a long letter to Fisher in April:

> It is very difficult to convince the ignorant or the foolish that swollen boundaries mean, or may mean, anything else than greater wealth, greater authority, greater solidarity. It may also be remembered that there may be territories which we must take because we do not want other countries to take them. Further too, there may be territories which we must take because there is no one else to give them to. The Turks may have disappeared. You cannot hand important pieces of land to savages and Great Britain may be forced to new responsibilities as reluctantly as she has on occasions been forced in the past ... But new territories require the expenditure of more money, and even more important, the expenditure of more men. We shall be short of both at the end of this war ... New territories will require new armies, new navies, new civil servants, new engineers, new teachers, new doctors, new nurses. Where are these to come from?
>
> ...
>
>   I believe that we have not the men or the money to make new countries out of barren and savage deserts; and if we try ... we shall arrest progress at home and in the other countries for which we are responsible, and we shall saddle the British taxpayer with huge liabilities for defence ...

Asquith was especially critical of Kitchener's call for the British acquisition of Mesopotamia. He went on to say:

> He thinks a new country in Asia can be made as quickly as a new army in England ... It has taken many years to make the Punjab, [but] it is yet not self-supporting ... How long will it be before Mesopotamia can give to the subjects of King George's great grandson some part of the expenditure which we today will have to bear for the fortifications of Alexandretta and the vast army necessary to defend it and the railway from there to Basra.[42]

The position taken by the War Council on 19 March was vague and reflected the differences of opinion among its members. Apart from providing for the establishment of a Muslim state in the Middle East, there was general agreement that it was premature to discuss the future partition of Turkey in Asia.[43] But Grey, in view of his upcoming informal discussions

1 Herbert Henry Asquith, 1st Earl of Oxford and Asquith (1852–1928), in about 1914
(*Imperial War Museum*)

2 Margot Asquith (1864–1945), by John Singer Sargent (*National Portrait Gallery*)

3 Venetia Stanley in about 1914 (*Milton Gendel*)

4 Lord Bertie, Asquith and Grey on their way to the Quai d'Orsay

5 Hugh O'Beirne and Asquith at the Vatican, 1 April 1916

6 Asquith watching men adjusting fuses. Outside Contay, 7 August 1916
(*Imperial War Museum*)

7 General Joffre, President Poincaré, George V, General Foch and Sir Douglas Haig,
at Château Val Vion, Beauquesne, 12 August 1916 (*Imperial War Museum*)

8 Field Marshal Lord Kitchener (1850–1916) at Anzac, 13 November 1915, returning through the trenches to the beach. With him is General Birdwood.
(*Imperial War Museum*)

9 Kitchener at Helles, 12 November 1915, with General Birdwood, Colonel Watson and General Davies (*Imperial War Museum*)

10 Sir Edward Grey (1862–1933)

11 Winston Churchill (1874–1965)
(*Imperial War Museum*)

12 Field Marshal Sir John French, 1st Earl
of Ypres (1852–1925) (*Imperial War Museum*)

13 Admiral John (Jackie) Fisher, 1st Baron
Fisher (1841–1920) by Francis Dodd 1916
(*National Portrait Gallery*)

14 David Lloyd George, (1863–1945) by an unknown artist, in about 1917
(*National Portrait Gallery*)

with Delcassé,[44] thought it desirable to ascertain more clearly Britain's war aims, particularly in the event of an emergency partition of the Ottoman state. Accordingly, in early April, Asquith appointed a special inter-departmental committee under the chairmanship of Sir Maurice de Bunsen, Assistant Under-Secretary of State at the Foreign Office. The committee presented its report on 30 June 1915.[45]

During March and April the government's absorption over the issue of war spoils presupposed an early victory against Turkey. The course of the fighting in the Dardanelles hardly justified such optimism. Trouble began early in March when Carden's ships engaged the intermediate defences and had to operate inside the narrow Straits.

Back in London, Churchill grew impatient and anxious at the lack of progress. His outlook brightened on 10 March when Kitchener ruled that the military situation was now sufficiently secure to warrant the despatch of the 29th Division. The next day Kitchener informed his colleagues that he had assigned General Sir Ian Hamilton to command the growing military force – 70,000 with the arrival of the 29th Division.[46]

The circumstances leading to Hamilton's appointment are unclear. It is known that Kitchener gave the matter considerable thought and discussed it with both Asquith and Churchill before making the actual selection. Of the various officers under consideration, Kitchener at first favoured General Leslie Rundle, a close friend and an officer whose services in Egypt and the Sudan had earned him a high military reputation. What caused him to change his mind? The answer is probably political pressure. Churchill expressed a preference for General Hunter-Weston but when his suggestion was turned down lobbied on behalf of Hamilton, with whom he had been on intimate terms for over twenty years. Churchill alone, however, would not have won over Kitchener as evidenced by the rejection of his first choice. It was apparently the Prime Minister who had the final say in the matter. According to Violet Asquith (later Lady Bonham Carter), it was at her father's insistence that Hamilton was sent to the Dardanelles. Her unpublished diary at this time contains the following entry:

> Tuesday I dined with Ava Astor and talked to Ian Hamilton afterwards. – I knew he was to be sent in full command (K. had suggested Trundle [probably Asquith's nickname for Rundle] but Father was quite firm about I. H.) ... He dined with us a week later when he knew of his appointment – in an ecstasy – I think he probably has just the right dash of irregularity for the situation.[47]

Kitchener evidently did not see any harm in deferring to the Prime Minister's wishes. He certainly considered Hamilton more than qualified to deal with the anticipated mopping up operations. More puzzling, however, was Asquith's endorsement of Hamilton, a soldier he had earlier described as having 'too much feather in his brain'.[48] Asquith had recently been in charge of the War Office and he knew most of the senior generals. It is conceivable that he was not so much enthusiastic about Hamilton as unenthusiastic about Rundle. Violet Asquith's last remark may hold the key. Did Asquith think that this was a job which required a rather unusual kind of soldier? To be sure Hamilton, who combined a quick wit and an abundance of charm with a flair for painting and a keen appreciation of music and poetry, did not fit the mould in which career officers were cast. It is also worth remembering that Hamilton was a popular figure in Liberal circles. He had stood by the government during the pre-war controversies, particularly in 1910 when he lent Haldane his fluent pen to state the case against conscription.[49] These were considerations which may have overborne the view that Hamilton had 'too much feather in his brain'.

In any case Asquith would have been well-advised to heed to his own dictum about amateur strategists foisting their opinions on men who had made soldiering their lives' work. Contrary to expectations, the army was called upon to undertake major operations in rugged terrain. Hamilton, despite impressive military credentials, was ill-suited for such a command. His excessive optimism inclined him to underestimate the task at hand and he was not strong enough to take charge and impose his will on less competent subordinates.[50]

When Kitchener handed Hamilton his instructions, on the morning of 13 March, he was emphatic that the army was not to engage in military operations until the fleet had exhausted every effort to get through.[51] Among the members of the War Council, only Hankey was sceptical of the prospects of unaided naval action. On 16 March he wrote a very perceptive note to Asquith, underlining the hazards involved in a landing when all chance of surprise had been lost. He observed that the War Council ought to assure itself that preparations for a combined operation had been carefully worked out and he included a list of questions upon which it was desirable to cross-examine the naval and military authorities.[52]

Asquith discussed the memo with Hankey on 17 March and expressed his satisfaction at the arrangements made for any landing that might be required.[53] The Prime Minister did, however, ask Kitchener two days later whether a scheme for a possible disembarkation had been devised. Kitchener replied that the War Office did not have sufficient information to prepare a detailed plan and that the work would have to be done by the

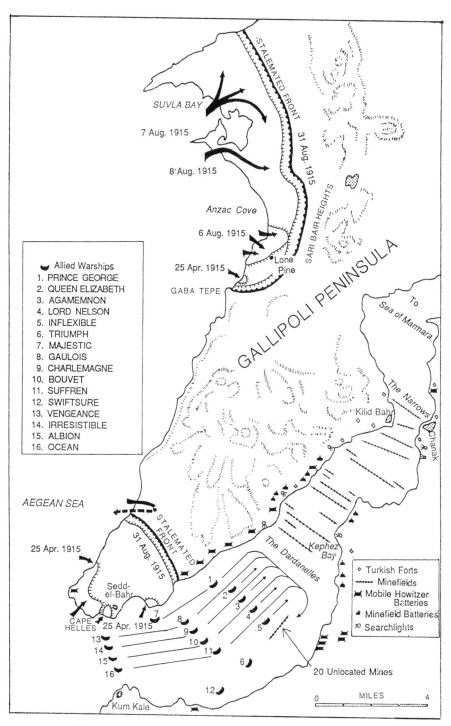

The Dardanelles: The Naval Attack and the Landings

general and admiral on the spot.[54] Since Asquith considered a large landing unlikely, he accepted this perfunctory answer and made no effort to press Kitchener on the other points raised by Hankey's memo.

On 18 March Rear-Admiral De Robeck, who had succeeded to the naval command when Carden suffered a nervous breakdown, made a bid to force the Narrows. After three ships were sunk and three others disabled, De Robeck halted the operation, leaving the guns of the forts comparatively untouched. An undetected row of mines had been responsible for most of the damage.

In London the Admiralty was disappointed over the action of 18 March but simply regarded it as a bad beginning, the first of what would be several days' fighting. Asquith was told that the ships lost were expendable and that steps had been taken to replace them. When the War Council met on the morning of 19 March, there was no thought of discontinuing the naval attack. The members raised few questions before authorizing Churchill to inform De Robeck to press forward with the operations 'if he thought fit'.[55]

After the meeting, Hankey wrote a memo to Asquith reiterating the concerns expressed in his earlier one. He felt that the opportunity for a *coup de main* in the Dardanelles had passed and that serious siege operations of a combined nature would be required. He attributed the naval setback to insufficient staff preparations, pointing out that it was essential in the joint operation to avoid the same mistake. Accordingly he urged the appointment of a technical naval and military committee – anticipating the Chiefs of Staff Committee set up in 1923 – at least to define the objectives of the expedition, in order to determine the forces needed to carry them out. Here Hankey had identified the basic flaw in the whole enterprise. Even at this late hour, much would have been gained by bringing together the two staffs. By pooling information and ideas a joint committee undoubtedly would have avoided some of the mistakes that subsequently occurred. As it was, Hankey's proposal was seen as too revolutionary to warrant consideration. Asquith probably discussed the idea with Kitchener and Churchill but, as Hankey conceded, if they objected to it, he could hardly overrule them.[56]

On 19 March De Robeck indicated he would try again as soon as he had reorganized his minesweeping force, but four days later decided to delay the attack until it could be undertaken in conjunction with military forces. Asquith heard the news directly from Churchill, who could hardly believe it himself. The First Lord added that he had drafted a telegram telling De Robeck to renew the attack at the first favourable opportunity but that the Sea Lords had taken the line that the opinion of the man on the spot had to be accepted. Asquith was sympathetic. He permitted himself a few thoughts on the subject:

> The ... Admiral seems to be rather in a funk. Ian Hamilton has not yet sent his report, but the soldiers cannot be ready for any big concerted operation before the 14th April. I agree with Winston & Kitchener that the Navy ought to make another big push, so soon as the weather clears. If they wait & wait, until the army is fully prepared, they may fall into a spell of bad weather, & (what is worse) find that submarines, Austrian or German, have arrived on the scene.[57]

With Asquith's support, Churchill returned to the Admiralty to restate his case, but his senior naval advisers, in particular Fisher, remained obdurate. Churchill again appealed to the Prime Minister, who noted:

> Winston came to talk about the Dardanelles. The weather is infamous there, & the Naval experts seem to be suffering from a fit of nerves. They are now disposed to wait till the troops can assist them in force, which ought to be not later than about April 10th. Winston thinks & I agree with him, that the ships, as soon as the weather clears, and the aeroplanes can detect the condition of the forts and the positions of the concealed guns, ought to make another push: & I hope this will be done.[58]

Unable to budge the senior admirals, Churchill had hoped that the Prime Minister would 'intervene and make his views effective'.[59] But it was unrealistic of Churchill to expect Asquith to allow his own instincts to override the judgment not only of the Admiralty experts but also that of the naval commander. As a layman with limited knowledge of naval matters, Asquith could not properly assess the dangers from mines and mobile howitzers, or the technical difficulties of dealing with them, and whether De Robeck had the resources at his disposal to do so. Had he, in defiance of logic, ordered a renewal of the naval attack, he would have forced Fisher's resignation and faced a major governmental crisis.

It remains a matter of controversy to this day whether the navy could have got through if it had resumed the attack. It is known that the Turks had expended much of their ammunition and that there were few mines left in the waters where the six Allied ships had been sunk or damaged. There was no possibility of the enemy making up these shortages for at least several months. Some naval officers on the spot, such as Commodore Keyes, agreed with Churchill that a great opportunity was lost. But there are as many who disagree and, as the naval assault was not resumed, it is impossible to be sure. It would have been, however, a gamble worth taking. The risks of land operations, to which the British were now committed, far outweighed the risks of further naval activity.

During the weeks of early spring, Asquith was beset by press attacks, by rumours of intrigue against him and loyal associates, and by dissension within the cabinet. In the wake of the recent failure in the Dardanelles, coupled with the absence of any hopeful signs on the Western Front, articles critical of Asquith's leadership appeared in *The Times*, the *Observer* and the *Morning Post*. This aroused suspicion in Liberal circles of a Tory conspiracy to discredit or weaken the Prime Minister in order to promote a coalition government. It was even alleged that the plotters were being abetted by at least one member of the cabinet. On 24 March H. W. Massingham warned Margot Asquith that Churchill was scheming to substitute Balfour for Grey at the Foreign Office.[60] He did not mention any movement against the Prime Minister himself but the inference was unmistakable. The two men had always stood together and it was well-known that Asquith would never consent to the removal of one of his closest associates. Was Churchill plotting to overthrow Asquith and clear the way for a coalition with the Tories?

Asquith had been alerted by Edwin Montagu, Chancellor of the Duchy of Lancaster, on 21 March that Churchill was broaching the suggestion to political allies that Balfour should 'be put in charge of the Foreign Office when Grey goes next week for his fishing holiday'.[61] The additional information passed on by his wife seems to confirm that the First Lord was intriguing with the Opposition. Asquith consulted Lloyd George the following day and asked him what he thought of Massingham's story. Lloyd George replied, rather to Asquith's surprise, that he believed it to be substantially true. After the meeting, Asquith wrote to Venetia Stanley revealing his growing disillusionment with Churchill:

> It is a pity, isn't it? that Winston hasn't a better sense of proportion, and also a larger endowment of the instinct of loyalty. As you know, like you, I am really fond of him: but I regard his future with many misgivings... He will never get to the top in English politics, with all his wonderful gifts; to speak with the tongues of men & angels, and to spend laborious days & nights in administration, is no good, if a man does not inspire trust.[62]

Matters took an unexpected turn when the *Daily Chronicle*, a Liberal newspaper, published an article on 29 March, implicating Lloyd George in a plot against Asquith. Before lunch that day, McKenna called at 10 Downing Street and accused Northcliffe of engineering a campaign to replace Asquith with Lloyd George. He claimed that he had evidence that Lloyd George and, perhaps Churchill, were involved in it. When Asquith confronted Lloyd George later that same day, he made no mention of the charges in the *Daily Chronicle* but simply referred to the sinister and, as he assumed, absurd tales now in circulation. Instantly Lloyd George became defensive and, in a rare display of emotion, vehemently disclaimed any involvement in the affair. The real culprit, he insisted, was Kitchener but as he was a Tory, or supposed to be one, the Tory press were afraid to criticize his shortcomings. Instead, they concentrated on the Prime Minister who was an easier target. Asquith's account of the meeting continues:

> As for himself (Ll.G.) he declared that he owed everything to me; that I had stuck to him & protected him & defended him when every man's hand was against him; and that he would rather (1) break stones (2) dig potatoes (3) be hanged and quartered (these were metaphors used at different stages of his broken but impassioned harangue) than do an act, or say a word, or harbour a thought, that was disloyal to me. And he said that everyone of our colleagues felt the same. His eyes were wet with tears, and I am sure that, with all his Celtic capacity for impulsive & momentary fervour, he was quite sincere ... Of course, I assured him that I had never for a moment doubted him – which is quite true: & he warmly wrung my hand & abruptly left the room.[63]

Certain that McKenna had inspired the article in the *Daily Chronicle*, Lloyd George insisted on a face-to-face encounter with him in the presence of the Prime Minister. It was no secret that Lloyd George and McKenna disliked one another and so Asquith, hoping to establish better relations between the two, arranged the tripartite meeting for 3.30 p.m. on 30 March. Churchill, invited by Lloyd George to attend, declined to do so. For an hour the two antagonists engaged in heated debate. Lloyd George accused McKenna of always seeing imaginary plots, as in Churchill's supposed campaign to oust Grey. To which McKenna replied that the real villain was Balfour, with whom Churchill was much too intimate. Asquith sat back for a while and simply listened to the exchanges but eventually intervened and managed to calm them down and restore a semblance of civility.[64]

That evening Asquith received a note from Churchill. In it the First Lord explained that he had refused Lloyd George's invitation to come to the interview because 'I feel that my case is safe in your hands'. In revealing the contents of the letter to Venetia Stanley, Asquith went on to say: 'That bears out what you said in your most darling letter – that (whatever happens) W. is really loyal to me. I am sure, & I have never doubted, that he is. So that silly "plot" is done with'.[65]

Asquith was not one to pay much heed to rumours and counter-rumours. Loyal and above board, he could not imagine that any of his colleagues would stoop to engage in sordid backroom intrigues. On this occasion he was correct in determining that neither Churchill nor Lloyd George had threatened his position. Impulsive by nature, Churchill did not always weigh the consequences of his actions. In view of Grey's lack of

vigour and rapidly failing eyesight, Churchill may well have expressed a
preference for Balfour at the Foreign Office, but criticism of a colleague or
even Prime Minister does not amount to a conspiracy. Nor is there any
evidence that Churchill was plotting to force his colleagues into a coalition.
It is true that in the past he had advocated such an arrangement but, after
observing the Tory leaders in the War Council discussions on 10 March
1915, his enthusiasm cooled and he became resigned to the continuance of
party government.[66]

As for Lloyd George, although he did not conceal his belief that Asquith
was deficient in driving power,[67] it is clear that he did not deliberately set
out to supplant his chief. On the other hand, it would be idle to pretend
that he did not covet the premiership or that he was incapable of
treachery. But in March 1915 he lacked the support to challenge Asquith
and he stood to gain little by promoting a coalition.

Asquith had barely reconciled the conflicting parties when the growing
feud between Kitchener and Lloyd George over the subject of munitions
supply threatened to produce a cabinet crisis. It became apparent during
the early weeks of the conflict that the amount of ammunition required
would be greatly in excess of what had been forecast. Kitchener, whose
ordnance department was responsible for supplying the army in the field,
realized from the beginning that the standing arrangements were
unsuitable for modern warfare. During the first six months of the conflict
his ordnance department organized a nineteen-fold increase in munitions.
Still the output could not keep up with the army's voracious appetite.
Asquith never understood that the basic problem was not Kitchener. Any
large-scale armament expansion was beyond the power of a sub-division of
the War Office: it required massive changes in labour relations as well as
in industrial and government practices.[68]

The first signs of uneasiness in the cabinet about munitions production
surfaced at the beginning of October 1914. On the 12th Asquith appointed
a committee under Kitchener's chairmanship to coordinate arms production.[69] Kitchener regarded the committee as something of a nuisance
and he effectively put an end to it at the beginning of 1915 by claiming that
he could no longer find time to attend its meetings.[70]

By then Lloyd George had concluded that War Office policy of
organizing production through the principal armament firms was inadequate and that the nation's entire engineering capacity needed to be
exploited to wage the war successfully. On 22 February he circulated a
long memorandum, warning of dire consequences unless the government
took steps to impose tight control over industry and manpower supply.[71]
The munitions issue was again discussed on 5 March at a conference at 10

Downing Street with Asquith presiding. Kitchener, Lloyd George and General Von Donop (Master General of the Ordnance) were among those in attendance. Kitchener and Von Donop acknowledged that the delivery of rifles and all types of munitions were seriously in arrears. The upshot was that the War Office was asked to investigate how much of the unexploited industrial capacity in the land could be utilized for war production and to report back as quickly as possible.[72] Lloyd George apparently approached Asquith, either after the meeting or the next day, and demanded that a special body be formed to take over the area of munitions production.[73]

As Asquith pondered the matter, he toyed with the idea of creating a Directorate of Army Contracts with a cabinet minister in charge. The man he first considered for the post was Edwin Montagu, who had prepared a scheme outlining the administrative machinery for the proposed operation.[74] Montagu had entered the cabinet in February 1915 as Chancellor of the Duchy of Lancaster at the unusually young age of thirty-six. He owed his rise in Liberal politics less to the good will of the Prime Minister (who was, by an odd coincidence, also his rival for the affections of Venetia Stanley) than to unmistakable ability and hard work. Upon further reflection, Asquith ruled him out and instead turned to Lloyd George as someone with enough weight to stand up to Kitchener. Lloyd George, however, would accept the office only if given complete control over the provision of munitions. Since Kitchener would not yield to such an arrangement, Asquith abandoned all thoughts of appointing a Director of Army Contracts.[75]

Instead Asquith turned to his other option – a new munitions committee invested with sufficient authority to answer Lloyd George's concerns. On 22 March he held a meeting with Lloyd George, Balfour, Churchill and Montagu to define the powers of the intended committee. Kitchener was not invited to attend the conclave. 'The discussion was quite a good one', Asquith told Venetia Stanley, 'and I think we came to some rational (and unanimous) conclusions.'[76] The purpose of the new committee under Lloyd George was to mobilize potential as well as existing sources of armament supply. It would be responsible to the cabinet rather than the War Office and would have the right, after due consultation with the service departments, to place contracts on its own authority.

The next day Asquith informed Kitchener of the conclusions of the meeting, assuring him of the 'minimum of interference with the normal contract work of the Departments'.[77] Kitchener was already fighting a rearguard action to maintain control over the production of munitions. A week earlier he had appointed his own Armaments Output Committee. Under the chairmanship of George Macaulay Booth, a Liverpool shipowner and industrialist, its principal task was to overcome the shortage of labour in the armament factories.[78]

In response to Asquith's note, Kitchener agreed in principle to the new munitions committee but insisted that it should not interfere with existing War Office contracts or divert labour from firms which had been, or were about to be, registered at the War Office as suppliers of war material.[79] Asquith showed this letter to Lloyd George who remarked, after reading it, that Kitchener's conditions would render the committee powerless and little more than an advisory body. This was not what he had in mind and he made his feelings known at once to the Secretary for War.[80]

The power struggle between Kitchener and Lloyd George erupted into the open on 28 March. Kitchener threatened to resign if the new committee had executive authority, while Lloyd George retorted that he would wash his hands of the whole business if it did not.[81] Asquith tried to find a way out of the dilemma by imposing a typically Asquithian solution. On 8 April he announced that a Munitions of War Committee would be established under the chairmanship of Lloyd George 'to ensure the promptest and most efficient application of all the available resources of the country to the manufacture and supply of Munitions of War for the Army and Navy'.[82] As it turned out, the new committee, popularly called the Treasury Committee, was never really in charge of munitions supply. Although the committee was nominally empowered to take any action deemed necessary, it had to look to the War Office for all its technical information and for final approval to any contract it might negotiate.[83] The compromise arrangement was quite unworkable, with the result that Kitchener and Lloyd George virtually went their own way. This division of effort lasted until the reconstruction of the government in May when Lloyd George left the Exchequer for the newly created Ministry of Munitions.

The inability of the Asquith government to put armament production on a satisfactory basis naturally had a bearing on the conduct of British operations in the West. After the onset of trench warfare, Sir John French complained at every opportunity that the gross inadequacy of his supply of field guns and shells was depriving him of the means necessary to do the job. There was an element of truth in French's lamentations: in his first major battle of 1915 at Neuve Chapelle his men certainly would have benefited from additional artillery support after they broke through the enemy line. But failure to exploit the gap was due to more compelling reasons, namely shortcomings in the planning and execution of the infantry attacks. Still the deficiency of munitions supply provided Sir John with a pretext to blame Kitchener.[84]

Back home rumours that the army had insufficient ammunition to conduct its operations added to the growing dissatisfaction with Asquith's management of the war. For months the party truce, which had tamed or muted discussion in parliament, and the patriotic restraint of the press (the Censorship Bureau exercised no control over editorials, suppressing only military and naval information that might prove useful to the enemy) had lulled the public into a false state of optimism. But by the early spring of 1915 the united front was breaking down. The Tory Party as a whole was disturbed by reliable accounts of munition shortages at the Front;[85] and by lack of military progress for which it saw no obvious explanation except the ineptitude of an administration it had always mistrusted. This prompted the Unionist Business Committee – formed in January by die-hard Tory backbenchers dissatisfied with the silence imposed upon them by their leaders – to press Asquith for a more aggressive war policy. While Bonar Law shared many of their concerns in private, he kept them from criticizing the government too sharply lest it seem to the public that the Unionist party was being unpatriotic.[86]

The press was less tolerant of the government's apparent inertia. Asquith's statesmanlike qualities, which it had acclaimed in the opening days of the war, were not seen as adequate to direct the war effort. It regretted that the Prime Minister had been unable to provide dynamic leadership, printed disturbing reports or letters from the Front, and began to give a more realistic picture of the war. As criticism of Asquith mounted, even Liberal newspapers joined the chorus.

Asquith had heard about the effect of the shells shortage on the BEF's operations. He obtained the information presumably from officers on leave who had first-hand experience of it. On 20 April he travelled to Newcastle to speak on behalf of the North East Coast Armaments Subcommittee – a body consisting of representatives from the service departments as well as employers and trade unions engaged in munitions production. The purpose of his talk was to spur the workers and employers to greater efforts.

Before making the trip, Asquith asked Kitchener to send for Sir John French and to obtain from him a concise report on the state of his ammunition.[87] On 14 April Asquith received the following note from Kitchener: 'I have had a talk with French. He told me I could let you know that with the present supply of ammunition he will have as much as his troops will be able to use on his next forward movement. '[88] Asquith had no reason to suspect its contents when he delivered his speech. He began by praising the munitions workers for what they had already accomplished and urged on them the need for increased endeavours. He then went on to refute the charges that his government had been lax in attending to the army's welfare:

> I do not believe that any ... army has ever either entered upon a campaign or been maintained during a campaign with better or more adequate equipment. I saw a statement the other day that the operations ... of our army ... were being crippled, or at any rate hampered, by our failure to provide the necessary ammunition. I say there is not a word of truth to that statement ... [89]

Asquith's address, in which he showed uncharacteristic poor judgment, was one of the major blunders of his wartime premiership. He had overstated Kitchener's assurance, applying it not to a projected attack but to past operations. Asquith sought to justify his calculated misstatements a year after the war ended: 'Operations of great possible moment ... were then impending, and it was of the utmost importance not to expose our own weaknesses or to give encouragement to the Germans – to let them think that we could not and were not able to do more than hold our own.'[90] It would be difficult to dispute such logic but Asquith was a master of the English language and he could have chosen his words more carefully at Newcastle.

As it happened, his statement ran counter to what too many people knew to be the truth, to say nothing of acknowledgments made in public by both Kitchener and Lloyd George, that munitions were in short supply. It raised doubts about the Prime Minister's integrity and ability to coordinate the war effort and reflected a sense of complacency at a moment when greater vision, resolve and dedication were needed to correct past inadequacies.

The British press struck with a vengeance. *The Times* expressed deep disappointment over the Prime Minister's petty attempts 'to prove that he and his colleagues have made no miscalculations and no mistakes'.[91] The *Daily Mail* wondered how Asquith could reconcile his remarks with those of Kitchener and Lloyd George proclaiming an acute shortage of munitions.[92] The *Scotsman* was astounded that Asquith had 'placed himself in the unfortunate position of denying and adversely criticizing, the grave and deliberate statements of his colleagues on a question of the highest possible moment'.[93] The speech, according to the *Daily Express*, was 'mischievous to a degree' for it was calculated to keep the nation in a fool's paradise.[94] Finally, the *Pall Mall Gazette* shrugged off Asquith's performance as too guarded and uninspiring and, adding insult to injury, compared it with Lloyd George's 'blunt and truthful' address on the drink question at Bangor the previous month.[95]

Asquith paid scant attention to the fallout from his Newcastle speech. At the time he was temporarily in charge of the Foreign Office (Grey had retired to his estate to rest for a few weeks) and was caught up in delicate negotiations with the Italian government. Italy was considered a major prize among the neutral nations and actively courted by the two groups of belligerents. The Salandra government had no qualms about flirting with both sides to see which would pay the higher price for Italy's services. Here the advantage lay with the Entente, since the territory which Rome coveted lay within the Austrian Empire. On 4 March 1915 the Italian ambassador in London announced Italy's readiness to intervene if its terms were granted: these included acquisition of Trent, Trieste, Cisalpine Tyrol, Istria and nearly all the Dalmatian coast with its offshore islands, a monetary subsidy, a share of the Ottoman Empire if it was partitioned, and equitable treatment in any distribution of colonies.[96]

Grey considered Italy's territorial demands exorbitant but on the whole had no objections to them as they did not conflict with British interests. Asquith was disgusted with the Italians, whose conduct had all the earmarks of a cynical bargain in *Realpolitik*. To Venetia Stanley, he described Italy as 'that most voracious, slippery and perfidious Power'.[97] Nevertheless, he believed that Italy was worth purchasing, for its entry in the war would precipitate similar action throughout the Balkans.[98] An agreement with the Salandra government was delayed because of Russia's refusal to concede the Dalmatian coast to Italy. A month later Asquith produced the compromise which had eluded Grey and Italy signed the Treaty of London on 26 April 1915. The pact bound Italy to join the conflict within a month.[99]

The elation over the Entente's only recent diplomatic success was dampened by tragic news from the Dardanelles. On 25 April Hamilton had commenced his landings on the Gallipoli Peninsula. His men secured a precarious hold on the southern tip and a small beachhead further to the north but they were unable to advance overland to positions that would dominate the Straits. Under skilful German leadership, the Turkish army showed immense courage and resolution, belying its performance on the Suez Canal and elsewhere.[100] By 8 May, when Hamilton's last offensive petered out, the British had incurred nearly 20,000 casualties.[101]

The events of the past few months had not brought Asquith much comfort. The addition of Italy to the Entente was the only bright spot in what was otherwise a bleak picture. Sir John French's attack at Neuve Chapelle had stalled, producing only a long casualty list. In the Dardanelles the navy's failure had been followed by that of the army, ending the hope of a quick victory over Turkey. Ahead lay a costly struggle of attrition, similar to the war in France. At the start of May the Austro-

German offensive in the East pierced the front at Gorlice and sent the Russian army in headlong retreat towards Warsaw. The deteriorating military situation was aggravated by dissension within the government and political pressures from without.

Asquith betrayed no outward signs of strain from his mounting difficulties. Alone in his office he may have experienced low moments but, in public or at cabinet meetings, he never gave anyone reason to suspect that his confidence had been shaken. 'All the Ministers look years older', Lord Esher wrote at the time, 'except the P. M. who seemed placid and confident.'[102] Asquith undoubtedly hoped that this stretch of bad luck had run its course and that things would soon improve. But, alas, there would be no ray of light ahead, only more dark clouds.

Chapter 6

The End of Liberal Rule

When the decision was made to capture the Gallipoli Peninsula, neither Asquith nor Kitchener gave serious thought to what would follow if, as had now happened, British forces proved unequal to the task. In view of what was at stake, Asquith favoured a continuation of the attack. But first he had to determine whether the requirements for another big offensive in the Dardanelles were within Britain's available military capability. Asquith asked Kitchener what he contemplated doing next. Kitchener was undecided. He admitted that he had underrated the difficulties in overcoming Turkish resistance. With such reinforcements as he could send, he held no hope that Hamilton, facing a reported 150,000 Turks, could capture the commanding heights. He wished he could withdraw from the Dardanelles but to do so would irreparably damage British prestige in the Muslim world.[1]

Asquith was beset with other problems relating to the Dardanelles enterprise. On 11 May Hankey informed him that a storm was about to break loose at the Admiralty. Fisher, it seemed, had flown into a rage over Churchill's proposal for a limited attack on the Narrows forts to cover the clearance of the Kepez minefield.[2] His patience almost exhausted with Churchill and the Dardanelles, the First Sea Lord paid a visit to Hankey. He gave Hankey a verbal message for the Prime Minister, the gist of which was that he would resign if the navy attempted to rush the Straits before the army had effectively occupied the adjacent shores. Asquith thought that Fisher was behaving foolishly but authorized Hankey to say that no naval action would occur in the eastern Mediterranean without his concurrence.[3]

The next day Fisher sent Asquith a copy of a memo he had written for Churchill, along with a note which read:

It will be your recollection that you saw me and the First Lord of the Admiralty in your
private room prior to a meeting of the War Council to consider my protest against the
Dardanelles undertaking when it was first mooted. With extreme reluctance, and
largely due to earnest words spoken to me by Kitchener, I by not resigning (*as I see now
I should have done*) remained a most unwilling beholder (and indeed a participator) of the
gradual draining of our naval resources from the decisive theatre of war.[4]

Asquith called in Hankey for advice on how to deal with Fisher. Hankey
replied that he had just seen Fisher and gathered that he had reconciled his
differences with Churchill. Asked to verify the facts, Hankey went to the
Admiralty to talk with James Masterton-Smith (Churchill's private
secretary), who confirmed that the navy would undertake no further
initiatives until the army had done its part.[5] When Asquith heard from
Hankey, he wrote Fisher a brief note, expressing satisfaction that he had
reached an accord with the First Lord.[6]

Asquith was therefore surprised the next day to receive a letter from
Fisher, whose complaints seemed incompatible with Hankey's information. Fisher indicated that, much as he wanted to help, he did not think
that he could stay on much longer in view of the First Lord's ceaseless
prodding of everyone in every department afloat and ashore in the
interests of the Dardanelles. He was writing to the one person who
understood his predicament and who 'I feel ought to know, *that I feel my
time is short*'.[7] Fisher followed up his note with a visit to 10 Downing Street.
The details of what transpired are not known but Fisher was delighted
with the interview, reporting to Hankey that the Prime Minister had told
him: 'Rely on me. I will never fail you.'[8]

Asquith had no sooner received Churchill's assurance that he was
abandoning the idea of a limited attack than he was drawn into an
interservice dispute. In view of the increasing U-boat danger in the
Mediterranean, Fisher insisted that the Royal Navy's super-dreadnought,
the *Queen Elizabeth*, be returned to home waters. Churchill, anxious to
placate the First Sea Lord, agreed to recall the *Queen Elizabeth* on condition
that two monitors with 14-inch guns be sent out as replacements. When
Kitchener was informed of this decision, his usual composure in trying
circumstances left him and he protested angrily at what he considered was
an act of treachery. But Churchill was prepared to endure Kitchener's
wrath if it meant keeping Fisher happy.

After leaving the Admiralty, Kitchener wrote to Asquith and pointed
out that the departure of the principal naval unit from the Dardanelles
would have a serious and depressing effect on the army. He was appalled
that, while Fisher talked about the risks of keeping the ship in unsafe
waters, he had to face the loss of 15,000 men in a campaign that had been

initiated to help the navy. He ended by accusing the navy of deserting the army at a critical moment.[9]

Asquith empathized with Kitchener but, like Churchill, did not want to risk Fisher's resignation. He was unsure of how to frame a reply to Kitchener, given that the issue lay entirely outside the area of his expertise. He solicited advice from Hankey, who suggested the following explanation:

> (1) The *Queen Elizabeth* was sent out to the Dardanelles when an attack by the Navy alone was contemplated, and she had the specific functions of smashing the forts at the Narrows by indirect fire over the Gallipoli Peninsula. Now that the army is cooperating with the Navy this necessity no longer exists, since the Fleet will not attempt to effect a passage of the Narrows until the Army has occupied, or dominated, the forts on either side.
> (2) The Army can equally well be supported by the Monitors which have guns of equal calibre with the *Queen Elizabeth* and were built for the specific purpose of operations against shore batteries and have no value for purely naval operations.[10]

Asquith's note to Kitchener contained Hankey's arguments word for word.[11] He had no idea of how Kitchener would react to it but when he woke up the next morning he had a far more serious problem on his hands. *The Times* on 14 May featured a highly provocative item about the recent abortive offensive against Aubers Ridge under the headline: 'NEED FOR SHELLS. BRITISH ATTACKS CHECKED. LIMITED SUPPLY THE CAUSE'. According to Lieutenant-Colonel Repington, its military correspondent, British soldiers died in droves because the field-guns were desperately short of high explosive shells. He went on to say: 'The Government, who have so seriously failed to organize adequately our national resources, must bear their share of the grave responsibility.' *The Times* piece was of considerable political significance, quite apart from its trenchant criticism of the Asquith government's conduct of the war. It contradicted Asquith's assertion at Newcastle that the supply of ammunition was equal to the army's needs and gave the impression that he was guilty of criminal deception.

The effects of the munitions controversy were already being felt when the War Council assembled on Friday, 14 May, its first meeting since 6 April. The atmosphere was, according to Churchill, 'sulphurous'.[12] Asquith had his hands full in trying to keep recriminations and bickering to a minimum. Before adjourning, the War Council authorized Kitchener to ask Hamilton what force he required to achieve success – a question, as Hankey later observed, 'that ought to have been put to him before ever a man was landed'.[13]

The morning of 15 May commenced for Asquith as the previous day had ended. Around 9.30 a.m. Churchill hurried in with the news that Fisher had resigned.[14] He explained that it was in reaction to his proposal to send to the Dardanelles two submarines which De Robeck had urgently requested. Churchill said that he wanted to discuss the problem with Fisher but that he had been unable to find him either at the Admiralty or at his home. At first neither Asquith nor Churchill took Fisher's resignation very seriously. During the past six and a half months Fisher had threatened such action on many occasions but, in the end, a friendly conversation with him had always set matters right. Nevertheless, it was a grave dereliction of duty for the First Sea Lord to be absent from his post in time of war, particularly in view of reports that the German High Seas Fleet had emerged from its safe harbourage into the North Sea.

Later in the morning Asquith interrupted his work to attend the wedding of Geoffrey Howard, a Liberal whip, at St Margaret's, Westminster. Shortly after Asquith returned to 10 Downing Street, Lloyd George called to say that several hours earlier he happened to run into Fisher who had grimly announced that he had resigned. Asquith replied that he already knew about it and that there was no reason for alarm. 'Fisher is always resigning,' he declared. 'This is nothing new.'[15] The Welshman was convinced that Fisher really meant it this time and thought it was important that Asquith should make an effort to try to persuade him to remain at his post. Half persuaded, Asquith sent several aides, including Lloyd George, to track down the First Sea Lord. Located in the sanctuary of the Charing Cross Hotel, he was ordered, in the King's name, to return to duty at once.[16] With great reluctance Fisher agreed to see the Prime Minister that afternoon.

Asquith spent an hour with Fisher and found him genial and relaxed but extremely upset with Churchill. Asquith's daughter Violet later disclosed the highlights of the meeting:

> Father ... told me that Fisher had been very friendly and mellow but complained that he found W. quite impossible to work with. He was always doing things without consulting him (Fisher), was overbearing, etc. etc. Father told him that if he wished to resign he must do so in the proper way and state his reasons in writing.[17]

Calling upon his magisterial talents, Asquith wrung from Fisher a promise that he would remain in London but was unable to persuade him either to withdraw his resignation or to return to the Admiralty. Asquith, however, got the impression that the First Sea Lord was beginning to waver. He then sent for Churchill and advised him to do everything he could to patch things up with Fisher. Asquith knew that his government, already rocked by a munitions scandal, would face a political crisis if Britain's most trusted and respected admiral resigned in protest.

On Sunday, 16 May, Asquith drove to The Wharf, his country home at Sutton Courtenay, Oxfordshire. Churchill came over in the afternoon to announce that Fisher's resignation was final.[18] He too would leave if the Prime Minister wanted a change at the Admiralty. 'No, I have thought of that', Asquith replied. 'I do not wish it, but can you get a Board?' Churchill indicated that the other members of the Admiralty Board had agreed to remain and that Sir Arthur Wilson would replace Fisher.[19] Asquith gave his tentative approval to the arrangement. But, as he subsequently explained to Maurice Bonham Carter, the combination of *The Times* article about the shells shortage and Fisher's resignation was so potentially damaging that he would need to consult with Opposition leaders.[20] Asquith asked Churchill to stay for dinner and the two spent a pleasant evening together. It only remained for Churchill to appear before the House of Commons, explaining the grounds for Fisher's resignation and presenting the nominees of the new Admiralty Board. Asquith was confident that Churchill could defend his record at the Admiralty against any challenge but he was not so certain that his young colleague would weather the storm.

Important developments elsewhere confirmed Asquith's worst fears. Fisher, having refused Churchill's overtures, contrived to alert Bonar Law that he was leaving the Admiralty.[21] The Tory leader approached Lloyd George early on Monday, 17 May, to ask if it was true that Fisher had resigned. Told that it was, Bonar Law exclaimed, 'Then the situation is impossible'. He pointed out that dissatisfaction among his followers was so intense that they would not tolerate the continued presence of Churchill at the Admiralty if Fisher persisted in his resignation. Were such an announcement to be made in the House, he warned, the Unionists would feel it their duty to break the political truce and deliver an attack upon the government's conduct of the war regardless of the consequences.[22] Bonar Law must have been surprised at the reaction of Asquith's chief lieutenant. His recollection of what followed was recorded by Austen Chamberlain:[23]

> Lloyd George burst out passionately, saying that he entirely agreed with Bonar Law – that it was impossible that things should go on as they were, and inveighing against much in the conduct of the war. In particular he said that Kitchener had 'put lies into his mouth' as to the supply of munitions and that the situation was altogether intolerable.[24]

Despite conflicting accounts it is almost certain that it was Bonar Law who first proposed a coalition and not Lloyd George or Asquith. That same day Lloyd George told his mistress, Frances Stevenson, that a crisis was in the making because 'the Tories demanded a national government'.[25] Asquith always maintained that Bonar Law had forced his hand. In order to keep the lid on intra-party disputes, it was evidently to his advantage to convey that impression but, as seen above, Lloyd George confirmed his version of the incident. For his part Bonar Law told friends and party members that the initiative came from Asquith, not himself.[26] However, Bonar Law's survival as Unionist leader depended on his ability to carry a united party behind him into a coalition. Most of his associates in the shadow cabinet remained unalterably opposed to joining the government, even though they were disillusioned by Asquith's leadership. On the other hand, Bonar Law had reluctantly concluded that a coalition was the only way to exert effective influence over the conduct of the war. This is evident from a letter written on 14 May to his associate Walter Long,[27]: '... I think you are right in considering that a coalition may become necessary. Indeed if the outlook does not improve I do not think that things can go on as they are and as it would be impossible for us to form a government I suppose a coalition is the only alternative'.[28] Since Bonar Law wanted to undercut his opposition and ease problems with his party, it suited him to say that he was only responding to pressure from the other side. After all the Tories could not, without appearing disloyal to the electorate, refuse an invitation to cooperate in the formation of a national government.

When Bonar Law went over to the Treasury on the morning of 17 May, he was thinking not only about a coalition but also about a change in the occupancy of 10 Downing Street. As a possible replacement for Asquith he suggested three names: Balfour, Grey or Lloyd George. The first two were quickly passed over. It was seen that the Liberals, in view of their relative strength, would never accept a Unionist premier. Grey's eyes were failing and he had less drive than his chief. As for the third option, Lloyd George himself rejected the invitation, pointing out that 'he would be too much exposed to jealousy and criticism'.[29] A more likely explanation was that, even if he commanded the allegiance of the entire Unionist party, he did not stand much chance of creating a new government. By including Lloyd George's name in the list, Bonar Law was either being tactful or uninformed about the degree to which the Welshman was disliked and distrusted by the Liberals.

It may be argued that Lloyd George conceived of coalition as a means to oust and replace Kitchener at the War Office or, at the very least, gain a more central role in the direction of the war. How else can one explain his collusion behind Asquith's back with the Leader of the Opposition?

Any loyal member of the Liberal cabinet would have, as a matter of course, tried to play down the events of the past few days. When confronted by Bonar Law could Lloyd George not have replied, for instance: 'This country is greatly indebted to Fisher for his earlier services but it was a mistake, on account of his advanced age, to bring him back. He is unable to cope with the strains of war which have made him quarrelsome, overly cautious and driven him to the verge of a nervous collapse. In truth he is a liability and his departure will bring a fresh and energetic approach to naval policy. Churchill has selected a first-rate replacement and will give the full details this afternoon in the House at which time he will answer all questions'. By being positive and striking an optimistic note, Lloyd George might have defused the political time-bomb. At the very least it was worth a try. Bonar Law disliked the idea of a coalition with the Liberals and he had no wish to be the cause of dividing the nation by pursuing party warfare. The effect of a sobering talk might have induced him to restrain his followers, as he had done since the start of the war. Of course it might have been impossible, even if he had so wished, to keep the restive Tory backbenchers in check. At any rate it was Lloyd George's duty to defend the government, not engineer its downfall.

Having joined forces with Bonar Law, Lloyd George asked him to wait while he went next door to speak to the Prime Minister. As far as is known, Asquith did not reveal the details of the meeting to anyone. Lloyd George was less circumspect. During a conversation with Lord Riddell, a leading newspaper proprietor, he observed that he told Asquith that 'things had reached a stage when we could not carry on and that a Coalition was the best way out'.[30] He continued the account in his own memoirs: 'The Prime Minister at once recognized that in order to avert a serious Parliamentary conflict, which would certainly lower the prestige of the Government, if it did not actually bring about its defeat, it was necessary to reconstruct the Cabinet and admit into it some of the leaders of the Unionist Party.' Lloyd George conveniently omitted to disclose the nature of the pressure that he had exerted in order to bring Asquith to his way of thinking. From what he subsequently told Churchill, this included the threat of resignation.[31]

While Asquith pondered the consequences of his decision, Lloyd George returned to the Treasury to summon Bonar Law. The three men then sat in the cabinet room and in less than a quarter of an hour an agreement was made to reconstruct the government, ending nearly a decade of Liberal rule.

New information on the May political crisis has not kept pace with the avalanche of literature that followed Lord Beaverbrook's celebrated study

Politicians and the War in 1928.[32] The historian's task has been complicated by a paucity of records, conflicting accounts and deliberately distorted testimony. Certain questions are likely to defy an answer, unless relevant testimony by one of the three major participants is found in collections of papers as yet unknown to researchers.

The reasons that led to the establishment of a coalition government have been fiercely debated by historians. Asquith's own accounts, published as well as private, are remarkably consistent.[33] He claimed that the first coalition was in response to the alleged deficiency of high explosive shells and the resignation of Fisher. It was vital, the Prime Minister felt, to forestall a renewal of party conflict, not only because it would undermine national morale but also because it might ruin all chance of Italy joining the Entente. The non-interventionist mood in the Italian parliament had deterred the Salandra government from declaring war. On 12 May Rennell Rodd, the British Ambassador at Rome, notified the Foreign Office that he feared the Italian government might be compelled to renege on the Treaty of London. The next day the outlook became even more ominous when Salandra resigned.[34] Clearly Asquith was worried that the latest problem posed by the shells shortage and the schism at the Admiralty would be the subject of an acrimonious parliamentary debate, souring the attitude of the wavering Italians. Asquith placed the highest hopes on Italian entry, convinced that it would bring the end of the war in sight.

Asquith believed that, sooner or later, another such crisis was bound to occur and that it was asking too much of the Conservatives to remain silent spectators to events that justified the gravest anxiety. By taking some of their leaders into the government and making them equally responsible for the conduct of the war, it would mitigate press and party-inspired criticism and avoid the need for a wartime general election which was bound to be divisive.

How accurate is Asquith's explanation? For one thing he did not reveal all that he knew. In particular he gave no hint whether he entered forcibly or willingly into the coalition. Some writers are troubled not only by his omissions but also by his stated reasons for dissolving his own government. They have maintained that the munitions controversy and Fisher's resignation were not the cause of the coalition but only provided the justification for it. They have disputed Asquith's claim that he acted out of concern for Italy. It has seemed to them that the collapse of the ministry, followed by a period of confusion and uncertainty, was more likely to project an image of instability than a mere parliamentary debate. His allegation that a national administration was the best way to hasten Italy's entry into the war, as they saw it, was in fact a smoke-screen to conceal his real reason. A number of them substituted their own version of the events.

Lord Beaverbrook wrote the first comprehensive treatment of the May political crisis. He maintained that the real cause of the coalition was Fisher's resignation, not the munition shortages. Asquith would probably have agreed. While he never ranked the crises in order of importance, he evidently felt he could have survived the first one but not the two combined. Beginning in the 1950s other interpretations followed but none, in my view, has supplanted Beaverbrook's account.[35]

Another point that requires investigation is the allegation made by several historians[36] that during the critical days Asquith's judgment was impaired by acute emotional distress. On 12 May Venetia Stanley had suddenly announced that she would marry Edwin Montagu. Her acceptance of a marriage proposal from a man she did not love reveals the extent of her desperation to escape from an emotional relationship that had become too burdensome.[37] Asquith was devastated by the news, which came on the eve of one of the worst weeks of his whole premiership. The woman he loved passionately, who had shared the cares of his office and provided him with emotional comfort during trying times, was about to commit the cruellest act that destiny could devise. 'This is too terrible', he wrote to her despondently. 'No Hell can be so bad.'[38] To Sylvia Henley, Venetia's elder sister, he confided:

> I am in the stress of the most arduous and exacting things that you can imagine and I miss (more than I could say) what has helped and guided me so often during these last three years. I cannot describe to you the depth of the unbridged gulf... It is not easy to reconcile one's self to such a breach. I feel almost like one half of a pair of scissors. And it cannot be supplied and replaced.[39]

There has been much discussion whether Asquith's private grief rendered him helpless, or nearly so, during the political crisis. Opinions cover the entire spectrum, from Gilbert who claims that it did to Koss who takes the exactly opposite view.[40] My own position lies somewhere in between. In the past Asquith had shown remarkable ability to compartmentalize his public and private activities, never allowing one to impinge on the other. But the fact that he could control, to an unusual degree, his personal feelings during periods of political turbulence does not mean that he might not temporarily falter under certain circumstances. Asquith had just been rejected by the greatest love of his life at a moment when he needed her most. The loss of a loved one is a particularly wounding experience. The evidence suggests that it did affect Asquith. His uncharacteristic note of self-pity, his tendency to draw attention to his

troubles and sacrifices in his conversation and correspondence, indicate
that he suffered from periods of deep gloom. Undoubtedly his personal
anguish began creeping into his public life and distracting him from the
difficult problems that had to be faced. If Asquith was not up to his usual
form there is no reason to suppose that his judgment and grip had deserted
him completely. In the end it was Lloyd George's disloyalty, not the sad
end of his romance with Venetia Stanley, that undermined his resolve.

For some time before 17 May Asquith had thought that coalition might
eventually become necessary, but it was a prospect that he did not relish.
As recently as 12 May he had, in answer to a question in the Commons,
declared that coalition was 'not in contemplation'.[41] His mind remained
unchanged when Churchill visited him at The Wharf four days later. Yet
Lloyd George would have us believe that by 17 May Asquith was as
much in favour of a coalition as he was. If so, why did he threaten to leave
the cabinet? It was out of character for Asquith abruptly to reverse a
firmly-held position on a vital issue. Granted that the war deprived him of
the luxury of time, it seems extraordinary that he should not have taken at
least a few hours to weigh the pros and cons and consider the options. But
despondent as he was, the threatened resignation of his chief lieutenant
took the fight out of him. What Asquith needed in a time of trial was for
his right-hand man to stand beside him, not desert him. Asquith acquiesced
in the call for a coalition because it was the path of least resistance. In the
short run it did resolve his political difficulties but only at a heavy cost.

Asquith had coped with many crises since 1908 and if he had shown the
same qualities of leadership on this occasion as before his beleaguered
government might have emerged with renewed strength. Besides a
coalition, he had several feasible options. One solution was to create a
small War Council and reshuffle his cabinet, replacing Churchill and
several other unpopular ministers. This was perhaps the least troublesome
approach and might have been enough to appease the Tories. The other
alternative was to put the matter before a secret session of parliament. It
is difficult to see how the Tories could have made political capital out of
their two grievances. In the first place, the manner of Fisher's departure
was vulnerable to criticism. As Asquith succinctly put it on 20 May:
'Fisher deserted his post, without leave or warning, at a time when the
stress of war, and the appearance of the German Gr. Fleet in the North
Sea, made it his imperative duty to remain at his duties...Strictly
speaking, he ought to be shot.'[42] How could the Tories have effectively
defended a man who had behaved so irresponsibly?

They would have had no better luck in exploiting the munitions
shortages. The debacle at Aubers Ridge was partially offset by the success

of a British night attack, which was reported in *The Times* on Monday morning, 17 May, under the headline: 'GERMAN LINE BROKEN. GERMAN LINE STORMED. A MILE OF GROUND WON.' Even without Sir John French's latest gains, Tory backbenchers, despite their animosity towards Asquith, would in all likelihood have tempered their condemnation of the administration. They could not afford to risk a popular backlash, which would almost certainly have occurred if they had inveighed, even indirectly, against Kitchener. But regardless of how the debate went, Asquith was virtually assured of a vote of confidence. His majority remained intact and was now de facto larger, since there were more than three times as many Unionists MPs as Liberals serving at the front (98 to 29). According to Long's estimate early in 1915 the Liberals and their allies had 270 members available to vote as against 189 for the Unionists.[43] No can say for sure how long the Liberals could have continued in office after May. The only certain thing was that the Liberal administration was a far better instrument for carrying on the war than the one that succeeded it.

Asquith's decision to embark on a coalition was made so quickly that, except for Lloyd George, he had not consulted with his colleagues, let alone the rank and file of the Liberal Party. In the afternoon of 17 May he broke the news to Crewe and Grey, his two most trusted advisers. With Lloyd George at his side, he explained the circumstances that had led him to invite the Opposition into the government. He was convinced that he could not restructure the ministry entirely from among members of the party without weakening it and aiding the enemy. Visibly upset, Grey asked to be left out of the new ministry. Asquith would not hear of it, saying that his services were indispensable.[44] After the meeting Asquith wrote a memo to his cabinet colleagues, essentially repeating what he had told Grey and Crewe and asking for their resignations.[45]

Once the shock of the announcement had worn off, reaction among the Liberal ministers ranged from annoyance to outrage. No one confronted Asquith directly with his objections, but there was considerable private grumbling. Pease told Runciman, 'I am sorry he acted as he did in asking for our resignations before calling us together'.[46] Seething with anger, Hobhouse wrote: 'Nothing will persuade me that that this is not the end of the Liberal party as we have known it.'[47]

If Asquith's decision caused mere ripples in ministerial ranks, it produced a near revolt among backbenchers. On 19 May Liberal rebels gathered in a committee room of the House. There was a consensus that the Prime Minister should have consulted with his party beforehand and that, at the very least, he owed them an explanation.[48] W. M. R. Pringle, one of the ringleaders, asked his fellow MPs to support a motion which amounted to a vote of no confidence in Asquith. While the motion was being debated, Asquith, alerted to what was going on, entered the room. He rallied the disgruntled Liberals to his side in a moving speech which he described to Sylvia Henley:

> I was of course unable to tell them the whole, or even half the truth, so I had to go more for their affections than reason. I can assure you it was a difficult job ... I suppose I spoke about ten minutes or a quarter of an hour, & I have good reason to be satisfied with the effect. Several of them were on the verge of tears, & they all rose & cheered wildly & declared that they were absolutely satisfied.[49]

Far more painful and delicate for Asquith was the task of allocating offices in the new government. Old friends had to be dropped in order to make room for the newcomers. Asquith worked in close collaboration with Lloyd George and Crewe in effecting the administrative changes. Asquith consulted no one else, not even Grey whose poor health disqualified him from participating in the tedious negotiations. The meagre spoils that the Unionists obtained showed that the Prime Minister was in possession of his political faculties. He was nearly over his *crise de coeur*. He found in Sylvia Henley a new epistolary confidante, though he wrote to her less frequently and informatively than he had to Venetia.

When the Unionists offered to coalesce with the Liberals, they demanded equal representation in the new ministry, that is ten cabinet posts. Asquith had seemed to agree in principle. The basis of the provisional arrangement was the removal of Kitchener as Secretary for War. According to Pease, Asquith claimed that Kitchener had repeatedly ignored French's demands for high explosive shells, concealed them from the cabinet and refused to allow civilian help to tidy up the muddle at the War Office.[50] Kitchener's place was to be filled by Lloyd George, who longed to move on to the War Office. As for the Tory leaders, Bonar Law was to become Chancellor of the Exchequer, Balfour First Lord of the Admiralty and Lansdowne Lord President of the Council, while Chamberlain would be offered the Colonial Office. Asquith also expressed an interest in finding a portfolio for Carson but he was equally anxious to exclude Curzon.[51]

Had Asquith's original proposals been implemented the Unionists would have occupied a favourable position in the coalition. But on 17 May Asquith was not at his best when he was rushed into a cabinet-making blueprint. In the days that followed he quickly regained his spirits and bearing. By 18 May it became apparent to Asquith that Kitchener's hold on public opinion at home and abroad was too great to permit his supersession.[52] In a recent biography of Lloyd George, Professor Bentley Gilbert has inferred that Asquith's decision to keep Kitchener as Secretary for War was prompted by the Welshman's reluctance to take the post.[53] His evidence is unconvincing, drawn from dubious sources.[54] In fact, Asquith retained Kitchener for political reasons. He reached this decision on his own, without taking into account, one way or another, Lloyd George's feelings about going to the War Office.

As soon as Asquith agreed to form a coalition, efforts were made from different quarters to induce him to make a change at the War Office. The Northcliffe press mounted a vicious campaign to discredit Kitchener. Lloyd George wrote to Asquith on 19 May to complain about Kitchener's supposed mismanagement of munitions supply. His letter contained half truths and such bald-faced lies as the following: 'Private firms cannot turn out shrapnel because of the complicated character of the shell; but the testimony is unanimous that the high explosive is a simple shell and that any engineering concern could easily produce it' (in fact the reverse is true).[55] Sir John French recited a list of grievances against Kitchener in a letter he forwarded from General Headquarters on 20 May.[56] However, Northcliffe's press campaign led to a violent public reaction (during which copies of the *Daily Mail* and *The Times* were burned at the London Stock Exchange) and eliminated any lingering misgivings Asquith may have harboured about keeping Kitchener at the War Office.

When it became clear that Kitchener could not be supplanted, Asquith fastened on an idea, to which the King had given expression on 18 May,[57] that munitions supply should be removed from the War Office's control. But Asquith hesitated to take the next logical step of creating a separate Ministry of Munitions. He told the King that a new minister was not needed since it would take only about three months to systematize the entire munitions operation.[58] There was another reason, a more important one, which he could not reveal to the King.

Although at the outset Asquith had conceded that the Opposition was entitled to parity in controlling the war effort, he went back on his word and attempted to distribute the offices in such a way as to ensure Liberal dominance and leave the Tories without a definite leader to represent them. Since Asquith decided there should be no change at the Foreign Office and at the War Office, the only other key vacant positions in the cabinet were the Exchequer and the new Ministry of Munitions. Obviously Bonar Law, with his vast business experience and as the leader of a coequal force in the government, was entitled to have one of these offices. This did not suit Asquith, who aimed to relegate the Unionist chieftan to the Colonial Office, a post of secondary rank. What were Asquith's motives for

wanting to exclude Bonar Law from either Munitions or the Exchequer?
He distrusted Bonar Law's abilities and found him personally uncongenial.
He also objected to him on political grounds. Asquith saw that his own
position would be secure if he reduced Bonar Law's status and limited his
opportunities to act as a rival.[59]

A case could be made that it would be illogical to assign Bonar Law to
the Exchequer because he was a Tariff Reformer in a House of Commons
that contained a large Free Trade majority. But Bonar Law's claims to the
Ministry of Munitions could not be rejected on grounds of unsuitability.
To circumvent this anticipated problem, Asquith proposed to leave Lloyd
George at the Exchequer as well as to place him in charge of the section of
the War Office which dealt with arms production. A better solution, Lloyd
George thought, would be for the Prime Minister to look after the
Exchequer during his temporary absence. This suggestion was abandoned
after the Tories raised strenuous objections, saying that it was impossible
for Asquith to combine the two offices in wartime. Nor would the Tory
leaders accept Asquith's proposal to let Lloyd George superintend
munitions output while remaining Chancellor of the Exchequer.[60] During
a meeting between Asquith, Lloyd George and Crewe a new arrangement
was devised: Lloyd George would head a new Ministry of Munitions with
McKenna moving to the Treasury, on the understanding that he would
step aside if the former wished to return.[61]

Asquith and his associates held a conference with the Tory leaders on 24
May. There was much haggling and bargaining over the various offices
and it seemed to Asquith that the Opposition was making unreasonable
demands. The Unionists saw things differently. Against their own best
interests they had come to the rescue of a failing government and they
deserved to be treated as equals, not as subordinates. They were especially
indignant that Bonar Law was not offered a more important post than the
Colonial Office. They insisted that if Lloyd George took over Munitions
their leader ought to get the vacated Exchequer. The Liberals argued that
it would be intolerable to have a Tariff Reformer as Chancellor of the
Exchequer or to have the Unionists control all the departments most
concerned with directing the war. (Balfour had been earmarked for the
Admiralty and Kitchener, although not offically belonging to any party,
was regarded as a virtual Tory.) At one point someone suggested
Runciman for the Ministry of Munitions but both sides quickly ruled him
out on account of his lack of stature in the country. The meeting broke up
without arriving at any settlement.[62]

The next morning Asquith commissioned Lloyd George to meet Bonar
Law privately to try to resolve the impasse. Lloyd George found the

Unionist leader 'very unyielding' about allowing either the Prime Minister or McKenna to succeed him at the Exchequer. When reminded of Liberal concern that the Tories should not run all the fighting departments, Bonar Law replied that his party regarded Balfour 'as much more belonging to the government'. In the end Bonar Law indicated that, unless Asquith was prepared to accept his terms, he might opt out of the coalition.[63]

When Lloyd George returned to 10 Downing Street, he found Asquith, who had arranged to see the King that evening, conferring with Lord Stamfordham. He went ahead and made his report. The Welshman did not express much concern over Bonar Law's threat and already had in mind an arrangement under which the Prime Minister would bring into the government some non-party peers. Other options were discussed. Stamfordham suggested a 'return to the *status quo ante* minus W. Churchill at the Admiralty, plus a Munitions Minister'. Asquith judged the proposal to be unfeasible because of the difficulty of finding someone to replace Churchill and the unlikelihood that Balfour would break with his party to take the appointment.[64]

Patience was an asset which Asquith had in abundance and it was his style to allow events to play themselves out with a minimum of intervention. But on this occasion he was compelled to take the initiative, for the country could not remain without a government indefinitely. He made a last-ditch effort to win over the Unionists, but he did so not by offering additional concessions but by laying down an ultimatum. He reportedly instructed Lloyd George to tell Bonar Law: 'There are my terms, you can take them or leave them.'[65] In conveying this message (presumably in softer language), Lloyd George begged the Unionist leader not to put party or personal ambition before his patriotic duty. Bonar Law yielded to the appeal and, ignoring the advice of his Conservative friends, took the Colonial Office.[66] When Bonar Law met Asquith to finalize arrangements, he remarked: 'You mustn't think I am doing this because I am compelled to. I know very well I can have what I want simply by lifting my little finger. But I won't fight. I am here to show you how to run a Coalition Government by forbearance and concession.'[67] Bonar Law might not have been nearly as accommodating if his bargaining position had not been weakened by the Jacks Affair.[68] As the memoirs of his private secretary reveal, he was very bitter at being given a second-rate post when he had been led to believe that he could expect a major ministry.[69]

Bonar Law was not the only one whose place in the new government was a matter of contention. The Unionists tried hard to exclude McKenna, Haldane and Churchill. Their grievance against McKenna was that he lacked zeal in hunting down enemy aliens. They were adamant that he be removed from the Home Office but reluctantly conceded that Asquith had a right to place him elsewhere.[70] Asquith not only saved McKenna but raised him from the Home Office to the Treasury.

Asquith had no room to manoeuvre when it came to Haldane, whom the Tories condemned as pro-German. They made his exclusion an absolute condition of their entry into the Coalition. Jenkins believes that Asquith capitulated too easily, as does Koss.[71] As no definitive conclusion can be made from the available evidence, it becomes a matter of interpretation. Asquith always insisted that he reluctantly accepted the inevitable and dropped his old friend because the Tories refused to sit with him in the cabinet.[72] After several meetings with Bonar Law and other Unionist stalwarts, Lloyd George, who was not in the habit of shielding Asquith, told Lord Reading, then Lord Chief Justice, that 'Haldane would have to go'.[73] Grey subsequently tried to intercede on behalf of Haldane but the Tory leaders, to whom he appealed, were quite inflexible.[74] Lloyd George's corroborative statement, plus Grey's action, leads me to believe that Asquith was telling the truth. Where Asquith can be faulted was the manner in which he handled Haldane's exclusion from the cabinet. To other Liberals who were not reappointed Asquith sent letters expressing deep regrets with hopes that before long they would again be working together.[75] He wrote in the warmest terms to Crewe and Lloyd George for their help in the reorganization of the government.[76] But to his oldest political ally, to the one person he should have explained in person what he felt so deeply, not even a few written words of apology or regret. He left Haldane to learn the news from others. It was unracharacteristic of Asquith to show such callous disregard towards a friend or colleague, and one can only surmise that he was too anguished and ashamed over what he had done to face or write to him.

After an interview with Asquith on 22 May, Haldane knew and accepted that his sacrifice was a political necessity: 'I have told the Prime Minister not to think of me anymore', he told Pease. 'Bonar Law has pointed out that many of his party regard me as suspect, though [he] ... does not share these views.'[77] On the same day he wrote to his mother: 'I regard it as certain that I shall go. But I am quite happy, for I think it best for the nation at this moment.'[78] Haldane left quietly but he was understandably aggrieved at the manner in which he was dispatched and the gulf that opened between him and Asquith was never quite bridged.[79]

Asquith did somewhat better in the case of Churchill, another object of Tory wrath. Bonar Law and his colleagues not only disliked Churchill on personal grounds but genuinely believed that he had failed at his post.

While their veto on Churchill's exclusion was less firm than that on Haldane, they were determined to keep him out of the Admiralty at all costs. Asquith remained favourably disposed towards Churchill, although his relationship with his young colleague had deteriorated since the turn of the year. On the advice of Lloyd George, Asquith considered assigning Churchill to the Colonial Office, but abandoned the idea in the face of mounting opposition from Liberals as well as Conservatives.[80] In the end Asquith relegated Churchill to the lowest cabinet post, the Chancellor of the Duchy of Lancaster, but with a promise that he would be allowed to retain his seat in the reconstructed War Council.

Unlike Haldane, Churchill did not accept his fate with good grace. He complained loudly that he had been shabbily treated and conducted a private vendetta against Asquith, forgetting that he was the one man who for years had been his chief supporter and untiring defender. He failed to understand how discredited he had become in the estimation of his own party and the press. Churchill's real fault, one which he never acknowledged, was his massive ego. If few were prepared to lift a finger to keep him in office, it was on account of his flamboyance, excessive confidence, contempt of the opinions of others, craving for publicity and undisguised ambition to reach the top. It is difficult to avoid the conclusion that he courted his own downfall.

Asquith had not abandoned hope that, with the imminent reconstruction of the government, Fisher might be persuaded to return to the Admiralty. He had refused formally to accept the admiral's resignation and indeed, in a letter on 17 May, had encouraged him to sit tight.[81] Fisher, convinced that his services were indispensable, addressed an ultimatum to the Prime Minister on 19 May. In it he demanded, as a condition for his return, dictatorial powers to run the Admiralty, reducing the functions of the First Lord to those of an under-secretary. His terms also included the ejection of Churchill from the cabinet; a refusal to serve under Balfour, the First Lord designate; the dismissal of the Second, Third and Fourth Sea Lords; and the authority to choose a new Board of Admiralty.[82] Fisher had clearly overplayed his hand. His conditions would have been intolerable to any democratic government, even one headed by the weakest of Prime Ministers. Asquith was furious, telling the King that the document 'indicates signs of mental aberration'.[83] To Balfour he wrote, as we have already noted, that Fisher ought to be shot for deserting his post knowing that the German High Seas Fleet had put to sea. (As it turned out, the German fleet's sortie was only intended to cover mine-laying operations in the Dogger Bank.)

There was every reason to believe that Fisher had become unhinged under stress and that his departure from the Admiralty was a foregone conclusion. Yet on 21 May Asquith sent J. A. Spender, editor of the *Westminster Gazette*, to see Fisher. His purpose in doing so is not clear but it would seem unlikely that he was making a final effort to reach an accommodation with Fisher. Even if Fisher had withdrawn his offensive memorandum, there were two things he could not undo. He could never regain the trust of the Sea Lords whom he had earmarked for the chopping block or erase the memory of having abandoned his post in time of war. It is possible that Asquith was trying to determine whether it might become necessary to throw a net over Fisher, for in his excited state there was no telling what foolish things he was liable to say or write.

At any rate Spender, a long-time admirer and defender of Fisher, had a painful interview with him. Fisher evinced little interest in what he heard. He lashed out against the politicians, releasing all his pent-up bitterness and accumulated grievances, and threatened to 'tell the facts' in the House of Lords. He made it clear that he would serve under Bonar Law or McKenna but not Balfour, holding him more to blame than Churchill for the Dardanelles.[84] Fisher did not help his case, as Asquith considered Balfour irreplaceable at the Admiralty. On 22 May Asquith gave Fisher his official release in a brief and curt statement: 'I am commanded by the King to accept your tendered resignation of the Office of First Sea Lord of the Admiralty.'[85] Sir Henry Jackson, an officer in whom the navy trusted and respected, replaced Fisher as First Sea Lord.

Asquith revealed the composition of the new cabinet to the King on the evening of 25 May, one week after the crisis had begun. All but one of the key offices remained under Liberal control. Kitchener and Grey stayed at their old posts. Lloyd George went to the new Ministry of Munitions, McKenna was transferred to the Treasury and Simon became Home Secretary. Balfour, who succeeded Churchill as First Lord, was the only Conservative occupying a senior position. Other incoming Unionists had to be content with lesser offices. Bonar Law was shunted to the Colonial Office, a poor base from which to direct the Unionist forces in the national government. His rivals for the Unionist leadership in 1911, Long and Chamberlain, were given more important portfolios, the Local Government Board and the India Office respectively. Curzon was made Lord Privy Seal, Selborne President of the Board of Agriculture, and Lord Lansdowne, as an elder statesman, Minister without Portfolio. Sir Edward Carson, a controversial figure on account of his threat to provoke civil war in Ireland a year earlier, was appointed Attorney General. John Redmond, the Irish Nationalist leader, declined an invitation to join, while strongly protesting at the inclusion of Carson. Arthur Henderson, as the voice of the

Labour Party, took over the Board of Education. The new twenty-two man cabinet consisted of twelve Liberals, eight Unionists, one Labour and one non-party (Kitchener).

If Asquith had allowed another man's initiative to decide the issue of coalition for him, the manner in which he had apportioned the offices demonstrated that he had regained his strength and skill. He was determined to give the Tories only the minimum of concessions and to establish none of them, least of all Bonar Law, as a potential challenger to his own leadership. He resented the necessity of coalition, partly because he felt it would hinder the war effort and partly because he was forced to jettison a number of old colleagues.[86] If coalition was unavoidable he wanted it to operate as much as possible as a normal party government with all ministerial lines leading directly to the Prime Minister. In the long run, however, Asquith's best chance of remaining Prime Minister would have been to turn the Unionist leader into a specially-trusted lieutenant and to have headed a genuine national ministry.

As it was, the Asquith coalition was from the outset a suspicious and divided body. Kitchener disliked Curzon, with whom he had engaged in a historic row in 1905, even more than Lloyd George. Both sides had their own intra-party feuds. McKenna and Lloyd George were mutually antagonistic. Most of the Unionists were irritated by Curzon's arrogance and pomposity. Selborne, Chamberlain and Curzon had misgivings about Bonar Law's capacity for leadership. There were, moreover, strong resentments between the old and new ministers. 'I loathe the idea of a Coalition Gov't', Long wrote to H. A. Gwynne, editor of the *Morning Post*. 'How on earth are we going to work with men of whom we hold as low opinion as we do of the present administration?'[87] Augustine Birrell, who remained as Chief Secretary for Ireland in the new cabinet, told Redmond, 'you cannot imagine how I *loathe* the idea of sitting cheek by jowl with these fellows'.[88]

The backbenchers on both sides mirrored their leaders' attitude regarding the coalition. The Liberal Party was annoyed at the abrupt demise of the previous government, about which Asquith had said precious little beyond an appeal for trust in his judgment, and was bitter at the sacrifice of Haldane to a right-wing witch-hunt. The Unionists in parliament wanted to wait until the next general election, when they expected they could form an independent ministry or at least a coalition on their own terms. To the Liberal and Conservative rank and file the coalition appeared to be a conpiracy of their leaders against their supporters – a compact between the two front benches against the back.

No one expected the coalition to last. Bonar Law remarked in retrospect:

'It had been regarded merely as a stop-gap arrangement and both parties were watching each other closely all the time.'[89] The new ministry, therefore, never functioned together as a team and the conflicting forces within made it a much more cumbersome and inefficient body than its predecessor. It was difficult to see how Asquith, with this combination, could properly direct the country through the stressful times ahead.

Chapter 7

Muddling Through under the Coalition

The Coalition altered the composition of the cabinet but brought no immediate change in the direction of the war. Asquith was still head of the government and he remained wedded to doing business in a certain way. He set up a new body, known officially as the Dardanelles Committee, to replace the War Council. It considered policy not only for the Dardanelles but for all theatres of war. There were thirteen members on this committee, six Liberals, six Unionists and one non-party. Serving under Asquith's chairmanship were Kitchener, Crewe, Lloyd George, Grey, Churchill, McKenna, Bonar Law, Selborne, Curzon and Lansdowne. Carson was included in August.[1] Like its predecessor, the new committee lacked final authority. Its decisions were referred to the full cabinet where they were again debated. Moreover, it contained too many powerful personalities, each with definite ideas and more often than not pulling in different directions. The absence of unanimity on controversial issues meant that an aggrieved minority could and did resurrect the fight in the cabinet, imposing further delays. Asquith recognized the importance of restricting the inner council to a selected few but he felt compelled to take in additional members on account of personal or party claims.

Kitchener wanted the War Council replaced by a smaller committee consisting only of Asquith, Balfour and himself, with Hankey as secretary. Asquith, however, considered the suggestion impractical. It was apparent, after the stalemate set in on the Western Front, that the heads of the service departments could not run the war without reference to other departments of state. Moreover, it was a virtual certainty that the Unionists would not delegate authority to a body on which they were represented only by Balfour, whom they viewed as too closely associated with the previous government.[2]

The new cabinet assembled for the first time on 27 May. Shortly after the meeting Asquith informed Kitchener that he was going to France to visit Sir John French and inspect the front. Asquith was unaware of the devious role French had played in the events of May and he refused to give any credence to charges made by Kitchener and others that Repington's story had been inspired by General Headquarters.[3] He and French had always got along well. During the recent political crisis he had received a letter from Sir John who wrote: 'You have shown me so much true generous kindness throughout this trying campaign that ... I am sure in the whole history of war no General in the field has ever been helped in a difficult task by the head of his Government as I have been supported and strengthened by your unfailing sympathy and encouragement.'[4] Asquith could not bring himself to believe that the man who had written to him in such cordial and fulsome terms could simultaneously be plotting to destroy him.

On 29 May Kitchener sent for Hankey, who was to accompany the Prime Minister to France. Kitchener's purpose was to prime Hankey on the line he wanted Asquith to take in discussions with Sir John and the French leaders. On no account, Kitchener stressed, was the Prime Minister to give any commitment or even hint of the time at which the New Armies would proceed to France. In defending the government's policy he was to offer two reasons. First, the output of munitions was considerably below the present needs of the army. To send reinforcements, with their proper complement of artillery, would mean that the number of rounds per gun would be even less. Secondly, the operations in May had shown that the line in the West could not be broken. To continue to launch major offensives would simply play into the enemy's hands. For the time being it was preferable to pursue a policy of attrition (an active defence in this context),[5] waiting for the Germans to weaken themselves through costly efforts to shatter the Anglo-French line.[6]

Asquith and his party left Charing Cross on the evening of 30 May, arriving at midnight at General Headquarters (GHQ) in Saint-Omer. The next day he motored to Second Army Headquarters and chatted with the commander, General Plumer. From there he was taken to a hill top overlooking Ypres, the site of a recent battle in which the Germans had used poison gas. Peering through glasses, he could see no devastation or trace of war except for the British and German trenches running parallel at about 100 yards apart. At Bailleul Asquith lunched with General W. P. Pulteney, commander of the Third Corps, and went over to visit the wounded at the hospital. Afterwards he delivered a brief but stirring address at a farewell parade for the men of the 16th brigade, who were about to depart for Ypres, and they responded by giving him three deafening cheers. Returning to Saint-Omer, he dined with French who was relaxed and in good humour. Later in the evening the two had a long *tete-à-tete* which Asquith described as 'on the whole quite satisfactory'.[7] Curiously enough, Asquith does not appear to have raised the munitions issue.

On the second day Asquith motored across territory occupied by the First Army. He was cordially welcomed by its commander, General Sir Douglas Haig, who introduced him to his senior staff officers. After lunch the Prime Minister was given an extensive tour of the Headquarters area, with an explanation of how each section operated. He then inspected some army units and, moving as far forward as his host would let him, examined the trench system. Haig wrote in his diary: 'Mr Asquith was most enthusiastic about all he had seen, and on bidding good-bye, he asked me to write to him whenever I could spare the time.'[8]

On the morning of 2 June Asquith had another protracted discussion with Sir John French. Asquith reported that Kitchener wanted the Allies in France to husband their resources and to abandon all major offensives for the remainder of the year. Consequently he intended to hold back the bulk of the New Armies and use them as a reserve in another theatre of war or in case of an emergency in France. The Field Marshal argued that experience in the spring of 1915 had shown that the German line could be pierced and he was confident of achieving decisive results if provided with more men and ammunition. Asquith brought up the touchy subject of French's relations with Kitchener. Sir John expressed a willingness to settle his differences with Kitchener and asked that he be allowed to go home before the Prime Minister, so as to give the impression that he was acting on his own initiative. Asquith remained in France an extra day to accommodate the Field Marshal.[9] 'He goes early tomorrow to London to breakfast on Friday with K.', Asquith confided to Sylvia Henley at the end of the day: 'And if I have done nothing else on my mission here, I am satisfied that I have dispelled the miasma of doubt & suspicion between the two Field Marshals.'[10] But, alas, the meeting between the two soldiers did not produce the rapprochement which Asquith had worked and hoped for.

In mid afternoon (on 2 June) a French delegation, consisting of Millerand and Generals Joffre and Foch, paid Asquith a visit. Millerand asked if it was possible to know when the New Armies would be crossing over so that Joffre could frame his future plans. Asquith replied that it was a matter for Kitchener to decide. The French generals chimed in, saying that the Germans in the West had been weakened by the temporary absence of many of their divisions now engaged on the Russian front. They lost no time in pointing out that unless the Allies acted at once the opportunity to expel the Germans from France and Belgium might never reoccur. The French were much too sanguine to impress Asquith and even Sir John admitted that they 'appear to throw all logical argument to the winds when their ideas are in the least degree opposed'.[11]

Asquith went out for a stroll after the French left and returned to General Headquarters shortly before dinner. Sir John had invited Henry Wilson and some members of his staff to dine with him and the Prime Minister.[12] Seated at the table, Asquith was engaged in small talk when he suddenly turned to French and blurted out: 'It is a curious thing, Field Marshal, that this war has produced no great generals.' Asquith may have been thinking about the French when he made that statement but, seeing who his host was, showed a singular want of tact. Wilson, who despised Asquith, broke the awkward silence by remarking, 'No, Prime Minister, nor has it produced a statesman'.[13]

Before leaving next day Asquith wrote to French, thanking him for his hospitality and lavishing praise on the army and the manner in which it was directed. He concluded by saying:

> My object in coming to you was to bring the Army a message of confidence and pride from the King, the Government and the people of the Empire. My last word ... is to assure you that they are never unmindful of the heroism and endurance, which is adding every day a fresh page to our glorious annals; and that they will spare no effort or sacrifice to support you to the end.[14]

The fog delayed Asquith's Channel crossing and he did not reach London until 2 a.m. on 4 June. It had been a gruelling but productive trip. Asquith had gained a better insight by seeing the army and the war at close quarters, had boosted morale wherever he went, and during discussions with Sir John and the French had laid down the broad principles of future British strategy. His report to the cabinet included three recommendations: that there should be an immediate study to determine the state of the army's defences and, in case of a disaster, its lines of retreat; that Sir John should come over, as soon as circumstances permitted, to discuss his military policy for the coming months; and that this be followed by a joint conference with the French.[15]

On 7 June Asquith held the first meeting of the Dardanelles Committee in his room at the House of Commons. The members were already in possession of three memoranda on the subject of the Dardanelles. One, by Kitchener, favoured replacing Hamilton's losses, leaving him to make what progress he could. The remaining two, one by Churchill and the other by Selborne, made an appeal for a vigorous prosecution of the campaign.[16] Prior to the meeting Asquith had asked Hankey for his views on Selborne's memo. Several hours later Hankey returned with detailed notes which he turned over to the Prime Minister. In supporting Selborne's position, Hankey observed that the reinforcements and stock of ammunition requested by Hamilton would not be missed in France but might achieve a victory against the Turks. Asquith discussed Hankey's appreciation with Kitchener and they agreed that another major effort at Gallipoli might prove decisive.[17]

The deliberations of the Dardanelles Committee got under way at 5 p.m. As Hankey was absent, no notes were taken. Asquith told the King, however, that it was unanimously agreed to send three divisions to the Dardanelles (in addition to the one already dispatched) so that Hamilton could mount a new offensive in mid July.[18]

Asquith became drawn into the debate over a landing site when Ellis Ashmead-Bartlett, correspondent for the *Daily Telegraph* at the Dardanelles, returned to London for a brief visit. A critic of Hamilton's tactics at Gallipoli, Ashmead-Bartlett favoured a landing in the vicinity of Bulair in order to cut off the defenders from Thrace and Constantinople. Ashmead-Bartlett discussed the idea with Churchill, who was quickly won over. Before lunch on 11 June both men saw Asquith at 10 Downing Street. Ashmead-Bartlett recorded the following entry in his diary:

> Winston produced the maps and we went over with him the scheme we had worked out the previous night. He followed all the points raised with the interest of a professional strategist, and agreed with everything we suggested. He finally expressed himself in favour of a landing ... just north of Bulair. Putting his finger on the narrow neck of the Peninsula, he said, 'It seems to be the only natural thing to do.' ... He asked me a great number of questions and, when I was about to leave, he said, 'I wish you would draw me up a short and concise memorandum on the whole situation, and let me have it some time this evening'.[19]

Asquith submitted Ashmead-Bartlett's memo for consideration at the Dardanelles Committee meeting the next day. On the whole it was well received. Asquith shared the general sentiment that it was preferable to aim for a 'starving' rather than a 'storming' operation and and he read an excerpt from a 1909 General Staff report on the defences of Constantinople describing several possible landing sites in the area. Kitchener agreed to consult Hamilton. But Hamilton was unalterably opposed to the operation. The presence of enemy submarines, he insisted, had made it impossible to give sufficient naval protection to the transports and supply ships as far north as Bulair. The committee gave no further thought to the proposal.[20]

As a matter of prudence Churchill urged his colleagues to provide

Hamilton with two more divisions for his projected offensive.[21] Asquith
supported such a move. He was confident that the dispatch of these
additional troops to the Dardanelles would make little difference to GHQ,
since he assumed no major attacks would occur in the West until the spring
of 1916. In discussing the matter with Kitchener, he conceded it was
advisable to wait until French had an opportunity to present his case and
a strategy for the Western Front had been adopted.

Sir John arrived in London on 30 June and the next day had a long
interview with Asquith at 10 Downing Street. Sir John wrote in his diary:

> The P. M. ... told me what he wanted me to bring before the Cabinet to-morrow. He
> asked me to give the Cabinet my views on the great strategic aspect of the campaign on
> the Western front. He expressed the opinion of himself and the Cabinet that *attrition*
> should be the controlling idea in our minds. He hoped I would give the Cabinet my full
> plans and ideas as to the state of the trenches and defences in rear of our first line; what
> I knew of German arrangements in this respect; and of the state of affairs in rear of the
> French and Belgian lines. He wished in fact to be fully posted so as to enable him to enter
> into a conference with Joffre and the French Ministers [scheduled early the following
> week] at Calais.[22]

The cabinet engaged in a thorough review of its war policy on 2 and 3
July. Sir John was present at both meetings during which he discussed his
position at length and fielded a multitude of questions. He announced that
he and Joffre had agreed to mount a joint offensive in August. In his
opinion it was practical and essential since, if it was delayed until 1916, the
Russians might be defeated. Wilson, who was also in attendance, added
that the French were grumbling that the British were not pulling their
weight and were beginning to doubt the determination of their ally to fight
through to victory. At the end of the second day's meeting, Asquith drew
up a memorandum outlining the cabinet's conclusions:

> We must keep our hands free in view of the unforeseeable contingencies of a war which
> is being carried on in so many different theatres. Every promise or assurance must be
> subject to that reservation.
>
> With that reserve, we regard the Western theatre as, for the time being, the dominant
> one, and we shall support the allied army there, with all the available strength we can
> command, as our new armies become complete in men and equipment. We are willing
> to indicate generally the numbers of troops which will be available at different dates so
> far as we can foresee.
>
> For the moment, we believe that the best service we can render may probably be to
> be ready to take over additional lengths of the French line, which will set free so many
> French troops either for offensive or defensive purposes.
>
> In view of the still imperfect equipment of our New Army in the matter of artillery
> ammunition, and of the uncertainties of the strategic situation, it should be strongly
> represented to the French that they should defer any offensive operations. If they

nevertheless think it necessary to undertake such an operation, Sir John French will lend such co-operation with his existing force as, in his judgment, will be useful for the purpose, and not unduly costly to his army.

We shall not depart from this arrangement without previous communication between the Allies.[23]

The British position was thus firmly set when Asquith selected a delegation to accompany him to the conference with the French leaders. Before leaving, Asquith called a meeting of the Dardanelles Committee at which a decision was taken to reinforce Hamilton with two more divisions.[24]

Asquith and his party arrived at Calais shortly before midnight on 5 July and stayed at the Hotel Terminus as guests of the French government. Around 8.30 the next morning Asquith was roused from bed by Hankey who informed him that the French wanted the conference to start at 9 o'clock. The other members of the British delegation were either in bed or having breakfast in their rooms. The only exception was Kitchener who had left the hotel at 7.45 to confer privately with General Joffre.[25] Asquith suggested that the start of the meeting be delayed an hour.[26]

The first Anglo-French conference of the war got under way at 10 a.m. Invited to take the chair, Asquith struggled to read a prepared statement in French. He outlined the British position and expressed the hope that there would be no more large-scale offensives during 1915. Kitchener, who spoke French fluently, made an excellent impression upon his hosts with his clear strategic exposition. Asquith thought Kitchener's bold diplomatic adroitness decisive in persuading the French that the campaign in the Dardanelles should enjoy priority over the Western Front.[27] As the British gained every major point they had wanted, Asquith was naturally delighted with the results of the conference.

After lunch Asquith, Kitchener and Hankey motored to Saint-Omer and stayed at GHQ. The next day Asquith again visited Ypres which was being shelled intermittently. As he walked through the deserted streets, he paused before the remains of Cloth Hall, once a celebrated Gothic monument, and lamented its destruction. Asquith could see no strategic reason why Ypres should be held. The recent battle had left the Allied line in front of Ypres in the shape of a salient which could be bombarded by German artillery from three sides. A far better defensive position would have been one on slightly higher ground just behind Ypres. But Asquith was told that there were political reasons for not abandoning the town.[28]

For the remainder of the day and for part of the next Asquith inspected French and Belgian positions to the north. In between trips to the Front he had several productive talks with Sir John on a number of issues. French asked Asquith if he felt that he had misled him on the ammunition question. Asquith's reply is recorded in French's diary as giving 'me quite satisfactory assurances on this point'.[29] The two men also discussed the Allied position in the Ypres area. Sir John was under the impression from the previous night's conversation that the Prime Minister had reservations about the wisdom of clinging to the salient. Asquith replied that he had not formed an opinion as he knew nothing about strategy and was quite content to leave such matters to Sir John's judgment.[30] Towards the end of the afternoon on 8 July Asquith and Hankey collected Kitchener at GHQ and returned to Calais where they boarded a steamer. From Dover Kitchener motored to his nearby home at Broome Park, while Asquith and Hankey went on to London, arriving a little after midnight.[31]

The understanding with the French at Calais enabled Asquith to shift his focus from the Western Front to the eastern Mediterranean. He continued to be both apprehensive and excited about the impending operations. This was, as he knew too well, the last chance for the Dardanelles. The growing opposition in the cabinet to the enterprise, to say nothing of the nation's limited resources, made it almost certain that Hamilton would not be reinforced again if he failed. Churchill harboured similar thoughts. Unencumbered by departmental responsibilities, he pressed to go on an official visit to the Dardanelles, ostensibly to provide the cabinet with first-hand information from the scene of battle but in reality to lend Hamilton the benefit of his expertise. Asquith agreed that it would be helpful to have a senior minister personally inspect and report on the future prospects at Gallipoli. Churchill, in his opinion, was the right man for the job and not only because he was more fully acquainted with the operation than almost anyone else. Asquith sensed Churchill's frustration at being isolated away from the centre of events and thought the chance of useful service would do wonders for his morale. Kitchener had no objections to Churchill's trip, providing he was accompanied by Hankey. Asquith agreed at once to Kitchener's condition.[32]

It never occurred to Asquith to put the matter of Churchill's mission before the cabinet for approval. After the cabinet meeting broke up on 19 July Churchill remained in the room to bid farewell to Asquith and Kitchener. Curzon returned unexpectedly as Churchill was shaking hands and having a last word with them. He naturally asked where Churchill was going and Asquith could not avoid telling him. Curzon said nothing but hurried off to convey the news to his Unionist colleagues. The upshot was that they protested so vigorously that it became evident to Asquith that Churchill's visit would have to be cancelled to avoid a cabinet crisis. It was a painful decision. He knew how excited Churchill had been at the prospect of involvement in the operation in which he had played so crucial a part. To be told at the last moment that he would not be going would 'almost break his heart'.[33] Hankey went off by himself as an agent of the Prime Minister with instructions to survey the situation and report back. His first communiqué from the Dardanelles was dated 28 July and he was present when Hamilton launched his second offensive.[34]

The operation began on 6 August. Hamilton's main thrust from Anzac was designed to seize Sari Bahr, a 1,000 foot ridge in the centre of the peninsula that would give him command of the Narrows. The plan was overly ambitious and if there existed any chance of success it was lost through poor generalship. On 17 August Hamilton admitted that his attack had been checked and that he required a total of 95,000 new men to provide the necessary superiority against a defending garrison estimated to number 110,000.[35]

Asquith had pinned such high hopes on the outcome of the operation that he was devastated when he heard the news, regarding the failure as his greatest disappointment since the start of the war.[36] His habitual composure left when he glanced over Hankey's account of the attack. Hankey was especially critical of the landing at Suvla Bay, which was intended to support the Anzac forces further south. When the troops disembarked on shore there was practically no Turkish opposition in the area. The local British commander ordered his men to consolidate the beachhead against an non-existent enemy rather than to advance inland to occupy the heights. His failure to exploit the advantages of surprise, in Hankey's view, ruined Hamilton's plan. Asquith's anger may be inferred from a note he wrote to Kitchener on 20 August: 'I have read enough to satisfy me that the generals and staff engaged in the Suvla part of the business ought to be court-martialled and dismissed from the Army.'[37]

Asquith was also inclined to lay part of the blame on Hamilton, whom Hankey had criticized indirectly for allowing unproved subordinates too much freedom and for failing to intervene even, when in his opinion, they were missing opportunities. He knew that Hamilton had received more troops than he had requested and he was annoyed that it was on the representation that victory was all but certain that he had opted for 'storming' the peninsula rather than the 'starving' operations at Bulair.[38] Now he was back facing the old struggle of competing claims between the Western and Eastern theatres of war.

Asquith had a talk with Kitchener before the Dardanelles Committee met on 20 August. As was customary, Kitchener briefed Asquith on his recent visit to France. Joffre was laying plans for his next attack in Champagne and expected to have the full cooperation of the BEF. The offensive was necessary, Joffre insisted, to relieve pressure on the faltering

Russians and he hinted, in unmistakable language, that a British refusal might lead France to make peace. In view of these circumstances, Kitchener reluctantly agreed to lay aside the Calais agreement and participate in Joffre's autumn offensive.[39]

Asquith reaction to the news is not recorded. From what he later told the King it is apparent that he had grave concerns about the proposed operation.[40] It did not help to hear Kitchener admit that the chances of the attack achieving anything tangible were remote. Still Asquith was unwilling to cancel Britain's commitment and risk losing France or Russia. The issue was resolved in the cabinet, which concluded that although an active defensive[41] in the West was eminently desirable it was no longer politically possible.[42] The change in British policy meant a substantial lessening of support for the Dardanelles operation. Henceforth the New Armies would be going to France. Just as Asquith and his colleagues were at their wits' end to find a means to extricate themselves from the morass in the eastern Mediterranean, their hopes were revived by an unexpected French offer on 31 August to land four divisions on the Asiatic side of the Straits.

The French announcement in London promised to breathe new life into the Dardanelles enterprise, generating enthusiasm even among those who had favoured an evacuation from Gallipoli. Asquith was somewhat astonished at the news, particularly when he remembered that only a fortnight ago Joffre had coerced the British into supporting his grand offensive on the Western Front. Whatever the French motive, he welcomed their decision. He assumed, as did his colleagues, that the transfer of large forces from France meant that Joffre would be postponing his autumn offensive. But Sir John French, who came over to London on 6 September, reported that Joffre had no such thought in mind.[43] Asquith was now unclear about the status of the French expedition. It was not until a week later that Kitchener, upon returning from a meeting with Millerand at Calais, was able to shed light on the matter.[44] He told Asquith that Joffre would not release the four divisions until after the results of his forthcoming thrust in Champagne had become known. Kitchener doubted that the proposed French expedition to the Dardanelles would ever materialize. Even if the troops were ultimately released they could not arrive on the scene before mid November, by which time the fierce winter storms would rule out a landing.

Asquith had rarely seen Kitchener looking so weary. The Field Marshal appeared to have aged overnight. Working long hours at the War Office day after day had taken its toll. Compounding the burdens of office was the strain of constant harassment by cabinet colleagues. Apart from Lloyd

George, Kitchener had made powerful enemies within the government. While the Liberal administration had tolerated Kitchener's methods and not obtruded itself unduly in the conduct of the war, the current one did not show the same forbearance. The Tories in particular brooded over Kitchener's secretiveness, his unwillingness to impart vital information to which they were entitled and which they required before making a decision. What started out as uneasiness changed first to resentment and then to antipathy. As Kitchener's standing fell in the cabinet, he came under greater scrutiny and much of his time was spent in defending his policies and opinions. Inarticulate and tongue-tied, he could easily be outmanoeuvred by practised debaters even when he was in the right. The nagging feeling that he was isolated and that his every move might invite criticism or ridicule seriously affected his judgment. He became indecisive, frequently changed his mind and lost touch with his war aims. Kitchener made it easier for Lloyd George to convince the cabinet that he had lost control of the direction of the war.

Asquith made no effort to narrow the gulf between Kitchener and the rest of the cabinet. Here was one instance when his talents as a mediator could have been used to good advantage. Asquith ought to have impressed upon his civilian colleagues the need to show more understanding in their dealings with Kitchener. After a lifetime of command on the frontiers of the empire the Field Marshal was accustomed to doing things auto-cratically and at the age of sixty-five was too old to change his ways. He might have reminded his colleagues that Kitchener had performed miracles of improvisation in the early months of the war and had been right much more often than they had. Asquith should have dismissed Lloyd George or, if he felt that was not politically feasible, taken him aside and directed him to refrain from interfering in matters about which he knew precious little. To drive home his message Asquith could have added that Lloyd George ought to apply his energy and creative ideas to his new department, so as to avoid the mess his neglect and prolonged absences had created at the Treasury.[45]

At the same time Asquith could have acquainted Kitchener with key elements in the system of cabinet government, especially the concept of collective responsibility, and why he needed to be forthright in what he told colleagues. He should have provided Kitchener with more help at the War Office. Before Kitchener actually took control of the War Office in August 1914, the General Staff had been fatally damaged when its leading lights dispersed to the Front, leaving ill-qualified deputies to learn vital tasks, untutored and in haste. Rather than reconstruct the General Staff, Kitchener pushed it into the background and tried to do everything himself. It was a burden that no single individual, however able and robust, could properly carry. In these circumstances Asquith ought to have recalled some of the senior members of the General Staff from France, so that they could relieve Kitchener of administrative work as well as guide him to make greater use of the machinery on hand. He could have, as he had done at the outset, acted as Kitchener's interpreter in the cabinet. The least that Asquith should have done was to shield Kitchener against unnecessary badgering and assist him to put his ideas in a coherent and argumentative form.

Unfortunately Asquith left Kitchener to his own devices and gradually distanced himself from the Field Marshal as his stock declined. The loss of confidence in Kitchener destroyed what little unity there was in the cabinet. Thereafter the coalition was like a rudderless ship on the high seas, unable to maintain a steady course and driven by winds, first in one direction and then in another.

During the first week in September Bonar Law, spurred on by Carson, approached Asquith about making changes in the higher direction of the war. What was needed above all, Bonar Law told Asquith, was a reconstituted General Staff at the War Office to assure the government of independent and sound strategic advice. In his opinion, the absence of such an organization had led to the haphazard selection of objectives which doomed military operations as in the case of the Dardanelles venture.[46]

Asquith did not act on Bonar Law's suggestion until the cabinet forced his hand on 22 September. Emboldened by Kitchener's absence from the meeting, the Tories raised the subject of the arrangements for the conduct of the war and took the lead in the discussions. They wanted a smaller War Council to manage the conflict, in addition to redefining the position of the General Staff in order to allow it to function again as an instrument of operational planning and control. Confronted with a ground swell of discontent with the existing machinery, Asquith agreed to institute the desired changes.[47]

Asquith wrote that same day to Kitchener, telling him that feeling in the cabinet was unanimous that it was essential to have a strong, functioning General Staff at home. The move, it was pointed out, would lighten the immense burdens of the Secretary for War and provide both him and the cabinet with the best possible intelligence 'for our common purpose'. Asquith suggested that General Archibald Murray, whom Kitchener was considering as his new CIGS, should be appointed at once; that he be assisted by three or four of the best staff officers who had seen service at the Front; that the General Staff draw up a weekly military appreciation for the benefit of the cabinet; and that a systematic interchange between staff officers at home and at the Front be created.[48]

Kitchener appointed Murray CIGS on 25 September but made no effort to carry out the other proposals and Asquith did not press him to do so. Although Murray was not a strong-willed individual, he worked hard to revive the place of the General Staff in cabinet government. During his brief term at the War Office, strategic and logistical problems were studied in a scientific manner for the first time. He was described by Hankey as a 'sort of John the Baptist to Robertson', who succeeded him three months later.[49] Murray's first major task was to advise on the Balkans, where a crisis was under way.

IN HAPPY DAYS TO COME.

The Coalition Owners (Mr. Asquith and Mr. Bonar Law) LEADING IN
A WINNER.

Chapter 8

A Confusion of Strategies

Early in September 1915 the Central Powers enticed Bulgaria into signing a military convention by promising large territorial gains at Serbia's expense. For this diplomatic defeat, Asquith blamed mostly the Serbians for refusing to make the necessary concessions sooner. Bulgaria probably could have been won over as an ally, he wrote to the King, but for Serbia 'whose obstinacy and cupidity have now brought her to the verge of disaster'.[1]

Because of conflicting intelligence reports, Asquith was uncertain until late in September whether another major offensive against Serbia was imminent. The Serbian government, viewing with alarm the concentration of troops across its eastern border, wanted to launch a preemptive strike on Bulgaria.[2] Asquith was reluctant to give his government's consent. On 1 October he told Grey that Serbia should be advised to hold off lest it be branded the aggressor and unite the Bulgarians behind their King.[3] Within twenty-four hours Asquith had changed his mind, concluding that it would be unwise to deprive Serbia of the strategic advantage of forestalling a Bulgarian attack. He now favoured sending 'nothing which could be interpreted either as encouraging or restraining Serbia'.[4] The cabinet also thought that was the best course.

Asquith immediately recognized that the collapse of Serbia would have dire military consequences. With the Germans able to move guns and supplies directly to Constantinople, the Turks could threaten Hamilton's position on the peninsula and even reopen the front against the Suez Canal. As much as Asquith wanted to deny the enemy that advantage, he reacted cautiously when Venizelos asked the Entente for 150,000 men,[5] so that Greece could fulfil the terms of the Greco-Serbian military convention.[6] As matters stood, Britain's quota of 75,000 men could be met only at the expense of the Dardanelles. A General Staff appreciation on 24

September weakened the case for involvement by implying there was little chance of saving Serbia even with Greek assistance.[7] The French, on the other hand, agreed at once to Venizelos' condition, realigning their sights from the Dardanelles to the Balkans. As they relied on the British government to follow their lead, it became impossible, Asquith reported, 'for us ... to hold back'.[8] As a preliminary step, arrangements were made with Hamilton to transfer the 10th Division to Salonika.

On 5 October, ironically as the Anglo-French troops from Gallipoli were disembarking at Salonika, King Constantine dismissed Venizelos and reaffirmed Greece's intention to remain neutral.[9] The last glimmer of hope for Serbia was gone, regardless of what the French and the British might do. In these circumstances, Asquith felt that the most sensible course for the Allied forces in Greece was to reembark and return home, even though it meant leaving Serbia in the lurch. That was the opinion of most of his colleagues in the cabinet but for a few die-hards who refused to face military reality.

As the British leaders debated, the Austro-German armies launched a massive offensive against Serbia on 7 October and within twenty-four hours captured Belgrade. On 11 October Bulgaria ended the guessing game in the Allied capitals when its forces struck from the east and moved to sever Serbia's link to Salonika.

The unfolding catastrophe in the Balkans increased the pressure on the British cabinet to define future strategy in the eastern Mediterranean. The British and French offensive in Loos-Champagne was ending in disappointment and, apart from the General Staff, there was no support for further operations on the Western Front for the remainder of 1915. This narrowed the choice to either the Dardanelles or Salonika. Asquith backed the first alternative but he was less committed to it than Kitchener, Churchill, Curzon and some others. He was prepared to send reinforcements to Gallipoli only if there was a reasonable chance of achieving decisive results. As a precautionary move he asked Kitchener to begin work on an evacuation plan.[10] Only Lloyd George, Bonar Law and Carson favoured the second course of action.

As noted earlier, Asquith wrote off Serbia the moment Greece turned its back on the Entente. He had read enough General Staff reports to understand that a purely Allied initiative in the Balkans, apart from presenting a logistical nightmare, ignored the enemy's advantage of interior lines, the limited capacity of Salonika and the difficulties of moving an army through mountainous terrain. He thought it incredible that the French were willing to send a major force all the way to Nish without any knowledge of the country or clear objectives. He considered

The Balkan States and the Salonika Campaign

their operation 'a wild goose affair', since it was clear to him that Allied goals in the Balkans could no longer be accomplished.

Asquith, like Kitchener, worried about opening a new front at a time when British resources were stretched to breaking-point.[11] The last thing he wanted was to be dragged into another side-show which was fraught with danger and would serve no purpose. He dismissed as fanciful the surmise advanced by the other side, that the presence of a large Anglo-French force at Salonika would encourage the neutral Balkan states to join the Entente camp.

Yet Asquith, regardless of his personal feelings, had to tread warily lest he alienate the French or wreck the coalition. At a meeting of the Dardanelles Committee on 11 October he worked out a formula under which 150,000 men would be sent from France to Egypt, leaving open whether they would be employed at Gallipoli or Salonika. A specially selected general was to be sent out to advise on the best policy.[12]

The pro-Salonika ministers refused to accept this compromise, which they correctly reasoned was tantamount to the abandonment of Serbia. All three wanted the troops now clinging forlornly to the Gallipoli Peninsula transferred immediately to Salonika. Blind to the complexities of politics in the Balkans and the military obstacles of waging war in that region, they never wearied of parading the same old arguments to the annoyance and puzzlement of Asquith and the other members of the cabinet.[13] For once Asquith had been ready to make a difficult choice and act on it without delay. But the pro-Salonika group, in particular Lloyd George, evaded making tough decisions, in fact doing the very thing they were most prone to criticize about the Prime Minister.

Asquith hoped to ease the growing tensions by sacking Hamilton and appointing an officer capable of reporting objectively on whether Galliopli should be abandoned. Hamilton's supersession had been under consideration for some time. From all the evidence that Asquith had seen, among which was a letter from his son 'Oc' who was recuperating from a wound suffered at Cape Helles, he was convinced that Hamilton had bungled the Suvla Bay operation and no longer enjoyed the confidence of his men. He urged his colleagues to recall Hamilton and to do so immediately. He foresaw a good deal of agitation once the results of the landing were fully known to the public and he wished to avoid the appearance that the government was merely reacting to external pressure.[14] The cabinet approved of the Prime Minister's recommendations. Hamilton's successor, General Charles Monro, formerly in command of the Third Army in France, was instructed to report fully and frankly on the military situation in Gallipoli.[15]

The change in command in the Dardanelles failed to mollify the dissenters in the cabinet. Carson submitted his resignation, citing, as his reasons, the abandonment of Serbia and general discontent with the machinery of war direction.[16] Asquith knew that Carson, with his forensic skill and single-mindedness of purpose, would become a dangerous critic on his return to the backbenches. He tried hard to persuade Carson to remain in the government but to no avail. Carson's departure left Lloyd George and Bonar Law as the only two firmly committed Balkanites in the cabinet. They continued the struggle alone but it is doubtful that their efforts would have paid dividends had it not been for the French. In the closing days of October, Joffre hurried to London and warned that Britain's failure to support the Balkan expedition would endanger both the Alliance and his own position as commander-in-chief. Confronted by the possibility of such dire consequences, Asquith and Kitchener yielded on condition that if communications with the Serbians could not be reestablished the entire Allied force would be withdrawn.[17]

Throughout the summer and autumn of 1915 the atmosphere of general crisis in the British cabinet had deepened divisions and strained old friendships. Asquith's personal relations with Lloyd George suffered as well. Their close association dated back to their early political careers and from 1908 onwards they had formed a truly formidable combination. They had much in common but more important each had essential qualities that the other lacked. Asquith never really trusted Lloyd George, finding him wanting in consistency, judgment and personal courage.[18] But of his great gifts he had no doubts. Asquith admired Lloyd George for his originality, stamina and ability to get things done. Until the middle of 1915 Asquith had frequently turned to Lloyd George for advice or active intervention to help resolve difficult problems. In turn Asquith had saved Lloyd George from being engulfed by the Marconi Scandal, lent weight to his practical proposals, given him the Ministry of Munitions and kept the Exchequer ready for him when he cared to return. But after the coalition was established an element of rivalry surfaced and, as the months slipped by, became steadily more apparent.

Asquith came to see Lloyd George as serving a largely negative function. He resented Lloyd George for playing the role of Cassandra and for his assertions of independence – advocacy of the Balkan campaign and especially of conscription[19] – which eroded the strength of, and confidence in, the government. Asquith could have dismissed Lloyd George earlier in the war but he no longer enjoyed that option. This was apparent when Bonar Law tried to use his good offices to patch things up between the two

Liberal leaders. Bonar Law had acquired genuine regard for Asquith by working with him and believed that he was the only conceivable Prime Minister. He was equally convinced that Lloyd George was indispensable, a point he underlined when he visited Asquith at 10 Downing Street. Asquith half-heartedly agreed, although he could not understand what Lloyd George had done to deserve his reputation. He was, according to Asquith, a 'very bad administrator and had muddled every Department with which he had been connected'. Bonar Law likened Lloyd George to Gladstone, observing that 'no matter how many mistakes he made he always came out greater than before, for the people trusted him'. Asquith did not dispute this observation but implied that Gladstone was motivated by nobler aims than Lloyd George.[20]

By the late summer of 1915 Asquith was so disenchanted with Lloyd George's disruptive ways that he was prepared to replace him as Deputy Leader of the House of Commons. In mid September Bonar Law, as a way to improve his standing with his own party, approached Asquith and requested that he be made Deputy Leader of the House. He had a strong claim to it since he actually led the largest party in the House. Asquith agreed to let him have the job. Apart from his growing estrangement from Lloyd George, Asquith saw an opportunity to make amends for having slighted Bonar Law the previous month by neglecting to include him in an important cabinet committee. Lloyd George was livid over the proposed move, which threatened his position as the heir apparent to the Liberal leadership. He protested vehemently against it to the Prime Minister and at the same time wrote a bitter letter to Bonar Law, accusing him of intriguing behind his back. In view of the furore created by Lloyd George, Bonar Law backed away from the post and there was no further discussion of it.[21]

Asquith could have isolated Lloyd George in the cabinet and reduced him to impotence if he had made an ally of Bonar Law – as he could easily have done. Relations between Asquith and Bonar Law had always been distinctly cool, a situation for which the former was largely to blame. Asquith regarded Bonar Law as a dull plodder and interpreted his reserve and caution as signs of weakness. Asquith was not above belittling Bonar Law, partly no doubt from political motives but mostly because he held him in low esteem.

Bonar Law, however, did not reciprocate these feelings. It is true he had not forgotten that at the time of the coalition he had been excluded from any office befitting his status as party leader. But his anger was directed at Lloyd George, not Asquith. It was Lloyd George's machinations that had kept him out of the Exchequer. He reasoned that Asquith would have been compelled to yield if Lloyd George had stood with him, instead of with McKenna. There is no evidence that he held Asquith accountable for his loss.[22] What is certain is that he respected and admired Asquith's parliamentary skills. Despite misgivings about the manner in which the war was being conducted, the Tory chief was convinced that Asquith was the only man who could unite the nation in the great struggle against Germany. Had Asquith taken the initiative and extended a hand of friendship to Bonar Law, his position would have been immeasurably strengthened and he would have avoided the later threat from Lloyd George.

Asquith committed a second major error when he ended Kitchener's reign as arbiter of British strategy. He did this by stages, each time to silence criticism of Kitchener and indirectly his own management of the war. Ironically Asquith failed in the long run, for while he sacrificed Kitchener's authority he was unable to win over his critics.

If Asquith's action was short-sighted, it was also ill-advised. Kitchener, for all his faults, had a coherent strategy. That fell apart when he ceased to enjoy the confidence of the cabinet. Without a guiding hand the coalition, which from its inception had never operated smoothly, degenerated into a ramshackle, quarrelsome and irresolute confederation. Its members, many of whom had definite ideas about what ought to be done, were divided on practically every issue that arose and, rather than seek solutions, devoted far too much time to debates, recriminations and postmortems. Asquith compounded matters by failing to provide strong leadership. As his government lurched from one crisis to another, he painstakingly devised and imposed compromises that were intended less to win the war than to satisfy all parties.

Everyone agreed that the Dardanelles Committee was too argumentative and cumbersome to be an effective instrument for the conduct of the war. It will be remembered that on 22 September the cabinet had decided to abolish the Dardanelles Committee and to replace it with a smaller body.[23] Asquith took no action. But at a cabinet meeting on 21 October, with Crewe deputizing for Asquith who was unwell, the matter was brought up again. As a result of the deliberations, Crewe was empowered 'to convey to the P. M. the drastic need for a change'.[24]

As Asquith turned to the task with which he was charged, there was no dearth of advice from colleagues. Crewe and Lansdowne wanted the committee limited to four members, the Prime Minister plus the heads of the fighting departments.[25] Balfour argued that no new committee would work effectively and he preferred to rely simply on the cabinet system, supplemented by occasional and informal conferences at 10 Downing

Street.[26] Curzon thought that the small committee should include at least three ministers without departmental responsibilities.[27]

The consensus in the cabinet favoured a committee of between three and five members.[28] Asquith decided to establish a body of three composed of himself and the heads of the War Office and Admiralty. Lloyd George was enraged to find himself excluded from the inner council while Kitchener, his arch enemy, was again in a position to dominate war policy. On 31 October Lloyd George sent Asquith a letter in which he recited his litany of familiar War Office grievances and threatened to resign if Kitchener remained in the government.[29]

Asquith had known for weeks that his colleagues were tired of Kitchener's obsessive secrecy, lack of candour and indecision. Lloyd George nagged him at every opportunity about dismissing Kitchener from the government. Bonar Law had echoed the same suggestion on several occasions. When the cabinet meeting ended on 21 October all the members present (Asquith, as noted above, was absent because of illness), except Kitchener, remained behind. During the conversation that ensued there was near unanimity that Kitchener was no longer fit to remain in office. Only McKenna held a contrary opinion. The cabinet's recommendation was passed on to Asquith who had reached the same conclusion some weeks before.[30] Yet Asquith was reluctant to remove Kitchener. He had no intention of alienating public opinion and leaving the War Office open to Lloyd George, who was emerging as a serious rival.

At the start of November the pressure on Asquith was so intense that he was forced to act. Lloyd George had obtained the backing of Bonar Law and both threatened to leave the cabinet unless a change was made at the War Office.[31] On 1 November Asquith promised Lloyd George, in the presence of two unnamed ministers, that he would get rid of Kitchener. As soon as Asquith left the room the two onlookers asked each another in disbelief, 'Will he do it?' Lloyd George himself doubted that he would and referred to the Prime Minister as a 'soft-nosed torpedo' lacking 'the steel point'.[32]

The only way that Asquith could keep his pledge without provoking a popular upheaval was to persuade the Field Marshal to leave of his own free will. Asquith wanted to send Kitchener to the Near East as generalissimo of all British forces outside of France. Kitchener rejected the offer. Although he had had his fill of politicians, he knew that his departure would affect national unity and would mean abandoning a great task unfinished. After other options were explored Kitchener agreed that, while remaining Secretary for War, he would go on a fact-finding mission to the Mediterranean.

Asquith did not really need a second opinion as to whether the Gallipoli campaign should continue: Monro had already pronounced himself unequivocally in favour of evacuation. He wanted Kitchener out of the way, if only temporarily, to prevent the cabinet from breaking up. Of course he hoped that ultimately Kitchener would resign from the government and return to Egypt, perhaps as Viceroy of the Near East with full command of the British armies in the Mediterranean and Asia.[33] Asquith proposed, in Kitchener's absence, to take charge of the War Office, as he had done in the wake of the Curragh Incident. 'We avoid by this method', he observed to Lloyd George, 'the immediate supersession of K. as War Minister, while attaining the same result. I suppose even B. L. would hardly object to such a plan.'[34]

Lloyd George resented Asquith's temporary occupation of the War Office but a night's reflection changed his outlook. He knew that Asquith could not hold down both offices for an extended period and that sooner or later he would be appointed Secretary for War. In the meantime he would allow Asquith to face the violent public reaction that was certain to follow Kitchener's resignation.

By contrast Bonar Law was unhappy with Asquith's arrangement and more than a trifle annoyed at the part Lloyd George had played in it. One cause of his disaffection was the belief that Asquith could not run the War Office in conjunction with his other duties. Bonar Law had consented to support Lloyd George's claims to the War Office which would then have opened the way for he himself to move into the Ministry of Munitions. He was surprised to hear that Lloyd George had backed out of their agreement and now approved of Asquith's proposal to assume temporary charge of the War Office. Again he felt that he had been tricked. He at once discerned the motive for Lloyd George's *volte-face* and in a fit of pique conveyed this to Asquith, who remained impassive. Beaverbrook, to whom the episode was related, asked Bonar Law why he had told Asquith his suspicions about Lloyd George. Because, the Tory leader replied, he had no use for people he could not trust.[35]

Another sore point with Bonar Law was over Asquith's decision to postpone the evacuation of Gallipoli pending the receipt of Kitchener's report. Bonar Law was convinced that, with the establishment of direct railway communications between Germany and Turkey, a great disaster would occur if the British army remained on the peninsula. He thought that sending Kitchener out was a waste of time, a pretext to avoid taking a painful but vital decision, and he hinted that he would resign unless the army was evacuated.[36]

Asquith was clearly irritated with Bonar Law, who had not objected to

Kitchener's mission when it was discussed in the cabinet. 'I really shdn't be sorry to part with him',[37] Asquith confided to Sylvia Henley in a moment of exasperation. Although these harsh words may have expressed his true sentiments, he recognized that Bonar Law's presence was indispensable to the survival of the Coalition. Asquith spent the next day or two in prolonged discussions with Bonar Law. His initiative was supported by key Unionists ministers, in particular Long and Chamberlain, who urged their leader to reconsider. Bonar Law succumbed to the pressure, consenting to wait for Kitchener's report.[38]

That matter resolved, Asquith was able to finalize the reorganization of the new and smaller War Committee. Asquith considered including Lansdowne, rather than Bonar Law, as the Tory representative. On the surface at least the step would seem incomprehensible, since the seventy-year-old Lansdowne lacked the determination and dynamism to serve on so vital a committee. In preferring Lansdowne to Bonar Law, Asquith was either a poor judge of human talent or playing politics by attempting to keep the Tories leaderless and in disarray. As it turned out Lansdowne refused the appointment, compelling Asquith 'to take on Bonar Law'.[39]

The War Committee was formally set up on 11 November and consisted of five (possibly six) members, not three as originally contemplated. Besides Asquith and Bonar Law, the others were Balfour, Lloyd George and McKenna. Asquith reserved another place for Kitchener 'if and when' he returned.[40] But the list of those who attended regularly soon swelled to eight or more. The War Committee had the same flaws as its predecessors: it was too large and it lacked executive authority.

Asquith's most notable ommission from the new body was Churchill. Without a voice in the direction of the war, Churchill resigned his sinecure office (although he retained his seat in the Commons) and asked to be put in command of the British forces in East Africa. Asquith accepted Churchill's resignation but, fearful of political repercussions, declined to send him where he wished.[41] The best that he could do under the circumstances was to give him command of a battalion in France. Before leaving for the Front, Churchill prepared to deliver a farewell speech before the House as was customary for all resigning ministers. 'I hope he will get through his performance', Asquith told Sylvia Henley, 'without lapses of taste and judgment.'[42] Churchill was more restrained than might have been expected and there was no reason to suppose that Asquith was unhappy with what he heard.[43]

By excluding from the War Committee the most ardent devotees of the Dardanelles campaign, Asquith gave the evacuationists a significant tactical advantage. Asquith himself was of two minds about the enterprise.

Gallipoli seemed hopeless and the bitter debates in the cabinet over its future were tearing the government apart. On the other hand, the country had invested so heavily in the campaign that he found it difficult to let go. He also had a nagging fear that heavy losses would be sustained during the evacuation and that an admission of failure would damage British prestige. He remained undecided until receiving reports, from Kitchener and the General Staff, recommending evacuation.[44] On 23 November the War Committee unanimously agreed to wind down the operation.[45]

To lessen the dangerous effect of withdrawal on Muslim opinion and to secure the defence of Egypt, Kitchener suggested using a portion of the Gallipoli force for a landing at Ayas Bay, opposite Alexandretta.[46] A bewildered Asquith forwarded the proposal to the War Office. The General Staff forcefully advised against the scheme, pointing out that it would require considerably more men than Kitchener had envisaged and place an intolerable strain on the nation's resources.[47] The French objected no less adamantly since the projected landing would place British troops near Syria, which they had traditionally regarded as their sphere of influence in the eastern Mediterranean.[48] On 19 November Asquith informed Kitchener that the War Committee had rejected the Ayas Bay scheme.[49]

Kitchener tried in vain to persuade Asquith that the operation was the only means to prevent a real calamity. Kitchener's fears for the safety of Egypt were exacerbated by a report that the Germans planned to attack the Suez Canal. The fall of Egypt, he predicted, would herald the defeat of the Allies. Asquith moved quickly to exploit the opening. In view of the anticipated difficulties, would it not be advisable for Kitchener to head for Egypt and personally direct its defence? Kitchener refused to take the bait, to Asquith's dismay. He replied:

> I think it is essential that I should return to England at once to give you full information of the situation out here, and to make the necessary arrangements to carry out the policy decided on. I personally can do no good in Egypt.[50]

Kitchener's imminent return prompted Asquith to carry through several major changes in the organization of the war. The first of these was the transfer of the Ordnance Board and Inventions Branch from the War Office to the Ministry of Munitions, ending a long-standing dispute between Kitchener and Lloyd George.[51] The second was the removal of Sir John French as commander-in-chief of the British forces in France. Asquith's confidence in French's capacity had declined throughout the summer and an investigation of the conduct of the battle of Loos convinced him that the burden of command was too great for a sixty-three-year-old man in failing health. Asquith did not raise the subject in the cabinet but few if any among those whose opinions he solicited doubted that French had outlived his usefulness. Asquith chose Lord Esher, frequently used by the government to run miscellaneous errands and a close friend of French, to tell the Field Marshal that he must relinquish his command. Sir John initially took the news reasonably well, but then his mood changed and he hurried over to London to see if he could engineer a revolt. When he discovered that he had forfeited his earlier political backing, he submitted his letter of resignation and accepted the command of the Home Forces. Asquith ignored French's recommendation of Sir William Robertson (then Chief of Staff at General Headquarters) as his successor and instead appointed Sir Douglas Haig.[52]

Asquith had already decided to use the services of Robertson at home in yet another change in the military machine. Asquith wanted the CIGS to be the sole adviser to the government on all matters of strategy and the current one, General Murray, was not a man to defy Kitchener. Asquith made an excellent choice in selecting Robertson to replace Murray. A blunt and forceful character, Robertson had risen from the ranks through ability and devotion to his profession. During the latter part of November Asquith had an interview with Robertson, who was in London to give the cabinet military advice. Robertson was not keen to take up the post but he agreed to do so if the powers of the CIGS were extended and defined in a written agreement with the Secretary for War. Asquith accepted the conditions and arranged to keep Robertson in London so that he would be available when Kitchener returned from Gallipoli.[53]

Kitchener arrived in London early on 30 November and drove straight from the railway station to the War Office. On learning that during his absence some of the MGO's functions had been tranferred to the Ministry of Munitions, he went to 10 Downing Street and told Asquith that he wanted to resign. Asquith no longer had any doubts that Kitchener's departure would be fatal to his government. A day after Kitchener left for the Dardanelles, the *Globe* had announced that he had resigned because of disagreements with his colleagues. 'Lord Kitchener', it blared, 'acting with a single eye to the interests of his King and country, has tolerated manoeuvres and machinations which none but the patriotic soldier would have endured for a day.' The newspaper was suppressed and only allowed to reopen a fortnight later on condition that it print a retraction. In the meantime the country was in a uproar and Asquith had been at pains to reassure parliament that the allegation was unfounded.[54]

Asquith told Kitchener that his resignation was out of the question. He admitted that his colleagues had lost confidence in Kitchener's judgment and that he now wanted Robertson to take over as CIGS in an enlarged role that would make him the government's principal adviser on military strategy. Nevertheless, Asquith went on to say, he fully expected Kitchener to remain at his post. As a symbol of the nation's will to fight, he would be betraying the army, the public and the King if he did otherwise. Asquith knew that by appealing to Kitchener's sense of duty he could persuade him to accept any terms he proposed.

As Asquith requested, Kitchener met Robertson and accepted the condition that the ground-rules of their professional relationship should be laid down in writing.[55] After returning to France, Robertson spelt out how he viewed the duties and status of the CIGS in a memorandum dated 5 December. The main points of the paper may be summarized in the following demands: that the War Committee be the supreme direct-ing authority on matters dealing with military strategy; that it formu-late its policy only through information supplied by the CIGS; that all operational orders be signed by the CIGS under the authority of the War Committee and not of the Secretary for War; and that the func-tions of the Secretary for War be confined to raising and equipping the army.[56] The first of these conditions was unconstitutional and Kitchener could not stomach the third and fourth on personal grounds. He decided to persist in his resignation rather than have to submit to further indignities.

Kitchener took Robertson's proposals to 10 Downing Street with the recommendation that they be accepted. He indicated, however, that it was impossible for him to continue as Secretary for War and proposed instead that he become a sort of roving generalissimo of the British army. Asquith was attracted to the idea. 'This would solve a lot of difficulties,' he told Sylvia Henley, 'if we could precisely define & circumscribe the functions of the G.(with a very big "G").'[57]

Asquith had already received a copy of Robertson's memo and, although making only a few passing remarks to Kitchener about its contents, was troubled at the implication of one or two points. He turned to Curzon, the Lord Privy Seal, for advice.[58] Curzon had misgivings about the document. The first thing that caught his eye was that it elevated the status of the War Committee at the expense of the cabinet. He was also concerned that the new CIGS might be seen abroad as the real commander-in-chief. Finally it would compel the government to find a post abroad for Kitchener. He found it difficult to imagine how Kitchener could remain at the War Office in view of the increased status of the new CIGS and the imminent arrival in London of another luminary, Sir John French. Curzon went on to say:

Where would he sit? What would be his office? Who would be under him & what would he do? He would have no seat in the War Council & therefore no voice in the control or direction of the war. The GOCs all not to be under him or even to report to him. It seems to me that he would be left in command of Sir George Arthur and Col. FitzGerald alone.[59]

Asquith had no intentions of allowing the War Committee to usurp a vital function of the cabinet but he wanted to create a system that would bring in Robertson and allow Kitchener to remain in a place of eminence but without real authority.[60] Asquith failed to understand that by removing Kitchener's protective umbrella he was undermining his own position.

Asquith hoped that Robertson's reputation and his practical, no nonsense approach to military problems would have a steadying influence in the inner councils of war. Asquith longed for the modicum of unity that had existed under Liberal rule. The past few weeks had been especially trying as the government struggled to decide where Britain should direct its efforts. The cabinet was convulsed by a memoranda war and ferocious debates. The contestants frequently threatened resignation. At times it seemed that the coalition could not survive.

Swayed by the advice of the military experts, Asquith had joined the others on the War Committee on 23 November in favouring the abandonment of Gallipoli. The matter was referred to the cabinet, where Curzon led a small die-hard group determined to block such a course. Asquith agreed to give them more time before calling for a final decision. At Curzon's suggestion, Asquith asked Hankey to produce a paper on the issue of future military policy in the Dardanelles. Hankey's appreciation, like his earlier ones, was polished and persuasive. It reinforced Curzon's arguments to hold on to Gallipoli by stressing the unfortunate consequences of withdrawal, not the least of which was the threat to Egypt and the possible signing of a separate peace by Russia. Hankey suggested that the four divisons at Salonika be used to strengthen the British position on Gallipoli, or better yet, to resume the offensive.[61]

Over the next few days there were signs that the cabinet might overturn the War Committee's verdict. Besides Hankey's expostulation, it had the benefit of a second paper by Curzon, graphically depicting the perils of evacuation, as well as a naval request to be allowed to rush the Straits.[62] Anti-evacuation sentiment gain further ground by the latest news from Mesopotamia.

After Turkey's entry in the war at the end of October 1914 the Indian government, at the insistence of London, had sent a small expedition to the head of the Persian Gulf to protect the Anglo-Persian oil installations on Abadan Island.[63] The mission was accomplished with so little difficulty

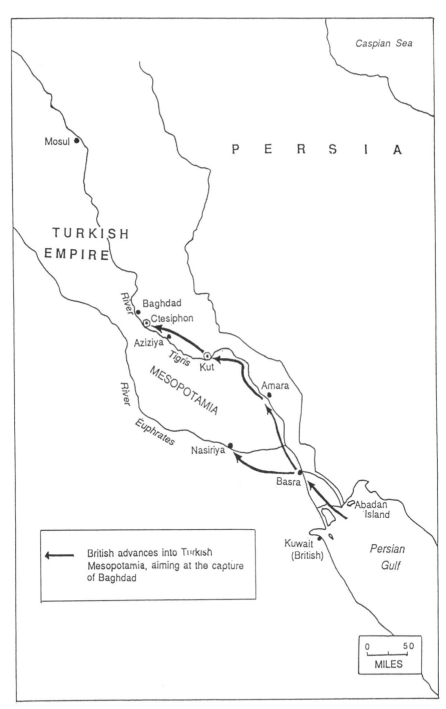

Mesopotamia, 1914–16

that the temptation to proceed further up the valley of the Tigris proved irresistible. Plausible arguments were advanced for each fresh advance but at no stage of the campaign were the ends and means clearly defined. By the summer of 1915 the Anglo-Indian force had completed the conquest of southern Mesopotamia and its ambitious commander, Sir John Nixon, was confident that he could push on to Baghdad.

Asquith's initial concern was to safeguard the oil supply and he had no interest in converting the operation from its original purpose to overthrowing Turkish power in Mesopotamia. The impetus for each forward move after the landing had come from the Indian authorities, not from London. Asquith had worried about overextending the British position but he found it difficult to deny his government's consent when the advances were limited and easy to achieve. Baghdad, however, presented potential logistical hazards and it is unlikely that Asquith would have sanctioned a further advance had circumstances been different. What Asquith needed at this time was a spectacular propaganda coup. The capture of Baghdad would impress opinion in the Muslim world and go far in offsetting the failure at the Dardanelles.

Early in October Asquith appointed a special inter-departmental committee, comprising of representatives of the Foreign Office, India Office, War Office and Admiralty, to consider whether there should be an advance on Baghdad. The committee reported that on both political and military grounds a permanent occupation of the city was 'most desirable'.[64]

The General Staff, to which Asquith also turned for advice, was less sanguine. It produced two papers on the subject, one on 6 October and the other eight days later. It concluded that any attempt to capture and hold Baghdad without forces larger than those presently available to Nixon would incur an unjustifiable risk.[65] Asquith was more confused than ever by the various memoranda and the relevant telegrams and correspondence exchanged between Nixon, the Indian government and the India Office. Accordingly he requested a joint study by the naval and military General Staffs. Their appreciation, dated 19 October, argued against occupying Baghdad 'with the intention of staying there until the end of the war'.[66]

As in the case of the naval attack on the Dardanelles, Asquith was so attracted by the political benefits that would accrue from victory that he minimized or ignored the practical difficulties that stood in the way. Kitchener, who was by far the best qualified in the cabinet to evaluate Nixon's chances, warned that it would be a terrible mistake to occupy Baghdad.[67] Asquith no longer placed much stock in Kitchener's advice. A majority in the cabinet wanted a further advance and it was to them –

particularly Balfour, Lansdowne, Churchill, Grey and Selborne – that Asquith turned his ear. The ministers, some of whom were convinced they knew more about strategy than the military experts, tended to accept advice from soldiers (such as Nixon) only if it was consistent with their own preconceived views. Although Baghdad was of negligible military value, they anticipated that its seizure would bolster the prestige of the government and help offset the misfortunes of Gallipoli and Germany's invasion of Serbia. They were concerned less about the long-range prospects of the expedition than the lure of several days of sensational newspaper headlines. As Grey stated, 'it was necessary to gain strength by eating *now*, even if it involved indigestion later on'.[68] Asquith could not have agreed more, anxious as he was to present the country with a dramatic victory for what seemed a small commitment.

Nixon received the go-ahead on 24 October, with an assurance that additional help would be despatched as soon as possible. General Townshend, the commander to whom the advance was assigned, had received some of the supplies but none of the reinforcements he expected when he moved out of Aziziya on 11 November. All went well until Townshend ran up against a heavily fortified Turkish position near Ctesiphon, twenty miles from Baghdad. His attack on 22 November was hurled back at a cost of 4,500 casualties out of a total strength of 14,000. In grievous straits, Townshend ordered a withdrawal three days later. On 3 December he reached Kut where, in view of the extreme exhaustion of his troops, he prepared to withstand a siege.[69]

The situation in Mesopotamia weighed heavily on Asquith's mind during the proceedings in the War Committee on 2 December and in the cabinet the following day. Kitchener no longer favoured evacuating the Dardanelles, stressing that the British could not afford another defeat. He then spoke of exploring the possibility of renewing the offensive at Suvla with the aid of troops from Salonika.[70] Kitchener's remarks influenced the thinking of Asquith as well as Balfour and F. E. Smith (the new Attorney-General). Asquith raised the question of Salonika and, together with his colleagues, concluded that the time had come to take a firm line with the new French government.[71] A conference was summoned for 5 December at Calais.

For obvious reasons Asquith did not include either Lloyd George or Bonar Law in his party. Kitchener was in fine form, as he usually was at Allied conferences. He pointed out that the retention of 150,000 men at Salonika was dangerous and likely to lead to a military disaster. It was too late to save Serbia or maintain communications with its army. He reminded the French that the conditions of his agreement with Joffre on 30

October had not been fulfilled and the best course now was to withdraw. Asquith followed with a prepared statement to the effect that military considerations dictated that the enterprise be liquidated. The French Prime Minister, Aristide Briand, claimed that it was in the interest of the Allies to remain in Greece. Not to do so would free 400,000 Bulgar-German troops pinned down in the Balkans for service on the Western and Russian Fronts. But Asquith and his colleagues remained adamant. With great reluctance the French bowed to British demands that the Allied troops at Salonika reembark immediately.[72]

The arrangements were not allowed to stand. When Briand returned to Paris the socialists were in an uproar and threatened to leave his government.[73] Briand hurriedly despatched Albert Thomas, his Minister of Munitions, to London to ask that the decision be reversed. Concurrently, at an Allied military conference at Chantilly, the Serbians, the Italians and the Russians supported the French policy of maintaining a presence in Greece.[74] Briand had outmanoeuvred and isolated the British. Asquith was clearly annoyed at the French. He told Sylvia Henley:

> The French have stiffened their backs, & claim to have the sympathy of both Russia & Italy. 'La Belle Alliance' has its drawbacks. We had here at lunch M. Thomas [who is] a delightful shaggy creature, full of *esprit* and good sayings. After lunch Grey & Ll. George & I had an hour with him. It is clear that the Briand Gov't would not survive an announcement that they had agreed with us...But *que faire?* Our joint 150,000 [men] are in real peril, which is impossible to make the Frogs realize or appreciate.[75]

For Asquith, the need to hold together the Briand government and maintain harmony in the Entente overrode all other considerations. The decision to keep the Balkan front open destroyed any hope of continuing operations at Gallipoli. Britain did not have the resources to sustain two major side-shows simultaneously. With his mind firmly set, Asquith put an end to vacillation and on 7 December the cabinet agreed to evacuate Suvla and Anzac, retaining Cape Helles for the present.[76]

The next day word arrived in London that the British 10th Division, while covering the French (under General Sarrail) retreat down the Vardar, had been mauled by the Bulgarians. As Asquith waited for further news, he vented his frustration to Sylvia Henley:

> I have had a pretty hellish day. The situation at & near Salonika could hardly be worse. Our poor 10th Division (the Irish) has been hammered & battered a lot in sustaining their self-denying role of guarding the French flank. Sarrail *est toujours optimiste* – & as far as I can see without any reason. It is no longer a question of retaining or evacuating Salonika as a policy; but of preserving the whole Allied force from the imminent menace of destruction. You can guess (& share) my feelings for the Frogs at this moment. We had a long War Council this morning, & after putting on one side a really insane

proposition of A. J. B. [Balfour] supported by Ll.G. to wash our hands of responsibility, & leave everything to the French,[77] we agreed to send K. & E. Grey to Paris ... to concert, with carte blanche, a joint plan for extricating our troops [from their immediate tactical difficulties]. The damned Alliance is costing us a heavy price.[78]

Asquith held little hope that Kitchener and Grey could persuade the French to leave Salonika. His pessimism was soon confirmed. Kitchener and Grey met Briand and General Galliéni, the new Minister of War, but because of the strained atmosphere they avoided raising the broad issue of evacuating Salonika. They only discussed ways on how best to defend the base and agreed to await developments. From Paris Kitchener reported to Asquith that their visit had restored good feelings and prevented a ministerial crisis.[79] On an unrelated issue, Kitchener indicated that he and Robertson had resolved the difficulties raised by his memorandum.[80] He added:

I feel he [Robertson] and I can work quite well together and his presence at the WO as CIGS will relieve me of a good deal of work and improve the relations of the office to the troops in the field besides giving great confidence.[81]

Asquith was surprised but not unhappy to learn that Kitchener and Robertson had reached an accommodation. Much as he wanted Kitchener out of the government, there were strong practical reasons, apart from public sentiment, why he should remain. The King enjoyed a close relationship with Kitchener and, while he favoured broadening the powers of the CIGS to include control over strategy, was adamantly opposed to replacing the Secretary for War.[82] British representatives in St Petersburg reported that rumours of Kitchener's removal were causing alarm in government circles and they suspected that any attempt to move him out of the War Office, even into another position, would threaten the fragile Anglo-Russian Alliance. Esher wrote to Asquith saying that the French deprecated Kitchener's departure from the War Office because he was a 'fixed point' in a dangerously fluid situation.[83] The final word came from Kitchener himself, who had made up his mind to stay. In truth Asquith had little cause to complain. From his own point of view he had the best of both worlds – Kitchener's new status would make him little more than a figurehead, while enabling the government to continue to draw benefits from his enormous prestige with the masses.

Asquith and Robertson met on 18 December to go over the details of the new arrangement. Each had different concerns. Asquith wanted Robertson to understand that executive authority on all matters must rest with the cabinet, as well as clarification of the measures designed to ensure that Kitchener did not interfere with strategy. Robertson for his part was anxious to 'make as sure of my ground as possible', not only 'about K. but also about the War Council'.[84]

Asquith promised Robertson that operations would be the exclusive province of the General Staff and that the CIGS would have a free hand in initiating proposals plus unrestricted access to his office and the War Committee. All he asked was that the CIGS refrain from impinging upon the constitutional powers and responsibilities of the Secretary of War. He impressed upon Robertson that the success of the new scheme largely depended upon his personal and professional relations with Kitchener. 'But I can see', Asquith later confided to Sylvia Henley, 'that his juxta-position with K. is a ticklish one & perhaps [a] hazardous experiment.'[85] As it turned out, Kitchener adhered faithfully to his compact with Robertson. The two became good friends and worked without strain until Kitchener met his death on the way to Russia in June 1916.[86]

For Asquith the hours following his interview with Robertson were a veritable nightmare, as the evacuation from Suvla and Anzac was set to begin on the night of 18 December. Military authorities had anticipated casualties of between 30 and 40 per cent of the total force. Asquith barely slept on the nights of 18 and 19 December. His mind raced back to the melancholy predictions of such men as Curzon and he saw terrible images of a panic withdrawal from the beaches. Contrary to general expectations, the evacuation from Anzac and Suvla was carried out with remarkable efficiency and without the loss of a single soldier. Asquith's relief was immense. He described the evacuation as without parallel in the annals of military history, 'far surpassing even Sir John Moore's at Corunna'.[87]

There remained the bridgehead at Cape Helles. The British position was growing more perilous with each passing day. The soldiers were sick, exhausted, disillusioned and unprepared for the severity of the winter on Gallipoli. To make matters worse, the Turks had received new German howitzers and were shelling the beaches with telling effect. Asquith, through his son Oc, was aware of the conditions at Helles.[88] It made him more determined than ever to remove the men from that beachhead.

Asquith learned, to his horror, that Churchill was back in London to protest against the evacuation of Cape Helles. Given the impact of Churchill's powerful speeches in the House, the last thing Asquith needed was more unrest among the backbenchers. He summoned Churchill to his office and, to use his own words, 'put a stopper on that'.[89] Churchill, already bitter at Asquith for a veto that deprived him of commanding a brigade in France, raged as he left 10 Downing Street. 'What could you expect of a drunken old rabbit with a Welsh weasel [Lloyd George] on its back', he reportedly exclaimed to an intimate.[90]

On becoming CIGS Robertson's first act was to place a memorandum before the War Committee on 23 December, arguing that to retain Helles would be a costly, dangerous and worthless undertaking. Asquith had no arguments with that assessment. Balfour wanted to deny the Turks a chance to claim victory but he stood virtually alone in opposing evacuation. On 27 December the cabinet confirmed the War Committee's action and orders went out for the final evacuation of the peninsula.[91] The operation on the night of 8–9 January 1916, like the earlier one, was completed without a hitch. The successful evacuation of the peninsula was given wide publicity. The efforts of Asquith and his government to represent it as a great victory was intended to obscure the unpleasant truth that Gallipoli had been a major defeat.

The liquidation of the Gallipoli venture laid to rest one of the cabinet's most divisive issues. But the Prime Minister's troubles were not over. During the closing days of December the long simmering debate over conscription reached boiling-point and Asquith found himself in the throes of a new crisis.

THE WINTER CAMPAIGN—AT HOME.

Mr. Punch (*to Mr. Asquith*). "THAT'S A GOOD START, SIR, BUT IT'S NOT ENOUGH. YOU'VE GOT TO TAKE A LEAF OUT OF THE ENEMY'S BOOK, AND ORGANISE THE WHOLE NATION."

Chapter 9

The Adoption of Conscription

When Britain went to war in August 1914 Asquith had no plan to regulate the economy or control the allocation of manpower. In accordance with standby arrangements, his government took charge of the the railways to facilitate the movement of troops and underwrote a war risk insurance scheme to keep the nation's merchant fleet at sea. Steps were also taken to settle urgent questions of monetary policy so as to prevent the collapse of the banking and international credit system. But these were isolated measures, not components of a comprehensive programme. Asquith and his ministers encouraged the impression that the war could be waged without seriously impinging on private business or individual liberties.[1]

The assumption that ordinary life in Britain would go on as before was short-lived. The deadlock on the Western Front brought a new urgency to accelerate the mobilization of the country's human and material resources in order to provide for the demands of the new type of warfare. Asquith, however, extended controls slowly and deliberately. Every step was improvised and in response to a specific problem. Necessity and not choice dictated where his government interfered in the nation's economic and social life.[2]

The cautious and haphazard nature of the transition to total war cannot be attributed to a reluctance to break with traditional *laissez-faire* principles. Asquith, as was true of most of the senior members of his party, was a pragmatist and not inhibited by dogmatic classical Liberalism. Signs of changes in political attitudes were apparent before the war. Between 1906 and 1914 the Liberals had enacted a host of social measures which involved an unprecedented degree of state intervention.

Asquith was ready to accommodate himself to the demands of war but he was unwilling to proceed at a pace faster than that which he believed the public would tolerate. His policy was intended both to ensure victory and to avoid compromising the delicate national consensus which in the bitterness of pre-war politics he had struggled to preserve. His aims were paradoxical in that he wanted to win the war without adopting any measures needed to do so that might endanger national unity.[3]

In the opening days of the war parliament, as a matter of course, enacted the Defence of the Realm Act which, with its subsequent amendments, granted the government broad powers, including the right to suspend civil liberties and requisition munitions factories. In March 1915 the authorities obtained concessions from trade unions in which they pledged to suspend restrictive practices that had the effect of impeding output; to abandon the right to strike in wartime and refer all disputes to arbitration; to and accept 'dilution', that is, the substitution of skilled labour by unskilled or semi-skilled men or women. These proposals were incorporated in the Munitions of War Act (2 July 1915) which further extended state control over the economy.[4]

What Asquith was unwilling to entertain during the Liberal administration was an arrangement that would compel able-bodied young men to serve where they would do the most good, either by going into the armed forces or by staying in their present occupation if engaged in work vital to the war effort. Late in August 1914 Churchill had argued that Britain should abandon its traditional reliance on voluntary methods and introduce conscription for unmarried men. But Churchill received no support whatsoever in the cabinet. Asquith felt that such a move would 'divide the country from one end to the other' and was unnecessary as long as men continued to volunteer in sufficient numbers.[5]

Asquith was probably correct in his estimate that compulsory service in any form was premature and politically dangerous. Hostility to compulsion was deeply rooted in British history and attitudes. The Liberals, practically to a man, considered enforced military service as incompatible with democratic principles. In their eyes the state had the right to request, but not demand, a citizen's services. The Irish Nationalists and Labour MPs were, if anything, more antagonistic to the measure. Among the Tories support for compulsion was negligible. Outside parliament the most vocal opponents of military conscription were the trade unions. They feared that it would foreshadow the implementation of industrial conscription in which they might lose their acquired rights and freedom of bargaining.[6] In short, the evidence is compelling that anyone who dared lead the nation in the direction of compulsory service would have been swimming against a powerful current of political and public opinion. It would have made no sense for Asquith to tackle so controversial an issue and risk dividing the country at an hour of the greatest national peril.

Although Asquith was temperamentally opposed to conscription, his response throughout the long controversy was always influenced by practical considerations. Early on he never anticipated that the time would come when there would be a military necessity to introduce universal service. In the Commons Asquith replied in the negative on the rare occasions he was asked whether the government intended to bring in a conscription bill. Content that the voluntary system would fulfil its purpose, he expected the war to be over before conscription became a pressing issue.

The first signs of dissatisfaction with the prevailing methods of raising manpower for the army came from the restive Opposition at the start of 1915. Some of the Tory leaders, notably Curzon and Long, felt that voluntary enlistment had served its turn and must give way to compulsion now that the nation faced the prospect of a long war.[7] During question time on 11 March 1915 the Prime Minister was asked whether the government was proceeding with or about to begin an investigation into the possible implementation of compulsory service. Asquith disarmed his interrogator by claiming that such a study had not yet become necessary.[8] Again on 20 April a Member of the House inquired if Asquith proposed to introduce universal military service as part of his government's declared policy to mobilize all the resources of the Empire to bring the war to a speedy and successful termination. Answering on behalf of the Premier, Lloyd George asserted that the government had no grounds to suppose that the war could be prosecuted more vigorously by means of conscription. To a question whether the government was satisfied with the current level of enlistments, the Welshman said: 'The Secretary of State is very gratified with the response which has been made to the appeal to the country for voluntary enlistment. '[9] Since Kitchener's appeal continued to draw more recruits than could be immediately armed and trained, neither the Asquith administration nor the public saw any reason to abandon the current system.

The mood in governing circles and in the nation began to change during the second half of 1915. The drop in enlistments, together with the manifest inefficiency and inequity of the prevailing recruiting methods, reconciled many to the idea that the voluntary system had lost its original virtue. Conscription became a contentious issue in the coalition government, dividing opinion mainly on party lines. The Tories tended to favour conscription, although with varying degree of fervour. The Liberals strongly objected to it, except for Churchill and later Lloyd George, who as Minister of Munitions had become disenchanted with the industrial implications of volunteerism. Asquith's overriding concern was to preserve the unity of the cabinet and the country. While at this stage he probably saw conscription as likely, if not inevitable, he was not about to be stampeded into a course of action which would require him to confront massive opposition from labour and an equally hostile reaction from his own party. He would back conscription only when its necessity had been proved and when there was universal demand for its adoption.[10]

Even with the cabinet split fairly evenly over conscription, Asquith could afford to chart his own deliberate course as long as he was sustained by Kitchener. Although Kitchener's power had diminished in the new administration, everyone recognized that the nation was more likely to accept conscription if it was he who stated the need openly. Kitchener was not averse to mandatory service in principle but favoured its delay. Loyalty to Asquith was an important consideration. But the most compelling factor was his desire to husband Britain's resources so that when the time came he would have enough troops on hand to deliver the decisive blow.[11]

Since the debates on conscription required a sound statistical basis, Asquith agreed to conduct a census of the total manpower resources in the country. A bill for this purpose was drafted by Walter Long, President of the Local Government Board, and introduced into the Commons on 29 June 1915. Asquith was suspicious of Long's bill because he saw it as a prelude to conscription (as indeed it was). Nevertheless it passed by an overwhelming majority and became law as the National Registration Act in mid July. The new act required both men and women between the ages of eighteen and sixty-five to complete a form, indicating their names, dates of birth, occupation, and whether they were skilled in work other than that in which they were currently engaged. The results of the register would provide the government with a record of the number and distribution of men throughout the country, enabling it to calculate the supply of manpower available for military service and war-related industries.[12]

To Asquith's dismay, the easy passage of the National Registration Act encouraged the conscriptionists to intensify their campaign. Leading the way outside of parliament was the National Service League which, under the chairmanship of Lord Milner, initiated a propaganda campaign to convince the nation of the desirability of adopting universal military service. The Unionist dailies, in particular *The Times*, *Daily Mail* and *Morning Post*, enthusiastically supported the endeavours of the league. More troubling to Asquith were the defections from within his own party. A small but vocal group of Liberal MPs, which included Frederick Guest and Josiah Wedgwood, had joined the Unionists to press for the immediate introduction of compulsion. On 28 July, the day before parliament adjourned for the summer recess, Asquith came under attack for his stand on compulsion. Guest wondered why the Prime Minister refused to change his policy in view of his admission that 'we must consider that this War may turn itself into a contest of endurance'. Wedgwood followed by insisting that in war it was the duty of the Prime Minister to provide aggressive leadership. 'I do not care whether he takes risks or makes mistakes', he thundered, 'but for God's sake give us a leader who will lead without fear of consequences.'[13]

Asquith always found the words to blunt criticism effectively but one thing that his rhetoric could not mask was the noticeable drop in the recruiting figures. In May the number of enlistments had been 135,263 but for June the figure was 114,679 and for July 95,413.[14] Asquith was on record as saying he would not hesitate to replace the voluntary system if it failed to meet the manpower needs for the army. Privately he objected to any compulsion bill as this excerpt from his memoirs shows:

> There are two vital matters, from a practical point of view, which it seems to me the compulsionists have never thought out, viz.: (1) How are you going to run financially and in the way of discipline a mixed army of volunteers and conscripts, and (2) Where are you going to draw the line of exemption? When you have made adequate provision for the economic needs of a country like ours in time of war, you may find that you have left for compulsion only a small residuum of the dregs of the nation: and you will have set aflame a blazing controversy – for nothing.[15]

As a means to gain time and a measure of relief from adversaries, Asquith appointed a cabinet committee in August to investigate if there was need for conscription and, if so, whether the nation could afford it.[16] He selected Crewe to chair the committee, which also included Henderson, Selborne, Curzon, Churchill and Chamberlain. Asquith evidently knew the feelings of these men and had deliberately opted to give the conscriptionists a four-to-two majority. But, assuming that Crewe and Henderson would oppose compulsion, he could claim that the absence of general consent made its implementation impractical.

The War Policy Committee, as it came to be called, held twelve meetings and interviewed various ministers and high-ranking army officers. Crewe reported to Asquith on 8 September that the War Policy Committee was unable to reach a firm conclusion on account of the conflicting evidence of the witnesses.[17] However, Churchill and the three Unionists on the Committee submitted a dissenting supplementary note. The signatories insisted that national resources permitted an army of at least seventy divisions – the number set by Kitchener – but that the desired level of military commitment to the war effort required the introduction of universal service.[18] Henderson, as spokesman for the working class, circulated his own supplementary memorandum in which he warned that the labour movement would accept conscription only if Kitchener called for it in public and even then subject to certain conditions.[19]

The committee's work amounted to a meaningless exercise – which was precisely what Asquith wanted. The official report was innocuous and gave no lead at all. The other two were unambiguous but their conflicting recommendations reduced their effectiveness. The result was that each side in the cabinet was able to take comfort. Yet what Asquith failed to foresee was that the evidence by the witnesses had forced the conscription issue into the open and exacerbated tensions in the cabinet. Hankey was accurate in his assessment that the committee's findings had 'put Asquith in a fix, as at that time any attempt on his part to force through compulsory service would have involved resignations, and the unity of the Coalition Government would have been lost'.[20]

Asquith had to contend with both factions almost on a daily basis. The Tories did not pass up any opportunity to beat him over the head with a stick. The Liberals, for their part, encouraged him to stand firm. Typical was the letter sent by Simon, one of the leading anti-conscriptionist in the cabinet:

> I do not believe that even your great authority could persuade trade unionists to acquiesce in Conscription. But if it were realized that the arguments against it appeared to you as of great weight it would become so obvious that this crusade threatens to divide the Nation that many who are now hesitating would decide on this ground against the change. A pronouncement from you that, having examined the contentions on either side, you are satisfied that the change could not be made without imperilling national unity to a degree for which no military reorganization would compensate, would have an immense effect. Are not those who have never wavered in their loyalty to you entitled to this much assistance from you?[21]

The full-scale onslaught of the conscriptionists had provoked opposition groups to intensify their own propaganda campaign. Both Simon and Henderson appear to have accurately gauged the attitude of the labour movement. At the annual conference of the Trades Union Congress (TUC) in Bristol on 7 September successive speakers were warmly applauded for their vigorous condemnation of national service during the debate on the question. A resolution passed unanimously that the TUC, while assisting in every possible way government efforts to bring the war to a successful conclusion, was unalterably opposed to conscription in any form.[22] Asquith could hardly ignore the resolution. The Congress alone represented 3,000,000 workers to say nothing of lesser trade organizations which had adopted a similar line. On 28 September Asquith told the

House of Commons that in the last three months he had received some 400 resolutions against compulsion from various labour bodies.[23]

As if Asquith's burdens were not heavy enough, Lloyd George at this moment released to the press the preface to his collection of war speeches, soon to be published under the title *Through Terror to Triumph*. In this piece Lloyd George hinted pointedly at his support for military and industrial conscription.[24] His comments created a 'great stir', drawing praise from *The Times* and condemnation from the Liberal press. The left-wing *New Statesman* questioned Lloyd George's motive in practically appealing 'to the country against his colleagues', concluding that he clearly intended to break up the government.[25]

Asquith was incensed with Lloyd George, perceiving his conduct as mischievous and as adding fuel to the raging fires rather than as an open challenge to his leadership. On 18 September he wrote to Balfour, the only firm volunteerist among the Tories in the coalition, to request his help. He reflected upon the latest controversy and claimed that Lloyd George was one of the two most unpopular and distrusted men in the Liberal Party (Churchill being the other). Asquith observed that, even if he were to announce his own reluctant conversion to conscription, it would be passionately resisted not only by organized labour but by the most powerful elements in his own party as well. After reiterating his faith in the traditional method of enlistment, he invited Balfour to comment on his assessment of the situation. He ended by saying: 'I have come to think that it is only by our joint efforts that a bridge can be constructed over a yawning & perilous chasm.'[26]

Balfour responded by submitting a cogently argued paper against conscription the next day. In it he questioned the readiness to accept the seventy divisions standard, arguing that the nation's contribution to the war should not be measured solely in terms of the size of its military commitment to the Western Front. He reminded his colleagues that Britain's traditional way of waging war within an alliance was to supply ships and money, not large numbers of men. Balfour's other main point was that national unity provided 'a moral contribution which is of incalculable military value, because it adds so enormously to the efficiency' of the national effort. He doubted whether national unity and conscription could coexist, a sentiment which he shared with the Prime Minister.[27]

Asquith welcomed Balfour's initiative which seemed to momentarily remove the sting from the Tory assault on volunteerism. But, after the deadlock in the Dardanelles and the immense losses during the unsuccessful Loos offensive, the need for men became glaring. The results of the National Register showed that slightly over 5,000,000 men of military age were not in the armed forces. Of these a considerable number were physically unfit or engaged in 'starred' (essential) occupations. Further reducing the number available by excluding married men, this still left a manpower pool of about 1,500,000.[28] Early in October Kitchener noted that the average number of weekly enlistments was well below the 35,000 he required simply to keep the existing units up to strength.[29] His admission that the voluntary system was breaking down was the signal for the Tories to return to the charge.

Before matters could be brought to a head, Asquith, with Kitchener acting as go-between, persuaded the Earl of Derby to become Director-General of Recruiting, in a great campaign to rejuvenate the voluntary system. A prominent Unionist and avowed conscriptionist, Derby was an extremely wealthy landed aristocrat and undisputed master of the county of Lancashire, where his public appearances evoked the excitement of a royal visit. On the outbreak of war he had raised five battalions of the King's Regiment and no one in the land, except Kitchener himself, was more effective as a recruiter. Derby accepted the daunting task of recruiting director as a favour to Kitchener and after receiving a written pledge from Asquith that, if his drive failed to make a significant impact on enlistments, a compulsion law would follow.[30]

The choice of Derby was an astute political move on the part of Asquith. The Tories, however unhappy, could hardly rebuff a man who was one of their own as well as an immensely popular national figure. On the other hand, Derby might pull it off and offer Asquith a way out of his predicament. If not, Asquith could justly claim that the voluntary system had been given every chance and found to be wanting. The criteria he had laid down for compulsion could be met only after it was clear that the voluntary system had run its course:

> Compulsion, to be effective, must be adopted with substantial general assent. If the prescribed minimum is not forthcoming by voluntary means, the Cabinet believe that the objection, which now so widely exists, would be largely modified if not entirely removed, and hopes that such general assent would be secured.[31]

The Tories, unable to persuade Derby to withdraw his acceptance of the post,[32] refused to give up and carried the fight into the cabinet. At the meeting on 12 October Kitchener requested a weekly recruiting level of 35,000 men up to the end of 1916 to maintain a field army of 1,400,000. This required over the next sixty-four weeks the enlistment of some 2,200,000 men, a figure that exceeded the highest estimate of the recruitable reservoir. A group of Liberals, led by Runciman and McKenna, challenged the desirability of a force of seventy divisions on the grounds that the costs and risks were too great. Lansdowne, Curzon, Long and the two Liberal mavericks, Lloyd George and Churchill, accepted the numbers proposed by Kitchener, observing that the statistics proved that the voluntary system could not attract the necessary number of recruits. Asquith had no qualms with the concept of a seventy-division army, but took the line that even if the Derby scheme failed to accelerate recruiting to the required level there was no guarantee that any form of compulsion would produce better results.[33]

The Unionists were more conciliatory when the cabinet convened on 15 October. For all their bluster and threats of resignation they had no wish to end the coalition which they perceived would damage the cause of conscription as well as their party's standing with the public. Several Tories spoke in favour of giving Derby a six-week trial on condition that the government had a Conscription Bill in hand and ready for implementation in case his efforts proved inadequate. Asquith argued against the proposal in the strongest terms:

> To introduce in Parliament such a Bill would be to strangle Lord Derby's scheme in the cradle: it would arouse all the animosity of the anti-conscriptionists, every clause would be debated and even [then] it might be finally rejected – meanwhile the necessary number *may* have been secured: if so all the turmoil and bitterness engendered in passing or discussing the Bill would have been unnecessary.[34]

Asquith was pleased that the cabinet as a body had behaved in a thoroughly professional manner even though some of its members held strongly opposed views. Lloyd George, he felt, struck the only discordant note. He subsequently told Stamfordham what happened:

> ... Lloyd George ... said that there were two parties in the country: one which realized the seriousness of the situation, the dangers that were being incurred and the urgent need for action: the others who were satisfied to let things be and sat twiddling their thumbs and [he] expressed doubts whether it was not his duty to free himself and go to the country to tell the people the truth! 'A blackmailer's speech'.[35]

The incident reflected the growing estrangement between Asquith and Lloyd George. As noted in the previous chapter, the rift developed because of their differences over strategy and the overall direction of the war, in addition to conscription. Asquith's sinking political fortunes had left him less sure of his grip over the government and this, in turn, led him to misread Lloyd George's intentions. On 16 October Bonar Law demanded that Asquith publicly commit himself to accept conscription as the price of the failure of the Derby scheme. Refusal to make such an announcement, Bonar Law warned, would compel the Unionist section of the cabinet

(Balfour was not among the names listed), along with Churchill and Lloyd George, to resign.[36] Asquith at once saw Lloyd George's conspiratorial hand behind the ultimatum. That same day he told Hankey he felt certain that the Welshman was determined to break up the government.[37]

There is no evidence that Lloyd George was trying to engineer a revolt against his chief. Lloyd George confided to his mistress that he had no wish to become Prime Minister yet, because he anticipated a string of disasters ahead and wanted Asquith to take responsibility for them.[38] His statement is only partially correct. His reluctance to challenge Asquith had more to do with lack of political support. His alliance with the Tory leaders was shaky at best. Although the Tories and Lloyd George were frequently in agreement on matters of policy, they found him an insincere and unattractive companion. But even if he could have relied on the Conservatives, it was unlikely that he could have pulled in enough Liberals to form a coalition.

The man who could have upset Asquith's dextrous juggling act was not Lloyd George but Kitchener, who appeared to be siding with the conscriptionists.[39] Kitchener's defection would doom the Derby scheme before it could be launched. To forestall that possibility, Asquith sent Kitchener a somewhat hysterical letter on Sunday, 17 October. He alluded to the intimate working relationship and mutual confidence that existed between them as a prelude to identifying their fates as being completely intertwined. He warned that the current crisis was fomented by Lloyd George and Curzon, whose real objective was to get Kitchener out of the War Office. Asquith concluded by saying:

> They know well that I give no countenance to their projects & consequently they have conceived the idea of using you against me ... So long as you & I stand together, we carry the whole country with us. Otherwise, the Deluge! Cannot you say that, while you aim at & wd like to obtain 70 Divisions, the thing should be done gradually & with general consent, & that if you can get under the voluntary system (say) 750,000 men by March 31st ... you would be satisfied ... I ... am certain in the interests of the country & of the effective prosecution of the war that it is essential that you and I should stand together, & that the intrigue which has as its main object both to divide & discredit us both, shd be frustrated.[40]

What was disturbing about this letter was not its tone – understandable under the circumstances – but its contents. It portrays Asquith in the worst possible light, as a man of questionable decency and integrity. Asquith was disingenuous when he claimed that the whole crisis was brought on because of his loyalty to Kitchener. He was at best stretching the truth when he maintained he reposed the utmost confidence in the Field Marshal and had always lent him unstinting support. But the *pièce de résistance* was that, at the very moment Asquith was urging Kitchener to stand by him, he was devising ways to reduce him to a cipher.

On Monday Asquith postponed the cabinet meeting until after lunch so that he could confer privately with Kitchener in the morning. No record of the talks exist but it is known that Kitchener bowed to Asquith's entreaty. Kitchener regarded Asquith as his only friend in the cabinet and was unaware of his double-dealing. Out of a misplaced sense of loyalty to Asquith, the Field Marshal destroyed his remaining credibility with the Tories.[41]

Fortified by Kitchener's assurance, Asquith was in a relaxed mood when the cabinet convened in the afternoon. He conducted business impassively and shortly after the subject of conscription was raised he passed a note to Lansdowne and left the room. Lansdowne read the note, then informed his colleagues that the Prime Minister felt sick and was obliged to retire.[42] Asquith was confined to his bed for a week and altogether was absent from his official duties for nearly a fortnight. The doctor's diagnosis, according to his wife, was that 'overwork, hot rooms and no sort of exercise had gripped his liver and driven bad blood all over him'.[43] Margot's own analysis, revealed in a letter to ex-Liberal Chief Whip, Lord Murray of Elibank, was that Henry 'was not so ill physically' as he was 'stale and morally disgusted'. She recounted that Asquith had read to her the chapter in the New Testament of Simon Peter's betrayal of Christ and commented at the end that Peter was also a Celt – the scriptural parallel might have made more sense if he had equated Lloyd George with Judas rather than Peter.[44]

In retrospect the Prime Minister's illness may have been a blessing in disguise. It went some way towards allaying the agitation by preventing any serious discussion in the cabinet. By the time he resumed work the conscriptionist front was beginning to disintegrate. Carson and Churchill had resigned and the remaining conscriptionists were badly split over an Eastern strategy. By default the Derby scheme would have an opportunity to prove itself.

Announced on 21 October, the Derby scheme was based on information gleaned from the National Register and involved a personal canvass of every man between the ages of eighteen and forty-one. Each man was asked either to join or to attest his willingness to serve when summoned. The attested men were divided into two groups, married and single, and each of these subdivided into twenty-three classes according to age. Classes would be called up in strict order as required, beginning with the youngest single men. Married men would not be taken until all the bachelors had been summoned to the colours.[45]

Asquith had neglected to tell Derby at the time of his appointment how the success or failure of his scheme would be defined. After a few days at his post Derby requested that the Prime Minister determine the numbers that his scheme was expected to raise.[46] Asquith's memorandum on 16 October laid down as a minimum 500,000 men by 31 March 1916.[47]

Derby was fatally handicapped by the fact that most of the men likely to come forward through patriotism or a sense of adventure had already enlisted. From the outset it was apparent that the unmarried men, who were liable to be called up quickly after attestation, were not responding on an adequate scale. As long as many bachelors were holding back, there was reluctance on the part of married men to attest. To overcome this difficulty, Derby requested the Prime Minister's help on 28 October:

> Unless you make it perfectly clear that the young men have to come forward, preferably voluntarily but if necessary brought by compulsory means before the older men who are asked to actually join the Colours, the scheme will be a failure. It is trembling in the balance at the present moment as the older men are holding back until they have this assurance. Believe me you have only got to make the threat. I do not believe for one minute you would have to put it into execution.[48]

Asquith found himself on the horns of a dilemma. To consent to Derby's request might mean conscription, at least for single men. To do otherwise would ensure the failure of the new recruiting scheme which would be followed by immediate compulsion. Asquith chose the first option as the lesser of two evils, assuring his supporters in the Commons on 2 November that the introduction of national military service was 'a contingency which I do not think is ever likely to arise'. He added a promise that attested married men would not be called up until virtually all the single men had been recruited voluntarily or, as a last resort, conscripted by an act of parliament.[49]

The Prime Minister's assurances left his listeners uncertain as to whether he had made a personal pronouncement or acted on behalf of the government. To clear the air, Derby, with Asquith's approval, issued a statement to the press on 11 November in which he confirmed that the Prime Minister's pledge to married men was made in the name of the government.[50] The guarantee, with its implied threat to coerce hesitant unmarried men into the army, constituted a big step towards conscription. And yet, if it foreclosed future government options, it also provided the Prime Minister with a weapon, in case compulsion had to be enforced, to undermine Liberal opposition to the measure.

The canvass under the Derby scheme, originally scheduled to end on 30 November, was extended eventually to 15 December.[51] The initial effect on recruitment was salutary. The enlistment figure for October rose to 113,000 and that for November to nearly 122,000.[52] But the trend reversed itself at the start of December. Whatever encouragement Asquith may have drawn from the long queues at the recruiting stations disappeared when Derby announced his preliminary findings to the cabinet on 14 December. It was apparent to the Prime Minister that the voluntary system could no longer be preserved. Without waiting for the complete figures, he set up a cabinet committee under Walter Long to draft a bill for the compulsory recruitment of single men.[53]

Derby's official report was ready on 20 December and circulated the next day to the cabinet ministers. Married men of military age had presented themselves in considerable numbers (1,679,263 out of a total of 2,832,210), anticipating that they would not be called up before the single men. The bachelors responded less enthusiastically. Of the 2,179,231 unmarried men known to be available, only 1,150,000 had either enlisted or attested, leaving 1,029,231, or nearly half, who were unaccounted for.[54] Among the bachelors registered, exemptions had to be made for those who were medically unfit or worked in starred industries. Derby estimated that the net yield of single men would be only 318,533 (later revised upward to 343,386), well below the minimum prescribed by army authorities. Under the circumstances he concluded that if the Prime Minister wanted to redeem his pledge he could not 'hold married men to their attestation unless and until the services of single men have been obtained by other means ... '[55]

The Derby Report was considered in the cabinet for the first time on 22 December and remained on the agenda throughout the rest of the year. Asquith had to contend with a last-ditch effort by Liberals and the Labour representative, Arthur Henderson, to block conscription. Labour feared that universal military service would open the door to industrial conscription. Liberal opposition was more diverse. McKenna and Runciman were disturbed at the War Office target of seventy divisions, which they perceived could only be attained through compulsory service. Some felt that the timing of the measure was inappropriate. Only John Simon stuck firmly to the narrow principle that it was wrong to force an individual to bear arms against his will.

Sensing that the game was all but lost, the cabinet dissidents in their desperation directed their opening salvos at Derby, questioning the validity of his report. They claimed that local military authorities had no interest in preserving the voluntary system and that the Derby scheme had not been allowed to operate fairly in certain districts. They tried to show that the number of unattested single men was substantially lower than the figures claimed and that another canvassing campaign would further reduce the total. The debates were intense and from the outset the cabinet was split roughly on party lines. Pulled in opposite directions, Asquith could not see a resolution in sight. 'The impression left upon me is profoundly disquieting,' Asquith noted on the 22nd 'and to judge from to-day's experience we seem to be on the brink of a precipice. The practical question is – Shall I be able during the next ten days to devise and build a bridge?'[56] The threat to the viability of the government cast a pall over the holiday season.

By the 26th Asquith's efforts to reconcile opposites, or even narrow differences, had failed and he feared that his days were numbered. He told Sylvia Henley:

> I find it very difficult to imagine how a split can be avoided, & whatever course I resolve to take, I am pretty sure to be called either a promise breaker, or a procrastinator, or a renegade (according to the camp in which the particular critic is enlisted).[57]

Asquith's troubles were compounded by Lloyd George, who returned to the capital on 27 December after a five-day stint in Scotland where he had spoken to the workers and shop stewards in the munitions plants. Apprised of what had occurred in his absence, he tried to force Asquith's hand by threatening to resign unless the government honoured its pledge to the married men.[58] That afternoon Asquith opened the cabinet meeting by asking his colleagues to accept the War Committee's recommendation that Cape Helles should be evacuated. The discussion dragged on needlessly with, according to Lloyd George, each minister afforded an opportunity to express his opinion on the subject at least twice. After the vote was taken Asquith adjourned the meeting, saying that it was nearly 5 o'clock and there was not enough time to address the question of compulsion that day. This provoked Curzon into an angry tirade in which he accused the Prime Minister of deliberately stalling in order to avoid making a decision.[59] Asquith would have been the last person to dispute Curzon's observation but at least he had given himself another twenty-four hours to find a magic formula.

As it turned out, the delay might have been sufficient to help save the ministry. At the cabinet meeting on Monday morning, 28 January, Samuel proposed a modest instalment of compulsion. Under his scheme unattested single men of military age would be compelled to enlist unless they could persuade a local military tribunal that they should be exempted. The conscriptionists, including Lloyd George, accepted the compromise and Asquith coerced most of the Liberals into following suit.[60] Asquith was in his office after lunch, possibly reflecting on his good fortune, when Runciman and McKenna appeared unexpectedly at the door and announced their intention to resign. They made it clear that they were not opposed to Samuel's proposal in principle but could not consent to the army's demand for seventy divisions which, in their view, was beyond the financial resources of the country and would take more men than could be spared from industry. Asquith understood their concerns but questioned their timing. He wanted to know why they had raised no objections before he made his pledge to the Commons. They endorsed the pledge, they replied, as a matter of expediency and on assurances that it would not be implemented. Asquith tried a new line of argument. He maintained that the cabinet had not yet fixed the exact number of divisions and that, at any rate, he could not see the relationship between compulsion and the size of the army. The two men remained immovable and the interview ended on a chilly note, 'without even a handshake'.[61] Later in the day Asquith received more bad news. Simon submitted his resignation, claiming that the state had no right to compel men to fight.[62]

In the evening Asquith contacted Montagu, Reading, Samuel and other Liberal loyalists to ask them to use their influence to persuade the three dissident ministers to remain in the government.[63] At the same time he added his own personal pleas to each of them:

> We have fought side by side in all the great domestic controversies of the last ten years, & not one of you has ever failed me in loyal and unselfish devotion, or in the highest requirements of administration & policy. It is not a moment for argument ... but before you take an inevitable step, which if taken, must surely invalidate the authority of the Gov't with the country, & especially with our own party, I wish, as your old leader, to make an appeal to you to reconsider your determination. As you all know, I would gladly be released myself from the constant strain & over-burdening weight of Gov't. Nothing ties me to my task but the sense of national duty. Your simultaneous departure would be a shattering blow to the Gov't, & I honestly believe to the National Cause.[64]

Early next morning Asquith received a reply from Simon to the effect that his decision was irrevocable.[65] Within an hour the crisis reached its acutest point when Grey informed Asquith that, with his close friends leaving, the time had come for him to make way for someone more in sympathy with the prevailing spirit in the government.[66] Asquith was stunned and outraged by the imminent defection of one of his oldest and closest comrades at a moment when he needed him most. He replied to Grey at once and in terms which made it clear that he felt betrayed. He indicated that, if Grey and the others persisted in their determination to resign, he might seek release from his own responsibilities as well. He added that Grey's resignation on whatever ostensible ground would be interpreted universally as a German triumph.[67]

Asquith accepted Simon's loss as inevitable and concentrated his efforts on keeping the others in the government. After lunch he called in McKenna and Runciman and pleaded with them for two hours. He indicated that since their main objection involved the size of the army they were at liberty to raise the matter in the cabinet, hinting that they could count on the support of both himself and Balfour. Asquith's motives were too transparent for his arguments to carry conviction. At the end neither man showed any signs of wilting. Asquith confided to Sylvia Henley in the evening that he was in 'deep water'.[68]

Asquith had not overstated his difficulties. By 29 December four of his leading ministers had submitted their resignations, or proposed to do so, with a fifth, Augustine Birrell, saying that he accepted conscription as a disagreeable necessity but did not anticipate he could remain in the ministry after the others had departed.[69] If they all chose to leave, Asquith would be isolated and his ability to govern, already weakened by the formation of the coalition, would be called into serious question.

For that reason a number of Asquithian faithfuls worked assiduously to achieve a compromise. Hankey found the key to break the deadlock. He discovered on the 29th that Robertson, the new CIGS, was flexible on the question of the eventual size of the army.[70] Early next morning he visited McKenna and convinced him to see Robertson. The two men emerged from their meeting that morning believing that their differences could be settled. This encouraged Hankey to suggest to Asquith that it should be left to the military and economic authorities to determine how many divisions Britain could afford to maintain.[71] Asquith held out Hankey's idea to ease Grey's return to the fold and then convinced him to use his influence to conciliate McKenna and Runciman. Grey reported on the 30th that both McKenna and Runciman had agreed to attend the cabinet meeting on the following day.[72]

The cabinet met twice on the last day of 1915 with all the ministers present except John Simon. It was apparent from the frayed tempers that acute differences remained. The talks seemed to be leading nowhere when Balfour suggested that a cabinet committee, consisting of Asquith, Chamberlain and McKenna, be established to investigate how many divisions Britain could afford to put in the field. Asquith seized upon the idea and it was quickly approved.[73] The rest of the sitting was devoted to discussing and amending the draft of the Military Service Bill. Asquith's secretary, Bonham Carter, reported to Stamfordham at the end of the day that the political crisis was over.[74]

Asquith laid the Military Service Bill before the House of Commons on 5 January 1916. The benches and the galleries were filled to capacity, a rare sight in the Commons. The bill empowered the government to call up single men and widowers without children or dependents, between the ages of eighteen and forty-one. Provision was made to exclude the population of Ireland, those engaged in munitions or in other necessary national work, the sole supporters of dependents, and the medically disabled. A clause was later added for approved conscientious objectors. Local tribunals, appointed under the Derby scheme, were to decide claims for exemptions.[75]

Asquith's speech to a tense and expectant House was low-keyed and dull and obviously intended to be as inoffensive in tone as possible. Consistent with previous statements, he underlined that he was not announcing a historic change. He was simply redeeming his pledge to the married men and doing so without abolishing the voluntary system, which would continue to operate side by side with partially applied compulsion. He assured his listeners that the bill was designed to apply only for the period of the war and was not a back-door method of introducing compulsion on a permanent basis.[76] His rhetorical performance may not have been awe-inspiring but it achieved what he set out to do, namely to deflate the passions that the bill would arouse among ardent volunteerists.

The main opposition was led by John Simon, who tried to establish that the bill went beyond the Prime Minister's redemption of a promise and constituted nothing less than a revolution in the history of the nation.[77] Asquith found the speech 'on the whole vicious and rather vitriolic', without any 'trace of the old familiar impeccable,[78] who had fed for the better part of eight years out of my hand'. He added: 'I felt really like a man who had been struck publicly in the face by his son.'[79]

Simon managed to rally only a handful of Liberals to his side. This, however, did not accurately reflect Liberal hostility to the bill. Many felt betrayed but did not dare do anything that would further jeopardize Asquith's position. Liberal whips were quick to remind the headstrong that a measure of conscription was preferable to the annihilation of the party at the polls and the ascension to power of a Lloyd George administration. The Labour members were almost evenly divided. Only the Irish Nationalists were united in their hostility to the measure but they subsequently (after the first reading) abstained from voting when they were satisfied that it would not be extended to Ireland. The vote on the first reading showed that 403 members favoured the bill and 105 opposed it, with 150 abstentions. Without the Irish Nationalists, the opposition was reduced to thirty-four Liberals and eleven Labourites. Asquith's political skill had effectively neutralized resistance and brought him another great parliamentary victory – his last.

The size of Asquith's parliamentary majority did not undercut the trade unions' resistance to compulsion. On 6 January a special Labour conference held in London came out forcefully against the new bill, on the ground that it gave no assurances that conscription would not be extended to married men or to workers in industry.[80] In keeping with the resolution, Henderson felt that he had no option but to leave the government.[81] Asquith hastened to remove the last impediment to the bill.[82] Within a few days he received a delegation of Labour MPs and trade unionists and persuaded them that married men would not be called up and that their fears about industrial conscription were unfounded.[83] As a result Henderson withdrew his resignation and on 26 January the Labour Party's annual conference at Bristol quashed a motion pledging to work for the repeal of the legislation if it should become law. The vote meant that Labour reconciled itself to a *fait accompli*, for by then the Military Service Bill had passed easily through every parliamentary stage. It gained the royal assent on 27 January.[84]

After months of bitter political fighting the issue had been resolved, but not to the satisfaction of most of the interested parties. For the Liberals national service breached generations of voluntarist tradition and was seen as a humiliating political defeat, even though Asquith tried to cushion the blow by representing it as an extension of the Derby scheme. Unionists saw it as a partial victory at best. Failure to include married men in the bill meant that in the near future the nation and parliament would have to go through the same wrenching experience. Asquith, on the other hand, was pleased by his handiwork. He had brought in partial compulsion when he felt that the nation would accept it and had done so without destroying the coalition or his own position as Prime Minister.

The implementation of conscription came after Asquith had suitably prepared the way. He was never philosophically converted to the policy but saw it as an unpleasant necessity if he wanted to save the coalition and his job. Before he was convinced that it was politically safe to adopt mandatory service, he fudged the issue by stalling, manipulating conscriptionists and anti-conscriptionist alike, appointing carefully recruited committees and improvising stopgap measures. But throughout the long controversy he remained firmly in control of the situation and, as in the case of the formation of the coalition in May 1915, forced 'his own solution on all concerned.'[85]

Asquith's hopes for a political respite never materialized. Agitation for an extension of compulsion began almost immediately after the passage of the National Service Act. Asquith was reluctant to adopt a more comprehensive system and not only because he felt the country was not ready for it. Like McKenna and Runciman, he doubted the military necessity and worried that total compulsion would adversely affect industrial output and place an intolerable burden on the Treasury.

Asquith met the new challenge by resorting to the same delaying tactics that had worked so well for him in the past. They were less successful this time. The country and parliament had wearied of the Prime Minister's ploys. Moreover Robertson, unlike Kitchener, was single-minded about total compulsion and paid little heed to political repercussions. In his view the scale of the operations planned for the Western Front mandated that the army expand quickly – the Cabinet Committee on the Co-ordination of the Military and Financial Effort had recommended sixty-two divisions – and the existing system was simply not producing the requisite number of men.[86] Robertson had won over Kitchener and he enjoyed the support of Lloyd George and the Unionists in demanding that every man of military age who was physically fit and not needed for industry be made avaiable to the army.[87]

Reacting to the pressure from both the War Office and the Tories, Asquith reconvened the Military-Finance Committee in April. Its report recommended extending compulsion to all men who had reached the age of eighteen since 15 August and of keeping time-expired Regulars and Territorials with the colours (each month it was estimated that 5,000 non-commissioned officers and men were allowed to leave the army on the expiration of their engagement, as in pre-war days). It further favoured a more stringent investigation of men in reserved occupations.[88] The committee's conclusions were intended to reconcile the Prime Minister's pledge to the married men with the need to provide more recruits for military service.

At the cabinet meeting on 14 April Lloyd George was 'in a furious rage', regarding the report as an inadequate and illogical half-measure. Backed by most of the Unionists, he demanded that Asquith reach an accommodation with the Army Council. Asquith yielded to the pressure. By allowing the army to be the arbiter of a dispute to which it was a party, he was for all intents and purposes admitting defeat.

Around noon the next day Asquith and the other members of the Military-Finance Committee met the Army Council at 10 Downing Street.[89] Asquith explained his political difficulties and hinted that, unless a resolution was found, he might be forced to resign. Chamberlain begged the Army Council to take the wider considerations into account. Britain, he pointed out, was bearing the burden of financing the Allied war effort. It could continue to do so only if its industrial output and trade remained unimpaired.[90] The soldiers, however, remained adamant and confirmed their position in a paper they sent to the cabinet on the 16th.[91]

Asquith was at The Wharf for the week-end but returned to London on Monday, 17 April, to confront his critics. Lloyd George had spread the word that he would not continue in office without universal conscription. However, he was unlikely to carry out his threat unless he was certain that the Unionists would also leave the government. As it was, he commanded the support only of rabid Carsonites and a handful of Liberals.[92] Lloyd George was not one to resign on a matter of principle if it meant returning to the backbenches and forfeiting his ministerial salary.

What really mattered to Asquith, therefore, was the attitude of the Unionist Party. The rank and file were overwhelmingly in favour of broadening compulsion regardless of the political consequences; those in the cabinet were divided with some reluctant to force it through at the cost of breaking up the coalition. Bonar Law appreciated Asquith's predicament but he recognized that his own position as head of the party would become untenable if he turned his back on a policy recommended by the military experts.[93] On 17 April he wrote Asquith a long letter in which he argued for the enforced enlistment of all men of military age. He maintained that in the interest of national unity he had been prepared to side with the Prime Minister, despite his own personal views as well as those of most of his party on the matter of compulsion, but that the Army Council's verdict seemed to him to be conclusive. Bonar Law knew of the determination of the Unionist War Committee and of Asquith's unsurpassed talent in selling universal compulsory service to unwilling Liberal volunteerists. With these thoughts in mind he ended his letter by observing: 'I think it is easier for you to carry your supporters in favour of compulsion than it is for us to obtain the support of our Party against it.'[94]

Asquith continued to play for time and on 18 April two possible solutions were advanced. One by Lloyd George proposed that the state adopt universal compulsory powers, with the proviso that married men would be called up only in months the number of recruits fell below a specified quota. The other by Henderson suggested that the recommendations of the Military-Finance report be adopted: if at the end of a six-week trial period the War Office was unhappy with the results, he and his party would consent to legislation to conscript unattested married men of military age.[95]

Asquith held little hope that a consensus would form around either scheme. He told the King's secretary: 'I am afraid that there is not a good chance of Ll.G. & the Unionist Ministers agreeing to No. 2, and I feel certain that the Labour Party will not agree to No. 1.'[96] As there seemed little likelihood that the impasse would be broken, Asquith's mood darkened and on the morning of 19 April he contemplated stepping down. He had, as he reported to Lady Scott, laid out his frock-coat in readiness to deliver his resignation to Buckingham Palace that afternoon.[97] But as the day wore on he had a change of heart, detecting a slight improvement in the atmosphere.

Asquith sensed that Bonar Law had no desire to force the resignation of the government, if a way could be found to satisfy both his backbenchers and the Army Council. Lloyd George, in his view, was the villian of the piece. In contrast to the conciliatory attitude of the Unionists during cabinet deliberations, the Welshman had adopted a combative, uncompromising posture which was marked by intemperate outbursts. Asquith also suspected that Lloyd George was leaking detailed information to the newspapers concerning the squabbles in the cabinet to try to discredit him in the eyes of the public. He became convinced that Lloyd George was orchestrating the crisis in order to smash the coalition.[98]

On the 19th Asquith appeared before the House of Commons and publicly admitted – though it was hardly a secret – that the cabinet was deeply divided on the question of universal compulsion. He added that unless there was agreement soon on the outstanding points the coalition would collapse.[99] A number of Liberal stalwarts interpreted the thrust of the Prime Minister's speech as a veiled criticism of Lloyd George.[100] As a result Liberal MPs were hastily called to a meeting at which the following resolution was unanimously adopted: 'We desire to express to the Prime Minister our conviction that his continuance as head of the Government is a national necessity.'[101]

That afternoon Henderson reported to the cabinet that the executive committee of the Labour Party could not, with the information it presently possessed, agree to an extension of compulsion. From the wrangling that ensued, the only thing that the ministers could agree to was that Henderson should arrange to confer with Robertson. What seemed to be an act of desperation paid off. After some discussion, an understanding was reached on the basis of Henderson's compromise proposal. The essence of the formula was that unattested married men were to be given a further opportunity to come forward voluntarily but that unless 50,000 of them did so by 27 May, and 15,000 a week thereafter, general compulsion would be introduced. Lloyd George and the Unionists had no reason to complain if Robertson was satisfied with that arrangement. Confident that he had a workable compromise in hand, Asquith decided to bring the matter before both Houses in secret session after Easter.[102] With a sense of relief, he wrote to Sylvia Henley on the 20th:

Things have now straightened out, as they generally do, if you give them time, & don't strike before the hour. (This, I suppose, is the philosophy of 'wait & see' – that much abused formula.) At any rate the Crisis (with the biggest of 'C's) is over ... It has been a hellish experience, and I'm too old a hand to think that trouble is over.[103]

As it happened, Asquith's intuition was correct. He was at The Wharf during the Easter holiday, much of which he spent in consultation with Hankey and compiling material for his speech to parliament.[104] On 25 and 26 April parliament met in secret session and on the first day Asquith explained Henderson's plan to an attentive audience. His speech was badly received. Parliamentarians were fed up with complicated half-measures. On the 27th Long had the thankless task of introducing the bill (encompassing the new compromise) to a House seething with hostility. A group of Liberal compulsionists joined the anti-government chorus which was led by Carson and the Unionist War Committee. The onslaught was so unrelenting and intense that the embarrassed Prime Minister withdrew the bill.

In the past Asquith had rarely been offended by remarks made during the cut and thrust of parliamentary debates. On this occasion the strength of feeling against him personally, on top of criticism of his direction of war policy, left him badly shaken. His confidence waned, at least momentarily. On 28 April Lord Robert Cecil, Parliamentary Under-Secretary at the Foreign Office, took the view that Asquith ought to resign. He reasoned that the unlikelihood that anyone else could form a ministry would enable Asquith to return triumphantly at the head of a genuine national government, rather than continuing to manage a coalition of party representatives. The members should be selected, Cecil noted in his memorandum to Asquith, 'not because certain parliamentary interests must be placated but because [they] were the best persons available to fill the offices for which they were chosen'.[105] Cecil had placed his finger on one of the chief weaknesses of the coalition. It was composed of men concerned more in representing the interests of their parties than in pursuing what they believed was the proper course.

Asquith never seriously considered Cecil's advice. He called his colleagues together on 29 April and told them that under the circumstances they had no alternative but to proceed at once with legislation for general compulsion. His view won unanimous approval, although Henderson and Runciman warned of probable labour disturbances arising from a new conscription bill.[106] Asquith announced the impending measure in the Commons on 2 May and introduced it the next day. The atmosphere was noticeably cold. As Hankey perceptively observed, the people who wanted universal military service did not want Asquith, while those who supported him did not want conscription.[107]

The Second Military Service Bill extended conscription to all men, single and married, between the ages of eighteen and forty-one. It also permitted the War Office to retain the services of time-expired men for the duration of the war. The bill quickly passed through both Houses and received the royal assent on 25 May. The bill was not followed by labour disturbances as had been feared in some quarters. The country as a whole favoured it and was glad to see an end to this distracting controversy.

At the outset of the war Asquith was undoubtedly right in gauging that compulsion would be strenuously resisted by the general public. But he was at fault in thinking that he had to administer the medicine in small doses to condition the country to accept the final solution. The process would have been less painful to all concerned, and he would have served both himself and the Liberal Party better, if at some point, possibly the autumn of 1915, he had boldly called upon the country to accept a reversal of a historic Liberal principle on the grounds of patriotism and national necessity.

As it was, the manner in which Asquith carried through conscription hurt his own reputation and the unity of his party. The perception that he was bowing to political expediency each time he agreed to a fresh instalment of compulsion eroded the public's confidence in his courage and leadership. Moreover, the year-long struggle over compulsion took its toll on the Liberal Party, dividing it between those who were irreconcilable over the abandonment, or as they considered it a betrayal, of a fundamental principle and those to whom winning the war outweighed all else. The disaffection in Liberal ranks was a harbinger of things to come. Conscription had another important consequence. It created a mechanism to meet the generals' demands for greater and ever-greater numbers of men, ensuring that the nation would continue the policy of attrition on the Western Front.

"WAIT AND SEE."

Mr. Asquith. "WELL, AS WE SAY IN ROME, I HAVE BEEN, I HAVE SEEN——"

Mr. Punch. "THEN YOU NEEDN'T WAIT ANY MORE, SIR; ALL YOU'VE GOT TO DO IS TO GO IN AND CONQUER."

Chapter 10

Westerners in the Ascendancy

Asquith had not intended to abdicate control of strategy to the soldiers when he ordered the General Staff reformed and appointed Robertson as CIGS. But Robertson went beyond his role as the military adviser to the government, commanding greater influence in shaping war policy than Asquith could have imagined at the outset. This was due to Robertson's forceful personality, the broadened powers of the CIGS and the unstinting support he received from the King, the press and the Tories.

Robertson was an out-and-out Westerner – the only theatre of war that mattered to him was the Western Front. Less than a week after taking office, Robertson persuaded the government to confirm plans made by Allied military representatives at Chantilly from 6 to 8 December 1915. On 28 December 1915, the War Committee agreed to regard France as the main theatre of operations and to make preparations for a gigantic attack there in the spring of 1916 in cooperation with the French, Russians and Italians.[1] Later, the committee members had second thoughts about prematurely committing the British army to offensive operations on the Western Front and on 13 January amended the earlier resolution. While permitting preparations for an offensive to continue, they reserved the right to decide if and when it should be launched.[2]

Asquith had accumulated sufficient experience to understand that the generals had shown practically no interest in devising new methods to win the war: their plan of attack had not evolved beyond massing men and guns to capture strongly defended positions. He had no reason to suppose that British attacks in 1916 would fare any better than those at Neuve Chapelle, Aubers Ridge or Loos. What he needed above all was a big military victory to boost his waning prestige. He could ill afford another military defeat. Like his colleagues he wanted convincing proof in the viability of a Western strategy.

Robertson was not confident that the German line could be punctured in 1916. In fact he was careful not to raise false expectations. He wrote that in 'war it is impossible to guarantee success' and 'this plan may therefore fail', or meet only with 'partial success'. Instead he justified the operation on the grounds that it would hasten Germany's collapse by drawing in and consuming its reserves.[3] This policy of attrition was on the lines of the French offensives in 1915 which had produced unprecedented casualties and threatened to wear out the attackers first.

Since Asquith was unimpressed by Robertson's case, he examined other options. One possibility was to delay offensive operations until the British armies were properly supplied and fully trained. Another was to remain on the defensive and allow the Germans to do the attacking. Yet another was to deliver the main thrust in a theatre outside the Western Front. The last idea offered no prospect of inflicting severe damage on Germany or of succeeding in time to help the Russians. It had no support in the cabinet except for Lloyd George. The remaining choices, however attractive, were also ruled out. The British could not remain inactive in the West while the Germans completed the destruction of the Russian armies.[4] Thus Asquith had no choice but to return to Robertson's plan

The 'last trace of strategic flexibility vanished' when the Germans assaulted the French fortress of Verdun in February 1916.[5] As the battle of Verdun intensified in violence, Joffre looked to the growing British army, standing beside his own in apparent idleness, to mount a large-scale offensive to relieve pressure on his front. On 12 March Haig and Robertson attended an Allied military conference at Chantilly where it was unanimously agreed to press forward with the general offensive as recommended the previous December. The soldiers, however, left open the crucial question of timing.[6] With the Russians debilitated by a series of defeats, the French tied down at Verdun and the Italians complaining about everything, from exhaustion to lack of resources, it was apparent that whatever large-scale offensive effort the Entente might carry out in 1916 would have to be borne mainly by the British.

The failure of the Allied military representatives to achieve a common policy was a convenient pretext for Asquith to continue to drag his feet. At a meeting of the War Committee on 21 March Robertson found himself confronted by questions he could not properly answer. What was to prevent one member of the coalition from attacking before the others were ready? What was the condition of the Russian army? Did the French have a plan? All this was, Asquith said, 'very slippery and sloppy'. Before continuing the debate he wanted more information from the Russians and the French.[7]

Prior to the regular meeting, the War Committee had invited Grey, Runciman and Admiral Jackson to discuss the latest peace initiative by the United States. In the early winter of 1914–15 President Wilson, under pressure at home both to defend American rights on the seas and maintain a policy of neutrality, had offered to act as an impartial mediator to end the war. Wilson thought that a peace could be forged on terms that would restore the *status quo ante* with the Germans surrendering their European conquests in return for concessions elsewhere. At the end of January 1915 he sent his friend and trusted adviser, Colonel E. M. House, on a secret mission to sound out the belligerents.[8] It was a forlorn quest. The object of Wilson's diplomacy was incompatible with fundamental British war aims.[9]

Asquith, like Grey, was hostile to the idea of a premature peace which would leave the current German military regime in power and allow it to begin the war again at a favourable moment. Yet his government could not appear to be intransigent and standing in the way of peace without compromising the Allied cause. It was imperative to retain the good will of the United States, on which the Entente was rapidly becoming dependent for money, food, raw materials and munitions.[10] Asquith was convinced that the Germans merely wanted to use the talks to turn American public opinion against Britain and sow dissension among the Entente.

Asquith had not taken an active part in the earlier peace negotiations with House although he did meet him on several occasions in London in February 1915. He essentially repeated what Grey had said before, that German readiness to accept mediation was insincere. House, however, wanted to keep the door open in case Berlin really desired peace. Asquith felt certain that the Germans were no more interested in peace without victory than the British. He smiled and replied: 'You will be a very clever man if you can do that successfully.'[11]

As Asquith had predicted, House's discussions with the Germans got nowhere. House determined in due course that Berlin was unlikely to meet the minimum demands of either Britain or its partners. Welcoming the German response, Asquith ceased to worry about House's mission. He likened it to 'the twittering of sparrows amid the storms and tumult of a tempest which is shaking the foundations of the world'.[12]

House returned to the United States at the start of June 1915 but in the autumn he embarked on another attempt to bring off a negotiated peace. This time he came not merely as an intermediary but with a scheme for a settlement based on freedom of the seas and the curtailment of militarism.[13] The plan was vague and the British did not expect anything dramatic to come of it. Asquith regarded House as a naive electoral broker who, posing as a mediator, had come to Europe to play a role that would enhance the prospects of the Democratic Party and Wilson's own reelection bid in November. There were others in the cabinet who thought as Asquith did.[14]

Asquith saw no compelling reason to welcome Wilson's good offices unless the stalemate persisted and the country faced bankruptcy, or the Allies were on the verge of losing. Things were not so desperate at this time as to require a rescue operation from across the Atlantic. General Headquarters remained confident of victory, in which case the British government would be able to dictate the conditions of peace. Even if the Entente only improved its military position, Asquith was certain that the British would emerge from the conflict with better terms than Wilson could obtain for them now. All the same it suited him to play along with House, to humour him even to the point of entering into a non-binding agreement.

On this occasion Asquith was directly involved in the talks with House, as was Lloyd George, Balfour and, of course, Grey. The most crucial meeting occurred on 14 February 1916 at a dinner hosted by Lord Reading. House suggested, and Asquith and the others agreed, that when the moment was propitious Wilson should demand an end to the war and summon a peace conference. There was a division of opinion regarding the question of timing. Grey favoured immediate action. Asquith shared House's view that the right time would be when the Allies had dented the German line. Balfour and Lloyd George wanted to wait until the Allies had secured a clear military advantage.

There followed a general discussion about territorial adjustments at the end of the war. These included the return of Alsace-Lorraine to France, the restoration of Belgium and Serbian independence and an outlet to the sea for Russia. The group also exchanged views on the division of the Ottoman Empire and the fate of Constantinople. No one bothered to inform House that Britain had already agreed to cede Constantinople to Russia and that it was involved in negotiations with France to delimit their respective interests in Asiatic Turkey.[15]

It was getting late when Lloyd George introduced the idea that there should be a prior agreement with the United States on minimum peace terms acceptable to the Allies. In view of America's attitude towards British use of sea-power, Asquith did not want to commit himself to Wilson's plan without knowing what his terms of peace were. House was evasive but Asquith would not let him off the hook. How, he asked, would Wilson react at the conference if he judged the Allied peace proposals to be unjust? House replied that he would probably withdraw from the conference and leave them to their own devices. By contrast Asquith wanted to know what the President would do in the event he found Germany's position unacceptable and against the interest of humanity. House thought that in these circumstances Wilson would throw his weight behind the Entente and aim for a fair and reasonable settlement and guarantees against future wars.[16]

On 17 February Grey and House together drew up a memorandum embodying their agreements. The final draft, dated 22 February 1916 and known as the House-Grey Memorandum, was quickly approved by the British inner group and by Cambon, the French Ambassador. It was understood that, on hearing from France and Britain, Wilson would propose a peace conference to put an end to the war. If the Germans proved uncooperative, the United States would enter the war on the side of the Entente. The terms which would be put to the Germans would include the restoration of Belgian sovereignty, the transfer of Alsace-Lorraine to France and the acquisition by Russia of an outlet to the sea. The Germans would be compensated for loss of territory by concessions outside Europe. A post-war security system would be established to guard against renewed aggression.[17]

Grey revealed the contents of the memorandum to the War Committee on 22 February. He thought that American intervention would lead to the reestablishment of the status quo and therefore ought not be requested unless the Allies had concluded that they could not defeat the enemy. Since 1916 was an election year in the United States, Asquith was convinced that Wilson would avoid involvement in the war. Lloyd George believed that the Americans might enter the war later but for the present he preferred to leave them alone. McKenna considered that Wilson's policy was designed to bring peace without giving either side an advantage. That prospect troubled Asquith, who claimed that a draw would be equivalent to a defeat. Grey concurred, saying that the 'Germans might call it a victory'. Convinced that Wilson did not possess the power to carry through his policy, Asquith supported Lloyd George's suggestion that at this stage it was better to do nothing.[18]

House cabled Grey on 8 March that Wilson, except for a minor amendment, had confirmed their agreement.[19] A week later Grey forwarded House's message to Asquith with a request that the War Committee be convened.[20] Asquith was stricken with a severe attack of bronchitis the next day and the War Council meeting, originally set for 17 March, was delayed until the 21st. While resting in bed he had occasion to discuss the matter informally with several of his colleagues. To Hankey, he described House's diplomacy as 'humbug and a mere manoeuvre of American politics'.[21] Asquith had no doubts that Germany would never surrender their foreign conquests unless forced to do so. House's plan, it seemed to him, was impractical and ought not be taken seriously. Montagu, following a visit to Downing Street on 18 March, sent Asquith a note in which he passionately denounced the House-Grey Memorandum. Montagu was not one to bite the hand that fed him and it is reasonable to assume that his views coincided with or were close to those of his chief and mentor.

Montagu acknowledged that Wilson's initiative was an election stunt but added that there were more compelling reasons to discard the memorandum. First, he had doubts about House's good faith. Arriving in London as a neutral, the American had offered to enter into a subterfuge against Germany. He had also gone to Berlin and no one could be sure that he had not made similar proposals there. Secondly, there were no guarantees that Wilson would stand by the terms that House had negotiated. If at the conference Wilson showed himself to be generally unsympathetic to the Allies it would be pointless for them to allude to the existence of a secret bargain. Thirdly, the terms of the settlement might have the result of vindicating German militarism and could be justified only on the assumption that the Allies could not win the war.[22]

This is how matters stood when Asquith called a special meeting of the War Committee on 21 March. Grey opened the discussion by giving a summary of his agreement with House. He saw no need to act upon it, however, as long as there was a reasonable chance that the Allies could do the job on their own. Asquith turned to Robertson for his opinion on future Allied military prospects. The CIGS refused to predict when the war would end, although he did not conceal that his own instincts were opposed to House's mediation. Bonar Law maintained that a return to the pre-war status quo was equivalent to a defeat and that neither the government nor the public would have it. Asquith doubted that Wilson was strong enough to carry through his policy and he suggested that it should be put aside for the present. Balfour agreed, saying that the proposal was 'not worth five minutes thought'. Its object, he added, was to extricate the President out of his political difficulties. McKenna drove the last nail into the House-Grey Memorandum. He reported that the nation's financial situation was safe at least until July. Although the ministers did not currently favour American mediation, they remained open to the suggestion that it might be necessary one day.[23]

The British government's reluctance to accept the House compromise plan was based on the assumption that an Allied military victory was clearly within reach. The object of the British was not so much to satisfy the Allies' territorial claims as to defeat the Germans. A Wilsonian peace would enable the military autocracy in Germany to boast of its conquests and of its successful resistance of Britain's naval blockade. The hold of the military over the Reich's policy would be stronger than ever and there would be no security for Europe, no guarantees against further German aggression.

By discouraging mediation Asquith believed that the British not only kept alive their chances of complete victory but avoided taking serious risks. Although Wilson proposed to hold out terms of peace which the Allies considered as essential, Asquith knew that Germany would find them objectionable. It was unrealistic to expect the United States, particularly with Congressional and Presidential elections looming, to enter the war simply because Germany had rejected a pro-Allied peace plan. A more likely scenario would have had the President begin a process of bargaining, with the result that the Allies would have been under enormous pressure drastically to reduce their terms. Asquith could not allow American domestic politics to determine Allied interests. He recognized that if they attended a peace conference and then refused terms which Wilson considered as reasonable, they would have lost much American sympathy and assistance – in particular access to credit and supplies – plus imperilled the Entente's morale and solidarity.

After sacrificing so much Asquith felt that the Allies had no option but to continue fighting as long as there was hope that the Germans would crack before the end of the year. The House-Grey Memorandum was seen as a safety-net which would break the Entente's fall in case dire economic circumstances and continued military setbacks forced a negotiated settlement.

While the House discussions were going on, Asquith had to contend with Churchill, who had crossed over from France seemingly to shake up the political scene. During his leave, Churchill saw an opportunity to rescue his political career by taking part in the debate on Naval Estimates. Asquith's relations with Churchill had cooled somewhat in recent months but the two continued to see each other socially. Asquith and his wife went to a dinner party at 41 Cromwell Road (the Churchills' residence) on the eve of Churchill's speech in the Commons. Churchill appeared nervous though he did not comment about the contents of his proposed talk except to say that he would call for Fisher's return to the Admiralty.[24] Asquith could scarcely believe what he had just heard. Churchill wanted the return to power of an old man whose erratic behaviour had led to the ruin of the Liberal administration and to his own eviction from office. Asquith knew that Churchill would be laying himself open to devastating counterattack and ridicule. 'He has about as much judgment as an average hen', Asquith later told Sylvia Henley.[25] Margot pointed out that Churchill had created a good impression by sacrificing a substantial income and the security of Whitehall to serve in dangerous circumstances at the Front. She warned him not to spoil it by impetuous remarks. Asquith, in the spirit of benevolent paternalism, had a private talk with Churchill and also tried to dissuade him from talking a step that he felt sure was unwise and could do him nothing but harm.[26] But the advice of the Asquiths had no effect on Churchill, who was determined to speak his mind.

Asquith did not relish witnessing the disaster. Late on Tuesday afternoon, 7 March, Churchill rose from the front Opposition bench to deliver his speech. What for the most part was a constructive critique of his successor's naval policy ended with the extraordinary proposal that Fisher should be recalled to the Admiralty.[27] The audience was stunned. Balfour's reply exposed Churchill's flawed logic by calling in question his judgment in supporting a man he could not get along with and who had recently shown that he was unreliable.[28]

Asquith sat impassively through Churchill's speech and did not comment on it as he made his way to his room. Violet (Asquith) Bonham Carter, who had listened to the speech from the ladies' gallery, subsequently went to her father's room and found him 'speechless'. Asquith knew that his daughter was very fond of Churchill and simply refrained from saying anything. He was more revealing during an interview with C. P. Scott, editor of the *Manchester Guardian*, the following afternoon. Scott kept a record of Asquith's remarks:

> As for Churchill's speech it was a piece of gross effrontery. Did I know that only three months ago when Fisher was appointed as head of the Inventions Department both Churchill and his wife had been furious and had denounced it as an outrage, so much so that Mrs Churchill had almost cut him and his wife and would not speak to him. And now suddenly Churchill professed to have discovered Fisher's extraordinary merits and called for his reinstatement. It was a piece of 'impudent humbug'. Why when Churchill and Fisher were together they did nothing but quarrel and Fisher's resignations were a perpetual worry of his life. He had resigned eight times before the last time. Then he actually deserted his post and went away at a time too of some anxiety. Had he not gone there would, said Asquith, have been no Ministerial crisis and no Coalition. 'He deserved to be shot', shouted Asquith, 'and in any other country he would have been shot.' This was known in the navy and his recall now would be deeply resented.[29]

Asquith's anger with Churchill, it should be pointed out, was probably exacerbated by an event that occurred before he saw Scott. Earlier in the day Kitchener informed him that Churchill had asked to be relieved of his command as he intended to return to parliamentary life.[30] Asquith had asked Kitchener to delay answering the letter until he had an opportunity to discuss the matter with Churchill.

Asquith could not help but wonder if Churchill was bent on self-immolation. Whether out of pity or paternalism, he hoped to spare Churchill further humiliation by persuading him to return to his battalion. As he saw it, the only way that Churchill could rebuild his political career was to serve at the Front with distinction. In time all would be forgotten. He had nothing but Churchill's best interests at heart. To be sure Churchill, particularly after his destructive speech, was no threat politically. He was held in low esteem by his own party, despised by the Tories and, beyond the corridors of Whitehall, his support was confined to one or two newspapers. He was completely isolated. Churchill, however, thought otherwise. He believed that the government was on the point of collapse over conscription and confidently expected to play a major role in bringing about a political change that would again catapult him into prominence. He naively failed to appreciate the extent of ill-feeling against him or how low his stock had fallen. He attributed his inability to influence events as an indication that he must try harder, never to his own political ineptness or personal shortcomings. In refusing to admit defeat some observers have suggested that Churchill had unlimited tenacity and self-confidence; others less kindly disposed have seen it as the product of a monumental ego.

Asquith 'had a very serious talk' with Churchill at 10 Downing Street on 9 March.[31] Neither kept a written record of their meeting, but Asquith did tell his daughter the gist of what had taken place. Fifty years later Lady Bonham Carter wrote:

> He told me that he had reminded Winston how his father, Lord Randolph (to whom my father was devoted), had committed political suicide through one impulsive action. He had said, 'If I can, I want to save you from doing the same thing. You will know that nothing but affection prompts me. It is because I care for you that I shall save you'. He said that Winston had tears in his eyes when they parted and that he was sure that he would go back to France.[32]

Asquith was wrong. The more Churchill thought about his future prospects the more he saw himself as the nucleus of an effective opposition in parliament which would hasten the overthrow of the coalition and rescue Britain from defeat. He visited 10 Downing Street on 11 March and told Asquith that he had decided to stay in London. Asquith, without betraying impatience, 'wrestled with Satan for his soul', adding that 'rarely has any missionary exerted himself more in the up-hill work of salvation'. Finally, after the better part of an hour, he felt as if he 'had got an uncertain but restraining grip on the shoulder of a would-be suicide'.[33] Asquith promised Churchill that should he consider it his duty to return to political life no obstacle would be placed in his way.[34]

On reaching Dover, Churchill changed his mind once more and wrote to Asquith asking to resign his commission. Asquith's reaction can be inferred from his remarks to Sylvia Henley: 'That unstable little cur Winston has evidently fallen again under evil influences since our interview of yesterday ... Well, I have done my best to save him from a colossal blunder which may well ruin his own future, & henceforth, so far as I am concerned, he must stew in his own juice.'[35] Upon reflection Churchill felt that perhaps he had acted too hastily and from his headquarters at the front sent a wire to the Prime Minister withdrawing his letter of resignation. Asquith was relieved but admitted to Lady Scott that it was impossible to predict Churchill's 'next mood or move'.[36]

Toward the end of March the relative lull in the usual intense pressure of business enabled Asquith to take a trip abroad. He left London with his party early on 26 March and reached Paris that afternoon. The next morning he attended an Inter-Allied Conference. The schedule was hectic and at times Asquith found it uncomfortable to sit at a table with various Allied representatives and have to depend on his fractured French to communicate his views. He was not sorry when the last session ended on the afternoon of the 28th. The Allied statesmen had discussed wide-ranging issues but, oddly enough, made practically no reference to the ongoing German offensive against Verdun. The French did not raise the subject, presumably because they were still unaware of the long-term effects of the battle.[37]

The conference accomplished little except engendering good-will. Asquith created an excellent impression by his straightforwardness, unassuming manner and genial disposition. He and his associates tried hard to dispel the French perception that Britain was more concerned with preserving its trade and carrying on with business as usual than in defeating the Germans.[38]

Before proceeding to Rome, Asquith spent a day driving along the battlefield of the Marne where the French had checked the German advance in September 1914. The long lines of graves stretching nearly five miles were a grim reminder of the heavy price the French had paid for their victory. Asquith was surprised to learn of the proximity of the battlefield to Paris. 'Very few people', he wrote, 'realize that the Germans were as near Paris as Slough, or even Hounslow, is to London.'[39]

Asquith took with him Hankey, Bonham Carter and Hugh O'Beirne (a diplomat) when he was driven to the Gare de Lyon on the morning of 30

March. At 11 a.m. he left for Italy in the French President's train, which included a beautifully decorated saloon, an ultra-modern dining car and large-sized sleepers. Asquith had never travelled in such luxurious circumstances. When not playing bridge or writing letters, he gazed at the scenic beauty of countryside untouched by war. He arrived in Rome at 3 p.m. the next day and was personally welcomed by Antonio Salandra, the Italian Prime Minister.

On the way to the British Embassy Asquith and his party passed through crowded streets amid great popular enthusiasm. Hankey and O'Beirne were accommodated at the Grand Hotel in a magnificent suite of apartments at the expense of the Italian government. Asquith and Bonham Carter stayed at the Embassy, as guests of Rennell Rodd, the British Ambassador at Rome, and his wife. Asquith found Rodd, a historian and classical scholar, to be a charming and a delightful conversationalist, well-informed about Italy and its people. Hankey liked and admired the British Ambassador whom he had first met in Greece in 1898. He felt that Rodd was 'was a worthy companion to the P. M., whose vast store of knowledge on all classical and historical matters fills me with amazement and envy'.[40]

Asquith had no sooner settled in at the British Embassy than he set out on a round of official visits. Accompanied by Rodd, he saw in succession the Queen of Italy, the Duke of Genoa, who was acting as Regent during the King's absence at the Front, and the Queen Mother. On 1 April Asquith was received in audience by Pope Benedict XV, who expressed a desire for an end to the process of mutual destruction, hinting that he would be happy to mediate between the warring coalitions. Asquith gave the Pope no encouragement, saying that Britain intended to fight to the end.[41] There followed a number of official meetings and functions at which Asquith's speeches, delivered usually in English but occasionally in French, touched the right note, eliciting a warm and spontaneous response from his audience.

Asquith capped his stay in Italy by spending two days at Italian Headquarters near Udine. Here he met the King, Victor Emmanuel, who lived in a single room which served him both as bedroom and study. The King spoke English fluently and Asquith was impressed by his dedication and military knowledge. With the King as a guide, Asquith was shown a number of points along the Front. He visited an army service depot before proceeding to climb a long ascending road deep into the Alps. The road had only recently been completed and was one of many Italian engineering feats carried out in an incredibly brief time in mountaineous regions hitherto inaccessible to traffic. Asquith inspected gun emplacements, defence systems and a specially recruited and trained Alpine battalion. From an observation post, he had a wonderful view of the fighting to the east. Asquith was struck by much of what he saw, particularly the spirited manner in which the Italians were conducting their campaign.[42] He failed to appreciate that their effectiveness and zeal came mostly from fighting against their old enemy Austria and for territory which they regarded as *Italia Irredenta*.

Asquith had a remarkable understanding of the Latin spirit and his trip to Italy continued the personal success he had enjoyed in France.[43] On the journey home Asquith and his party stopped briefly in Paris, where they were met by Briand and Alexandre Ribot, the Finance Minister. The two Frenchmen requested a £60,000,000 loan and urged that the British attack with all the forces they could muster in order to take the weight off the defenders at Verdun. They were adamant that without that assistance France could not go on.[44] Asquith assured them that his government would do everything it could to aid France. In the afternoon Asquith departed from Paris and reached London (there was a seven-hour delay at Boulogne) in the early hours of 6 April.

On his return Asquith was immediately confronted by Robertson, who pressed for a definite decision as to whether there would be an general offensive in support of the French. The matter was aired at the War Committee on 7 April. Robertson read out a letter from Haig, who reported that Joffre fully expected the British to intervene and that he accepted the necessity for doing so. In these circumstances the ministers felt compelled to give their approval. However, the nature of the action was never properly defined. Robertson maintained that Haig should receive *carte blanche*, assuring everyone that he could be trusted to employ his forces prudently. Asquith, on the basis of what Kitchener had said, thought that the offensive would take the form of a series of minor attacks along the line. Unknown to him, Robertson and Haig had already agreed to Joffre's demand for a big and spectacular offensive on the Somme. Instead of placing restrictions on Haig's discretion, Asquith joined his colleagues in giving him the latitude that Robertson was asking for.[45]

Robertson felt that the government's commitment to an offensive in the West in 1916 made it more imperative than ever that the British forces languishing in Greece should be transferred to France where they could influence the war. Asquith, who had allowed British forces to continue to occupy Salonika in order to keep Briand in power, gave Robertson his blessing to reopen the issue with the French. However, all efforts by Robertson to withdraw from Greece met with such resistance from Briand that Asquith decreed that the British divisions should remain in place. To make matters worse the French suggested late in April that the Allies at Salonika should strike northwards against Bulgaria. Robertson thought the proposal was ludicrous. The War Committee agreed with the CIGS and summarily rejected the whole concept of a Macedonian offensive. Even Lloyd George, who had played no small role in initiating this meaningless campaign, recognized that any thrust from Salonika would be starved of the necessary resources and might result in a debacle.[46]

Asquith was in no mood to countenance further involvement in side-shows, particularly in light of the recent disaster in Mesopotamia. As the reader may recall, Townshend's advance on Baghdad had been halted and his troops driven into retreat, coming to rest at Kut where they awaited relief. A column led by Lieutenant-General Fenton Aylmer failed to break through in January 1916. Aylmer met the same fate when he tried again in March. Judged to have mismanaged the relief expedition, he was replaced by Lieutenant-General George Gorringe. In the meantime control of the Mesopotamian operation was transferred from the Indian Government to the War Office. This meant a greater application of British methods, resources and equipment to the campaign.

Asquith saw the change in leadership as perhaps marking the beginning of a new epoch in the campaign. He failed to grasp that the Indian army lacked the equipment and organization to undertake an expedition on any considerable scale outside India itself. He conveniently forgot that it was his government, with little consideration for the geography and conditions of Mesopotamia, that had authorized Nixon to take Baghdad. Rather it suited him to place the blame for the mistakes on the Indian government. He confided his thoughts to Curzon on 21 March 1916:

> The gross & criminal lack of preparation for the Mesopotamian venture on the part of the Indian Gov't is (I think) far the worst feature of the war.
>
> Since the campaign has been taken over by the CIGS there has been, I am glad to believe, a vast improvement. But their part is deplorable & the responsibility for it ought to be brought home. One of the things wh. impresses me most disappointingly is the absence in the Indian Army, not only of proper organization, but of good generals & leadership.
>
> As you know, we finally superseded Aylmer after his last fiasco. Townshend is, as I fear, at least two parts mad.
>
> At this moment, it is in my judgment, the danger spot in the whole arena of the war ... There is, however, still, I think, a fair chance that Townshend may be dug out ... [47]

Asquith's hopes were quickly dashed. After Gorringe's rescue operation was turned back on 22 April, Townshend did not feel justified in calling upon his troops to endure further hardship and suffering. He surrendered unconditionally on 29 April, after an offer to secure the release of his garrison of 11,000 for a £2,000,000 bribe had been spurned by the Turks.[48] Not since Yorktown in 1781 had a British commander yielded a major force to an enemy.

Contrary to expectations, the fall of Kut, in the same way as the final evacuation of the Gallipoli Peninsula, did not cause serious disturbances in any Muslim state under British rule. But it was a bitter blow to British pride and naturally aroused resentment at home. Asquith despatched Kitchener to the House of Lords to put the best possible face on the incident while he, with an emotional fervour that he seldom showed in public, appealed to the Commons to exercise forbearance.[49] As it happened, public attention turned quickly from Mesopotamia to events closer to home.

On Easter Monday, 24 April, Asquith was informed that a small group of extreme Irish nationalists had seized the General Post Office in Dublin and proclaimed Ireland an independent republic.[50] The rebels had little support among the Irish people and surrendered after four days of fierce and bloody street fighting. All in all the British authorities behaved moderately in circumstances of great difficulty. What was open to question was the piecemeal and seemingly random manner in which subsequent executions were carried out. The rebel leaders were executed singly or in batches of two or three over a period of nine days. A number of the leading rebels were spared, while others occupying lesser posts were not. The consequence of the British reprisals was to transform a rag-bag of insurgents into martyrs.

Asquith, who was mired in the conscription controversy, was slow to recognize the dangerous implications of military justice in Dublin. His first thought was to appoint a new Chief Secretary for Ireland to replace Birrell, who resigned after having ignored the warnings of the dangers of a Sinn Féin outbreak. Unable to find an immediate replacement, Asquith visited Ireland for a week to assess the situation personally. He came back to London on 19 May, having concluded that the existing system of government had broken down completely and that there needed to be a new approach to the Irish problem.[51] It was urgent, he felt, to concede at once a measure of Home Rule, both to undercut Sinn Féin and prevent the spread of anti-British feeling in the United States. Asquith entrusted Lloyd George with the unenviable task of working out a fresh settlement between Carson and Redmond.

The details of the ensuing negotiations are not relevant to this study. The Irish problem was a purely domestic issue and is briefly discussed here only because of its impact on Asquith and British politics. It is sufficient to say that Lloyd George secured from Carson and Redmond an agreement whereby Home Rule would be implemented immediately, with the six disputed counties remaining part of the United Kingdom until the end of the war, when a conference would settle their ultimate fate.[52]

In the cabinet the compromise plan divided the Tories. Bonar Law, at some cost to his prestige in the party, gave his grudging assent but Lansdowne, Selborne and Long raised strong objections. Selborne resigned and the remaining dissidents threatened to do likewise. Had Asquith made the issue one of confidence and stood firmly behind the agreement he might have split his government. He was not prepared to take such a risk. The plan foundered in storms of denunciation from extremists on both sides. Asquith thereupon restored the old system of government in Ireland and appointed a Unionist, H. E. Duke, to succeed Birrell. Asquith's weakness in handling the Irish problem further damaged his standing with his own party and fatally alienated the Irish Nationalists.[53]

Before the events in Ireland came to a sorry conclusion, there occurred the only significant naval battle of the war. It was fought off the Danish coast of Jutland on 31 May and ended inconclusively with the German fleet retiring hastily to port. When the first reports came in, Asquith 'showed no trace of anxiety or nervousness, but only delight at having brought them [the German fleet] to action with some fear that they might manage to flee without a fight'. Like the public, the Prime Minister had been conditioned to expect another Trafalgar when the opposing surface fleets met. As more information became available his heart sank at the depressing tale of British losses. By 3 June it was possible to form a more complete picture of the outcome and Asquith's spirits improved on being assured that the battle had been a strategic triumph for the Royal Navy.[54] That conclusion was not an overstatement. Although the Germans lost three fewer ships, they suffered heavy losses without any prospect of relieving themselves of the pressure of British sea power. Henceforth the German navy remained close to its bases and, except for one or two inconsequential episodes, did not venture out into the North Sea again.[55]

Asquith was somewhat disappointed with the result of Jutland in view of what he had generally expected from the fleet's action. Far more devastating, however, was the blow the sea brought within days of the naval battle. In May 1916 Tsar Nicholas had invited Kitchener, whom he greatly admired, to visit Russia. For about a month Asquith had contemplated sending a high-ranking emissary to inspect conditions on the Russian Front and to discuss the Tsar's huge demands for supplies and credit.[56] This need coincided with his eagerness to see Kitchener embark on a prolonged leave. Late on the afternoon of 5 June Kitchener left Scapa

Flow on the cruiser *Hampshire* en route to Archangel. That evening the ship struck a mine and sank in stormy seas west of the Orkneys. Kitchener was among those drowned. News of his death sent a wave of horror across the country.

The tragic circumstances of Kitchener's death saddened Asquith, as it did even those ministers who disliked him personally. Pease had it on good authority that Asquith wept all night when he received word that Kitchener had gone down with the *Hampshire*.[57] Lady Bonham Carter recorded that her father was moved to tears when he announced the melancholy news to his family.[58] By all accounts the Prime Minister was profoundly affected by the loss of his colleague. In addition to personal grief, the Prime Minister may have felt remorse over his ungrateful treatment of the man who had been unfailingly loyal to him. However, Asquith did not revise his ultimate estimate of Kitchener as an administrator and leader. In a similar way to his colleagues, he placed a disproportionate emphasis on the Field Marshal's shortcomings. For a man of unusual intellectual breadth it is strange that he never fully appreciated Kitchener's prescience, strategic talents and keen judgment, or acknowledged his greatest feat: that within a span of eighteen months he had transformed a nation traditionally reliant on sea-power into a military power capable of holding its own against the best army in the world. Several weeks after Kitchener's death, he told Pease:

> The world and history will never know as we know, Jack, what were his limitations – it is tragic – his reputation and ability for all times will be placed far higher than a true appreciation would place them ...[59]

Kitchener's death at a crucial moment in the struggle left a vacancy in what was still regarded as the second most important post in the land (in spite of the reduction of the powers of the Secretary of State). The aspirants to the office began jockeying for position almost immediately. 'All this canvassing & wire-pulling about the succession, while poor K.'s body is still tossing about in the North Sea, seems to me to be in the highest degree indecent', Asquith wrote disparagingly to Stamfordham.[60] Asquith was in no hurry to fill the post. He recognized what was at stake. He wanted to ponder the matter carefully and select someone who would neither threaten his own position nor upset his fragile coalition. A full month passed between the death of Kitchener and the selection of his successor. During the interval Asquith assumed the management of the War Office as he had on two previous occasions.

Among the likely candidates the two front-runners were Lloyd George and Bonar Law. Asquith was not enthusiastic about either man. Robertson urged Asquith to appoint Chamberlain, a man who could be relied upon to leave him in peace. The CIGS shuddered at the prospect of serving with Lloyd George, whose sharp criticism of the generals' prevailing strategy had made him anathema to the army.[61] The Prime Minister deemed Chamberlain a worthy candidate.[62] But Bonar Law scotched the idea because he considered it a slight if the post was offered to any Unionist other than himself.[63]

From the outset Lloyd George assumed that he was the obvious choice for the War Office. As a result, he felt he could dictate his own terms. What he wanted was total control of the War Office, which meant the abrogation of the special powers conferred upon Robertson as CIGS.[64] On 11 June he met Bonar Law at the home of Max Aitken (later Lord Beaverbrook) to discuss the matter. Both men were really competing for the same post and they were not on close personal terms. It was no secret that Bonar Law found the Welshman to be a disingenuous and thrusting colleague, much too preoccupied with self-aggrandizement. But he disliked even more the idea of leaving the post open to a satellite of Asquith or to a pliant man agreeable to the soldiers. At the end of the long discussion Bonar Law indicated he would step aside and support Lloyd George's claims.[65]

The next day the Tory leader motored to Sutton Courtenay to see Asquith, who was resting at his country home. He wasted no time in presenting Asquith with an ultimatum. Taken by surprise, Asquith countered by offering the post to Bonar Law himself. Bonar Law replied that he would have accepted it before his discussion with Lloyd George but now it was too late. In these circumstances, Asquith agreed to surrender the War Office to Lloyd George.[66]

Asquith had second thoughts after interviews with Lloyd George on 13 and 15 June. He was astounded that an amateur strategist like the Welshman should seek powers greater than those exercised by the late Field Marshal. Besides, he was almost certain that Robertson would resign rather than accept a modification of his compact with Kitchener. But Lloyd George was adamant, hinting that he would leave the ministry if his demands were not met.[67]

Asquith suspected that Lloyd George was bluffing. It was difficult to take seriously a man who threatened to resign each time he failed to get his own way. More significantly, Asquith recognized that Lloyd George would be committing political suicide if he actually carried out his threat to return to the backbenches. The public was certain to brand his move as selfish and unpatriotic. Asquith could afford to outwait his headstrong colleague.

A school of historians has advanced the view that Asquith procrastinated in order to slip in Derby, or some other accommodating occupant, but that his plan was frustrated when Bonar Law and Lloyd George delivered a joint ultimatum. This version of the events, as Jenkins points out, is only partially correct.[68] There is no evidence that Asquith seriously entertained anyone besides the two front-runners, or that he considered his hands tied after the interview with Bonar Law. At some point Asquith concluded that Lloyd George should have the job. He was influenced by two factors. With Kitchener gone, it was important that his successor should possess an international reputation to lend weight to the government's views at Allied conferences. Moreover, as Montagu noted, the best way to silence Lloyd George's constant carping about the conduct of the war was to make him more closely associated with it.[69]

As an added incentive Asquith offered Lloyd George the vice-presidency of the War Committee.[70] This was tantamount to making him Deputy Premier. In trying to find a way to mollify the Welshman one thing was certain. Asquith neither desired nor deemed practical any formal alteration in the role of the CIGS.

Even if the current arrangement was allowed to stand, Asquith knew that he would have difficulty in selling Lloyd George to the generals. Indeed there was an important element in the country which urged him to retain the War Office on a permanent basis, with someone like Derby as his second-in-command. This group included Sir John French, the Army Council, the King and key figures in the right wing of the Unionist Party. Asquith was fond of the War Office but he recognized that, even if the political objections could be overcome, he could not properly discharge the added responsibilities.[71]

Although Lloyd George was a skilful negotiator, he found himself with very little leverage, as friends, whom he consulted, were quick to remind him.[72] At a meeting with Asquith on 24 June he accepted the Secretaryship for War without any of the powers for which he had bargained. To make matters worse he was not permitted to choose his own undersecretary, as he had done at the Ministry of Munitions. Asquith appointed Derby, a great favourite of the army, to ensure that the Welshman did not interfere with strategy. Lloyd George's satisfaction at moving into the War Office was tempered by the knowledge that he had fallen far short of his own goals. Not only had he been outmanoeuvred into accepting a post which had no more control over war policy and strategy than before, but his every action would be carefully scrutinized by his chief lieutenant. As he could not fail to realize, his tenure could be brief if the war continued to go badly.

Asquith was taking no less a gamble than Lloyd George. Given the importance of the position of Secretary for War, his resignation from the government for whatever professional differences would be much more damaging to Asquith than if the head of another department left the ministry. Furthermore, an ambitious Secretary for War, particularly one who would stop at nothing to gain his end, was like a Prime Minister in waiting. It was clear to Asquith that if the war prospects should improve, or seem to improve, Lloyd George would claim credit and be in a strong position to make a bid for his own position. Asquith had an uneasy feeling after Lloyd George accepted the War Office. 'He thinks it is the mistake of his life',[73] Duff Cooper wrote in his diary while on a visit to The Wharf on 25 April.[74] Margot Asquith had no doubts whatsoever. Her often-quoted entry in her diary reads: 'We are out: it can only be a question of time now when we shall have to leave Downing Street.'[75] Events vindicated her baleful prophesy.

Asquith left Lloyd George and Robertson to work out their respective spheres of responsibility. The two exchanged views in conciliatory tones but Robertson did not give anything fundamental away.[76] For the time being Lloyd George had no option but to accept things as they stood. He formally took the seals of office on 7 July, one week after the battle of the Somme had begun. The Somme represented the first real test of the soldiers' Western strategy.

A NON-PARTY MANDATE.

John Bull. "I DON'T CARE WHO LEADS THE COUNTRY SO LONG AS HE LEADS IT TO VICTORY."

Chapter 11

Troubled Government

The Somme was the first major action by the British army on the Western Front. At 7.45 on the morning of 1 July 1916, after a preliminary bombardment of unprecedented fury, nearly 120,000 British infantrymen clambered out of their trenches and advanced in close formation, as the armies of Frederick the Great might have done in mid eighteenth century. Burdened with 66 lbs. of equipment, the men advanced at a slow walk across the shell-pocked No Man's Land. They were an easy, concentrated target and German machine gunners mowed them down, wave after wave, until the ground was littered with corpses. By the end of the first day Haig's army had suffered 57,000 casualties with more than 19,000 killed. This was the darkest day in British military history and the bloodiest suffered by any army during the war. The saddest part of the story was that Haig allowed the fighting to continue long after it should have been apparent that there was no longer – if there ever had been – a possibility of breaking through the German line.[1]

When news of the progress of the fighting gradually filtered back to London there was considerable anxiety about the endless casualty lists and the absence of tangible results. Asquith feared a repetition of previous Allied offensives in which catastrophic losses were exchanged for tiny morsels of enemy-occupied territory. Robertson, in an attempt to allay the cabinet's restiveness, pressed Haig for a statement of his achievements and objectives.[2]

Replying on 1 August, Haig gave no hint of the impending break-through which had been his main goal. Instead he focused on lesser objectives, asserting that his offensive had eased pressure on Verdun, assisted the Russians by tying down German troops in the West and destroyed 30 per cent of the enemy divisions. He expected the attacks to continue well into the autumn but conceded that another campaign in

1917 would be required to shatter German resistance completely.[3] There was little justification for Haig's claim that the Somme was paying handsome dividends to the Allies: the tide at Verdun had begun to shift before the opening battle; the Germans transferred nine divisions to the Eastern Front in July and August; and German losses at the time were considerably less than those of the Allies.

All of this was unknown to Asquith, who expressed himself satisfied with Haig's letter. Asquith noted that Briand had informed him that the British drive had saved Verdun and boosted the morale of the French government.[4] However, Haig's optimistic analysis of the Somme offensive was challenged by Churchill who was back at Westminister, trying to piece together the fragments of his once brilliant political career. In a strongly-worded memorandum circulated to the cabinet through F. E. Smith, Churchill warned that the prolonged slaughter on the Somme threatened to exhaust the British army.[5] The paper received a frigid reception.

Asquith had concluded in recent months that the bright, alert, imaginative, constructive Churchill of pre-war years was gone forever, destroyed by his own hand. He described his former colleague at this time as a 'tragic figure of failure and folly ... malignant, & clumsy to boot, without a friend or follower in the world (except perhaps F. E. and I suppose Clementine)', concluding that a 'man is not so unpitied as he is unless he lacks real character'.[6] Churchill's observations regarding the battle on the Somme only validated his judgment. Had his former colleague learned nothing from the Dardanelles fiasco? Once again the brash and egocentric Churchill was professing to be wiser than the experts. Asquith never gave Churchill's paper a fair reading. It did not help that the copy sent to him was annotated – possibly in Bonham Carter's hand – with quotations marks and such contempuous ejaculations as 'Rubbish'.[7] Thus Haig was assured that he could continue to count on Asquith's full support.[8]

Asquith had an aversion to large and costly assaults that only succeeded in pushing the enemy back a few miles to a new set of fortified lines. But he was heartened by recent signs that the Allied policy of attrition was making enormous inroads into German resources. The Sixth Battle of the Isonzo had given the Italians their first real gains of the war and, on the South-Western Front, the Russians under General Brusilov won a spectacular victory, destroying nearly half the entire Austro-Hungarian army and penetrating deep into enemy territory. In the latter stages of the Somme the Germans suffered more than the attackers because they stubbornly obeyed their High Command's orders not to yield an inch of ground. These losses, coupled with those at Verdun, both demoralized the

Germans and caused irreplaceable vacancies in their ranks. All in all the Allies were winning or holding their own on all fronts. The initiative had passed to them for the first time since August 1914.

Asquith's optimism was further heightened by the entry of Roumania into the war in the closing days of August 1916. It strengthened his hope that the Allies would shortly inflict such damage on Germany as to compel it to accept a settlement on their terms. With the likelihood of peace in the near future, Asquith faced demands from some of his colleagues for a comprehensive statement defining the nation's war aims.

Since the beginning of the war Asquith, except for making general statements on the conditions essential for peace, had avoided any systematic study or discussion of war aims. His unwillingness to do so did not reflect a lack of concern with the problem of a peace settlement. He did not believe that Britain should make demands in advance of Germany's defeat, lest it exacerbate differences among the Allies and cause them to slacken their effort against the common enemy. He preferred to wait for a decisive victory which he hoped would come in 1917 when Britain, as the leading power, would be able to impose its own terms. To counteract growing peace movements, he appealed to the public's emotion, stressing, as he did on 11 October 1916, that the enormous loss of life and hardships caused by the war could not be 'allowed to end in some patched-up, precarious, dishonouring compromise, masquerading under the name of Peace'.[9]

Asquith would have allowed matters to drift but for the impetus to act which apparently developed simultaneously and separately in various sectors of the government. In August the Foreign Office and the War Office each produced detailed reports devoted to the post-war settlement.[10] Asquith was told, erroneously as it turned out,[11] that the Briand government had formulated the terms of an eventual settlement as well as France's claims and post-war policies. It was pointed out that in the councils of the victorious nations France would enjoy a huge advantage unless Britain was similarly prepared. On 30 August the Prime Minister asked his colleagues to consider the terms upon which the country might be willing to conclude peace.[12] Asquith did little to encourage them to act on his request. Initially the only minister to undertake the exercise was Balfour.[13]

The various initiatives over the post-war settlement generally expressed the kind of terms that were current in official circles in the summer and early autumn of 1916. The War Committee did not discuss these, far less move toward a consensus on the nation's war aims. Asquith was anxious to avoid ministerial debates on the subject lest it further weaken his coalition.

He received assistance from an unexpected quarter. On 19 September the French Prime Minister made an impromptu speech in the Chamber of Deputies when, replying to a pacifist's accusation that he was needlessly prolonging the war, he flatly rejected any idea of a compromise peace. Briand's well-publicized oration delighted Asquith for, in addition to confirming French resolve, it removed the apparent motive which underlay his call for a consideration of peace terms.

Asquith's inaction prompted Hankey to take matters into his own hands. On 31 October he produced a statement of war aims based on Asquith's previous declarations and the points of agreement among the authors of the various memoranda. Hankey had hoped to force Asquith's hand. But his memorandum was never considered in the cabinet because the current strategic picture ruled out an early peace on British terms. What had occurred in recent months to tip the military balance against the Entente?

As a condition for securing Roumanian cooperation, the French and British had agreed to attack Bulgaria with their forces based at Salonika. Much to Lloyd George's chagrin, Robertson brusquely refused to move substantial detachments from France to Salonika. Robertson felt that the immediate objective of the Allied offensive was to contain the Bulgarian forces in the southern Balkans so as to ensure the safe and orderly mobilization of the Roumanian army. As far as he was concerned, Sarrail (appointed titular commander of the Allied Eastern Army early in 1916) had ample men to do the job.[14] To Lloyd George's argument that Britain could not afford another Serbian tragedy, the CIGS maintained that the best way to help Roumania was to continue to pound the Germans on the Somme.[15]

Asquith had not changed his mind about the futility of conducting large-scale operations in the Balkans. He proposed to do no more there than was mandated by Britain's treaty commitments. Asquith's attitude made it certain that Robertson would triumph over Lloyd George.

Asquith was also of the same mind as Robertson in approving Haig's deliberate and unhurried tactics at the battle of the Somme. He confided to Sylvia Henley that 'Haig is I think doing very well: sticking to his original plan and not allowing himself to be hustled'.[16] During the first week in September Asquith crossed over to France with Hankey and Bonham Carter 'to see things at first hand'.[17] They toured the Somme battlefield, which was intersected by roads choked with huge columns of lorries, ambulances, guns and troops. Near Fricourt they met the Prime Minister's eldest son, Raymond, who had ridden over on horseback and was waiting for them at a cross-road. As they passed through the town they were startled by a series of shell-bursts, one of which was no more than fifty yards away, forcing them to take shelter in a 'dug-out' where they remained until the bombardment was over. Hankey recorded that Asquith was as usual quite composed but thought he detected his hand trembling, adding 'and no wonder'.[18]

That evening (6 September) Asquith and his party dined with Haig at his advanced headquarters. Asquith had recovered from his earlier unsettling experience, aided undoubtedly by several glasses of brandy. He was relaxed and in a jovial mood. Haig wrote in his diary:

> Mr A. and I had a long talk after dinner. He said he and the Government are well pleased with the way the operations have been conducted here, and he is anxious to help me in every way possible ... He seems fully determined to fight on till Germany is vanquished.[19]

On 7 September Asquith and Hankey motored to Crécy and, while they were strolling by the cross commemorating the famous battle in 1346, they had a chance encounter with Edwin Montagu, the new Minister of Munitions, who was returning from a conference in Paris. Asquith took considerable delight at Montagu's apparent ignorance of the historical importance of the site. The two men drove on to look at a strange new invention called the 'tank', about sixty of which had just arrived in France complete with crews. Described by Asquith as the latest invention of 'the Devil',[20] they were Britain's answer to the trench barrier on the Western Front. These ungainly armoured vehicles, with weapons mounted in sponsons at the sides, were impervious to machine-gun fire and, crawling on caterpillar treads, could crush barbed-wire and cross trenches.

Haig intended to employ the tanks to exploit the anticipated breakthrough during his next big push on the Somme in mid September. Hankey was convinced that the secret of a powerful new weapon should not be thrown away on the Somme. He felt that the tank was intended to be used against normal defences, whereas on the Somme it would have to penetrate a tremendous artillery barrage and operate over ground dotted with gaping craters. Asquith felt that they risked nothing by raising the matter with the army leadership. Back at headquarters, Asquith approached Haig about massing the tanks against a new front. Hankey likewise pressed that idea on Haig's Chief of Staff. 'We made an impression,' Hankey recalled in later life, 'but failed to persuade them to alter their plans.'[21]

Asquith's view of the war up close reinforced his confidence in Haig. His anxiety over the extent of British losses was somewhat eased by the High Command's assurances that the enemy had suffered even more heavily.

He was especially encouraged by predictions that German reserves were practically depleted and that the battle was approaching a climax.

Asquith met Robertson shortly after returning to London. The CIGS complained that Lloyd George was trying to commit Britain more deeply in the Balkans than either he or the Imperial General Staff wished to go. He made it clear that if the War Committee adopted a Balkan plan which the General Staff deemed unsound, he would not be responsible for its execution. Asquith assured Robertson that under no circumstances would he allow events in the Balkans to jeopardize Haig's offensive. At the War Committee on 12 September Robertson's strategic view prevailed without opposition.[22] Lloyd George, who almost certainly would have cast a dissenting vote, was away on a tour of the Western Front.

Haig's renewed offensive on the Somme was launched on 15 September. The Germans were alerted to the approaching attack by the massive preliminary artillery bombardment but were unprepared for the appearance of the armoured tank. Of the forty-nine machines available (10 per cent remained in reserve) thirty-two reached the fighting line but, with inexperienced crews and soft, shell-torn ground, their effect was minimal. With them vanished Haig's last opportunity to achieve a breakthrough on the Somme. The battle continued until late autumn when a blizzard, followed by torrential rain, brought an end to the awful carnage. During the four-and-a-half-month campaign British casualties totalled 420,000 and the French 194,000, while German losses may have reached 450,000. The Somme, which was the glory and destruction of Kitchener's armies, may well have deprived Britain of a generation of leaders.

The Somme dealt the death-blow in Britain to the remaining idealistic and romantic attitudes to war. Few in Britain escaped losing a family member or close relative. The dimension of the losses was brought home personally to Asquith when Raymond, the eldest and most gifted of his four adult sons, was killed while leading his men during the first wave of the attack on 15 September. The sad news reached the Asquiths two days later while they were at The Wharf. Dinner was over and they were playing bridge with friends when Margot was called to the telephone. After putting down the receiver she sat down for a few minutes to collect herself, then rang the bell and asked a servant to summon her husband. Asquith entered the room and, as he looked at Margot's ashen, tear-streaked face, his heart sank. 'Terrible, terrible news', she said. Instantly he knew that it was about Raymond and that he was dead. 'He put his hands over his face', Margot's entry in her diary ran, 'and we walked into an empty room and sat in silence'.[23]

Asquith never fully recovered from this maiming blow. Raymond was a symbol of a talented generation. His high spirits, zest for life and unspoiled charm had made him a favourite with all his family. Raymond was very much unlike his father, although intellectually his equal if not his superior. Jenkins writes that, of Asquith's sons by his first marriage, Raymond was not the closest to him.[24] That may be so, but Asquith was captivated by Raymond's charismatic personality and intellectual prowess and had always regarded him with special affection. 'I can honestly say that in my own life he was the thing of which I was truly proud', Asquith wrote despondently to Sylvia Henley after the tragedy, '& in him and in his future I had invested all my stock of hope. This is all gone, & for the moment I feel bankrupt.'[25] Asquith's natural grief was undoubtedly aggravated by the belief that Raymond's life, like those of so many young men, had been sacrificed on the Somme for no apparent purpose.

Throughout early autumn Asquith missed a number of cabinet sittings and generally was unapproachable and incapable of sustained work. Gradually the dark clouds rolled away and he recovered enough to carry on his heavy duties. But his tragic loss reduced his concentration and efficacy and came at a time when he required his full powers to surmount growing difficulties. Asquith reemerged from his self-imposed isolation in about a fortnight and on 11 October gave what he described as a 'difficult and trying' speech in the House of Commons. It went better than he had expected 'as everyone was very kind and sympathetic'.[26]

Several days later Asquith was called upon to adjudicate a dispute between Robertson and Lloyd George. The Welshman wanted to send Robertson to Russia, supposedly to confer with Russian army leaders to determine their needs. The desirability of supplying Russia with war material was incontestable but it is probable that Lloyd George was more anxious to get Robertson out of the country and end his strangle-hold over military policy. Lloyd George's ruse would have been obvious to one far less astute than Robertson. Not surprisingly the CIGS adamantly refused to be bundled off to Russia. He could not be forced to do anything against his wish because his standing in the country was immense. Asquith thought he should go, but did not press the point.[27]

Asquith again took a less than authoritative stand when Lloyd George, in collusion with the French, lobbied for a major campaign in the Balkans. This time there was a good chance that the Welshman's efforts might pay off as the Roumanian army was in desperate straits and threatened with destruction. Asquith understood that the Entente's ability to rescue Roumania was no greater than it had been in the case of Serbia the year before. Given the isolation of Roumania, there was little the Entente could do in the way of direct help. He was therefore dismayed when Joffre announced on 10 October that with four additional divisions, two British and two Italian, he believed that the Eastern army would be able to break through Bulgaria's defences in the south and relieve the Roumanians. Joffre maintained that the mission of the Allied Eastern Army had been extended from simply covering the mobilization of the Roumanian army to driving the Bulgarians out of the war in cooperation with the Russians.[28]

At the War Committee on 12 October Robertson predictably refused to accept the enlarged role Joffre had unilaterally assigned to Sarrail's army, insisting that its function was to contain the Bulgarians and not to push forward. Asquith and the others on the committee agreed with Robertson that the Eastern army should not deviate from its original role but, as a sop to the French, proposed to send an extra division to Salonika.[29] Lloyd George was not one to accept defeat graciously and once again reached into his ample bag of tricks. At his instigation the French requested a conference on the Balkans.[30]

The conference was held at Boulogne on 20 October. The lines were drawn after the opening remarks by the two Prime Ministers. Briand favoured a major thrust from Salonika in an effort to save Roumania. To that end he argued that the Eastern army should be augmented from sixteen to twenty-three divisions. He promised that his government would send two more divisions to the Balkans and implored the British to commit yet another division (in addition to the one announced a week earlier). He hoped that Italy and Russia would make up the remaining three divisions.

Asquith admitted that the Allied cause would receive a serious blow if Roumania suffered the same fate as Belgium and Serbia. But he took a diametrically opposed view as to the best means to assist Roumania. He observed that the Eastern army was effectively fulfilling its designated assignment, namely to prevent the Bulgarians from diverting any of their forces in Macedonia to the north. To attempt now to inflict a decisive defeat on Bulgaria would, according to the British General Staff, require an additional ten to fifteen divisions as well as the corresponding artillery and ammunition. He was further advised that, even if the troops could be spared, they would arrive too late to be of significant military value. For those reasons he considered that the role of the Eastern army should not go beyond pinning down the Bulgarian forces in Macedonia.

Asquith could detect French hostility over his adamant stand. He was ill-at-ease and at an obvious disadvantage in presenting the British case in French. He was put in an even more awkward position by Lloyd George, who broke rank and sided with the French. Still his only concession was to promise to consider Briand's request that Britain contribute another division to the Balkans.[31]

The War Committee convened on 24 October to discuss whether to send an extra division to Salonika. Robertson was unmoved by the imminent collapse of Roumania, maintaining that it would be a grave strategic error to be drawn into a major campaign in the Balkans. Lloyd George unleashed a tirade against the military, observing that reinforcements sent two months earlier might have knocked Bulgaria out of the war. Although the Welshman acknowledged that it was probably too late to influence military events in the Balkans, he argued passionately for the additional division on political grounds. Asquith did not defend Robertson's position as he might have been expected to do. Instead he sided with Lloyd George and the others in overriding Robertson's objections, inclining to the view that the extra men would placate the French and hopefully stiffen the morale of the faltering Roumanians.[32]

  Asquith had shown a lack of courage, not because he suddenly reversed his position but because he did so more out of guilt than military logic. Asquith knew that with the resources that could be spared it was impossible for the Allies to break through the Bulgarian lines and rescue Roumania. The operation that Lloyd George had called for would have required an additional ten or fifteen divisions. Were they to be drawn, as seemed almost certain, from the Western Front? How were these troops to be supplied? Did it make sense to weaken the main front to undertake a forward push in the Balkans where, owing to the impossible terrain, the chances of success were at best slim? Asquith never tried to induce his colleagues to face these questions. Had he done so the cabinet might have seen the absurdity of the whole enterprise and voted to end Britain's commitment. Instead Asquith, against his better judgment, allowed Britain's involvement in the Balkans to continue. The forces in the malaria-infested Salonika region were for the most part limited to an equivocal and defensive role and never affected operations on the Western Front or against Roumania. By 1917 the Eastern army had swollen to 600,000 men with the British and the French providing the largest contingents. The Germans treated the whole affair as a big joke and derisively nicknamed Salonika 'the largest Allied internment camp'.

  Such illogical undertakings might have been averted if Asquith had taken a more active role in promoting the case for a Western strategy. Amateur strategists like Lloyd George had convinced themselves that the carnage on the Western Front was the result of faulty policy. They looked to fight the war on the periphery in the expectation that progress there would be easier and the cost in lives substantially less. What Asquith needed to do was to underscore some obvious truths. Germany with its powerful defensive position could not be materially weakened by side-shows, for even if it could not win it could almost certainly avoid defeat. France remained the vital theatre, for a victory here by either side would end the war. If the Allies could beat the Germans in France it mattered little what happened on the other fronts. Conversely, if the Allies were defeated in the West they would lose the war even if they were in control of all the subsidiary theatres. Simply put, it was not the generals' strategy that needed to be changed, only their tactics.[33]

Asquith might have made more of an effort to devise ways to help end the war. After the lesson of 1915 it should have been apparent to someone as perceptive as Asquith that mere mass would not produce victory. Clearly more pressure needed to be placed on the generals to develop new methods and tactics to counter the effects of machine guns. A second mistake of Asquith is that he failed to put forward a greater claim to shape Allied strategy, particularly after Britain had concentrated a huge army on the Western Front. At the very least the British were entitled to determine how and where their forces should be employed. Finally, Asquith ought to have taken advantage of Britain's advanced technology. Had he devoted more attention to the development of self-propelled armoured vehicles and other new weapons to assist the infantry, the war might have been shortened and countless lives saved. As it happened, the few technological contributions made by the British in the war owed more to individual enthusiasm than to government encouragement and sponsorship.[34]

During the last days of October Asquith took time from pressing business to read through a mass of memoranda and papers connected with the various phases of the Dardanelles operation in preparation for his appearance before a commission of inquiry. In the aftermath of Suvla and Kut parliamentary pressure had grown for the publication of papers relating to the Dardanelles and Mesopotamian campaigns. The government resisted these demands at first but on 1 June Bonar Law, acting in place of Asquith, told the House of Commons that all pertinent documents on the Dardanelles campaign would be assembled and laid before the country. Whether the matter had been discussed in the cabinet cannot, in the absence of records, be determined. Hankey thought the decision was ill-advised and penned a long memo to Asquith, alluding to the host of problems that would arise if the papers were published.[35]

The more Asquith reflected on the issue, the more he realized that Hankey was correct in his estimate of the military and diplomatic damage the revelation of confidential information would cause. On 18 July, with the War Committee's blessing, he rescinded the government's promise, announcing that it was not in the national interest to publish the documents on the Dardanelles.[36] His statement provoked such a row in the House that two days later he agreed to set up a commission which would hear evidence and present a report on the operation. A similar commission was established to inquire into the Mesopotamian campaign. 'It is infinitely better to have a couple of secret inquiries, which will do no harm & may even do some good,' Asquith confided to Sylvia Henley, 'than the publication of papers which, however edited, would have been in the last degree mischievous.'[37]

Hankey, on the other hand, saw the compromise in a different light and he had historical precedent on his side. Having spent many hours researching earlier campaign investigations, Hankey held out his findings in a desperate attempt to stiffen Asquith's resolve. The purposeless exercise of raking over dead coals, he feared, would lead to mutual recriminations in the cabinet, some resignations, government paralysis and perhaps even its fall, as well as injury to the morale of the army and the prestige of the Supreme Command. All of this, he concluded, would be occurring at a moment when the nation was fighting for its very existence.[38] Hankey's skilfully-argued case fell on deaf ears.

As so often happened, Asquith chose the most expedient option. Had he analyzed the long-range consequences carefully, he undoubtedly would have seen the obvious inherent dangers in submitting his government's performance to critical scrutiny. Asquith, in the eyes of the world, was not only acknowledging that grave mistakes had been committed but impugning his own leadership as well.

The Dardanelles and Mesopotamian Commissions were formally constituted in August 1916. Although the terms of reference were generally the same in both cases, the Mesopotamian inquiry concerned chiefly the India Office and the Indian government, which had controlled the campaign until nearly the end. On the other hand all the notables in the cabinet, plus the service leaders at the War Office and Admiralty, were directly involved in the Dardanelles campaign. The Dardanelles Commission began its work in earnest in September and the ever-faithful Hankey, who had prepared the government's case, was an early witness. Asquith was interviewed on 31 October. He presented the evidence in such a way as to justify his own role without throwing blame on others. At all times he remained in complete control, even under searching cross-examination. Hankey, who had accompanied Asquith, made the following observation:

> He was simply splendid. Answered all the questions with extraordinary promptitude – like a racket's ball coming back off the back wall – and with great dignity and

confidence, and perfect urbanity and good nature ... P. M. was very pleased with himself as we walked home.[39]

If Asquith made a serious parliamentary blunder in yielding to the pressure for the appointment of the commissions, his fate and that of his government ultimately rested on the course of the war. Had the Entente continued to make military gains, his political position would have been as secure as ever. But as the year was about to end, the Allies were less well placed than in the spring. The Brusilov offensive had been halted and Roumania was being overrun. The battle at the Somme was dying down amidst bitter disappointment. German submarines were increasing the radius of their activity and dangerously imperilling the life-line of the island kingdom. The number of British merchant ships sunk by U-boats had risen alarmingly, from a few a month at the start of the year to forty-one in October.[40] Admiral Jellicoe felt it necessary to warn the Prime Minister on 29 October that continued shipping losses on the present scale might compel the Allies to make peace in the early summer of 1917.[41] The President of the Board of Trade, Walter Runciman, was equally worried at the prospect of a shipping breakdown, in which case he predicted that the collapse would occur even before June of 1917.[42]

No less disheartening to Asquith were the reports that the German authorities were adopting measures to expand war mobilization.[43] Robertson admitted that he had underestimated Germany's resources and staying power and that he could not be sure when the war would end. He offered no novel approach to the war and simply stated that the only course was to continue to apply pressure on the Germans in the spring of 1917.[44] Robertson's sombre assessment played into Lloyd George's hands. He not only revived his suggestion to ship Robertson off to Russia but devised a plan for the Entente governments to decide strategy for 1917.[45] At the War Committee on 3 November, from which Robertson was conveniently absent, the Welshman roundly condemned the policy of attrition, stressing that it had permitted the Germans to recover the initiative and occupy more territory, and warned that without tangible victories the public would become demoralized and lend its support to peace groups campaigning to stop the war unconditionally.

Some ministers felt that Lloyd George was too pessimistic, but the Prime Minister was among those who shared some of his misgivings about the High Command's conduct of the war. The Somme offensive, it seemed to him, did not justify the more optimistic prophesies of its supporters. It is true Robertson himself had not promised that the offensive would defeat Germany but, apart from relieving Verdun, there was little to show for the horrendous casualty list. Even if the High Command's claim was accurate that the fighting had inflicted terrible punishment on the enemy, the price was too high if in the process the British army itself was being bled to death.

Asquith had no definite policy and as a rule he was more inclined than Lloyd George to leave questions of strategy to the soldiers. But during the latest action on the Western Front it had not escaped his attention that the French, attacking further to the south, had achieved more satisfactory results and at a significantly lower cost than the British.[46] The experience of his son 'Oc',[47] recently invalided from France, reinforced his view that the generals needed to concentrate more tanks and adopt more progressive tactics before launching another massive assault.

Given the the Prime Minister's reservations, it is not surprising that Lloyd George's recommendations prevailed. The ministers decided to postpone further major operations in France and explore whether a decision might not be reached in another theatre. Secondly, they agreed that a military conference should be held in Russia, to be attended by the principal generals from the West, including Robertson. Finally, they accepted the proposal that a political conference should precede the forthcoming meeting of Allied generals at Chantilly which was intended to discuss next year's campaign.[48] In this way the Entente politicians could frame plans for 1917 and then present them to the soldiers as a *fait accompli*.

By now Asquith was well aware that Robertson was not a man who could be mollified or would yield easily to persuasion. He was right in anticipating a sharp reaction from the CIGS when he discovered what had occurred behind his back. An indignant Robertson struck back immediately. Forewarning Joffre of the politicians' plan to pre-empt the military meeting, he ensured that the two conferences would take place simultaneously. On the second issue he threatened to resign if pressed to undertake a mission to Russia. He sent word to the King and canvassed his political friends and sympathetic newspaper editors. He appealed to the Prime Minister, observing that vital military matters required that he remain in London.[49] Asquith told the King that three months earlier Robertson could not have absented himself from the War Office for an extended period, but that 'circumstances were now different as our forces are on the point of going into winter quarters'. It was clear to Asquith that Robertson scented a plot to get him out of the way and, as in the case of Kitchener, reduced to a figurehead.[50]

Asquith was uneasy about the growing antagonism between Robertson and Lloyd George. He asked Hankey to assure the Field Marshal that the government had no ulterior motive in proposing that he attend the Russian conference. When Hankey's efforts failed, Asquith decided to meet Robertson personally.[51] He too found that the Field Marshal was immovable.[52]

Asquith saw that nothing would come of the proposal and that it was time to move on to more pressing business. His immediate concern was to prepare for the forthcoming political conference in Paris. Lloyd George set out his views of the military situation in a long memorandum which he presented to Asquith to read at the conference. The exercise was vintage Lloyd George, scornful of those with different viewpoints, short on specifics and lavish in self-praise. Specifically, the Welshman savagely condemned the policy of attrition. Yet while anxious that Allied strategy should adopt a new direction, he could give no definite leads except to call for close coordination between the leading political and military figures of East and West. A recurring theme was the clear implication that all along he had been right and everyone else (especially the soldiers) wrong.[53]

Asquith's response came as a disappointment to Lloyd George. The Prime Minister considered that the document would outrage Robertson and do no good. He flatly declined to include the greater part of it in his own statement to the French leaders.[54] On the way over to Paris Asquith, with considerable assistance from Hankey, worked practically until the last moment getting his speech into final shape and translated into French.

During the morning of 15 November, before the conference opened that afternoon, Asquith and Lloyd George held an informal and unrecorded conversation with Briand and his Minister of Marine, Admiral Lacaze, at the Quai d'Orsay, the French Foreign Ministry. For inexplicable reasons, Asquith read his statement at this meeting rather than at the conference. Although Asquith had softened the vitriolic tone permeating Lloyd George's paper and omitted the most offensive passages in it, his remarks still constituted a harsh indictment of the Anglo-French High Command.

In reviewing the past two years of the war, Asquith observed that the Entente had scored few successes and was on the verge of losing all of south-east Europe. The generals had no clear conception of how to win the war except to hammer away at the enemy's fortified lines. Such a policy was likely to continue the stalemate indefinitely in view of the Central Powers' ample reserves, which the British General Staff placed at between 3,000,000 and 4,000,000 with a further 1,000,000 young men becoming available for military service each year. He wondered how long the Alliance could bear the strain of a protracted war. As the war dragged on, casualties would become heavier, suffering would increase and nations would face bankruptcy. Not the least of the difficulties of a war of attrition was the effect of the submarine campaign, which threatened Britain's mastery of the seas and indeed its very existence. The Prime Minister hinted that the only way to avoid defeat was to devise a new strategy. Accordingly he recommended that an Allied conference be called as soon as possible.[55]

How much impact Asquith's remarks had on the French representatives is difficult to measure. Briand had his own reasons to be dissatisfied with Joffre's generalship. But just before the meeting with the British leaders he had been subjected to a scorching cross-examination by a committee of the Chamber of Deputies which was unhappy with certain aspects of the war. He was perhaps aware that he was not in a state of mind to give his undivided attention to what was being said. At the end he asked Asquith for a copy of his speech and promised to study it before the afternoon meeting.[56]

The first session of the formal conference, which was enlarged by the presence of Italian and Russian delegations, was devoted chiefly to a discussion of the relationship of governments to soldiers. There was broad agreement among the political leaders that they, not their general staffs, should decide policy. At a second meeting the following day they were joined by the generals, who had terminated their discussions at Chantilly. The generals presented their report, which was practically a carbon copy of the one written at Chantilly eleven months earlier. They held that France should remain the principal theatre of war and that a new offensive should be mounted no later than the middle of February 1917.

Intimidated by the surly scowl of the soldiers, none of the politicians found the courage to proclaim their right to direct future operations. Asquith waited for Briand to give the lead. When the French Prime Minister finally did, he urged the endorsement of the conclusions of the military conference. The other political leaders quickly fell into line, nullifying such resolutions as had been adopted the previous day.[57]

Asquith had no more reason to be happy than Lloyd George when he left the conference room. Although the outcome in the last session did not definitely prejudice the strategy for 1917, it was clear that the soldiers had stolen a march on the politicians. But much as Asquith wanted to avoid a repetition of the bloodbath at the Somme, he was not prepared to challenge the Allied High Command. He understood, if Lloyd George did not, that no policy favoured by the politicians was likely to succeed without the full support of the generals.

Asquith had left unsettled a number of problems which drew his attention on his return. Try as he might, he was unable to identify an acceptable nominee willing to undertake the onerous responsibility of the newly-created post of Food Controller. On 28 November a desperate Asquith offered the job to Lord Milner, a gifted administrator but one of his most outspoken critics. Milner became the fourth man to turn down the appointment.[58]

At the Admiralty the counter-measures taken to deal with the submarine challenge had proved inadequate. A shake-up among top-level naval officials was inevitable. Asquith wanted Sir Henry Jackson, on whom much of the odium had fallen, replaced as First Sea Lord by someone with more recent sea experience and greater drive. His favoured candidate was Admiral Jellicoe, the supreme naval commander. Balfour was reluctant to make the change until the press agitation had died down. However, the Prime Minister's insistence that the situation was too critical to permit further delay prompted Balfour to act on 27 November. With Jellicoe installed as First Sea Lord, command of the Royal Navy passed to Admiral Beatty.[59]

Another issue facing Asquith was the growing manpower crisis. As the direct result of the staggering losses incurred at the Somme, the army found itself desperately short of men – about 80,000 below authorized strength. Robertson felt that the government had not adopted tough enough measures to find the necessary recruits, allowing far too many exemptions to men whose civilian work was not vital. As the ultimate solution, he advocated applying conscription to all forms of war employment, not just the army. He suggested that the military age should be raised from forty-one to fifty-five and that all men up to that age should be available for such work as the government deemed essential for the effective prosecution of the war.[60]

Asquith feared that a policy of compulsory national service would damage his authority with organized labour. But when the issue was discussed again on 30 November he had changed his mind. It was apparent that he preferred to take his chances with the trade unions rather than appear to deny the army the means to win the war. After a brief discussion the War Committee went beyond the Army Council's demand, agreeing in principle to introduce compulsory national service for every adult male up to sixty. Asquith appointed a new committee under Montagu to write the new national service law.[61] Britain, it seemed, was about to take a decisive step towards total war.

Asquith had acted in response to the changing conditions of the war. He was confronted by the impending defeat of Roumania, the gradual depletion of French reserves, the measures taken by Germany both to increase and reorganize its manpower, and an announcement that the New York Reserve Bank might refuse to grant further loans to Britain's allies. His government needed not only to stifle criticism that it was floundering, but also to prosecute the nation's war effort more effectively.

Asquith had no remedy to check the spreading anxiety inside the upper echelons of government. The conflict was entering its third winter and the prospects of victory were as remote as ever. How long could Britain continue to fight? The recent battles had produced casualties on a scale unprecedented in British experience. Moreover, the war was costing the gvernment about £5,000,000 a day. The nation's supply of gold and convertible securities was nearly exhausted and soon it would have to finance the war with American loans. The Treasury was concerned about the implications of Britain's dependence on American supplies and credit. 'If things go on as at present,' McKenna warned late in autumn, 'I venture to say with certainty that by next June or earlier, the President of the American Republic will be in a position, if he wishes, to dictate his own terms to us.'[62]

Although there was probably no one in the cabinet who worried about defeat, there were some who questioned whether the price of outright victory was becoming too high. One such person was Lord Lansdowne, the bland but respected Minister without Portfolio, who produced a belated reply to Asquith's request for thoughts on peace terms. In his long, pessimistic paper, dated 13 November, he doubted that Britain could stay the course to victory and suggested a compromise peace such as Colonel House had put forward earlier in the year.[63]

Asquith considered that Lansdowne had performed a faithful and courageous act but he did not share his gloomy outlook. He felt that talk of peace was premature and should be contemplated only if there was no hope of victory, in which case it would make sense to wind up the war on the best terms available. He was certain, however, that the Allied military situation would improve and that it would be better to fight on until satisfactory terms could be achieved. A lasting peace, he told an audience at the Guildhall on 9 November 1916, was contingent on an Entente victory, which he frankly admitted was not likely to come soon:

> I wish to declare on behalf of the Government of Great Britain ... that the Allies are fighting for a common cause ... and that a victory which will secure them all is, in our judgment, the essential condition of a lasting, enduring peace ... And the peace when it comes, be it soon, or be it late – and I will not disguise from you for a moment my convictions that the struggle will tax all our resources and our whole stock of patience and resolve – ... must be such as will build upon a sure and stable foundation the security of the weak, the liberties of Europe, and a free future for the world.[64]

Asquith never believed there was any real danger that the cabinet would abandon its commitment to total victory. Robertson swept away any defeatist sentiment when he replied to Lansdowne in somewhat bellicose terms on 24 November. Entertaining no doubts as to the

Entente's ability to win the war, the CIGS heaped scorn on the 'miserable members of society' who lent their support to a negotiated peace settlement.[65] On 28 November Asquith, anticipating a fresh initiative by Wilson to mediate, asked the War Committee to frame a response. The speakers adopted much the same line, leading Asquith to conclude that 'the time has not yet come for peace feelers'.[66]

Such a consensus was strikingly uncharacteristic of the government's conduct of affairs at this time. In November the pressure on the War Committee became so acute that it met on fifteen separate occasions, a sharp increase from the monthly average of five or six between January and October.[67] But even frequent meetings could not clear up the backlog of unfinished business. The explanation for this is obvious. Asquith had steadily increased the membership of the War Committee, from five to seven, later to nine and finally to eleven. It did not help matters that its members were badly overworked for, in addition to devising war policy, they had important departments of their own to administer. Its deliberations, marred by tension and disputes, were usually long, tedious and inconclusive. Such decisions as were taken were apt to be blocked in the cabinet, which contained far too many powerful, clashing personalities.

The defects in the instruments of government were aggravated by Asquith's style of leadership and declining powers. His methods in avoiding irreconcilable divisions among his ministers had obvious advantages in normal times but they were more likely to be a liability in the abnormal conditions of war, when events could not always tarry on the process of debate and discussion to produce a compromise. For about a year Asquith showed remarkable skill in holding together his ramshackle coalition but, as the second half of 1916 wore on, he began to lose his grip, partly because of mounting problems and partly because the loss of his son and the mental and physical strain of the war affected his judgment and drained his resilience and spirit.[68]

The continuous and calamitous loss of life, to no apparent gain, inevitably had its effect on the nation's spirit. What was needed in these circumstances was a war leader who could foster confidence in the outcome of the struggle, strengthen the waverers and impart a new inspiration to the staunch of heart. The public needed to be reminded that there was a competent captain at the helm. Oratory was natural to Asquith and words set to the music of war would have had a tonic effect on the British people. Unfortunately Asquith never tried to shed his image of Olympian detachment and to establish a rapport with the public. If, in the fashion of Churchill during the Second World War, he had built an image the public could rally around, he might have averted the challenges to his leadership.

As head of the government Asquith was held accountable for the nation's setbacks, even though most of these were not his fault. To make matters worse the Lansdowne Memorandum was leaked to the press and the impression was conveyed that the Conservative elder statesman was actually acting as Asquith's stalking-horse. Newspapers controlled by Northcliffe led the cry and attacked Asquith relentlessly, sometimes unjustly and cruelly, with the avowed object of driving him from office. Everything that went wrong was laid at his door. He was accused of sloth and lethargy, of adopting policies calculated more to prevent the break-up of the coalition than to winning the war, and of devoting excessive time to social pursuits. Asquith typically made no reply to the press's criticism. His refusal to defend himself or highlight the achievements of his admin-istration left him open to unscrupulous attacks which further eroded public confidence in his leadership.

There were signs in the latter part of 1916 that Asquith's control over the House of Commons was failing. Within his own party he faced a hostile body of about forty MPs, popularly known as the Liberal 'Ginger Group'. These Liberals, willing to subordinate traditional values to the demands of war, wanted more dynamic leadership than Asquith now provided.[69] Asquith's alliance with the Irish Nationalists had collapsed since the failure over Home Rule. However, discontent with the government as a whole and Asquith in particular was deepest among the Tory back-benchers. Many at odds with their party elders had rallied around Carson who had become the *de facto* leader of the Opposition. The split in Tory ranks became apparent during a debate in the Commons over the disposal of enemy property confiscated in Nigeria. As Colonial Secretary, Bonar Law had to defend the government's scheme to sell the properties to the highest bidders. Carson insisted that only British subjects should be eligible. The issue itself was irrelevant but provided Carson with an opportunity to humiliate Bonar Law and force him to end his alliance with Asquith. The government easily overcame the challenge but it brought a sense of foreboding to Bonar Law, who had managed to carry only a narrow majority of Conservatives (73 voted with him, 65 against, and 148 either abstained or were absent). The result of the debate imperilled both the unity of the Unionists and Bonar Law's own standing as party leader.[70]

Inside the cabinet the mounting dissatisfaction threatened to produce a national crisis. The partnership between Liberals and Conservatives, uneasy in the best of times, was on the verge of falling apart in the existing climate of disillusionment and despair.[71] The extent of disharmony in the cabinet was demonstrated by Asquith's casual acknowledgment to Lady Scott on 1 November that six resignations were looming.[72] A kind of paralysis was setting in at the upper levels of government. Britain's weary leaders, despite their best efforts, had seemingly reached a dead end.

The inability to devise a formula for victory no doubt accounted for much of the frustration and rancour in the cabinet. But there was a growing conviction, particularly among the Unionists, that Asquith was inadequate as a war leader. The Prime Minister had never shown much creative vision or drive, but now that the war was going badly he seemed almost a passive spectator of the events. Hankey complained that the Prime Minister was frequently inattentive at meetings and that he refused to countenance any interference in his normal social activities, with the result that the business of the War Committee fell increasingly in arrears.[73] Chamberlain described the cabinet as 'the worst managed of any which I have ever heard' and Asquith as 'incurably haphazard in his ways and ... content to preside without directing'.[74] The Unionist Lord Crawford, who had succeeded Selborne in July 1916 as President of the Board of Agriculture, was no more charitable. He recorded his impressions after attending his first cabinet meeting:

> It is a huge gathering, so big that it is hopeless for more than one or two persons to express opinions on each detail – great danger of side conversation and localized discussions. Asquith somnolent – hands shaky and cheeks pendulous. He excercised little control over debate, seemed rather bored, but good-natured throughout.[75]

There followed similar entries in his diary. On 4 November he went to see Asquith about a matter relating to agricultural labour. That evening he wrote:

> He wasn't very helpful. His eyes were watery and his features kept moving about in nervous twitching fashion. I thought he looked ill and frail – also weak and undecided. He is one of those men whose reputation reposes entirely upon intellectual power and fertility of language – but to expect firmness or initiative from him would be quixotic ... At cabinets he is calm and urbane – but as for ruling his colleagues or abridging idle or wasteful discussions he is hopeless.[76]

In sum, Asquith's inability to exert energetic control in the face of the deteriorating military situation had not only exhausted the public's patience, but had also widened the dangerous divisions in cabinet ranks and allowed the government's downhill slide to gather momentum. During November the perception grew that the current system could no longer cope with the problems and perils facing the country. It was the feeling that there had to be a change in the management of the affairs of state that sparked a palace revolt against Asquith.

Chapter 12

The Fall of Asquith

The developments that led to Asquith's eviction from 10 Downing Street have been chronicled exhaustively, day-by-day, indeed almost hour-by-hour. All the main actors and even some members of the supporting cast have left their impression of what happened.[1] As might be expected, no two accounts coincide exactly. It is precisely these discrepancies which have kept interest in the political upheaval alive among subsequent generations of historians.[2]

The acute period of the political crisis began shortly after the Nigerian debate from which Bonar Law emerged, so Asquith told Lady Scott, 'with teeth chattering'.[3] During the second week in November Bonar Law spoke to Asquith and predicted disaster unless there was a drastic change in the cumbrous method of deciding war policy. Asquith treated the matter lightly, saying that his discontent was due to the want of military success and would soon pass. Always feeling a little insecure in Asquith's presence, Bonar Law found it difficult to argue with him. While clinging to his opinion, he indicated that there was no object in pursuing the issue until he had something concrete to propose.[4]

Asquith's impatience with Bonar Law is perhaps understandable. He was beset with enormous difficulties, both external and internal, and Bonar Law's concern appeared to him to be a trivial one. Still he had not made things easier for his political counterpart. Up to this point the Tory chieftain had been a loyal and unselfish member of the coalition, firm in his conviction that the unity of the nation mandated that Asquith remain at the helm. But he could not ignore the recent storm signals. If he continued his partnership with Asquith, it would mean sacrificing control over his own party. Alternatively his departure from office would precipitate the fall of the government and, unless another Liberal could be found who was acceptable to most Conservatives, there would be a return to party strife and a general election. His close friend Max Aitken, a self-made millionaire and Unionist MP for Ashton-under-Lyne, rescued him from his dilemma. Aitken tried to persuade Bonar Law on 14 November that he should abandon the discredited Prime Minister and join Lloyd George and Carson, who were acting in close collaboration. Aitken was aware that the two malcontents had agreed on a plan to overhaul the machinery of war. The idea was to place executive control of war policy in the hands of a small committee of three or four instead of the traditional cabinet. Lloyd George would serve as its chairman. Although continuing as Prime Minister, Asquith would be excluded from membership in the new body. When Aitken gave an outline of the scheme, Bonar Law's reaction was guarded and unenthusiastic but he did agreed to meet Lloyd George and Carson.[5]

All the same the Tory leader was determined not to be drawn into a sordid plot against Asquith. On 15 November he went to 10 Downing Street and told Asquith of what was in the wind. The Prime Minister did not appear surprised. He expressed doubts that even if Lloyd George got his way he would remain satisfied with anything less than complete power. He was also sceptical of Carson's constructive abilities on the basis of his performance while a member of the coalition. Asquith clearly disliked the plan but raised no objections to its informal discussion.

Bonar Law met Lloyd George and Carson to discuss the subject for the first time in Aitken's room in the Hyde Park Hotel on 20 November. There were further meetings on the following three days. Suspicious about Lloyd George's motives, the Tory chief was adamantly opposed to the intended exclusion of Asquith from what would be the most important instrument of government. However, on Saturday morning, the 25th, he accepted a compromise formula prepared by Aitken. The plan envisaged Asquith as president of the new War Council. Lloyd George was designated as its chairman, which meant that he would preside at meetings whenever Asquith was absent. The names of the remaining two members were left blank, but Carson and Bonar Law were the obvious candidates. It was understood that the War Council would have executive authority except in circumstances when the Prime Minister deemed it desirable to refer its decisions to the whole cabinet.

With this document in hand, Bonar Law went to see the Prime Minister in the afternoon. Asquith had his bags packed and was about to repair to The Wharf for the week-end. He glanced at the document and made a few preliminary remarks. He reiterated what he had said earlier, namely that he was certain the terms did not represent Lloyd George's last demands and that he was not keen on Carson rejoining his administration. Although not attracted to the proposed arrangement, he promised to give Bonar Law his final answer on Monday.[6]

In all probability Asquith had made up his mind before leaving for the week-end. By now he felt certain that a plot was in the making. On 23 November the *Morning Post*, a newspaper that Asquith habitually read, created a great stir by publishing a leader depicting Lloyd George as the only man fit to lead the nation through to final victory. Its editor, H. A. Gwynne, who was known to be a mouthpiece for Carson, had in the past been a harsh critic of Lloyd George. His sudden volte-face was an obvious signal that an alliance existed between Carson and Lloyd George.[7]

Asquith's reply was set out in a long letter which he handed personally to Bonar Law on Monday morning. In it he rejected unequivocally the triumvirate's scheme. His arguments for doing so were measured, precise and reasonable. While he was open to any suggestions for the improvement of the War Committee, he could not imagine how such a body could operate effectively without the heads of the Admiralty and War Office among its members. Moreover, the inclusion of Carson at the expense of others with better claims would be deeply resented by both Liberals and Conservatives. It would be universally interpreted, Asquith correctly observed, as 'the price paid for shutting the mouth of our most formidable parliamentary critic – a manifest sign of weakness and cowardice'. Asquith directed his heaviest blows at Lloyd George, depicting him as an unscrupulous opportunist who had devised the plan in question, 'with the purpose, not perhaps at the moment, but as soon as a fitting pretext could be found, of his displacing me'. He concluded by saying that the proposal could not 'be carried out without fatally impairing the confidence of loyal and valued colleagues, and undermining my own authority'.[8]

Bonar Law discussed Asquith's reply with Lloyd George and Carson at the Colonial Office in the afternoon. No clear consensus emerged from the meeting. Carson favoured declaring full-scale war against Asquith but Lloyd George had not yet reached this point and, if anything, began to back-pedal. Bonar Law wanted to arrange a reconciliation between Asquith and Lloyd George and, as a way of solidifying his leadership of the Tory party, to bring Carson back into the government.

Bonar Law again visited 10 Downing Street to see whether he could persuade Asquith to reconsider the matter. His recollection of the interview ran as follows:

> I ... told him that in my opinion the facts made it absolutely necessary to carry out such a change. I added that as far as I could judge he had no idea of the extent of the unpopularity of his Government, and, indeed, from the nature of the case anyone in his

position would find it difficult to realize the exact facts … for no one would be likely to tell him.[9]

The interview did not prove very productive. Asquith missed what was perhaps his best opportunity to strike a bargain with the Unionist leader and short-circuit the movement for his removal. The triumvirate at this moment was in a state of confusion. More importantly, Bonar Law had good reason to believe that his Unionist colleagues would be chary of the whole business. They were unlikely to accept a scheme which they would see as devised to further Lloyd George's ambitions. They were also hostile towards Carson, regarding him with almost as much distrust as Lloyd George. Thus Bonar Law was desperately in search for an arrangement that would bring about a change in the running of the war and essentially leave Asquith in control. Had Asquith taken the initiative then and shown a willingness to compromise, he might well have detached Bonar Law from his two partners and circumvented the political crisis. As it happened, he sat back and characteristically waited upon events.

On 29 November Asquith acknowledged in the cabinet something that everyone had known for a long time, namely that the existing system was not operating smoothly and that it required modification. Cecil suggested that there ought to be an executive council to deal with the non-military aspects of the war. He believed that the war could be prosecuted more effectively if there were drastic changes in the organization of the nation's civil life. Together with compulsory national service, he anticipated that the government would have 'to make great innovations in our industrial organization'. Under the pressure of events the government had slowly and haphazardly extended its grip over a sector of the economy. Most agreed, however, that a further extension of state control of industries was necessary to ensure the most economical use of manpower. Cecil observed that the operation of state-controlled industries would be improved through the establishment of a three-man cabinet committee on civilian organization. Such a committee, he envisaged, would work in close collaboration with the War Committee.

Asquith fastened onto the idea at once. He indicated that there were many matters outside the purview of the War Committee requiring firm control and constant examination. He maintained that orders from above had too often been ignored or evaded. It was essential, in his view, to set up a machinery to ensure that the departments concerned carried out their orders. General sentiment in the cabinet favoured such a proposal and it was accepted in principle.[10] After the meeting Asquith wrote to Sylvia Henley:

I am setting up, as a counterpart to the War Committee, a Civil Committee of the Cabinet to deal with such things as food, coal and general national organization. At the same time I think we shall have to cut down the numbers of the War Committee.[11]

Asquith was confident that with the proposed changes in the policy-making apparatus he had beaten back any challenge to his leadership. Both Lloyd George and Bonar Law had sat passively in the cabinet and apparently made no effort to resist an arrangement they obviously abhorred. Asquith interpreted their silence as accepting, or at the very least acquiescing in, the cabinet's decision.

On 30 November Bonar Law belatedly called together his Unionist colleagues to inform them what was happening. He ran into strong opposition when he explained the nature of the contemplated changes. Cecil openly accused him of dragging the Conservative party on the coat-tails of Lloyd George. Long, Chamberlain and Lansdowne were equally hostile. Feeling sadly isolated, Bonar Law's resolve weakened.[12]

Lloyd George had reached a crisis point. He knew that he would have to act quickly if he wished to keep the triumvirate intact. He drew up a new memorandum to present to the Prime Minister at their interview fixed for Friday morning, 1 December. The proposals were significantly different than those Bonar Law had carried with him to 10 Downing Street on 25 November. In Lloyd George's plan, the Prime Minister was to be excluded from the War Council's deliberations but retained the discretion to refer any matter to the full cabinet for ratification. On the other hand, the Welshman acceded to Asquith's wishes that the new body should include the two service ministers.[13]

Lloyd George made an additional demand when he discussed his memorandum with Asquith. He considered it essential to eject Balfour from the Admiralty, citing as the reason his failure to devise an antidote to the worsening submarine crisis. Little else is known of what passed between them. Hankey, who saw both men later in the day, recorded that during the interview Lloyd George had hinted at resignation unless his terms were accepted.[14] Even if the Welshman had made such a statement, Asquith would not have taken him seriously. On many past occasions Lloyd George had threatened to resign but when he did not get his way always had found a justification, or a face-saving formula, to draw back at the eleventh hour. There was no reason to suppose that he would act differently now. Whatever the case, the talks were amicable enough. Asquith raised no immediate objections to the plan, not even to the provision that would relegate him to the position of an arbiter in the background. He promised to give Lloyd George his answer after he had reflected on his terms.

Asquith forwarded his counter-proposals to Lloyd George late in the afternoon. He admitted that the system needed revision but insisted that the cabinet must in all cases retain ultimate authority. He wanted the War Committee restructured under his own chairmanship as well as the establishment of a parallel home front body to concern itself with domestic war problems.[15]

Asquith refused to consider anyone but himself as head of the committee directing war policy. He reasoned that if he was not fit to manage the war he was not fit to be Prime Minister.[16] His unyielding position placed Lloyd George in a quandary. If he had chosen to go forward on his own he almost surely would have either suffered a serious humiliation or been forced to resign. It was clear to him that he could not hope to challenge Asquith successfully without the unqualified support of Bonar Law. An earlier meeting with the Tory leader had ended on an inconclusive note.[17] In the evening Aitken brought the two men together at the Hyde Park Hotel. There Bonar Law committed himself to support Lloyd George as chairman of a small council, providing the Prime Minister selected the remaining members. Lloyd George accepted the condition.[18]

Before 2 December there was every reason to expect that all the parties would come to terms. Bonar Law continued to believe that Asquith's retention as Prime Minister was indispensable. Lloyd George, hardly one to act on principle alone, feared being outmanoeuvred and forced into the wilderness. As for Asquith, he was preoccupied with a host of problems and the last thing he wanted was to see the dispute developing into a political crisis. In fact he was so confident that differences could be bridged that he left on Saturday for Walmer Castle.

The pace of events quickened over the week-end after the press entered into the dispute. On the morning of 2 December the front pages of the *Daily Chronicle* and the *Daily Express* were dominated by stories of the political infighting, in which the names of the likely members of the new War Council were given.[19] Later in the day Northcliffe's *Evening News* ran an article entitled 'Lloyd George Packing Up'. On 3 December *Reynolds' News* carried a sensational story under the headline 'Grave Cabinet Crisis: Lloyd George to Resign'. The article announced that Lloyd George intended to resign as Secretary for War unless his terms were accepted and it implied that if he went Bonar Law would follow suit. The picture of the inside struggle was presented with such clarity and detail that it required little imagination to determine who had inspired the story. Nowhere were the effects of the revelations felt more acutely than in the ranks of the

Unionist ministers. As they gathered in Bonar Law's home for a critical meeting, they bristled at Lloyd George's tactics which they considered were calculated to force their hand while delicate negotiations were still in progress. They took turns in venting their spleen at Lloyd George. In this heated atmosphere Bonar Law again found himself in a minority of one. From then on what happened is obscure except that in the end they all agreed on a resolution which Bonar Law was to transmit to Asquith. It read:

> We share the view, expressed to you by Mr Bonar Law some time ago, that the Government cannot go on as it is.
>
> It is evident that a change must be made, and in our opinion the publicity given to the intentions of Mr Lloyd George makes reconstruction from within no longer possible.
>
> We therefore urge the Prime Minister to tender the resignation of the Government.
>
> If he feels unable to take that step, we authorize Mr Bonar Law to tender our resignation.[20]

The different impressions carried away by the Unionist ministers in attendance[21] make it unclear as to the motives behind their action.[22] The only common thread in the confused and ambiguous discussion was the Unionists' determination 'to strive for an arrangement in which they would have maximum influence'.[23] They were inclined to stand aloof from the quarrel and let the Liberals alone decide whom they wanted to follow. Much as the Tories disliked Lloyd George, they disliked even more the notion of being unable to shape events. There was no hint that under the right conditions any would refuse to serve under Lloyd George if he were asked to form a government. After lunch Bonar Law went to see Asquith.

Alerted to potentially troublesome developments, Asquith interrupted his week-end in the country and hurried back to London on Sunday morning. Montagu was on hand to greet him when he arrived at 10 Downing Street around 2 p.m. They sat down to a late lunch and, during the course of their conversation, Asquith sent word to Crewe to join them. The two men had barely concluded their lunch when Bonar Law walked in and asked to speak privately to the Prime Minister.[24]

Arguments still rage over exactly what occurred at the meeting. Since neither of the participants recorded what was said, we must rely chiefly on Beaverbrook's account, which needs careful scrutiny. One thing is clear: Bonar Law did not transmit the Unionist resolution to Asquith as he was supposed to do. He may have felt that the clause rebuking Lloyd George for his disclosures to the press would weaken his hand. The Unionist leader claimed that he forgot to hand Asquith the actual document, an unlikely explanation in view of the purpose of his visit. Be that as it may, he did reveal its essential contents. But what really mattered was whether he gave the correct impression about the Unionists' aim in calling for Asquith's resignation.

Jenkins, in my view, is mistaken in saying that Bonar Law, whether by accident or design, seriously misled Asquith. As a result, he observes, the Prime Minister took the resolution to mean that the Unionist ministers were about to desert him.[25] It is not certain that Bonar Law revealed the extent of the gulf between him and his Tory colleagues over the merits of Lloyd George. But from what Asquith himself admitted to intimates,[26] it is clear that in due course Bonar Law explained the significance of the resolution, underlining that it did not imply that the Unionists had gone over to Lloyd George. That would account for Asquith's combative attitude after his initial reaction of disbelief. It surprised Bonar Law. When the Unionists convened at his house at 4 p.m. for a second conference he gave them the following account:

> He [Asquith] positively refused to serve with Ll.G. until his own position of control was assured. He would not dream of being Chancellor of the Exchequer or Lord Chancellor.[27] He said no government could stand which did not contain both himself and Lloyd George. He almost indicated that he would fight, call a meeting of his party for a vote of confidence – and let Ll.G. do his best or worst in isolation.[28]

Asquith was evidently stunned by the Unionist resolution, which came as something of a bombshell. He could hardly believe that, in less than twenty-four hours, matters had taken such a turn that he was actually in danger of being jockeyed out of office. He seemed unaware of the extent of his unpopularity, attributing the latest developments to a ploy to force him to give the chairmanship of the new War Council to Lloyd George. He wanted to avoid resignation as much as he wanted to avoid losing Lloyd George. If he resigned there was no guarantee that the Tories would again accept his leadership or that he would even be asked to form the next ministry. In any case he could not see how a reconstructed government could survive without Lloyd George.

Asquith discussed his predicament with Montagu and Crewe after the Unionist chief left. Crewe, who arrived at 10 Downing Street while Asquith was closeted with Bonar Law, had been distracted in recent days by a heavy schedule of public engagements and had only a hazy notion of what was going on – unlike Montagu who was caught between Asquith and Lloyd George and from the outset of the crisis had tried to act as a peacemaker. Asquith felt that he could reach an accommodation with Lloyd George that would allow him to retain supreme control of war policy. He was much less certain, however, that they could agree on the composition of the new War Council. Asquith believed that the inclusion of Balfour was as essential as the ostracization of Carson.[29]

At approximately 4 p.m. Bonham Carter called Lloyd George and informed him that the Prime Minister wished to see him. On his way over, Lloyd George stopped at the War Office and, while smoking a cigar, rehearsed his arguments in the presence of Aitken who had briefed him on the latest developments.[30] When the Welshman walked across to 10 Downing Street he was as eager as Asquith for a compromise settlement.

As far as can be determined, the conversation between Asquith and Lloyd George was reasonably civil and free of rancour. What followed was a tentative agreement to set up a small War Committee, although there was still some uncertainty about its membership. Lloyd George would preside as its chairman but, at least in principle, the Prime Minister would retain ultimate direction of the war. He would receive daily reports from the chairman as well as be free to attend its meetings whenever he wished and veto any of its conclusions.[31] From the sketchy evidence available, there is nothing to suggest that any mention was made of the Civil Committee. But if one conclusion can be drawn from Asquith's subsequent discussions with Crewe on the matter, it is that he had not abandoned the two committee scheme as agreed upon at Wednesday's cabinet meeting.[32]

Asquith appeared satisfied at the end of his conference with Lloyd George. The new formula, however, left him in a much weaker position than he apparently realized. As Professor Wilson has pointed out, Asquith's authority was merely on paper, for he was unlikely to exercise his power of veto lest it bring on the collective resignation of the War Council.[33]

At 5 p.m. Asquith recalled Bonar Law and went over the terms of his understanding with Lloyd George. Bonar Law was relieved to hear that the two Liberal leaders had buried the hatchet. Asquith indicated that the Welshman was waiting in another room and suggested that he should join them. In Lloyd George's presence Asquith repeated his statement that, except for personnel, complete agreement had been reached on all matters relating to the War Council. In the end it was decided that the Prime Minister should request the resignation of all cabinet ministers in order to facilitate his task of reconstructing the government.[34]

Bonar Law went back to tell his Unionist colleagues (who had gathered at the home of F. E. Smith) the news of the compromise which he thought would end the crisis. That judgment, however, was premature. Lloyd George's determination to substitute Carson for Balfour was an insuperable obstacle. Balfour had restored stable and orderly administration at the Admiralty in the wake of the turbulent Churchill era. He was easy to work with, enjoyed the confidence of his professional officers and, given his long association with the CID, possessed a sound grasp of strategy and warfare.[35] The main criticism against him, a valid one to be sure, was that he lacked physical stamina and imagination and made decisions only after leisurely reflection.[36] But Lloyd George was disturbed more by his assets than by his liabilities. As Hankey correctly discerned, the Welshman wanted to be the virtual dictator of war strategy and knew that Balfour was 'too strong and too skillful to allow this'.[37] Asquith would have preferred Henderson in place of Carson and felt that Balfour should be included as a dependable counterweight to Lloyd George. Asquith did hint to the King that, if Balfour submitted his resignation, he would not oppose it.[38] But with or without Balfour in the picture it is almost certain that the Prime Minister would have insisted on his own nominees. He considered Lloyd George too erratic to be left unfettered. As it turned out, Asquith and Lloyd George never had a chance seriously to discuss the matter of personnel. All the same, if the compromise had hinged on that issue it is questionable whether they could have resolved their differences.

Besides the composition of the War Council, Asquith had to deal with another major problem. He had yet to confront the Liberals in the cabinet, most of whom were unaware there was a crisis brewing. Gaining their approval of the compact was uncertain in view of their antipathy to Lloyd George and their own exclusion from the main seat of power.

Although Asquith was guardedly optimistic when he wrote on the evening of 3 December that the crisis showed 'every sign of following its many predecessors to an early & unhonoured grave',[39] he did not consider his agreement with Lloyd George as final.[40] Nor did Lloyd George feel that anything definite had been settled. He made that admission to Arthur Lee, with whom he had dinner on 3 December, and in a letter to the Prime Minister the next day.[41] Earlier at the War Office (late afternoon on 3 December) Lloyd George had urged Montagu to 'persuade Asquith to put the agreement in writing that night, in order that there might be no watering down or alterations, and in order that it might not be misconstrued'.[42]

On the evening of 3 December the Asquiths dined with Montagu (Venetia was away in the country) at his home in Queen Anne's Gate. Margot was uncharacteristically subdued while the others engaged in small talk. She may have been reflecting upon the arrangement to reconstruct the government through which she feared her husband had surrendered the substance of power. While dressing for the dinner-party she had admonished her husband for the haphazard nature of his negotiations with Lloyd George.[43]

Reading and Crewe came in after dinner and the topic of conversation turned to the question on everybody's mind. Asquith felt that an accommodation with Lloyd George could be reached without sacrificing his own position as chief of the War Council.[44] Among the changes he contemplated was replacing Balfour with Runciman at the Admiralty.[45] Montagu urged Asquith to send Lloyd George the substance of the accord in writing in order to avoid any misunderstanding. Asquith promised to do so.[46] He also agreed to issue a statement to the press that he intended to reconstruct the government.

It was late at night when the Asquiths returned to 10 Downing Street. Margot was not ready to go to sleep. She loved the atmosphere of power and the thought of being deprived of it darkened her mood and charged her with nervous energy. Lashing out at her husband, she berated him again for failing to defy Lloyd George. She dwelt on that theme until the early hours of the morning.[47]

Margot was not alone in deprecating the political formula between her husband and Lloyd George. There were others who shared her sentiment, although for different reasons. A group of prominent politicians and journalists – among whom were Carson, Milner, Northcliffe and Aitken – suspected that Asquith had engineered yet another compromise which would permit him to sail on until the next crisis. Determined not to allow this to happen, they embarked on a campaign to overthrow Asquith and to elevate Lloyd George in his place.[48]

The ministerial accord began to unravel with Monday morning's headlines. 'Cock Robin' was dead pronounced the *Morning Post*. The Liberal *Manchester Guardian* reported that Asquith's options were either to accept humiliation or to resign. The most damaging blow came from *The Times*, which pilloried Asquith in a front-page article. Describing him as temperamentally unfit to manage the war, it explained with glee that he had abjectly endorsed his own supersession and that henceforth he would be Prime Minister in name only.[49]

The suggestion by some of the leading newspapers that effective power had been transferred to Lloyd George made for painful reading in 10 Downing Street. It would have been relatively easy for Asquith to shrug off most of the offensive stories in the newspapers but the one in the columns of *The Times* was intended to make the compromise unworkable. Since it was openly proclaimed that Lloyd George had held a pistol to his head, it is difficult to see how he could have introduced the necessary changes and still maintained his prestige and sense of dignity.

Asquith was bristling with anger when he laid down his copy of *The Times*.[50] The article was remarkably accurate and detailed and could only have been written by someone with good inside contacts. Asquith knew that Northcliffe had visited the War Office the previous evening and he drew the conclusion that Lloyd George had been his informant. As it happened, it was Carson who had leaked the information to the editor of *The Times*, Geoffrey Robinson.[51] Whether it was done with the connivance of Lloyd George (who presumably was Carson's source) is a question that cannot be answered with certainty. In all probability Carson acted on his own, since Lloyd George was seemingly content with the accord. What mattered, however, was that Asquith believed that Lloyd George had inspired the disclosures in *The Times* to humiliate him and to redefine the terms of their bargain. Asquith had no objections to delegating some of his executive functions but only as long as his final authority was unimpaired.

Asquith immediately wrote a curt letter to Lloyd George, reminding him of the terms of the agreement that 'we considered yesterday' and warning him that he would not implement them unless the impression was corrected that he was being relegated 'to the position of an irresponsible spectator of the War'.[52] Lloyd George had achieved his goal and had no wish to break with Asquith. He had just asked Hankey to draft a set of rules for the new War Council,[53] a sign that he was at least willing to give the new arrangement a fair trial. His reply to Asquith was conciliatory. He disclaimed any responsibility for the leader in *The Times* and accepted the Prime Minister's summary of the 'suggested arrangement', subject to the personnel of the War Council. He concluded by emphasizing his loyalty to Asquith.[54]

Lloyd George followed up his letter by requesting an interview with the Prime Minister. He waited at the War Office for Bonham Carter's phone call. It did not come. On making inquiries he was told that the Prime Minister was preoccupied and temporarily unavailable. But the Welshman persisted and a meeting was provisionally set for 6 p.m.

Before 4 December Asquith had taken only a few of his Liberal colleagues into his confidence. The announcement in the press that the government was to be reconstructed naturally came as a shock to the rest. A number of the uninformed ministers – Grey, McKenna, Harcourt and Runciman – hurried over to 10 Downing Street early on Monday morning. Their resentment at being kept in the dark paled in comparison with their hostility to the compromise which they saw would effectively eliminate their control over events. McKenna, who despised Lloyd George, was the most forceful, arguing that Asquith should stand firm and fight, otherwise he would be reduced to the humiliating position of a nominal Prime Minister.[55]

Following the interview Asquith saw several Unionist ministers. Exactly who they were is not clear. The extant sources suggest that he talked to Curzon, Lansdowne (late in the afternoon or early in the evening) and possibly Cecil.[56] They reportedly told him that their intention was not to oust him from the premiership but to help him defeat the machinations of Lloyd George. Their call for Asquith's resignation was simply to afford Lloyd George a chance to form a government which they were certain he could not do. Curzon went so far as to assure Asquith that in no circumstances would he, 'or those acting with him, take office under Lloyd George or Bonar Law'. But Curzon was playing both ends against the middle.[57] His unprincipled behaviour was designed to ensure that he remained in the government regardless of who emerged on top.

At 12.30 p.m. Asquith went to Buckingham Palace. The King expressed his absolute confidence in his ability and gave him authority to form a new ministry.[58] After a quick lunch with Margot, Asquith walked over to the House of Commons where he moved its adjournment until 7 December so that he might reconstruct the government. Bonar Law followed Asquith to his room and asked if he intended to stand by the provisional plan. Asquith replied that he was reconsidering the arrangement because Lloyd George had broken faith by intriguing with the press and because of the hostility of his colleagues, both Liberal and Unionist, to it. Their conversation was interrupted when Asquith was called to the Front Bench to answer questions. At the end of the question time Asquith headed straight to 10 Downing Street, pursued by Bonar Law and most of his Liberal ministers. Because of the waiting queue of Liberal ministers, Bonar Law remained only a few minutes with the Prime Minister. Still he left no doubt that he would leave the administration if Asquith repudiated Sunday's agreement.[59] Asquith sat silently with an inscrutable expression on his face.

By now Asquith was beginning to regret the concessions he had made to Lloyd George. It looked more and more like a bad bargain. Asquith imagined that he would be discredited in the eyes of the nation, that he would be perceived as lingering on shamelessly as nominal Prime Minister until it suited Lloyd George to turn him out altogether. Would it not be better to challenge Lloyd George and force him either to fall into line or leave the government? The encouragement that he received from Liberals and Unionists alike during the day led him to believe that his position was stronger than he had previously imagined.

After Bonar Law left, Asquith told Bonham Carter to cancel his appointment with Lloyd George.[60] Instead he summoned all his leading Liberal ministers, except Lloyd George, to a meeting at 10 Downing Street. Henderson, who was also invited to attend, arrived late and does not appear to have participated to any extent in the discussions.

Asquith asked his colleagues if they thought that acceptance of Lloyd George's proposals would be inconsistent with his constitutional responsibilities as Prime Minister. They all agreed that it would. The general view among the Liberal ministers was that, unless Lloyd George was put in his place, such crises as the present one were sure to reoccur at short intervals. They recommended that Asquith ought to call Lloyd George's bluff by resigning. In so doing he would force Bonar Law or Lloyd George to try to form a government and, when they failed, it would be proof that he was the only possible Prime Minister. Asquith expressed fears that if a Lloyd George–Carson government were formed, Labour would break away and the pacifist movement would become formidable. At the end he deferred his final decision, saying only that he would not accept terms that meant a surrender of his authority.[61]

After the meeting Hankey saw Asquith, who admitted his uncertainty about whether he should resign or call for Lloyd George's resignation. The entry that followed in Hankey's diary is worth quoting:

> He seems to think that Lloyd George and Carson have compounded with the Irish, and that if Ll.G. cannot get his way about the War Ctee., he will form an odd hotch-potch Govt. of Carsonite Unionists, Ll.G. Liberals, Nationalists, and Labour, who will be bribed by several seats in the Cabinet.[62]

Asquith had made up his mind about one thing. If he was to remain Prime Minister, the government would be reconstructed on his, and not on Lloyd George's, terms. He knew that he would be bringing the crisis to a head if he rejected Lloyd George's demands and sought no further accommodation with him. He was cautiously optimistic, however, that he could win in a showdown with the Welshman. His support among the Liberal Party was solid and he anticipated that he could count on a fair number of Unionists. But he had no sure way of knowing how the struggle would turn out in light of the probable defection of Bonar Law, who controlled the party machine if not his Unionist colleagues in the cabinet. Asquith preferred to take that risk rather than stay on merely as a shadow Prime Minister.

Before dinner on 4 December Asquith wrote to Lloyd George, rejecting the compromise of the previous day. He explained that, after full consideration, he now felt it essential that the Prime Minister should be the permanent chairman of the War Council. Furthermore he insisted that the Prime Minister alone should select its personnel. As such he was adamant about not displacing Balfour from the Admiralty and he refused to accept Carson as a member on the grounds that there were others in the cabinet with better claims.[63]

There is no justification in criticizing Asquith for veering away from a provisional transaction. The bargain had not yet been sealed and he was perfectly entitled to cancel it irrespective of his reasons. Whether he should have done so is another matter. Asquith acted the way he did apparently because he felt, on the basis of *The Times* article, that Lloyd George attached a different meaning to what he had provisionally accepted. Moreover, he seems to have formed the impression – in large measure due to the strong assurances of Liberals like McKenna – that he could retain office without conceding the direction of the war to Lloyd George.

Asquith sent off his letter to Lloyd George and then proceeded to Queen Anne's Gate to dine again with Montagu. He was in good spirits but refused to discuss the political situation, knowing full well that Montagu would be extremely upset with his latest action. Montagu naturally suspected the worst.[64]

Lloyd George received Asquith's letter the next morning. The events of the last twenty-four hours must have prepared him for its contents. He may have been indignant but not as surprised as he later professed. His first move was to contact Bonar Law. The letter resolved the ambivalence of the Unionist chief, who could no longer hope to keep both Asquith and Lloyd George working together under a new relationship. He now had to choose. Since Asquith had reneged on the tentative compromise, he felt he had no option but 'to back Lloyd George in his further action'.[65]

Definitely assured of Bonar Law's support, Lloyd George formally handed in his resignation to Asquith. His letter, evidently meant for publication at an early date, included a long preamble. In it he reproached Asquith for going back on their agreement, paraded his familiar list of grievances regarding the government's conduct of the war, and gave notice that he intended to launch a campaign to inform the people of the true state of affairs and to give them an opportunity, before it was too late, to save their country from certain disaster.[66] Lloyd George, it was clear, did not mean to leave office gracefully.

Asquith anticipated that Lloyd George would create mischief at every opportunity. What he did not expect was Balfour's unsolicited letter at midday announcing his resignation as First Lord of the Admiralty. Balfour, although confined to his sick-bed for the past few days, had managed to keep abreast of developments and was aware of Lloyd George's hostility to his administration at the Admiralty. He was leaving, he told Asquith, in order to give the new system a fair trial.[67] Asquith does not appear to have grasped the implications of Balfour's subtle signal. If he had, it is inconceivable that he would have written back to urge him to reconsider his decision.

At 12.30 p.m. Crewe called on Asquith after attending a Privy Council at Buckingham Palace. He reported that the King was hopeful that a solution could be reached without a change of Prime Minister. Asquith showed him Lloyd George's letter of resignation and asked him what he thought. Crewe replied that Lloyd George's challenge must be resisted but acknowledged that everything depended on the attitude of the Tories. If the Tories refused to participate in a reconstructed government, it would be impossible for Asquith to continue.[68]

Such was also the opinion of the Liberal ministers summoned for a meeting at 1 p.m. Since it was understood that the Tories had insisted on Asquith's resignation before a new ministry could be created, there was near unanimity that this was the only sensible course. Montagu alone dissented, urging Asquith not to resign but to ask the King to convene a conference of party leaders. His suggestion was ridiculed.[69]

When the Liberal gathering broke up, Asquith wrote to Lloyd George accepting his resignation.[70] At 3 p.m. he sent for Curzon, Chamberlain and Cecil to gain an idea of the degree of his support among the Unionists. He asked the three 'Cs', as Beaverbrook dubbed them, whether they would serve in an administration that did not include Bonar Law and Lloyd George. To his shock, they answered unequivocally that they would not. They explained that their position had been altered by Bonar Law's decision to throw in his lot with Lloyd George and Carson. They saw no prospect of any government surviving if this formidable trio went into opposition, backed, as they were certain to be, by the Tory press and party machine. What may also have influenced the three 'Cs' were rumours, erroneous at the time, that Lloyd George had secured the adherence of the Labour Party and probably a majority of Liberal MPs.

Asquith, barely able to maintain his composure, followed up with a second question. What would be their attitude to Lloyd George if he tried to form an administration? Their reply, in view of their recently expressed distrust of Lloyd George, was an even more serious blow to Asquith. Their only object, they asserted, was to get a stable administration capable of winning the war. They were under no obligation to Lloyd George but they would serve under anyone who promised to meet that qualification. They had no way of predicting the future but considered it essential that both Lloyd George and Asquith cooperate in the next administration. Cecil felt that the most patriotic thing that Asquith could do was to accept office in a Lloyd George ministry. Asquith dismissed the suggestion with contempt.[71]

There can be little doubt that the Unionists had misled Asquith, at least concerning the extent of their antagonism towards Lloyd George. It was evident that under the right circumstances their reluctance to serve under him could be overcome. In fact all along they had considered the Asquith-Lloyd George struggle as a family affair from which they should remain aloof, holding themselves free to transfer their allegiance from one Liberal to another as their interests dictated.

The axiom that politics makes strange bedfellows was seldom more evident than in the imminent rapprochement between Balfour and Lloyd George. A few minutes after 4 p.m. Asquith received a second note from Balfour. This time the shift in his allegiance was clear:

> I still think (a) that the break up of the Government by the retirement of L. G. would be a misfortune, (b) that the experiment of giving him a free hand with the day-to-day work of the War Committee, is well worth trying, & (c) that there is no use trying it except on the terms which enable him to work under the conditions which, in his own opinion, promise the best results. We cannot, I think, go on in the old way... I am therefore still of opinion that my resignation should be accepted, & that a fair trial should be given to the new War Council à la George.[72]

As Asquith paused to reflect he could see two alternatives to resignation. The first was to accept the principles of Lloyd George's scheme. To do so would have carried the process of humiliation beyond tolerable limits. Asquith not only would have have been robbed of the direction of the war but he also would have had to put up with Carson, an implacable adversary. The second was to ask the King to dissolve parliament. But a wartime general election would have divided the nation and in all likelihood ended in a Liberal debacle.

Asquith had accepted the inevitable before he again met his Liberal colleagues at 5 p.m. He gave them a summary of his encounter with the three 'Cs' and read his correspondence with Balfour. After reviewing his options he indicated that he had decided to resign, even though he found it odious to capitulate to a rebellious minister. Everyone agreed that he could not carry on without Lloyd George and the Unionists 'and ought not to give the appearance of wishing to do so'.[73]

At the conclusion of the meeting Curzon appeared at 10 Downing Street with a formal Unionist resolution signed by Bonar Law. The Unionists' collectively called for Asquith's immediate resignation, adding that if he failed to do so he was to accept theirs.[74] Asquith informed Curzon that the decision had already been taken. As a car waited outside the door to take him to Buckingham Palace, Derby made a last ditch effort to persuade him to reach an accommodation with Lloyd George. Asquith declined to discuss the matter and simply said that his mind was already made up.[75] At 7 p.m. he submitted his resignation to the King.[76]

It has been suggested by Beaverbrook and others that Asquith left office

with the supreme confidence that he would be recalled once it was shown
that no one else could form a government. There is tantalizing first-hand
testimony to buttress that view. J. H. Thomas, a Labour MP, recalled a
conversation with Asquith at the time of his resignation:

> What ... influenced him was the advice of a number of close friends that it was
> impossible for Lloyd George to form a Cabinet. He himself told me this, and I, wanting
> him to continue, pointed out that this advice was sheer madness. In fact, I remember
> saying (and I made a note of it at the time): 'Do remember, Asquith, that anybody
> can form a cabinet with the patronage at their disposal that exists in this country.'
> But he was resolved, believing that the King would send for him before the day was
> out.[77]

There is yet another witness. Cynthia Asquith, who was married to
Asquith's second son, Herbert, was present at dinner on 5 December. She
made the following entry in her diary:

> Of course, the whole evening was spent in conjecture and discussion – most interesting.
> I tried to absorb as much as I could, but I am not quick about politics. I gathered that,
> before dinner, Mr Asquith had said he thought there was quite a chance of Lloyd
> George failing to form a Government at all. The Tories – in urging him to resign – had
> predicted such a failure. In any case, most people seemed to think that any Government
> he could succeed in forming would only be very short-lived.[78]

There is no reason to doubt these sources. All the same it is difficult to
accept the sweeping conclusion that Asquith expected his departure from
office to be only temporary. The above authors were probably recording
the words of a defeated man at the time engaged in wishful-thinking rather
than reflecting on what he knew to be the true state of affairs. Asquith
resigned, not as a tactical manoeuvre, but because he no longer had a base
on which to maintain a government.

There were many Liberals who doubted that Lloyd George would be
able to form a government, or having formed one make it last. This was not
the opinion of well-informed party members – like Montagu, Reading,
Samuel, Pease – or Asquith. On 6 December (presumably on the very day
that the ex-Prime Minister told J. H. Thomas that his would-be successors
would fail to form a government and that he would soon be recalled),
Asquith wrote to Sylvia Henley and, as usual, bared his innermost
thoughts. He practically conceded that the opposition had won:

> It is impossible yet to say what is likely to happen [but] the probabilities point to a
> junction of the Unionists plus Carson with Ll.G. I confess to feeling a certain sense of
> relief. Nothing can be conceived more hellish than the experience I have gone through
> during the last month. Almost for the first time I have felt that I was growing old.[79]

Historians have observed that, as the crisis unfolded in the first days of December, Asquith made a number of tactical errors. He may have but it is easy to be wise after the event. My own feeling is that the outcome would not have been affected, regardless of what he did. It was Asquith's perceived inadequacies that ended his premiership. Simply put, he no longer possessed the requisite confidence of the nation and parliament to beat back a major challenge to his leadership.

Asquith's resignation left the way opened for either Bonar Law or Lloyd George. The two contenders reached a formula that practically guaranteed Lloyd George the premiership. Bonar Law would try to form a government if he could persuade Asquith to serve in a subordinate office. If not, Lloyd George would assume the task.[80]

As leader of the single largest political party, Bonar Law was invited to form the next administration. On leaving Buckingham Palace he headed straight for 10 Downing Street and asked Asquith if he would join a ministry headed by a neutral Prime Minister, meaning either himself or Balfour. His inclusion of Balfour's name is puzzling in view of his earlier arrangement with Lloyd George. It proved to be irrelevant in any case. Asquith had no more interest in serving in a Balfour government than in a Bonar Law government.[81]

The next day, 6 December, the King arranged a conference of political leaders to see if a national government could be constructed. It took place at Buckingham Palace at 3 p.m. and was attended by Asquith, Balfour, Lloyd George, Bonar Law and Henderson. There was a consensus among the central figures that things had now gone too far to contemplate a return to the Sunday arrangement. Henderson doubted that Labour would support any government that did not include Asquith. Balfour pleaded with Asquith to serve under Bonar Law on patriotic grounds in order to maintain an appearance of national unity. Lloyd George thought that Asquith should form a government from among his own supporters. Asquith spoke at length, his words sometimes tinged with bitterness, as he alluded to the virulent attacks made against him by the press and refuted charges that he had mismanaged the war. He gave no encouragement to the proposal that he accept a position in a Bonar Law ministry but reserved a final decision pending consultation with his supporters.[82]

After returning to 10 Downing Street Asquith hurriedly summoned Henderson and all the ex-Liberal ministers, save Lloyd George, to a late afternoon meeting. A. C. Murray, a Liberal MP and youngest brother of Lord Murray of Elibank, was with Eric Drummond (Grey's Secretary) when several key Liberals stopped at the Foreign Office on their way over. He recorded in his diary:

> He [Asquith] has not made up his mind whether he will join. The Chief Whip, John Gulland, is very averse to this course, saying that the Liberal Party would not stand it, & that it would be humiliating. While I was in Eric D.'s room McKenna came in to see Grey. It appears that McKenna is afraid that Asquith is going to agree to the... proposition, & wishes Grey to dissuade Asquith from it. Grey himself was in two moods about it, but on the whole against Asquith joining the new Gov't.[83]

The Liberal assemblage first dealt with the suggestion advanced by Lloyd George at the conference. It was unanimously agreed that, without Lloyd George and Bonar Law, Asquith would have no chance of constituting a viable government. The next subject of discussion centred on whether Asquith should join an administration in a subordinate capacity. Henderson and Montagu felt that Asquith's presence would serve as a unifying force. All the others either urged him to stay out, or by their silence showed they endorsed this view. Asquith entirely concurred with the majority's position.[84]

Crewe's account maintains that Asquith's decision was in no way based on 'personal dignity or *amour propre*'. This statement goes perhaps too far. Although Asquith was neither vindictive nor insecure, it is difficult to believe that his pride was not hurt by what had happened. It must be remembered that he was invited to occupy a secondary post in a ministry controlled by the very two men who had collaborated to drive him out of office while they were still members of his administration. But in all likelihood Asquith was influenced by more compelling reasons.

In the first place the new government would be in the hands of his critics, who were certain to exclude him from the policy-making process. He foresaw friction developing between himself and Lloyd George, resulting in an even more damaging political crisis. Secondly, Asquith felt that by playing a passive and unproductive part in the succeeding administration his authority with both his colleagues and the public would disappear. Thirdly, Asquith perceived that if he entered the new government, even as a lesser official, the press attacks would continue and he would be held accountable for every failure. This would further diminish his standing in the country and in parliament. The Liberal gathering concluded that it would be preferable in the national interest if Asquith created a 'sober and responsible opposition' and, as last resort, offered an alternative administration.[85]

At 6 p.m. Asquith forwarded his reply to Bonar Law.[86] Within the hour the Tory leader appeared at Buckingham Palace and declined the royal commission. Thereupon the King sent for Lloyd George and invited him to form a government. The Welshman agreed to try. Much as he wanted to be Prime Minister, he was not certain that he could command the necessary votes in parliament.[87]

Of vital concern to Lloyd George was the attitude of Liberal backbenchers, since it was clear that he could not, any more than Bonar Law, expect the support of ex-Liberal ministers. His ally Dr Christopher Addison, the Liberal MP for Bedford and his former right-hand man at the Ministry of Munitions, undertook a discreet canvassing of party members to determine how many would back him as Premier. Addison reported on the evening of 6 December that there were 49 for certain and another 126 could be counted on as soon as his position was secure.[88] No less important to Lloyd George was the cooperation of Labour whose leader, Arthur Henderson, had publicly endorsed Asquith a few days before. On 7 December he enlisted the support of Henderson and the Labour Party by vague and attractive-sounding promises.[89]

Similarly the Welshman bought off the Conservative leaders known to be sympathetic to Asquith.[90] One of his first moves on receiving the King's commission was to offer the Foreign Secretaryship to Balfour, who accepted without a moment's hesitation. Balfour's instinct for self-preservation overrode any sentiments of loyalty to Asquith. 'He passed from one Cabinet to another', Churchill commented cynically, 'from the Prime Minister who was his champion to the Prime Minister, who had been his most severe critic, like a powerful, graceful cat walking delicately and unsoiled across a rather muddy street.'[91] Balfour's defection was a major coup for Lloyd George. As a former Prime Minister and the leader of the Conservative Party, his membership in the new regime lent it an aura of respectability and authority. It also went a long way towards influencing the views of other Unionists.[92]

Asquith was understandably shaken by the news. Should he have divined Balfour's attitude earlier as some writers have suggested? Balfour's letters on the day before, it must be remembered, merely stated that Lloyd George should be given a chance to run the war. There was no hint, or reason to expect, that he would be prepared to accept a post from the man who had been an unrelenting critic of his administration at the Admiralty.

Within the span of twenty-four hours Lloyd George succeeded in securing a comfortable majority and forming a government. It was a remarkable feat but it was not as if he had been unprepared for the task. During the past two years he had not only railed against the system of war direction but also exchanged views and given thought to what he would do if he were in Asquith's place. Before Asquith actually resigned both he and Bonar Law had discussed a possible roster of cabinet appointments.[93] That said, it does not necessarily follow that the Welshman set out to overthrow Asquith. For one thing he feared that Asquith's sway over parliament was still relatively unimpaired. For another he lacked the finesse to orchestrate a complex plot against his chief. Clearly Lloyd George's intention initially was to gain control of strategy as chairman of a small War Council. Given his personal craving for power, there was of course no guarantee that he would not have made further demands until he had reached the end of the road to the premiership. But it is reasonably safe to say that when he attained his lifelong ambition it was at a time and in a manner which he had not anticipated.

Before leaving 10 Downing Street, Asquith attended a meeting of Liberals of both Houses at the Reform Club. He spoke about the events that led to his downfall and defended his actions in a typically statesmanlike and unprovocative manner. He concluded by advising his party members to support the new government 'in words that appealed to the patriotic instinct of all present'. After sustained and thunderous applause a motion was unanimously passed thanking him for his services to the nation and expressing unbounded confidence in his leadership.[94] To his followers, he would always be fondly remembered as 'the last of the Romans', the symbol of discarded virtues.

Asquith was sixty-four years old when he fell from power. He had been Prime Minister for eight years and 241 days – the longest unbroken term between the Earl of Liverpool and Margaret Thatcher. Although he remained head of the Liberal Party until 1926, he never again returned to office.

Chapter 13

Asquith as War Leader

Asquith's professional reputation, already under heavy fire during the last stages of his premiership, continued to suffer in the flood of post-war literature. Asquith made no effort to answer his detractors, not even in his so-called memoirs,[1] nor would he authorize one word to be written on his behalf. The closest he came to justifying his war administration was during his maiden speech as Leader of the Opposition in the House of Commons on 19 December 1916. It was a weak and half-hearted statement, given his abhorrence of any form of self-advertisement.

In his remarks, Asquith offered no apologies for the manner in which he and his government had conducted the war. Although conceding that errors of judgment had probably been committed, he emphatically denied that his administration had managed the war with a want of energy, foresight and purpose. On the contrary, he claimed, he and his colleagues had pursued aggressive policies with regard to the army, navy and economy, the three areas most vital to winning the war. Asquith confined himself to general remarks, saying that the full story could not yet be told. But it is clear that he never intended to pursue the theme again in public. As he told his audience on 19 December, he was 'quite content, when all the facts come to be disclosed, to leave my administration and the part which I played in it to the judgment of history'.[2]

History has dealt too harshly with Asquith as a war-time leader. His manifest failings have received more than their fair share of attention while his achievements have been largely ignored or dismissed as irrelevant. It is commonplace to regard Asquith as a brilliant parliamentarian, a man of honour and dignity but lacking in creative vision and temperamentally unsuited to the exigencies of war leadership. True he had none of the dynamism and resourcefulness of the elder Pitt. In cabinet he continued the peace-time practice of leisurely discussion, frequently allowing matters requiring rapid decision to drag on.

Asquith acted more as a conciliator than as a leader after the coalition came into existence. The war by cabinet government, which on the whole had worked well enough under Liberal rule, proved ineffective in a ministry composed of headstrong men divided by suspicion, conflicting ambition and party loyalty. The removal of Kitchener from the centre of power left the government without a coherent strategy. Ministers with little or no technical knowledge of war vied with one another in trying to fill the vacuum. Half a dozen dominant personalities had to be consulted on every great issue, which meant that decisions were reached only after prolonged and heated discussion. Far too often the cabinet laboured through unsatisfactory compromises. The chaotic ministerial direction of the war led to faulty policies, not the least of which resulted in two costly and useless side-shows. As the coalition was buffeted by one crisis after another, only the absence of a credible alternative allowed it to survive for eighteen months.

Asquith, who lacked the authority he had enjoyed in the previous administration, was unable successfully to manage such powerful and quarrelsome colleagues. Given the circumstances it would have been beyond the ability of most men to do so. All the same he devoted too much time and energy in trying to patch up rifts. He would have been well-advised to concern himself more with winning the war than devising ways to keep his critics at bay and to paper over the cracks.

Glaring as Asquith's shortcomings may have been, it would be wrong to conclude that his administration of the war was a failure. The record shows a list of significant accomplishments, particularly when his party was in sole control of the government. Immediately before and during the opening days of the conflict he was indispensable as Prime Minister. In August he brought the country into the war without civil disturbance or political schism, a feat which in the beginning had seemed impossible. His high statesmanship and imperturbability inspired the needed confidence in a people feeling the first twinges of uncertainty about the war's outcome. His controversial appointment of Kitchener as Secretary for War was a master-stroke.

By any standard, the Asquith government handled the initial phase of the war with remarkable skill. Government measures and guarantees to support financial institutions prevented panic and allowed business to carry on without disruption in war-time. At its station during the critical moment, the navy proceeded to drive the enemy's merchant marine from the high seas and to enforce a strict blockade of Germany and its allies. The

British Expeditionary Force was safely transported across the Channel and took its assigned place on the left of the French Front. Superbly trained and equipped, it played a key role in halting the German juggernaut in September 1914. Under Kitchener a programme was launched to expand both the army and the output of munitions vastly. Had the war ended in 1915, Asquith would probably have been hailed as the saviour of civilization.

The Asquith government, like those of the other belligerent nations, was utterly unprepared for the devastating struggle that followed. All the governments were confronted with major and unprecedented problems spawned by the grim war of attrition. In each country economic and social life had to be changed to keep the war machine from grinding to a halt. Victory would depend as much on material resources and productive power as on the men in the fighting line.

In the beginning, Asquith had expected to fulfil his nation's commitment to its allies without departing from the cherished policy of 'business as usual'. He had no consistent philosophy or overall blueprint to mobilize manpower and industries for total war. After the stalemate set in, he introduced controls slowly and in an *ad hoc* fashion. Throughout both his administrations, the means always lagged behind the ends.

Asquith was cautious about waging all-out war because he wished to preserve, as much as possible, the pre-war social order and its values. His concern was understandable enough but waiting for events to change the nation's mood risked compromising a military victory. There were instances, such as conscription, where he actually fell behind public and political opinion. In most cases, however, he failed to exert sufficient leadership to reconcile national sentiment to war-time necessities.

Asquith tried to find a balance between doing just enough to win the war and adopting measures so extreme that they would destroy the fragile national consensus on which all future social and political progress depended. He had pinned his hopes on a decisive military victory, but the army proved unable to extricate him from his predicament. After the Somme, which was judged a costly failure, he ran out of time.

Yet Asquith, even in the face of his self-imposed limitations, continued to make vital contributions to the war effort. His government carried through essential measures of national organization. It exerted increasing control over vital industries and met rising industrial production needs by working out arrangements with unions that provided for compulsory arbitration and for the dilution of skilled labour. The transition from voluntary recruiting to conscription was accomplished without disrupting the political unity of the nation. In other areas Asquith strengthened the

Entente with France and, to a lesser extent, with Russia. Britain's wealth was used to finance the Allied cause. Finally, it was Asquith who decreed that the Western Front would be the pre-eminent theatre of combat for Britain's growing army.

As the conflict wore on, Asquith's authority weakened. The bloody repulse at the Somme coming on the heels of a series of political mistakes on his part – his handling of the conscription crisis, his failure to push through the Irish deal, and his decision to set up commissions to enquire into the Dardanelles and Mesopotamian campaigns – had badly tarnished his reputation. With no apparent end to the war in sight, the growing anxiety about the human and material costs, and even about the capacity of the nation to survive, inevitably led to pressures for a change in the leadership of the government. At the same time Asquith was showing the strains of eight and a half stormy years as Prime Minister, more than two of them during the war. The excruciating apprehension he felt for his sons at the Front, climaxed by the blow of the death of his eldest son, had also taken its toll. He was weary and aging rapidly: the periodic bronchial sicknesses, from which he began to suffer in late 1915, were symptomatic of the deterioration of his general health. He had given as much as he could and the time had come for him to make way for someone who could instill a new spirit in the nation.

During the the twenty-eight months that Asquith managed the war, he faced problems of an unprecedented nature and of much greater difficulty than those of his successor. To make matters worse he had to deal with his political opponents throughout much of that period, to say nothing of the blatant disloyalty of Lloyd George, who undermined him whenever it suited his purpose. Nevertheless, he resolved the big questions of munitions supply and manpower and established the means for the expansion of production. All the strategic elements that would produce victory, save for the convoy system, were in place when he passed the mantle of leadership to Lloyd George. His achievements are sufficiently impressive to earn him a place as one of the outstanding figures of the Great War.

Notes

Notes to Chapter 1

1 Unless otherwise indicated, the material for this section was culled from J. A. Spender and Cyril Asquith, *Life of Herbert Henry Asquith, Lord Oxford and Asquith* (London, 1932), i; Roy Jenkins, *Asquith* (London, 1978); Stephen Koss, *Asquith* (London, 1976).

2 Samuel R. Williamson, *The Politics of Grand Strategy: Britain and France Prepare for War, 1904–1914* (Cambridge, MA, 1969) remains the best detailed account of the informal contacts between French and British staff officers. Also useful is John Gooch, *The Plans of War: The General Staff and British Military Strategy, c. 1900–1916* (New York, 1974); Keith Robbins, *Sir Edward Grey* (London, 1971); K. A. Hamilton, *Bertie of Thame* (Woodbridge, 1990); and his two articles 'Great Britain and France, 1905–1911' and 'Great Britain and France, 1911–1914', in F. H. Hinsley, ed., *British Foreign Policy under Sir Edward Grey* (London, 1977).

3 John W. Coogan and Peter F. Coogan, 'The British Cabinet and the Anglo-French Staff Talks, 1905–1914: Who Knew What and When Did He Know It?', *Journal of British Studies*, 24 (1985), pp. 117–18.

4 On this issue see Trevor Wilson, 'Britain's "Moral Commitment" to France in August 1914', *History*, 64 (1979), pp. 380–90.

5 Coogan and Coogan, 'The British Cabinet and the Anglo-French Staff Talks', p. 118.

6 A. J. A. Morris, *Radicalism against War, 1906–1914* (Totowa, NY, 1972), pp. 295–99; H. S. Weinroth, 'The British Radicals and the Balance of Power, 1902–1914', *Historical Journal*, 13 (1970), pp. 676–77.

7 David French, *British Economic and Strategic Planning, 1905–1915* (London, 1982), passim.

8 Franklyn A. Johnson, *Defence by Committee* (London, 1960), ch. 2; John P. Mackintosh, 'The Role of the Committee of Imperial Defence before 1914', *English Historical Review*, 77 (1962), pp. 490–92; John Ehrman, *Cabinet Government and War, 1890–1940* (London, 1958), passim; Lord Hankey, *The Supreme Command, 1914–1918* (London, 1961), i, ch. 5; G. R. Searle, *The Quest for National Efficiency* (Berkeley and Los Angeles, 1971), pp. 216–35.

9 The invasion inquiries are described in Gooch, *The Plans of War*, pp. 284–85, 293–95.

10 The best account of Haldane's army reforms is Edward M. Spiers, *Haldane: An Army Reformer* (Edinburgh, 1980).

11 The reforms in the Royal Navy during the Fisher and Churchill eras are impressively chronicled in Marder, *From the Dreadnought to Scapa Flow* (London, 1961), i. Jon T. Sumida, *In Defence of Naval Supremacy: Finance, Technology and British Naval Policy, 1889–1914* (Boston, 1989), is also useful.

12 The development of air power in Britain is carefully examined in A. M. Gollin, *No*

Longer an Island: Britain and the Wright Brothers, 1902–1909 (Stanford, CA, 1984) and the sequel, *The Impact of Air Power on the British People and their Government, 1909–1914* (Stanford, CA, 1989).

13 On imperial defence see Hankey, *The Supreme Command*, i, ch. 13; Gooch, *The Plans of War*, ch. 5; H. H. Asquith, *The Genesis of the War* (London, 1923), chs 16–17; Donald C. Gordon, *The Dominion Partnership in Imperial Defense, 1870–1914* (Baltimore, MD, 1965), passim; Richard A. Preston, *Canada and 'Imperial Defense'* (Durham, NC, 1967), chs 12–14.

14 Sheila Sokolov Grant, 'The Origins of the War Book', *Journal of the Royal United Service Institute*, 117 (1972), pp. 65–69; Hankey, *The Supreme Command*, i, ch. 12.

15 French, *British Economic and Strategic Planning*, ch. 4; Edwin A. Pratt, *British Railways and the Great War* (London, 1921), i, chs 5–6;

16 On pre-war Liberal policy, see especially K. M. Wilson, *The Policy of the Entente: Essays on the Determinants of British Foreign Policy, 1904–1914* (Cambridge, 1985), chs 2–3.

17 The story of the conflict, with its deeper causes and tragic consequences, is told perceptively and poignantly in George Dangerfield, *The Damnable Question: A Study in Anglo-Irish Relations* (Boston, 1976); See also Sheila Lawlor, *Britain and Ireland, 1914–1923* (Totowa, NJ, 1983); and Patricia Jalland, *The Liberals and Ireland* (Brighton, 1980).

18 On the Curragh Incident see A. P. Ryan, *Mutiny at the Curragh* (London, 1956); Sir James Fergusson, *The Curragh Incident* (London, 1964); Elizabeth Muenger, 'The British Army in Ireland, 1886–1914' (unpublished Ph.D. thesis, University of Michigan, 1981), ch. 7; Ian F. W. Beckett, ed., *The Army and the Curragh Incident, 1914* (London, 1986); John Gooch, 'The War Office and the Curragh Incident', *Bulletin of the Institute of Historical Research*, 46 (1973), pp. 202–7.

19 Robert Blake, *The Unknown Prime Minister: The Life and Times of Andrew Bonar Law, 1858–1923* (London, 1955), chs 12–13; H. Montgomery Hyde, *Carson* (London, 1953), pp. 370–72; Denis Gwynn, *The Life of John Redmond* (London, 1932), pp. 336–42. Asquith to Venetia Stanley, 22 and 24 July 1915, in Michael and Eleanor Brock, ed., *H. H. Asquith: Letters to Venetia Stanley* (Oxford, 1982), pp. 109, 122. Henceforth referred to as Brocks, ed., HHA.

Notes to Chapter 2

1 Asquith to Venetia Stanley, 30 June 1914, in Brocks, ed., HHA p. 93.
2 Asquith to Venetia Stanley, 24 July 1914, in Brocks ed., HHA, pp. 122–23.
3 For Grey's views and policy during this period see Keith Robbins, *Sir Edward Grey*, ch. 14; Michael Ekstein and Zara Steiner, 'The Sarajevo Crisis', in Hinsley, ed., *British Foreign Policy*; Zara Steiner, *Britain and the Origins of the First World War* (New York, 1977); Michael Ekstein, 'Some Notes on Sir Edward Grey's Policy in July 1914', *Historical Journal*, 15 (1972), pp. 321–24; idem, 'Sir Edward Grey and Imperial Germany in 1914', *Journal of Contemporary History*, 6 (1971), pp. 121–31; notes of Professor Temperley's talk with Grey (1929), Spender papers, Add. 53686; Arthur C. Murray, *Master and Brother* (London, 1945), pp. 116–20; G. P. Gooch and Harold Temperley, ed., *British Documents on the Origins of the War, 1898–1914* (London, 1926), vol. xi. Henceforth referred to as BD.
4 Asquith to Venetia Stanley, 24 July 1914, in Brocks, ed., HHA, pp. 122–23.
5 Asquith to King George V, 25 July 1914, Asquith papers, vol. 7.
6 Asquith to Venetia Stanley, 26 July 1914, in Brocks, ed., HHA, pp. 125–26.
7 Ibid., p. 126. Asquith spoke in similar terms to others. See Robert Gathorne-Hardy, ed., *The Memoirs of Lady Ottoline Morrell, 1873–1915* (New York, 1964), p. 256.
8 Dangerfield, *The Damnable Question*, pp. 119–21.
9 Robert Blake, *The Unknown Prime Minister*, p. 217.
10 Given the rapid march of events during these fateful days, it may be important to note that the cabinet met after 4 p.m., not in the morning as stated by Martin Gilbert in *Winston S. Churchill: The Challenge of War, 1914–1916* (Boston, 1971), iii, p. 7.
11 Asquith to King George V, 28 July 1914, Asquith papers, vol. 7; Almeric Fitzroy, 'Memories' (unpublished), 28 July 1914, Fitzroy papers, Add. 48377; Burns diary, 27 July 1914, Burns papers, Add. 46308; Gilbert, *Churchill*, iii, pp. 7–8; Trevor Wilson, ed., *The Political Diaries of C. P. Scott, 1911–1928* (Ithaca, NY, 1970), pp. 91–92.
12 BD, xi, no. 185.
13 Winston S. Churchill, *Great Contemporaries* (Freeport, NY, 1971), p. 123.
14 Hankey, *The Supreme Command*, i, p. 154.
15 Asquith to Ventia Stanley, 29 July 1914 in Brocks, ed., HHA, p. 132; Haldane to his mother, 29 July 1914, Haldane papers, MS 59991.
16 Pease diary, 29 July 1914, Gainford papers.
17 Pease, 'War Reminiscences' (unpublished), pp. 2–5, Gainford papers, vol. 42; Pease diary, 29 July 1914, ibid; Asquith to King George V, 30 July 1914, Asquith papers, vol. 7.
18 Pease, 'War Reminiscences', pp. 2–5, Gainford papers, vol. 42.
19 Asquith to Venetia Stanley, 29 July 1914, in Brocks, ed., HHA, p. 133.
20 Pease, 'War Reminiscences', p. 4, Gainford papers, vol. 42; See also Samuels to his wife, 29 July 1914, Samuel papers, A/157; McKenna to Spender, 8 May 1929, Spender papers, Add. 46386.
21 Pease diary, 29 July 1914, Gainford papers; Asquith to King George V, 30 July 1914, Asquith papers, vol. 7.
22 Hankey, *The Supreme Command*, i, pp. 155–57.
23 Asquith to Venetia Stanley, 29 July 1914 in Brocks, ed., HHA, p. 133.
24 BD, xi, no. 293.
25 Viscount Grey of Fallodon, *Twenty-Five Years* (New York, 1925), i, pp. 317–19.
26 Pease diary, 31 July 1914, Gainford papers; Asquith to Venetia Stanley, 31 July 1914, in Brocks, ed., HHA, p. 138.

27 Asquith to Venetia Stanley, 31 July 1914 in Brocks, ed., HHA, p. 138.

28 G. K. A. Bell, *Randall Davidson: Archbishop of Canterbury* (London, 1935), ii, pp. 733–35.

29 Asquith to Venetia Stanley, 1 August 1914, in Brocks ed., HHA, pp. 139–40.

30 Paul G. Halpern, *The Mediterranean Naval Situation, 1908–1914* (Cambridge, MA, 1971), ch. 4.

31 Asquith to Venetia Stanley, 2 August 1914, in Brocks, ed., HHA, p.146.

32 Asquith to Venetia Stanley, 1 August 1914, ibid., p. 140.

33 BD, xi, no. 426; King George diary, 1 August 1914, Royal Archives; Charles Trevelyan, 'Personal Account of Beginning of the War, 1914', p. 1, Trevelyan papers, CPT 59. Trevelyan mentions an encounter with Runciman (which he inadvertently misdates) who informed him of the decision against sending the BEF.

34 Asquith to Venetia Stanley, 1 August 1914, in Brocks ed., HHA, p. 140; Burns diary, 1 August 1914, Burns papers, Add. 46336.

35 Winston S. Churchill, *The World Crisis* (New York, 1951), i, p. 231.

36 Asquith to Venetia Stanley, 2 August 1914, in Brocks, ed., HHA, p. 146.

37 Bonar Law and Lansdowne to Asquith, 2 August 1914, Bonar Law papers, 37/4/1.

38 Austen Chamberlain, 'Diary on England's Intervention, August 1914', Chamberlain papers, AC 14/2/2.

39 Grey, *Twenty-Five Years*, ii, pp. 10–11; Lucy Masterman, *C. F. G. Masterman* (London, 1968), p. 265; Runciman, 'Cabinet-Sunday, 2 August 1914', Runciman papers, WR 135.

40 Asquith to St Loe Strachey, 11 August 1918, Strachey papers, box 11, fol. 6.

41 See for example Blake, *The Unknown Prime Minister*, p. 223; Cameron Hazlehurst, *Politicians at War, July 1914 to May 1915* (New York, 1971), pp. 41ff; and David Lammers, 'Arno Mayer and the British Decision for War, 1914', *Journal of British Studies*, 1 (1973), pp. 155–62. K. M. Wilson, 'The British Cabinet's Decision for War, 2 August 1914', *British Journal of International Studies*, 1, (1975), pp. 148–59, takes a different position, arguing that the Tory memo did in fact determine some ministerial decisions.

42 Pease diary, 2 August 1914, Gainford papers; Runciman, 'Cabinet-Sunday, 2 August 1914', Runciman papers, WR 135; John Viscount Morley, *Memorandum on Resignation, August 1914* (London, 1928), p. 11. Morley's memory betrayed him on points of details, as a result of which his account must be approached with caution.

43 Asquith to Venetia Stanley, 2 August 1914, in Brocks, ed., HHA, p. 46; Lord Beaverbrook, *Politicians and the War, 1914–1916* (London, 1960), pp. 19–20; Hazlehurst, *Politicians at War*, ch. 5. There is moreover a note (A/45), written by Samuel and found among his papers, listing the members of the three groups. It is on the whole consistent with other sources.

44 Asquith to Venetia Stanley, 2 August 1914, in Brocks, ed., HHA, p. 146.

45 Samuel to his wife, 2 August 1914, Samuel papers, A/157; Pease diary, 2 August 1914, Gainford papers; Morley, *Memorandum on Resignation,* p. 12.

46 BD, xi, no. 531.

47 Pease, 'War Reminiscences', p. 9, Gainford papers, vol. 42; Pease diary, 2 August 1914, Gainford papers.

48 Asquith to Bonar Law, 2 August 1914, Bonar Law papers, 34/3/3.

49 Asquith to Venetia Stanley, 2 August 1914, in Brocks, ed., HHA, p. 146.

50 Wilson, ed., *Political Diaries*, pp. 96–97.

51 Samuel to his wife, 2 August 1914, Samuel papers, A/157.

52 Viscount Herbert Samuel, *Memoirs* (London, 1945), p. 104.

53 Crewe to King George V, 2 August 1914, Asquith papers, vol. 7; Pease diary, 2 August 1914, Gainford papers; Samuel to his wife, 2 August, 1914, Samuel papers, A/157; Morley, *Memorandum on Resignation*, p. 21.

54 R. B. Haldane, 'Memorandum of Events between 1906–1915', Haldane papers, MS 5919.

55 Maj.-Gen. Sir Frederick Maurice, *Haldane* (Westport, CT, 1970), i, pp. 354–55.

56 BD, xi, no. 514.

57 Chamberlain, 'Diary on England's Intervention, August 1914', Chamberlain papers, AC 14/2/2.

58 Pease diary, 3 August 1914, Gainford papers; Asquith to King George V, 3 August 1914, Asquith papers, vol. 7; Morley, *Memorandum on Resignation*, pp. 24–25; Edward David, ed., *Inside Asquith's Cabinet: From the Diaries of Charles Hobhouse* (New York, 1977), p. 180.

59 Pease to his wife, 3 August 1914, in 'War Reminiscences', p. 21, Gainford papers, vol. 42; Geoffrey Robinson, 'Note of a Discussion with Morley', 18 January, 1915, Dawson papers, vol. 64. The editor of *The Times* later changed his surname to Dawson.

60 Churchill, *The World Crisis*, i, p. 234.

61 Williamson, *The Politics of Grand Strategy*, p. 357; Beaverbrook, *Politicians and the War*, pp. 22–24; John Grigg, *Lloyd George: From Peace to War, 1912–1916* (London, 1985), pp. 142–48; Lord Riddell, *War Diary, 1914–1918* (London, 1937), pp. 4–6. See also Bentley B. Gilbert, 'Pacifist to Interventionist: David Lloyd George in 1911 and 1914. Was Belgium an Issue?', *Historical Journal*, 28 (1985), pp. 863–85. Gilbert argues that at this time Lloyd George, while publicly proclaiming pacific principles, worked behind the scenes for compromises that would keep the cabinet intact. My examination of the sources leads me to a different conclusion, namely that Lloyd George's main concern was to devise a formula that would keep him in the ministry without seeming to betray the cause he symbolized.

62 Robbins, *Sir Edward Grey*, pp. 296–97; Williamson, *The Politics of Grand Strategy*, pp. 357–60. For the full text of the speech see Grey, *Twenty-Five Years*, ii, pp. 308–26.

63 Asquith to Venetia Stanley, 3 August 1914, in Brocks, ed., HHA, p. 148.

64 Grey received the telegram after his speech, whereupon he read it to the House.

65 Spender and Asquith, *Life of Herbert Henry Asquith*, ii, p. 92.

66 Pease diary, 3 August 1914, Gainford papers.

67 Ibid.; Pease, 'War Reminiscences', p. 12, Gainford papers, vol. 42; Samuel to his wife, 3 August 1914, Samuel papers, A/157.

68 Crewe to King George V, 4 August 1914, Asquith papers, vol. 7; Asquith to Simon, 3 August 1914, Simon papers, box 2; Simon to Asquith, 4 August 1914, ibid; Morley, *Memorandum on Resignation*, pp. 27–31; Asquith to Stamfordham, 4 August 1914, Royal Archives, GV K731/1; Asquith to Venetia Stanley, 4 August 1914, in Brocks, ed., HHA, p. 150; Asquith, *Genesis of the War*, pp. 218–21.

69 Pease to his wife, 4 August 1914, in 'War Reminiscences', p. 22, Gainford papers, vol. 42; Asquith to Venetia Stanley, 4 August 1914, in Brocks, ed., HHA, p. 150; BD, xi, nos 573 and 594. It is unclear whether the first telegram was sent before or after the cabinet meeting.

70 Lady Violet Bonham Carter, *Winston Churchill: An Intimate Portrait* (New York, 1965), p. 255.

71 Jenkins, *Asquith*, p. 330.

72 David Lloyd George, *War Memoirs* (London, 1938), i, pp. 45–48; A. J. P. Taylor, ed., *Lloyd George: A Diary by Frances Stevenson* (New York, 1971), p. 37; Mark Bonham Carter, ed., *The Autobiography of Margot Asquith* (London, 1962), p. 294.

Notes to Chapter 3

1 *Nation*, 30 November 1914.
2 Spender and Asquith, *Life of Herbert Henry Asquith*, i, p. 213.
3 Jenkins, *Asquith*, p. 95; Daphne Bennett, *Margot* (London, 1984), pp. 129–30.
4 A. G. Gardner, 'Mr Asquith', *Spectator*, 149 (1932), p. 527; H. N. Brailsford, 'The Last of the English Liberals', *Foreign Affairs*, 11 (1932–33), p. 635; Don M. Creiger, 'The Last English Whig: Herbert Henry, Lord Oxford and Asquith', *Duquesne Review*, 11 (1966), p. 2.
5 Spender and Asquith, *Life of Herbert Henry Asquith*, i, pp. 208–10; Herbert Asquith, *Moments of Memory* (New York, 1938), p. 89.
6 Henry W. Nevinson, *Last Changes, Last Chances* (New York, 1929), p. 303; Hector Bolitho, *Alfred Mond, First Lord Melchett* (London, 1933), pp. 154, 255.
7 Churchill, *Great Contemporaries*, p. 116.
8 Viscount Cecil of Chelwood, *All the Way* (London, 1949), p. 135.
9 A. G. Gardiner, *Prophets, Priests, and Kings* (London, 1914), p. 59.
10 Lord Selborne 'The War Cabinet', *c.* July 1916, Selborne papers, file 80.
11 Francis Boyd, ed., *The Glory of Parliament* (London, 1960), p. 24. A compilation of articles written by Harry Boardman for the *Manchester Guardian*.
12 James Johnston, *Westminister Voices: Studies in Parliamentary Speech* (London, 1923), pp. 53, 64; Samuel, *Memoirs*, p. 87.
13 Earl of Birkenhead, *Contemporary Personalities* (London, 1924), pp. 28–29; Creiger, 'The Last English Whig', p. 8.
14 Its object was the gradual reduction in the number of public houses by one-third. The measure passed through the House of Commons but was rejected by the House of Lords on 27 November 1908.
15 Brig.-Gen. John Charteris, *At GHQ* (London, 1931), pp. 133–34; Sir Lawrence Guillemard, *Trivial Fond Records* (London, 1937), pp. 34–35; J. L. Hammond, *C. P. Scott of the Manchester Guardian* (London, 1934), p. 297.
16 Sir Alexander Mackintosh, *Echoes of Big Ben: A Journalist's Parliamentary Diary, 1881–1940* (London, 1945), p. 111; A. G. Gardiner, 'Asquith', *Nineteenth Century*, 112 (1932), p. 616; Creiger, 'The Last English Whig', p. 5.
17 Gardiner, 'Mr Asquith', p. 528; Samuel, *Memoirs*, p. 87.
18 Viscount D'Abernon, *An Ambassador of Peace* (London, 1929), ii, pp. 32–33; Creiger, 'The Last English Whig', pp. 7–8.
19 Gardiner, 'Mr Asquith', p. 528.
20 Jenkins, *Asquith*, pp. 344–46.
21 Spender and Asquith, *Life of Herbert Henry Asquith*, ii, p. 176.
22 Beaverbrook, *Politicians and the War*, pp. 215–16; Spender and Asquith, *Life of Herbert Henry Asquith*, i, p. 217.
23 See for example, David, ed., *Inside Asquith's Cabinet*, p. 79.
24 Alan Clark, ed., *A Good Innings: The Private Papers of Viscount Lee of Fareham* (London, 1974) p. 98; Kenneth O. Morgan, ed., *Lloyd George: Family Letters* (Cardiff and London, 1973), p. 155; Randolph Churchill, *Churchill: Young Statesman, 1901–1914* (Boston, 1967), p. 332.
25 Robert Blake, ed., *The Private Papers of Douglas Haig, 1914–1919* (London, 1952), p. 164. After Asquith visited GHQ, Haig wrote to his wife: 'The P. M. seemed to like our old brandy. He had a couple of glasses (big sherry glass size) before I left the table at 9.30, and apparently he had several more before I saw him again. By that time his legs were unsteady, but his head was quite clear, and he was able to read a map and discuss the

situation with me. Indeed he was most charming and quite alert in mind.' Haig's impression corroborated other sources.

26 Jenkins, *Asquith*, p. 258.
27 See for example Philip Ziegler, *Diana Cooper* (London, 1981), p. 60.
28 Brocks, ed., HHA, p. 3.
29 Ibid., pp. 10–11.
30 Walter Bagehot in the *Economist*, 2 January 1875.
31 Cameron Hazlehurst, 'Asquith as Prime Minister', *English Historical Review*, 85 (1970), p. 506.
32 J. A. Spender, 'Lord Oxford and Asquith', *Contemporary Review*, 130 (1926), pp. 683–84.
33 Asquith to Venetia Stanley, 26 February 1915, in Brocks, ed., HHA, p. 452.
34 Selborne, 'The War Cabinet', c. July 1916, Selborne papers, file 80.
35 Jenkins, *Asquith*, p. 341.
36 David, ed., *Inside Asquith's Cabinet*, pp. 120, 230; Hankey, *The Supreme Command*, i, pp. 184–85; K. M. Wilson, 'Grey', in K. M. Wilson, ed., *British Foreign Secretaries and Foreign Policy: From Crimean War to First World War* (London, 1987), ch. 7 passim.
37 Stephen McKenna, *Reginald McKenna, 1863–1943* (London, 1948), passim; Jenkins, *Asquith*, passim.
38 David, ed., *Inside Asquith's Cabinet*, p. 121.
39 Robert Rhodes James, ed., *Memoirs of a Conservative: J. C. C. Davidson's Memoirs and Papers, 1910–1937* (New York, 1970), pp. 52–53.
40 Ziegler, *Diana Cooper*, p. 91.
41 Along with several other prominent politicians, Lloyd George was accused of taking advantage of inside information to profit from share dealings in the Marconi Company. The reader who wishes to follow the story of the episode in detail may be referred to Frances Donaldson, *The Marconi Scandal* (London, 1962) and Bentley B. Gilbert, 'David Lloyd George and the Great Marconi Scandal', *Historical Research*, 62 (1989), pp. 395–417.
42 David, ed., *Inside Asquith's Cabinet*, p. 230; Jenkins, *Asquith*, passim; Samuel, *Memoirs*, pp. 88–89; Birkenhead, *Contemporary Personalities*, pp. 34–39; Grigg, *Lloyd George*, passim.
43 Beaverbrook, *Politicians and the War*, pp. 125–27; Birkenhead, *Contemporary Personalities*, pp. 114–18; David, ed., *Inside Asquith's Cabinet*, p. 121; Sir Almeric Fitzroy, *Memoirs* (New York, 1925), ii, p. 594; A. G. Gardiner, *Pillars of Society* (London, 1916), pp. 153–58; Charles Eade, ed., *Churchill: By His Contemporaries* (London, 1955), passim.
44 George H. Cassar, *Kitchener: Architect of Victory* (London, 1977), passim.
45 Asquith to Kitchener, 3 August 1914, Kitchener papers, PRO 30/57/76.
46 Lady Bonham Carter, *Winston Churchill*, p. 257.
47 Pease, 'War Reminiscences', p. 9, Gainford papers, vol. 42.
48 Stephen E. Koss, *Lord Haldane* (New York, 1969), p. 115.
49 Haldane to his sister, 5 August 1914, Haldane papers, MS 6012.
50 Chamberlain, 'Diary on England's Intervention, 3 August 1914', Chamberlain papers, AC 14/2/2; Selborne to his wife, 4 August 1914, Selborne papers, fol. 102.
51 Gilbert, *Churchill*, iii, p. 28.
52 Cassar, *Kitchener*, p. 174.
53 Haldane to his sister, 5 August 1914, Haldane papers, MS 6012; Haldane to his mother, 5 and 6 August 1914, ibid., MS 5992.
54 Minutes of the Council of War, 5 August 1914, CAB 42/1/2; Haig diary, 5 August 1914, Haig papers; Wilson diary, 5 August 1914, Wilson papers; Hankey, *The Supreme Command*, i, pp. 169–72; Churchill, *The World Crisis*, i, pp. 248–50.
55 Asquith to Venetia Stanley, 6 August 1914, in Brocks, ed., HHA, p. 158.
56 Pease diary, 6 August 1914, Gainford papers.

57 Asquith to Venetia Stanley, 6 August 1914, in Brocks, ed., HHA, p. 158.
58 Hankey to Asquith, 5 August 1914, CAB 21/3; Hankey, *The Supreme Command*, i, pp. 168–69; Maj.-Gen. Sir C. E. Callwell, *Experiences of a Dug-Out, 1914–1918* (London, 1920), pp. 171–72; W. Roger Louis, *Great Britain and Germany's Lost Colonies, 1914–1919* (Oxford, 1967), pp. 36–37; Sir Julian Corbett, *Naval Operations* (London, 1920), i, pp. 131–32.
59 Asquith to Venetia Stanley, 5 August 1914, in Brocks, ed., HHA, p. 157.
60 Asquith to Venetia Stanley, 3 November 1914, ibid., p. 306.
61 Minutes of the Council of War, 6 August 1914, CAB 42/1/3.
62 Cassar, *Kitchener*, pp. 229–31.
63 Asquith to Venetia Stanley, 11 August 1914, in Brocks, ed., HHA, p. 165.
64 Haig wrote in his diary on 11 August 1914: 'In my own heart, I know that French is quite unfit for this great command at a time of crisis in our Nation's history.' Wilson in his own diary often referred to Sir John as a fool or idiot. Murray would write in later life: 'I had been so many years with him, and knew better than anyone how his health, temper and temperament, rendered him unfit, in my opinion, for the crisis we had to face.' Murray to Deedes, 18 December 1930, Spears papers, 2/3/79.
65 David French, *British Strategy and War Aims, 1914–1916* (London, 1986), chs 1–2 passim.
66 By far the best book on the subject of the New Armies is Peter Simkins, *Kitchener's Army* (Manchester, 1988).
67 Cited in Blake, *The Unknown Prime Minister*, p. 232.
68 Asquith to King George V, 4 November 1914, CAB 41/35/57.
69 Asquith to Venetia Stanley, 4 November 1914, in Brocks, ed., HHA, p. 309.
70 Asquith to Venetia Stanley, 27 October 1914, ibid., p. 287.
71 Lord Stamfordham, Memorandum of events 27–30 October 1914, Royal Archives, GV Q711/1.
72 Asquith to Venetia Stanley, 29 October 1914, in Brocks, ed., HHA, p. 296.
73 David, ed., *Inside Asquith's Cabinet*, p. 197; Hankey, *The Supreme Command*, i, p. 213.
74 Minutes of the CID, 7 October 1914, CAB 38/28/47.
75 Cassar, *Kitchener*, pp. 257–58; Gilbert, *Churchill*, iii, pp. 138–39; Churchill, *The World Crisis*, i, pp. 409, 419–20, 490–91; David, ed., *Inside Asquith's Cabinet*, pp. 200–1; Asquith to Venetia Stanley, 21 October 1914, in Brocks, ed., HHA, p. 281.
76 George H. Cassar, *The Tragedy of Sir John French* (Cranbury, NJ, 1985), pp. 100ff.
77 Asquith to Venetia Stanley, 24 August 1914, in Brocks, ed., HHA, p. 191.
78 Asquith's four sons of military age had all joined the colours in the early months of the war. Raymond received a commission in the Queen's Westminister Rifles but subsequently transferred to the Grenadier Guards and was posted to France. Wounded four times, Arthur, nicknamed 'Oc', saw action at Antwerp with the Royal Naval Division, in the Dardanelles and on the Western Front. Herbert ('Beb') was an artillery officer in France. Only Cyril ('Cys') the youngest, was relatively safe, relegated by ill-health to a home defence battalion.
79 Asquith to Venetia Stanley, 25 August 1914, in Brocks, ed., HHA, pp. 194–95.
80 Cassar, *Sir John French*, pp. 126–31.
81 French to Kitchener, 30 August 1914, Kitchener papers, PRO 30/57/49, .
82 Asquith to Venetia Stanley, 31 August 1914, in Brocks, ed., HHA, p. 209; David, ed., *Inside Asquith's Cabinet*, pp. 185–86; Sir George Arthur, *Life of Lord Kitchener* (London, 1920), iii, pp. 51–52.
83 Kitchener to French, 31 August 1914, Kitchener papers, PRO 30/57/49.
84 French to Kitchener, 31 August 1914, ibid.
85 Grey to Kitchener, 31 August 1914, ibid., PRO 30/57/77.
86 Cited in Cassar, *Sir John French*, p. 134.
87 Asquith to Venetia Stanley, 1 September 1914, in Brocks, ed., HHA, p. 213; Pease diary, 31 August 1914, Gainford papers.

88 Asquith to Venetia Stanley, 6 September and 27 October 1914, in Brocks, ed., HHA, pp. 224, 287.
89 Asquith to Venetia Stanley, 8 September 1914, ibid., p. 226.
90 Asquith to Venetia Stanley, 17 August 1914, ibid., p. 171.
91 Cited, ibid., p. 172, n. 5.
92 Cassar, *Sir John French*, ch. 6.
93 Idem, *Kitchener*, pp. 249–50.
94 Asquith to Venetia Stanley, 6 November 1914, in Brocks, ed., HHA, p. 311. Asquith was wrong in describing Kitchener's feelings towards Hamilton. In fact Kitchener liked Hamilton personally and thought highly of his abilities as a soldier.
95 Cassar, *Sir John French*, p. 176.
96 Asquith to French, 6 November 1914, Asquith papers, vol. 46.
97 French to Asquith, 9 November 1914, French papers, 75/46/3.
98 Desmond MacCarthy, ed., *H. H. A.: Letters of the Earl of Oxford to a Friend, 1915–1922* (London, 1933), p. 13.
99 Cassar, *Sir John French*, pp. 190, 203.
100 Asquith to Venetia Stanley, 30 October 1914, in Brocks, ed., HHA, p. 298.
101 Pease Diary, 28 October 1914, Gainford papers.
102 Asquith to Venetia Stanley, 28 October 1914, in Brocks, ed., HHA, p. 291.
103 Asquith to Venetia Stanley, two letters dated 30 October 1914, ibid., pp. 298–99.
104 For Lloyd George's perspective of the affair, see Taylor, ed., *A Diary by Frances Stevenson*, pp. 7–9.
105 Asquith to Venetia Stanley, 19 September 1914, in Brocks ed., HHA, p. 247.
106 Gilbert, *Churchill*, iii, pp. 74–75.
107 Cassar, *Kitchener*, pp. 261–63; Asquith to Venetia Stanley, 4, 18 and 19 December 1914, in Brocks, ed., HHA, pp. 325, 329, 330.
108 Asquith to Venetia Stanley, 3 October 1914, ibid., p. 260.
109 Asquith to Venetia Stanley, 5 October 1914, ibid., p. 262.
110 Ibid., pp. 262–63.
111 Churchill, *The World Crisis*, i, pp. 384–88; Cassar, *Kitchener*, pp. 245–49; Gilbert, *Churchill*, iii, pp. 115–19.
112 Asquith to Venetia Stanley, 10 October 1914, in Brocks, ed., HHA, p. 271.
113 Asquith to Venetia Stanley, 7 October 1914, ibid., pp. 266–77.
114 Asquith to Venetia Stanley, 13 October 1914, ibid., p. 275.
115 Mackintosh, 'The Role of the Committee of Imperial Defence', pp. 502–3; Parliamentary Debates, *House of Commons*, 2 November 1915, col. 526, vol. 75.
116 Lady Scott diary, 26 July 1916, Kennet papers.
117 Hankey, *The Supreme Command*, i, pp. 237–39; *First Report of the Dardanelles Commission* (London, 1917), pp. 5–6; H. H. Asquith, *Memories and Reflections* (London, 1928), ii, pp. 87–88.
118 Minutes of the War Council, 25 November 1914, CAB 42/1/4.
119 Paul Guinn, *British Strategy and Politics, 1914 to 1918* (London, 1965), p. 44.

Notes to Chapter 4

1 Memo by Hankey, 28 December 1914, CAB 37/122/194; Churchill to Asquith, 29 December 1914 in Gilbert, ed., *Companion*, pp. 343–45; Asquith to Venetia Stanley, 30 December 1914, in Brocks, ed., HHA, pp. 345–46.

2 Lloyd George, 'The War – Suggestions as to the Military Situation', 1 January 1915, CAB 42/1/8; Grigg, *Lloyd George*, pp. 194–97; Asquith to Venetia Stanley, 1 January 1915, in Brocks, ed., HHA, pp. 357–58.

3 Gilbert, *Churchill*, iii, p. 228.

4 Asquith to Venetia Stanley, 30 December 1914, in Brocks, ed., HHA, p. 345.

5 French to Kitchener, 3 January 1915, Kitchener papers, PRO 30/57/50.

6 Minutes of the War Council, 8 January 1915, CAB 42/1/12.

7 Cassar, *Kitchener*, p. 270.

8 Minutes of the War Council, 13 January 1915, CAB 42/1/16.

9 The plan was essentially the same one Churchill had submitted to Asquith at the end of December 1914. It called for the seizure of the island of Borkum as a preliminary step to the invasion of Schleswig-Holstein. The object was to open the Baltic to the British fleet which would then enable a Russian army to land within ninety miles of Berlin.

10 Asquith to Venetia Stanley, 20 January 1915, in Brocks, ed., HHA, pp. 387–88.

11 Asquith to Dardanelles Commission, 31 October 1916, CAB 19/33.

12 Churchill, *The World Crisis*, ii, pp. 157–60. The date on the memo is given as 27 January, but it is a misprint.

13 Gilbert, *Churchill*, iii, p. 265.

14 Arthur J. Marder, ed., *Fear God and Dreadnought: The Correspondence of Admiral of the Fleet Lord Fisher of Kilverstone* (London, 1959), iii, pp. 147–48.

15 Gilbert, *Churchill*, iii, p. 269.

16 Asquith to Venetia Stanley, 28 January 1915, in Brocks, ed., HHA, p. 405.

17 Minutes of the War Council meetings at 11.30 a.m., 4 p.m., and 6.30 p.m., 28 January 1915, CAB 42/1/26, 27 and 28; Lord Fisher, *Memories and Records* (New York, 1920), i, pp. 89–90; Fisher to Dardanelles Commission, 11 October 1916, CAB 19/33; Churchill, *The World Crisis*, ii, pp. 162–64.

18 Marder, *From the Dreadnought*, ii, p. 219.

19 On 20 July 1916 Asquith set up a commission to inquire into the conduct of the Dardanelles campaign. It interviewed everyone involved in the planning and execution of the operations, with the exception of Kitchener who had drowned the previous month. The commission published two heavily censored reports in 1917 and 1918. The full proceedings were never published but became available on 1 January 1968.

20 Asquith to Dardanelles Commission, 31 October 1916, CAB 19/33.

21 Hankey, *The Supreme Command*, i, pp. 42, 279.

22 Hankey diary, 19 March 1915, Hankey papers; Hankey to Balfour, 10 February 1915, Balfour papers, Add. 49703.

23 Hankey, 'Attack on the Dardanelles', 2 February 1915, CAB 42/1/30.

24 David French, 'The Origins of the Dardanelles Campaign Reconsidered', *History*, 68 (1983), pp. 213–17.

25 Churchill clearly overplayed his hand. He misjudged the effects of naval firepower, overruled professional experts who disagreed with him, and refused to wait until troops were available to accompany the fleet. He dazzled the War Council with visions of a world-shattering coup and the rewards that it would bring. He never properly defined the political and military ends of the campaign. Had he done so it would have been obvious that he had insufficient means to achieve the desired objectives.

26 On the pre-war investigations of the Dardanelles see Brig.-Gen. C. F. Aspinall-Oglander, *Military Operations: Gallipoli* (London, 1929), i, ch. 2.

27 Asquith to Stamfordham, 22 January 1915, Royal Archives, GV Q838/5.

28 R. J. Crampton, *The Hollow Detente: Anglo-German Relations in the Balkans, 1911–1914* (London, 1979), passim; Keith Robbins, 'British Diplomacy and Bulgaria, 1914–1915', *Slavonic and East European Review*, 49 (1971), pp. 563–66; Michael G. Fry, *Lloyd George and Foreign Policy* (Montreal and London, 1977), i, pp. 268–70; G. E. Torrey, 'Rumania and the Belligerents 1914–1916', *Journal of Contemporary History*, 1 (1966), pp. 171–72.

29 Noel Buxton, an influential Liberal backbencher, had gone to Bucharest with his brother Charles, ostensibly to attend the funeral of King Carol of Roumania but in fact to investigate whether the Balkan states could be mobilized against Austria. They left without the blessing of Grey, although both Churchill and Lloyd George were enthusiastic about their mission.

30 Charles and Noel Buxton, 'Notes on the Balkan States', January 1915, Masterman papers, CFGM A 3A/2/2; Asquith to Venetia Stanley, 15 January 1915, in Brocks, ed., HHA, p. 380; Fry, *Lloyd George*, i, pp. 279–82; T. P. Conwell-Evans, *Foreign Policy from a Back Bench, 1904–1918* (London, 1932), pp. 94ff.

31 Asquith to Grey, 17 January 1915, Grey papers, FO 800/100; Asquith to Venetia Stanley, 15 January 1915, in Brocks, ed., HHA, pp. 380–81.

32 Asquith to King George V, 21 January 1915, CAB 41/36/2.

33 Asquith to Venetia Stanley, 21 January 1915, in Brocks, ed., HHA, p. 389.

34 Asquith to Grey, 21 January 1915, Grey papers, FO 800/100.

35 Asquith to Venetia Stanley, 21 January 1915, in Brocks ed., HHA, p. 389.

36 Asquith to Grey, 21 January 1915, Grey papers, FO 800/100; Asquith to Venetia Stanley, 21 January 1915, in Brocks, ed., HHA, pp. 388–89.

37 Asquith to Stanfordham, 22 January 1915, Royal Archives, GV Q838/5 ; Asquith to Venetia Stanley, 22 January 1915, in Brocks, ed., HHA, p. 390.

38 Esher diary, 22 January 1915, Esher papers.

39 Asquith to Venetia Stanley, 22 January 1915, in Brocks, ed., HHA, p. 391.

40 David R. Woodward, *Lloyd George and the Generals* (Newark, NJ, 1983), pp. 37–38; Grigg, *Lloyd George*, pp. 205–6; Lloyd George, *War Memoirs*, i, pp. 240–45.

41 Asquith to Venetia Stanley, 8 February 1915, in Brocks, ed., HHA, pp. 418–19; Hankey, *The Supreme Command*, i, p. 277.

42 Minutes of the War Council, 9 February 1915, CAB 42/1/33.

43 George B. Leon, *Greece and the Great Powers, 1914–1917* (Thessaloniki, 1974), p. 120; Robbins, 'British Diplomacy and Bulgaria, 1914–1915', pp. 571–72; Keith Neilson, *Strategy and Supply: The Anglo-Russian Alliance, 1914–1917* (London, 1984), p. 69.

44 Asquith to Venetia Stanley, 17 February 1915, in Brocks, ed., HHA, p. 433.

Notes to Chapter 5

1 Asquith to Venetia Stanley, 13 February 1915, in Brocks, ed., HHA, p. 429.
2 Minutes of the War Council, 16 and 19 February 1915, CAB 42/1/35, 36.
3 Asquith to Venetia Stanley, 17 February 1915, in Brocks, ed., HHA, p. 434.
4 Minutes of the War Council, 19 February 1915, CAB 42/1/36.
5 For a detailed description of the naval operations, see Marder, *From the Dreadnought*, ii; Corbett, *Naval Operations*, ii, iii; Paul G. Halpern, *The Naval War in the Mediterranean, 1914–1918* (Annapolis, MD, 1987).
6 The full statement has been reproduced in Hankey, *The Supreme Command*, i, pp. 282–83.
7 Lady Bonham Carter, *Winston Churchill*, p. 294; Asquith to Venetia Stanley, 28 February 1915, in Brocks, ed., HHA, p. 454.
8 Minutes of the War Council, 24 February 1915, CAB 42/1/42.
9 Asquith to Venetia Stanley, 24 February 1915, in Brocks, ed., HHA, pp. 445–46. The date is inaccurately given as 23 February.
10 Cassar, *Kitchener*, pp. 295–99; Minutes of the War Council, 26 February 1915, CAB 42/1/47.
11 Asquith to Venetia Stanley, 26 February 1915, in Brocks, ed., HHA, p. 449.
12 Asquith to Venetia Stanley, two letters on 26 February 1915, ibid., pp. 449–50.
13 French, *British Strategy*, pp. 35–36.
14 V. H. Rothwell, *British War Aims and Peace Diplomacy, 1914–1918* (Oxford,1971), pp. 19–20.
15 Parliamentary Debates, *House of Commons*, 6 August 1914, vol. 65, cols 2079–80; H. H. Asquith, 'The War: Its Causes and Its Message' (London, 1914); idem, 'The Justice of Our Case' and 'The Duty of Everyman' (London, 1914); Lorna S. Jaffe, *The Decision to Disarm Germany* (Boston, 1985) pp. 10–11.
16 Minute by Asquith, *c.* 23 September 1914, Grey papers, FO 800/84. Asquith's thoughts were scribbled on the back of a Foreign Office telegram.
17 The relevant excerpt can be seen in Asquith, *Memories*, ii, pp. 38–39.
18 George W. Egerton, *Great Britain and the Creation of the League of Nations* (Chapel Hill, NC, 1978), pp. 24ff.
19 H. H. Asquith, 'What Britain is Fighting For' (London, 1916); idem, 'A Free Future for the World' (London, 1916).
20 Pease diary, 1 March 1915, Gainford papers.
21 Centuries-old treaties ensuring European privileges and extra-territorial rights and protection by their own government agencies.
22 Asquith to King George V, 20 October 1914, CAB 41/35/54.
23 Basil Herbert, ed. and comp., *Speeches by the Earl of Oxford and Asquith* (London, 1927), p. 224.
24 Asquith to Venetia Stanley, 31 October 1914, in Brocks, ed., HHA, p. 300.
25 Bernard Wasserstein, *Herbert Samuel: A Political Life* (Oxford, 1992), pp. 198ff.
26 Herbert Samuel, 'The Future of Palestine', 21 January 1915, CAB 37/123/43.
27 Asquith to Venetia Stanley, 28 January 1915, in Brocks, ed., HHA, p. 406.
28 Herbert Samuel, 'Palestine', 11 March 1915, CAB 37/126/1.
29 Asquith to Venetia Stanley, 13 March 1915, in Brocks, ed., HHA, p. 477.
30 Spender and Asquith, *Life of Herbert Henry Asquith*, ii, p. 353.
31 Montagu to Asquith, 16 March 1915, Asquith papers, vol. 27. Discussion and partial excerpt of the note are given in Isaiah Friedman, *The Question of Palestine, 1914–1918* (New York, 1973), pp. 22–24.

32 Asquith to Venetia Stanley, 13 March 1915, in Brocks, ed., HHA, p. 478.
33 Russia's opposition encouraged the Greek king, Constantine I, who had been impressed by the arguments of his General Staff as to the strategic dangers of Greece's entry into the war, to reject Venizelos' policy.
34 Michael Ekstein, 'Russia, Constantinople and the Straits, 1914–1915', in Hinsley, ed., *British Foreign Policy*, pp. 428–29; C. Jay Smith, 'Great Britain and the 1914–1915 Straits Agreement with Russia: the British Promise of November 1914', *American Historical Review*, 70 (1965), pp. 1015–34; Leon, *Greece*, pp. 134–39; Hankey, *The Supreme Command*, i, pp. 286–87; Churchill, *The World Crisis*, ii, pp. 202–05.
35 William A. Renzi, 'Great Britain, Russia and the Straits', *Journal of Modern History*, 42 (1970), pp. 5–12; Ekstein, 'Russia, Constantinople and the Straits, 1914–1915', pp. 428–33; Gregory Paget, 'The November 1914 Straits Agreement and the Dardanelles-Gallipoli Campaign', *Australian Journal of Politics and History*, 33 (1987), pp. 253–58.
36 Asquith to Venetia Stanley, 6 March 1915, in Brocks, ed., HHA, p. 463.
37 Asquith to King George V, 9 March 1915, CAB 41/36/9; David, ed., *Inside Asquith's Cabinet*, pp. 227–28.
38 Minutes of the War Council, 10 March 1915, CAB 42/2/5; Churchill, *The World Crisis*, ii, pp. 199–200.
39 Minutes of the War Council, 10 and 19 March 1915, CAB 42/2/5, 14; Jukka Nevakivi, 'Lord Kitchener and the Partition of the Ottoman Empire, 1915–1916', in K. Bourne and D. C. Watt, ed., *Studies in International History* (London, 1967), pp. 321–25; Kitchener, 'Alexandretta and Mesopotamia', 16 March 1915, CAB 42/2/10; Kitchener, 'The Future Relations of the Great Powers', 21 April 1915, CAB 37/127/34; A. K. Wilson, 'Russia and Constantinople', 15 March 1915, CAB 42/2/9; Fisher to Kitchener, 11 March 1915, Kitchener papers, PRO 30/57/80; The Admiralty, 'Alexandretta and Mesopotamia', 17 March 1915, CAB 42/2/11; H. B. Jackson, 'Alexandretta: Its Importance as a Future Base', 18 March 1915, CAB 42/2/13; General Barrow, 'Note on the Defence of India', 16 March 1915, CAB 42/2/8; A. Hirtzel, 'The Future Settlement of Eastern Turkey in Asia and Arabia', 14 March 1915, ibid; Hardinge to Crewe, 8 April 1915 in Gilbert, ed., *Companion*, pp. 785–86.
40 Asquith to Venetia Stanley, 25 March 1915, in Brocks, ed., HHA, p. 509. Haldane was also opposed to the dismemberment of Turkey.
41 Minutes of the War Council, 19 March 1915, CAB 42/2/14.
42 Asquith to Fisher, 22 April 1915, Asquith papers, vol. 27.
43 Minutes of the War Council, 19 March 1915, CAB 42/2/14.
44 Grey, *Twenty-Five Years*, ii, p. 236.
45 Of the various types of arrangements examined, it recommended that the Turkish Empire, except for Constantinople and Basra, be preserved as an independent federal state. The committee recognized that the dismemberment of Turkey might be unavoidable, in which case it favoured British acquisition of territory running from Acre to Ruwandiz in the north and from Aqaba to Kuwait in the south. This area included Haifa, rather than Alexandretta, as the requisite British port on the Mediterranean and the terminus of a possible connecting line with Mesopotamia. Since France would be left with Alexandretta, it would have less reason to claim the south of Syria and advance its frontier close to the Suez Canal. Finally the committee, in acknowledging the universal character of the Holy Places, advocated that Palestine be neutralized and internationalized. Report of the Committee on Asiatic Turkey, 30 June 1915, CAB 42/3/12; Rothwell, *British War Aims*, p. 23.
46 The French had agreed to contribute a squadron and a division in support of the operation.
47 Violet Asquith diary, reference to date is early March 1915.
48 Asquith to Venetia Stanley, 30 September 1914, in Brocks, ed., HHA, p. 257.

49 For a sympathetic treatment of Hamilton see the biography by his nephew and namesake, Ian B. Hamilton, *The Happy Warrior* (London, 1966).

50 Robert Rhodes James, *Gallipoli* (London, 1965), pp. 318–20.

51 *Final Report of the Dardanelles Commission*, pp. 10–11.

52 Stephen Roskill, *Hankey: Man of Secrets* (London, 1970), i, pp. 163–64.

53 Hankey diary, 17 March 1915, Hankey papers.

54 Minutes of the War Council, 19 March 1915, CAB 42/2/14.

55 Ibid.; Churchill, *The World Crisis*, ii, p. 234; Hankey, *The Supreme Command*, i, pp. 292–93.

56 Ibid., i, pp. 293–95.

57 Asquith to Venetia Stanley, 23 March 1915, in Brocks, ed., HHA, pp. 500–1.

58 Asquith to Venetia Stanley, 24 March 1915, ibid., p. 506.

59 Churchill, *The World Crisis*, ii, p. 239.

60 Asquith to Venetia Stanley, 25 March 1915, in Brocks, ed., HHA, p. 508.

61 Asquith to Venetia Stanley, 21 March 1915, ibid., p. 495.

62 Asquith to Venetia Stanley, 25 March 1915, ibid., p. 508.

63 Asquith to Venetia Stanley, 29 March 1915, ibid., p. 519.

64 Asquith to Venetia Stanley, 30 March 1915, ibid., p. 522; Taylor, ed., *A Diary by Frances Stevenson*, pp. 42–43.

65 Asquith to Venetia Stanley, 30 March 1915, in Brocks, ed., HHA, p. 523.

66 Churchill to Fisher, 15 March 1915, Fisher papers, 1/18.

67 Riddell, *War Diary*, p. 70.

68 Cassar, *Kitchener*, pp. 332–35; Chris Wrigley, 'The Ministry of Munitions: an Innovatory Department', in Kathleen Burk, ed., *War and the State* (London, 1982), pp. 36–39.

69 *History of the Ministry of Munitions* (London,1920), i, ch. 4, pt 1; 'Notes on the Supply of Guns Prior to the Formation of the Ministry of Munitions, August 1914–June 1915', MUN 5/6/170/30.

70 R. J. Q. Adams, *Arms and the Wizard: Lloyd George and the Ministry of Munitions, 1915–1916* (College Station, TX, 1978), p. 20.

71 Lloyd George, 'Some Further Considerations on the Conduct of the War', 22 February 1915, CAB 37/124/40.

72 Minutes of the meeting, 5 March 1915, MUN 5/6/170/22.

73 Lloyd George to Balfour, 6 March 1915, Balfour papers, Add. 49692. See also Lloyd George, *War Memoirs*, i, pp. 104–05.

74 Montagu to Asquith, undated, Lloyd George papers, C/14/3/3.

75 Grigg, *Lloyd George*, p. 240.

76 Asquith to Venetia Stanley, 22 March 1915, in Brocks, ed., HHA, pp. 497–98.

77 'Provisional Conclusions of the Proposed Committee on War Supplies', 22 March 1915, Lloyd George papers, C/14/3/4; Asquith to Lloyd George, 22 March 1915, ibid., C/6/11/36; Asquith to Kitchener, 23 March 1915, Kitchener papers, PRO 30/57/82.

78 Duncan Crow, *A Man of Push and Go: The Life of George Macaulay Booth* (London, 1965), p. 91.

79 Kitchener to Asquith, 25 March 1915, Kitchener papers, PRO 30/57/82.

80 Lloyd George to Kitchener, 25 March 1915, ibid, PRO 30/57/82.

81 Asquith to Venetia Stanley, 28 March 1915, in Brocks, ed., HHA, p. 514.

82 Asquith, Memorandum on the Munitions of War Committee, 8 April 1915, Kitchener papers, PRO 30/57/82.

83 Ibid.

84 David French, 'The Military Background to the "Shells Crisis" of May 1915', *Journal of Strategic Studies*, 2 (1979), pp. 199–200; Cassar, *Sir John French*, pp. 210–14.

85 The information came from high-ranking soldiers, such as Sir Henry Wilson, and Tory MPs attached to the general staffs of the BEF.

86 W. A. S. Hewins, *The Apologia of an Imperialist* (London, 1929), ii, pp. 11–27; Blake, *The Unknown Prime Minister*, pp. 231–32; A. J. P. Taylor, *Politics in Wartime* (New York, 1965), pp. 17–18; Grigg, *Lloyd George*, p. 243.

87 H. H. Asquith, 'Mr Asquith's Reply to Lord French', *Living Age*, 302 (1919), p. 71.

88 Kitchener to Asquith, 14 April 1915, Asquith papers, vol. 14.

89 A copy of the speech can be found in the Asquith papers, vol. 49.

90 Asquith, 'Mr Asquith's Reply to Lord French', p. 71.

91 *The Times*, 21 April 1915. The next day the editorial was equally scathing.

92 *Daily Mail*, 22 April 1915.

93 *Scotsman*, 21 April 1915.

94 *Daily Express*, 1 May 1915.

95 *Pall Mall Gazette*, 21 April 1915

96 W. A. Renzi, *In the Shadow of the Sword: Italy's Neutrality and Entrance into the Great War* (New York, 1987). See especially ch. 11.

97 Asquith to Venetia Stanley, 23 March 1915, in Brocks, ed., HHA, p. 501.

98 Ibid.; Asquith to King George V, 24 March and 8 April 1915, CAB 41/36/12, 15.

99 C. J. Lowe, 'Britain and Italian Intervention, 1914–1915', *Historical Journal*, 12 (1971), pp. 541–48.

100 During the first week in February a Turkish force of about 20,000, having crossed the inhospitable Sinai Desert, attempted to seize the Suez Canal. The attack was poorly executed and was repulsed easily.

101 There are many accounts of the military operations but the most useful, in my view, are Rhodes James, *Gallipoli*; Aspinall-Oglander, *Gallipoli*, 2 vols; John Laffin, *Damn the Dardanelles*, (London, 1980).

102 Esher to Bertie, 16 April 1915, Bertie papers, FO 800/167.

Notes to Chapter 6

1 Kitchener said the same thing at the War Council on 14 May
2 Marder, *From the Dreadnought*, ii, p. 275; Churchill, *The World Crisis*, ii, pp. 350–54; Gilbert, *Churchill*, iii, p. 419.
3 Hankey diary, 11 May 1915, Hankey papers.
4 Marder, ed., *Fear God*, iii, p. 220.
5 Hankey diary, 12 May 1915, Hankey papers.
6 Asquith to Fisher, 12 May 1915, Fisher papers, 1/19.
7 Marder, ed., *Fear God*, iii, pp. 220–21.
8 Hankey diary, 13 May 1915, Hankey papers; Fisher to Hankey, 14 May 1915, ibid, 5/2B.
9 Kitchener to Asquith, 13 May 1915, Kitchener papers, PRO 30/57/72.
10 Hankey to Asquith, 13 May 1915, CAB 63/5.
11 Asquith to Kitchener, 13 May 1915, Kitchener papers, PRO 30/57/72.
12 Churchill, *The World Crisis*, ii, p. 364.
13 Ibid., pp. 365–67; Hankey, *The Supreme Command*, i, p. 306; Minutes of the War Council, 14 May 1915, CAB 42/2/19.
14 Not long afterwards a messenger brought in a copy of Fisher's letter of resignation with an accompanying minute: 'As I find it increasingly difficult to adjust myself to the increasing policy of the First Lord in regard to the Dardanelles, I have been reluctantly compelled to inform him this day that I am unable to remain as his colleague and I am leaving at once for Scotland so as not to be embarrassed or embarrass you by any explanation to anyone'. Fisher to Asquith, 15 May 1915, 1/9 Fisher papers.
15 Riddell, *War Diary*, p. 93.
16 Asquith to Fisher, 15 May 1915, CAB 1/33.
17 Lady Bonham Carter, *Winston Churchill*, pp. 318–19.
18 For the correspondence exchanged between Churchill and Fisher see Churchill, *The World Crisis*, ii, pp. 375–79; Gilbert, *Churchill*, iii, pp. 439–43; Richard Hough, *First Sea Lord: An Authorized Biography of Admiral Lord Fisher* (London, 1969), pp. 337–39; Marder, ed., *Fear God*, iii, pp. 228–34.
19 Churchill, *The World Crisis*, ii, pp. 379–80.
20 Lady Bonham Carter, *Winston Churchill*, p. 322.
21 Beaverbrook, *Politicians and the War*, pp. 105–6; Blake, *The Unknown Prime Minister*, p. 243.
22 Beaverbrook, *Politicians and the War*, p. 106; Blake, *The Unknown Prime Minister*, p. 243; Lloyd George, *War Memoirs*, i, p. 136.
23 Joseph Austen Chamberlain (1863–1937). Conservative MP, 1892–1937. Postmaster-General, 1902–3. Chancellor of the Exchequer, 1903–05. Unsuccesssful candidate for the leadership of his party, 1911. Secretary of India, 1915–17. Chancellor of the Exchequer, 1919–21. Secretary of Foreign Affairs, 1924–29.
24 Chamberlain, 'Memorandum on Events of 17–18 May 1915', Chamberlain papers, AC 2/2/25.
25 Taylor, ed., *A Diary by Frances Stevenson*, p. 51. See also Riddell, *War Diary*, pp. 93–94.
26 Rhodes James, ed., *Memoirs*, pp. 24–25.
27 Walter Hume Long (1854–1924). Conservative MP, 1880–1921. Government Board, 1900–5, 1915–16. Colonial Secretary, 1916–18. First Lord of the Admiralty, 1919–21. Created Viscount, 1921.
28 Bonar Law to Long, 14 May 1915, Long papers, Add. 62404.

29 Chamberlain, 'Memorandum on Events of 17–18 May 1915', Chamberlain papers, AC 2/2/25; Reading diary, 18 May 1915, Reading papers, EUR F118/153; Taylor ed., *A Diary by Frances Stevenson*, p. 51; Riddell, *War Diar*, p. 94.

30 Riddell, *War Diary*, p. 109.

31 Lloyd George, *War Memoirs*, i, p. 136; Churchill, *The World Crisis*, ii, p. 381.

32 William Maxwell Aitken (1879–1964). Born New Brunswick, Canada. Self-made millionaire. Conservative MP, 1910–16. Canadian military representative at the Front, 1915–16. Created Baron Beaverbrook, 1916. Newspaper proprietor. Chancellor of the Duchy of Lancaster and Minister of Information, 1918. Minister of Aircraft Production, 1940–41. Minister of Supply, 1941–42. Lord Privy Seal, 1943–45.

33 Stamfordham Memorandum (Asquith's explanation of the circumstances that lead to the reconstruction of the government) for the King, 19 May 1915, Royal Archives, GV K770/3; Pease diary, 18 May 1915, Gainford papers; Asquith, memorandum for the cabinet, 17 May 1915, Kitchener papers, PRO 30/57/76; Asquith, *Memories*, ii, pp. 97–98; Lady Bonham Carter, *Winston Churchill*, p. 323.

34 French, *British Strategy*, p. 87; Renzi, *In the Shadow of the Sword*, ch. 14.

35 A. J. P. Taylor, in a Raleigh Lecture given before the British Academy in 1959, was among the first to challenge Beaverbrook. Entitled 'Politics in the First World War', it can be found, along with other essays by Taylor, in *Politics in Wartime* (New York, 1965). Other historians who have contributed different interpretations include Bentley B. Gilbert, *David Lloyd George: The Organizer of Victory, 1912–16* (London, 1990), ch. 5; Trevor Wilson, *The Downfall of the Liberal Party, 1914–1935* (London, 1966), pp. 53–64; Stephen Koss, 'The Destruction of Britain's Last Liberal Government', *Journal of Modern History*, 40 (1968), pp. 257–77; idem, *Lord Haldane*, ch. 7; Martin D. Pugh, 'Asquith, Bonar Law and the First Coalition', *Historical Journal*, 17 (1974), pp. 813–36; Peter Fraser, 'British War Policy and the Crisis of Liberalism in May 1915', *Journal of Modern History*, 54 (1982), pp. 1–26; A. M. Gollin, *Proconsul in Politics* (New York, 1964), ch. 11. See also Gollin's article in the *Spectator* of 28 May 1965 and the running dispute between him and Robert Rhodes James in the following issues.

36 Jenkins first raised that possibility.

37 Adelaide Lubbock, *People in Glass Houses* (London, 1977), pp. 82–83.

38 Asquith to Venetia Stanley, 14 May 1915, in Brocks, ed., HHA, p. 596.

39 Asquith to Sylvia Henley, 17 May 1915, Asquith/Henley papers, C542/1.

40 Gilbert, *Churchill*, iii, pp. 446–47; Koss, *Asquith*, pp. 186–87.

41 Parliamentary Debates, *House of Commons*, 12 May 1915, vol. 71, col. 1642.

42 Asquith to Balfour, 20 May 1915, Balfour papers, Add. 49692.

43 Long to Balfour, 27 January 1915, ibid., Add. 49693.

44 Pease, 'War Reminiscences', p. 117, Gainford papers, vol. 43; Robbins, *Sir Edward Grey*, p. 320; Lady Bonham Carter, *Winston Churchill*, p. 323.

45 Asquith, memorandum for the cabinet, 17 May 1915. A copy can be found in the Kitchener papers, PRO 30/57/76.

46 Pease to Runciman, 9 June 1915, Runciman papers, WR 135.

47 Hobhouse to Runciman, 28 May 1915, ibid.

48 A. MacCallum Scott diary, 19 May 1915, MacCallum Scott papers; Richard Holt diary, 19 May 1915, Holt papers; Christopher Addison diary, 19 May 1915, Addison papers.

49 Asquith to Sylvia Henley, 19 May 1915, Asquith/Henley papers, C542/1.

50 Addison diary, 17 May 1915, Addison papers. There is a similar version in Chamberlain, 'Memorandum on Events of 17–18 May 1915', Chamberlain papers, AC 2/2/25.

51 Chamberlain, ibid.

52 Ibid.

53 B. Gilbert, *David Lloyd George*, p. 199. According to Gilbert, Lloyd George initially

wanted the War Office merely as a means to correct the munitions problem. Supposedly he changed his mind after it became apparent that an independent ministry of munitions would be set up. Gilbert's theory is difficult to reconcile with Lloyd George's known ambition and lust for power.

54 Gilbert's claim is based on remarks made by Lloyd George.

55 Lloyd George to Asquith, 19 May 1915, Asquith papers, vol. 14; Lloyd George, *War Memoirs*, i, pp. 121–22.

56 French to Asquith, 20 May 1915, Asquith papers, vol. 27.

57 Stamfordham to Asquith, 18 May 1915, Royal Archives, GV K770/2. The King was prepared to stand by Kitchener, irrespective of the consequences. He wanted a separate Ministry of Munitions to shield Kitchener from future attacks and to lighten his crushing load.

58 Stamfordham, memorandum for the King, 22 May 1915, Royal Archives, GV K770/11.

59 Jenkins, *Asquith*, pp. 367–68; Stamfordham, memorandum for the King, 22 May 1915, Royal Archives, GV K770/11; Blake, *The Unknown Prime Minister*, pp. 249–52.

60 Stamfordham, memorandum for the King, 22 May 1915, Royal Archives, GV K770/11; Blake, *The Unknown Prime Minister*, pp. 249–50; Taylor, ed., *A Diary by Frances Stevenson*, p. 54.

61 Crewe to Lloyd George, 24 May 1915, Lloyd George papers, C/4/1/22; Beaverbrook, *Politicians and the War*, p. 132.

62 Stamfordham, memorandum for the King, 25 May 1915, Royal Archives, GV K770/12; Llewellyn Smith to Runciman, 24 May 1915, Runciman papers, WR 136.

63 Stamfordham, memorandum for the King, 25 May 1915, Royal Archives, GV K770/12; notes by Asquith, 26 May 1915, Asquith papers, vol. 27.

64 Stamfordham, memorandum for the King, 25 May 1915, Royal Archives, GV K770/12.

65 Addison diary, 26 May 1915, Addison papers.

66 Stamfordham, memorandum for the King, 25 May 1915, Royal Archives, GV K770/12; notes by Asquith, 26 May 1915, Asquith papers, vol. 27; Beaverbrook, *Politicians and the War*, pp. 134–35; Rhodes James, ed., *Memoirs*, p. 25.

67 Beaverbrook, *Politicians and the War*, pp. 134–35.

68 The Unionist chief's brother, John, was an active partner in the firm of William Jacks & Co., which was under criminal prosecution for having traded with the enemy. Although Bonar Law no longer had any executive connection with the firm, there were scurrilous rumours that both he and his brother were implicated. He was extremely upset over the accusations and vowed that if his brother was proved guilty he would resign from public life. After the trial got under way it was apparent that neither he nor his brother were in any way responsible for what had happened. See Blake, *The Unknown Prime Minister*, pp. 257–59.

69 Rhodes James, ed., *Memoirs*, p. 25.

70 Long to Bonar Law, 23 May 1915, Long papers, Add. 62404.

71 Jenkins, *Asquith*, p. 362; Koss, *Haldane*, p. 203.

72 Lady Bonham Carter, *Winston Churchill*, p. 323; David, ed., *Inside Asquith's Cabinet*, p. 246.

73 Reading diary, 18 May 1915, Reading papers, EUR F118/153.

74 Jenkins, *Asquith*, p. 361.

75 See, for example, Asquith to Pease, 26 May 1915 in 'War Reminiscences', pp. 122–23, Gainford papers, vol. 43; David, ed., *Inside Asquith's Cabinet*, p. 247.

76 Asquith to Crewe, 25 May 1915, Crewe papers, C/40; Asquith to Lloyd George, 25 May 1915, Lloyd George papers, D/18/2/1.

77 Pease to his mother, 22 May 1915, Gainford papers, vol. 522.

78 Haldane to his mother, 22 May 1915, Haldane papers, MS 5993.

79 Spender and Asquith, *Life of Herbert Henry Asquith*, ii, p. 167.
80 Reading diary, 19 May 1915, Reading papers, EUR F118/153; Stamfordham, memorandum for the King, 19 May 1915, Royal Archives, GV K770/3; Emmott to Asquith, 20 May 1915, Asquith papers, vol. 27; Pringle to Asquith, 20 May 1915, ibid., vol. 27; Gilbert, *Churchill*, iii, ch. 14.
81 Asquith to Fisher, 17 May 1915, Fisher papers, 1/19.
82 Marder, ed., *Fear God*, iii, pp. 241–43; Fisher to Asquith, 19 May 1915, Fisher papers, 1/19.
83 Stamfordham, memorandum for the King, 19 May 1915, Royal Archives, GV K770/3.
84 J. A. Spender, *Life, Journalism and Politics* (London, 1927), ii, p. 71; Marder, *From the Dreadnought*, ii, p. 285.
85 Hankey, *The Supreme Command*, i, pp. 317–18; Ruddock F. Mackay, *Fisher of Kilverstone* (London, 1973), p. 504.
86 Besides Haldane, Asquith was compelled to exclude from the cabinet seven previous members: Samuel, Pease, Emmott, Lucas, Hobhouse, Beauchamp and Montagu.
87 Long to Gwynne, 20 May 1915, Gwynne papers, MS 20.
88 Gwynn, *John Redmond*, p. 425.
89 Hankey, *The Supreme Command*, i, p. 319.

Notes to Chapter 7

1 Final Report of the Dardanelles Commission, p. 24; Hankey, *The Supreme Command*, i, p. 336. Hankey neglected to list McKenna's name.
2 Hankey, *The Supreme Command*, i, p. 337.
3 Cassar, *Sir John French*, p. 244; D'Abernon to his wife, 4 June 1915, D'Abernon papers, Add. 48936. 'The general view here is that the *Daily Mail* intrigue against K. – in which he [French] appears to have participated – makes him almost impossible.'
4 French to Asquith, 20 May 1915, Asquith papers, vol. 27.
5 The term is elusive and changed in meaning over time and depending on who was using it. Here Kitchener, in contrast to Joffre's policy of large and costly frontal assaults, hoped that the Germans would obligingly wear themselves out by attacking the strongly entrenched Allied line in the West. For an engaging discussion on the subject of attrition see David French, 'The Meaning of Attrition, 1914–1916', *English Historical Review*, 103, (1988), pp. 385–405.
6 Memorandum by Hankey for the Prime Minister, 29 May 1915, WO 159/7; Hankey to Asquith, 29 May 1915, Asquith papers, vol. 27.
7 Spender and Asquith, *Life of Herbert Henry Asquith*, ii, p. 173; Hankey to his wife, undated, *c*. 2 June 1915, Hankey papers, 3/20; Hankey diary, 30–31 May 1915, ibid.
8 Haig diary, 1 June 1915, Haig papers.
9 Hankey diary, 3 June 1915, Hankey papers; Lambton (French's military secretary) to King George V, 3 June 1915, Royal Archives, GV Q832/229.
10 Asquith to Sylvia Henley, 2 June 1915, Asquith/Henley papers, C542/1.
11 French diary, 2 June 1915, French papers; Hankey diary, 3 June 1915, Hankey papers.
12 After Sir John appointed Robertson as his chief of staff, Wilson became principal liaison officer at French Headquarters.
13 Callwell, *Sir Henry Wilson*, i, p. 230n.
14 Spender and Asquith, *Life of Herbert Henry Asquith*, ii, pp. 173–74.
15 Asquith, note prepared after a visit to Sir John French, June 1915, Asquith papers, vol. 27.
16 Kitchener, 'The Dardanelles', 28 May 1915, CAB 37/128/27; Churchill, 'A Note on the General Situation', 1 June 1915, CAB 37/129/1; Selborne, 'The Dardanelles', 4 June 1915, CAB 37/129/10.
17 Hankey diary, 7 June 1915, Hankey papers.
18 Asquith to King George V, 9 June 1915, CAB 41/36/25. See also *Final Report of the Dardanelles Commission*, pp. 25–26; Churchill, *The World Crisis*, ii, pp. 410–11.
19 E. Ashmead-Bartlett, *The Uncensored Dardanelles* (London, 1928), pp. 124–25.
20 Minutes of the Dardanelles Committee, 12 June 1915, CAB 42/3/2; Cassar, *Kitchener*, p. 375.
21 Churchill, *The World Crisis*, ii, pp. 415–16; Minutes of the Dardanelles Committee, 17 June 1915, CAB 42/3/4.
22 French diary, 1 July 1915, French papers.
23 Asquith to King George V, 3 July 1915 (letter and accompanying minute), CAB 41/36/31; French diary, 2 and 3 July 1915, French papers; Wilson diary, 3 July 1915, Wilson papers; Asquith to Sylvia Henley, 2 July 1915, Asquith/Henley papers, C542/1.
24 Minutes of the Dardanelles Committee, 5 July 1915, CAB 42/3/7.
25 For details of the meeting see Cassar, *Kitchener*, pp. 381–82.
26 Hankey diary, 5 and 6 July 1915, Hankey papers.

27 Stamfordham, memorandum for the King, 9 July 1915, Royal Archives, GV Q921/3; Crewe to Bertie, 8 July 1915, Grey papers, FO 800/58; Hankey, 'Draft of Conclusions of Anglo-French Conference Held at Calais', 6 July 1915, CAB 28/9; French diary, 6 July 1915, French papers; Cassar, *Kitchener*, pp.380–82; Neilson, 'Kitchener', pp. 220–21.

28 Asquith, *Memories*, ii, pp. 107–8; Stamfordham, memorandum for the King, 9 July 1915, Royal Archives, GV Q921/3.

29 French diary, 8 July 1915, French papers.

30 Ibid.

31 Stamfordham, memorandum for the King, 9 July 1915, Royal Archives, GV Q921/3; Hankey diary, 8 July 1915, Hankey papers.

32 Cassar, *Kitchener*, p. 386; Gilbert, *Churchill*, iii, pp. 510–12; Lady Bonham Carter, *Winston Churchill*, p. 340; Kitchener to Asquith, 17 July 1915, Asquith papers, vol.14; Asquith to Churchill, 16 July 1915, ibid, vol. 46.

33 Asquith to Sylvia Henley, 19 July 1915, Asquith/Henley papers, C542/1.

34 The other reports were sent on 5 and 12 August. The originals are in vol. 117 (and the printed vol. 28) of the Asquith papers, but Hankey disclosed the greater part of all three in *The Supreme Command*, i, pp. 378–402.

35 *Final Report of the Dardanelles Commission*, p. 51; Rhodes James, *Gallipoli*, p. 307.

36 Asquith to Sylvia Henley, 15 August 1915, Asquith/Henley papers, C542/2.

37 Asquith to Kitchener, 20 August 1915, Kitchener papers, PRO 30/57/76.

38 Spender and Asquith, *Life of Herbert Henry Asquith*, ii, pp. 181–82.

39 For the details of Kitchener's trip to France see Cassar, *Kitchener*, pp. 387–88.

40 Asquith to King George V, 20 August 1915, CAB 41/36/40.

41 The term implies remaining on the defensive with occasional local attacks to keep the enemy off balance.

42 Asquith to King George V, 20 August 1915, CAB 41/36/40; Minutes of the Dardanelles Committee, 20 August 1915, CAB 42/3/16; Asquith to Sylvia Henley, 20 August 1915, Asquith/Henley papers, C542/2.

43 Asquith to King George V, 10 September 1915, CAB 41/36/43.

44 For the details of the meeting see 'Note of a Conference Held at the Terminus Hotel, Calais', 11 September 1915, CAB 28/1.

45 It is acknowledged by both and Grigg and Gilbert that, except for the opening weeks of war, Lloyd George spent little time on Treasury business. His budget in May 1915 was seriously flawed and, when he left the Treasury, it was in a state of utter chaos. For more details see see Grigg, *Lloyd George*, pp. 237–38 and B. Gilbert, *David Lloyd George*, pp. 200–1.

46 Sarah Melville notes, 4 September 1915, Melville papers. Lady Melville was secretary to Bonar Law from 1907 until 1916.

47 Asquith to King George V, 23 September 1915, CAB 41/36/45; Melville notes, 23 September 1915, Melville papers.

48 Asquith to Kitchener, 23 September 1915, Kitchener papers, PRO 30/57/76.

49 Hankey, *The Supreme Command*, ii, p. 445.

Notes to Chapter 8

1 Robbins, 'British Diplomacy and Bulgaria, 1914–1915', pp. 575–81; C.J. Lowe, 'The Failure of British Diplomacy in the Balkans, 1914–1916', *Canadian Journal of History*, 4 (1969), pp. 85–89; French, *British Strategy*, pp. 139–40; Guinn, *British Strategy and Politics*, pp. 97–98; Spender and Asquith, *Life of Herbert Henry Asquith*, ii, p. 185.
2 Cyril Falls, *Military Operations: Macedonia* (London, 1933), i, p. 31.
3 Asquith to Grey, 1 October 1915, Grey papers, FO 800/100.
4 Note by E.Drummond, 2 October 1915, ibid.
5 Leon, *Greece*, pp. 207–24.
6 The convention obligated Greece to come to Serbia's assistance in case it was attacked by Bulgaria. Serbia, for its part, had to concentrate 150,000 men opposite the Bulgarian frontier. Serbia, however, was unable to meet that condition as its forces were deployed to meet an Austro-German as well as a Bulgarian offensive. Venizelos was prepared to activate the treaty as long as the Entente powers in the West provided the 150,000 men themselves.
7 'Appreciation of the Situation in the Balkans by the General Staff', 24 September 1915, CAB 42/3/29.
8 Spender and Asquith, *Life of Herbert Henry Asquith*, ii, p. 185; George H. Cassar, *The French and the Dardanelles* (London, 1971), pp. 197–201; Jan K. Tanenbaum, *General Maurice Sarrail, 1856–1929* (Chapel Hill, NC, 1974), p. 66.
9 Leon, *Greece*, pp. 242–44.
10 Minutes of the Dardanelles Committee, 7 and 11 October 1915, CAB 42/4/4, 6.
11 Minutes of the Dardanelles Committee, 4 October 1915, CAB 42/4/2.
12 Minutes of the Dardanelles Committee , 6 and 11 October 1915, CAB 42/4/3, 6.
13 Memorandum by Bonar Law, 12 October 1915, CAB 37/135/23; memorandum by Lloyd George, 14 October 1915, CAB 37/136/9; Minutes of the Dardanelles Committee, 11 and 14 October 1915, CAB 42/4/6, 9,; Lloyd George, *War Memoirs*, i, pp. 295–97; D. Woodward, *Lloyd George*, p. 63.
14 Minutes of the Dardanelles Committee, 14 October 1915, CAB 42/4/9; Margot Asquith to Hankey, 15 October 1915 in Gilbert, ed., *Companion*, pp. 1219–20; Cooper, *Old Men Forget*, p. 56; Asquith to Dardanelles Commission, 29 March 1917, and Lansdowne to Dardanelles Commission, 7 March 1917, CAB 19/33.
15 *Final Report of the Dardanelles Commission*, p. 53.
16 Carson to Asquith, 12 and 17 October 1915, Asquith papers, vol. 15; Bonar Law to Asquith, 15 October 1915, Bonar Law papers, 53/6/44.
17 'Note of a Conference Held at … 10 Downing Street', 29 October 1915, CAB 28/1; memoranda by Kitchener, 30 October 1915, and by Joffre, 29 October 1915, ibid. ; Hankey diary, 29 October 1915, Hankey papers.
18 Asquith to Venetia Stanley, 16 and 28 November 1914, in Brocks, ed., HHA, pp. 316, 321; Jenkins, *Asquith*, pp. 337–38.
19 See next chapter.
20 Note by Beaverbrook of a conversation with Bonar Law, 15 September 1915, Beaverbrook papers, G/5, fol. 7.
21 Blake, *The Unknown Prime Minister*, pp. 262–64; Note by Beaverbrook of a conversation with Bonar Law, 16 September 1915, Beaverbrook papers, G/5, fol. 7. Blake is not certain from whom the suggestion originated. Replying to Lloyd George, Bonar Law denied that he had raised the matter with the Prime Minister. However, in a private conversation with Beaverbrook he admitted that he had taken the initiative.

22 Wilson, *Downfall*, pp. 385–86.

23 See above p. 272.

24 Crewe to King George V, 22 October 1915, CAB 41/36/49.

25 Lansdowne to Crewe, and Crewe to Lansdowne, 11 November 1915, Crewe papers, C/30.

26 Balfour to Asquith, 23 September 1915, Asquith papers, vol. 28.

27 Curzon to Asquith, 22 September 1915, ibid., vol. 28. See also Lansdowne to Asquith, 5 and 9 November 1915, ibid.; Middleton to Asquith, 4 November 1915, ibid.; Selborne to Asquith, 23 September 1915, ibid.; Long to Bonham Carter, 1 November 1915, ibid., vol. 15.

28 Asquith to Sylvia Henley, 28 October 1915, Asquith/Henley papers, C542/2; Asquith, 'Conduct of the War', 28 October 1915, CAB 37/136/36.

29 Lloyd George to Asquith, 31 October 1915, Lloyd George papers, D/18/2/11.

30 Gilbert, *Churchill*, iii, pp. 558–59; note by Beaverbrook of a conversation with Bonar Law, 15 September 1915, Beaverbrook papers, G/5, fol. 7; Addison diary, 2 and 9 November 1915, Addison papers; Hankey diary, 1 November 1915, Hankey papers.

31 Bonar Law to Lloyd George, 1 November 1915, Lloyd George papers, D/17/8/9.

32 Wilson, ed., *Political Diaries*, p. 153.

33 Cassar, *Kitchener*, pp. 413–17; Beaverbrook, *Politicians and the War*, p. 191; Taylor, ed., *A Diary by Frances Stevenson*, p. 72.

34 Asquith to Lloyd George, 3 November 1915, Lloyd George papers, D/18/2/12.

35 Note by Beaverbrook of a conversation with Bonar Law, 2 and 3 November 1915, Beaverbrook papers, G/5, fol. 7.

36 Bonar Law to Asquith, 5 November 1915, Asquith papers, vol. 15.

37 Asquith to Sylvia Henley, 5 November 1915, Asquith/Henley papers, C542/2.

38 Bonar Law to Asquith, 5 November 1915, Asquith papers, vol. 15; Asquith to Bonar Law, 5 November 1915, ibid.; Bonar Law to Asquith, 8 November 1915, ibid.; Balfour to Bonar Law, 7 November 1915, Bonar Law papers, 51/5/15; Chamberlain to Bonar Law, 7 November 1915, ibid., 117/1/22, 23. Beaverbrook states in his book (pp. 162–63) that Asquith won over Bonar Law by promising to support his demand for the evacuation of Gallipoli irrespective of what Kitchener might recommend. Contemporary evidence, however, does not confirm this claim.

39 Asquith to Sylvia Henley, 10 and 11 November 1915, Asquith/Henley papers, C542/2; Asquith to King George V, 11 November 1915, CAB 41/36/51; Lansdowne to Asquith, 9 November 1915, Asquith papers, vol. l5.

40 Asquith to Sylvia Henley, 10 November 1915, Asquith/Henley papers, C542/2.

41 Gilbert, *Churchill*, iii, pp. 563–66.

42 Asquith to Sylvia Henley, 13 November 1915, Asquith/Henley papers, C542/2.

43 For the full text see Parliamentary Debates, *House of Commons*, 15 November 1915, vol. 75, cols 1499ff.

44 Kitchener's telegrams from the Dardanelles can be found in the Asquith papers, vol. 121 ; General A. Murray, 'General Staff Arguments For or Against the Complete or Partial Evacuation of Gallipoli', 22 November 1915, CAB 42/5/20. Appended to the minutes of the War Committee, 23 November 1915.

45 Minutes of the War Committee, 23 November 1915, CAB 42/5/20.

46 Kitchener to Asquith, 10 November 1915, Asquith papers, vol. 121.

47 Asquith to Kitchener, 12 November 1915, ibid., vol. 121.

48 Asquith to Kitchener, 14 November 1915, ibid., vol. 121; 'Conference tenu au Ministère des Affairs Etrangères a Paris', 17 November 1915, CAB 28/1; Cassar, *The French and the Dardanelles*, pp. 220–21.

49 Asquith to Kitchener, 19 November 1915, WO 33/747.

50 Kitchener to Asquith, 22 November 1915, Asquith papers, vol. 121.

51 Minutes of the Army Council, 27 November 1915, WO 163/21; Von Donop to Kitchener, 29 November 1915, WO 159/4.
52 The events leading to French's resignation are explored in depth in Cassar, *Sir John French*, ch. 14.
53 Jenkins, *Asquith*, pp. 383–84; Field-Marshal Sir William Robertson, *From Private to Field Marshal* (Boston, 1921), p. 236; Cassar, *Kitchener*, pp. 427–28.
54 Parliamentary Debates, *House of Commons*, 11 November 1915, vol. 75, col. 1389ff.
55 Robertson, *From Private*, pp. 236–37; Cassar, *Kitchener*, pp. 429–30.
56 Memorandum by Robertson, 5 December 1915, Kitchener papers, PRO 30/57/55.
57 Asquith to Sylvia Henley, 7 December 1915, Asquith/Henley papers, C542/2; Kitchener to Robertson, 7 December 1915, Kitchener papers, PRO 30/57/55.
58 Asquith to Curzon, 8 December 1915, Curzon papers, EUR F112/114.
59 Curzon to Asquith, 8 December 1915, Asquith papers, vol. 15. Arthur and FitzGerald were Kitchener's secretaries.
60 Hankey diary, 8 December 1915, Hankey papers.
61 Hankey, 'The Future Military Policy at the Dardanelles', 29 November 1915, CAB 42/5/25.
62 Curzon, 'Evacuation of Gallipoli', 29 November 1915, CAB 37/138/22; Corbett, *Naval Operations*, iii, pp. 212–14; Aspinall-Oglander, *Gallipoli*, ii, pp. 435–36; Rhodes James, *Gallipoli*, pp. 336–37.
63 On the Mesopotamian campaign see A. J.Barker, *The Neglected War: Mesopotamia, 1914–1918* (London, 1967); Brig.-Gen. F. J. Moberly, *The Campaign in Mesopotamia, 1914–1918* (London, 1923–24), i, ii; Sir Arnold T. Wilson, *Loyalties: Mesopotamia, 1914–1917* (London 1930), i; *Report of the Mesopotamia Commission* (London 1917); S. A. Cohen, 'The Genesis of the British Campaign in Mesopotamia, 1914', *Middle Eastern Studies*, 12 (1976), pp. 119–32; John S. Galbraith, 'No Man's Child: The Campaign in Mesopotamia, 1914–1916', *International History Review*, 6 (1984), pp. 358–85; Douglas Goold, 'Lord Hardinge and the Mesopotamia Expedition and Inquiry, 1914–1917', *Historical Journal*, 19 (1976), pp. 919–45.
64 Report of an inter-departmental committee on the strategical situation in Mesopotamia, 16 October 1915, CAB 42/4/12.
65 *Report of the Mesopotamia Commission*, p. 24.
66 Jackson and Murray, 'The Present and Prospective Situation in Syria and Mesopotamia', 19 October 1915, CAB 42/4/15. Appended to the minutes of the Dardanelles Committee, 21 October 1915.
67 Minutes of the Dardanelles Committee, 14 and 21 October 1915, CAB 42/4/9, 15.
68 Hankey to Asquith, 22 October 1915, Asquith papers, vol. 120.
69 For a detailed chronicle on the siege of Kut, see Ronald Millar, *The Death of an Army: The Siege of Kut, 1915–1916* (Boston, 1970) and Russell Braddon, *The Siege* (New York, 1970).
70 Hankey diary, 2 December 1915, Hankey papers; Minutes of the War Committee, 2 December 1915, CAB 42/6/2; Asquith to King George V, 3 December 1915, CAB 41/36/53.
71 Viviani fell from power in the closing days of October. He was succeeded by Aristide Briand who also held the office of Foreign Minister. D. J. Dutton has ably examined the circumstances that led to the change of government in 'Union Sacree and the French Cabinet Crisis of October 1915', *European Studies Review*, 8 (1978), pp. 411–24.
72 Summary of the Conference held at Calais on 5 December 1915, CAB 28/1; D. J. Dutton, 'The Calais Conference of 1915', *Historical Journal*, 21 (1978), pp. 148–50.
73 Cassar, *The French and the Dardanelles*, pp. 231–33.
74 'Military Conference of Allies Held at the French Headquarters, 6–8 December 1915', CAB 28/1; meeting at Chantilly, 6 December 1915, WO 106/1454.
75 Asquith to Sylvia Henley, 7 December 1915, Asquith/Henley papers, C542/2.

76 Asquith to King George V, 8 December 1915, CAB 41/36/54.
77 Balfour and Lloyd George had suggested, not abandoning the French as Asquith implied, but giving them complete authority over the Balkan campaign.
78 Asquith to Sylvia Henley, 8 December 1915, Asquith/Henley papers, C542/2.
79 'Conference between Sir E. Grey and Lord Kitchener and M. Briand and General Gallieni at Paris', n.d., CAB 38/139/24; Kitchener to Asquith, 10 December 1915, Kitchener papers, PRO 30/57/76; Asquith to King George V, 15 December 1915, CAB 41/36/55.
80 The revised document has been reproduced in its entirety in Field Marshal Sir William Robertson, *Soldiers and Statesmen, 1914–1918* (London, 1926), i, pp. 168–71; and Victor Bonham-Carter, *Soldier True* (London, 1963), appendix 1.
81 Kitchener to Asquith, 10 December 1915, Kitchener papers, PRO 30/57/76.
82 Stamfordham to Asquith, 3 December 1915, Royal Archives, GV Q838/49.
83 Esher to Asquith, 10 December 1915, Asquith papers, vol. 15.
84 Robertson to Wigram (the King's equerry), 15 December 1915, Royal Archives, GV Q838/63.
85 Asquith to Sylvia Henley, 18 December 1915, Asquith/Henley papers, C542/2; Asquith to Stamfordham, 18 December 1915, Royal Archives, GV Q838/67.
86 Robertson, *From Private*, pp. 287–90.
87 Asquith to Sylvia Henley, 20 December 1915, Asquith/Henley papers, C542/2; Asquith, *Memories*, ii, p. 112.
88 Asquith to Sylvia Henley, 24 December 1915, Asquith/Henley papers, C542/2.
89 Asquith to Sylvia Henley, 23 December 1915, ibid.
90 MacCallum diary, 29 December 1915, MacCallum papers.
91 Minutes of the War Committee, 23 December 1915, CAB 42/6/13; Hankey, *The Supreme Command*, ii, p. 463.

Notes to Chapter 9

1 Samuel J. Hurwitz, *State Intervention in Great Britain* (New York, 1949), ch. 2; French, *British Economic*, ch. 2 and his article 'The Rise and Fall of 'Business as Usual'' in Kathleen Burk, *War and the State*, pp. 7ff; Trevor Wilson, *The Myriad Faces of War: Britain and the Great War, 1914–1918* (Cambridge, 1986), ch. 20.

2 Sir Llewellyn Woodward, *Great Britain and the War of 1914–1918* (London, 1967), pp. 453–54.

3 J. M. Bourne, *Great Britain and the Great War, 1914–1918* (London, 1989), p. 116.

4 Arthur Marwick, *The Deluge: British Society and the First World War* (Boston, 1965), passim; Chris Wrigley, 'The First World War and State Intervention in Industrial Relations, 1914–1918', in Chris Wrigley, ed., *A History of British Industrial Relations, 1914–1939* (Brighton, 1987).

5 Emmott diary, 25 August 1914, Emmott papers; Pease diary, 25 August 1914, Gainford papers; David, ed., *Inside Asquith's Cabinet*, pp. 184–85.

6 Denis Hayes, *Conscription Conflict* (London, 1949), passim; G. D. H. Cole, *Labour in War Time* (London, 1915), passim; Lloyd George, *War Memoirs*, i, pp. 426–27; Grey, *Twenty-Five Years*, ii, p. 72; Gollin, *Proconsul*, pp. 230–33.

7 R. J. Q. Adams and Philip P. Poirier, *The Conscription Controversy in Great Britain, 1900–1918* (London, 1987), p. 66.

8 Parliamentary Debates, *House of Commons*, 11 March 1915, vol. 70, col. 1553.

9 Ibid., 20 April 1915, vol. 71, col. 172–73.

10 Asquith, *Memories*, ii, pp. 123–24.

11 Cassar, *Kitchener*, pp. 445–46.

12 Gerald H. Jordan, 'The Politics of Conscription in Britain, 1905–1916', (unpublished Ph.D. thesis, University of California, Irvine, 1974), pp. 127–29; Adams, *Arms and the Wizard*, pp. 101–2.

13 Parliamentary Debates, *House of Commons*, 28 July 1915, vol. 73, cols 2395, 2408.

14 *Statistics of the Military Effort of the British Empire during the Great War, 1914–1920* (London, 1922), p. 364.

15 Asquith, *Memories*, ii, p. 108.

16 Memorandum by Crewe to the members of the War Policy Committee, 12 August 1915, in Gilbert ed., *Companion*, pp. 1132–34.

17 War Policy Committee Report, 8 September 1915, CAB 37/134/9.

18 Supplementary Report, 2 September 1915, CAB 37/134/3; Revised Supplementary Report, 7 September 1915, CAB 37/134/7.

19 Memorandum by Henderson, 7 September 1915, CAB 37/134/5.

20 Hankey, *The Supreme Command*, i, p. 427.

21 Simon to Asquith, 25 August 1915, Simon papers, box 51.

22 *Annual Register*, 1915, p. 154.

23 Parliamentary Debates, *House of Commons*, 28 September 1915, vol. 74, col. 833.

24 Grigg, *Lloyd George*, p. 328.

25 18 September 1915.

26 Asquith to Balfour, 18 September 1915, Asquith papers, vol. 28.

27 Balfour, 'Efficiency in War and Compulsion', 19 September 1915, CAB 37/134/25.

28 Memorandum by Derby, 20 December 1915, CAB 37/139/41.

29 Kitchener, 'Recruiting for the Armies', 8 October 1915, CAB 37/135/15.

30 Randolph Churchill, *Lord Derby: 'King of Lancashire'* (London, 1959), pp. 191–92.

31 Note by the Prime Minister, 16 October 1915, Asquith papers, vol. 28.

32 Churchill, *Lord Derby*, pp. 192–93.
33 Asquith to King George V, 12 October 1915, CAB 41/36/48.
34 Memorandum by Stamfordham, 16 October 1915, Royal Archives GV K869/1.
35 Ibid.
36 Bonar Law to Asquith, (copy) 16 October 1915, Kitchener papers, PRO 30/57/73; note by Beaverbrook of a conversation with Bonar Law, 16 October 1915, Beaverbrook papers, G/5, fol. 7.
37 Hankey diary, 16 October 1915, Hankey papers.
38 Taylor, ed., *A Diary by Frances Stevenson*, p. 69.
39 Riddell, *War Diary*, p. 126.
40 Asquith to Kitchener, 17 October 1915, Kitchener papers, PRO 30/57/76.
41 Cassar, *Kitchener*, p. 450.
42 Taylor, ed., *A Diary by Frances Stevenson*, p. 70.
43 Jenkins, *Asquith*, p. 376.
44 Margot Asquith to Murray, 20 October 1915, Elibank papers, MS 8803, fol. 251.
45 Memorandum from Lord Derby to Mayors, Lord Mayors and Chairmen of County Councils, 16 October 1915, Derby papers, 920 DER (17) 26/2; Lloyd George, *War Memoirs*, i, p. 435.
46 Derby to Kitchener, 8 October 1915, Kitchener papers, PRO 30/57/73.
47 Note by the Prime Minister, 16 October 1915, Asquith papers, vol. 28.
48 Derby to Asquith, 28 October 1915, Asquith papers, vol. 15; Adams and Poirier, *The Conscription Controversy*, pp. 128–29.
49 Parliamentary Debates, *House of Commons*, 2 November 1915, vol. 75, cols 523–24.
50 *The Times*, 12 November 1915.
51 Memorandum by Derby, 13 December 1915, CAB 37/139/26.
52 *Statistics of the Military Effort*, p. 364.
53 Asquith to King George V, 15 December 1915, CAB 41/36/55.
54 See table in Adams and Poirier, *The Conscription Controversy*, p. 135.
55 Memorandum by Derby, 20 December 1915, CAB 37/139/41.
56 Spender and Asquith, *The Life of Herbert Henry Asquith*, ii, p. 201.
57 Asquith to Sylvia Henley, 26 December 1915, Asquith/Henley papers, C542/2.
58 Taylor, ed., *A Diary by Frances Stevenson*, p. 89.
59 Ibid.
60 Samuel, 'Enlistments', 22 December 1915, CAB 37/139/45; Asquith to King George V, 28 December 1915, CAB 41/36/56; Asquith to Sylvia Henley, 28 December 1915, Asquith/Henley papers, C542/2; Runciman to his wife, 27 and 28 December 1915, Runciman papers, WR 303. Asquith referred to the scheme in correspondence as his own, possibly because he may have suggested its broad outlines to Samuel.
61 Asquith to Sylvia Henley, 28 December 1915, Asquith/Henley papers, C542/2; Runciman to his wife, 28 December 1915, Runciman papers, WR 303; Lady Scott diary, 28 December 1915, Kennet papers.
62 Simon to Asquith, 27 December 1915, Simon papers, box 52.
63 Asquith to Montagu, 28 December 1915, Montagu papers, AS 1/1/4s; Runciman to his wife, 28 December 1915, Runciman papers, WR 303.
64 Asquith to Simon, McKenna and Runciman, 28 December 1915, Simon papers, box 52.
65 Simon to Asquith, 29 December 1915, Asquith papers, vol. 28.
66 Grey to Asquith, 29 December 1915, ibid.
67 Asquith to Sylvia Henley, 29 December 1915, Asquith/Henley papers, C542/2; memorandum by Stamfordham, 29 December 1915, Royal Archives, GV K869/3; G. M. Trevelyan, *Grey of Fallodon* (Boston, 1937), pp. 369–70.
68 Asquith to Sylvia Henley, 29 December 1915, Asquith/Henley papers, C542/2; Runciman to his wife, 29 December 1915, Runciman papers, WR 303.

69 Birrell to Asquith, 29 December 1915, Asquith papers, vol. 28.

70 Hankey diary, 29 and 30 December 1915, Hankey papers.

71 Ibid., 30 December 1915.

72 Memorandum by Stamfordham, 29 December 1915, Royal Archives, GV K869/3; Asquith to Sylvia Henley, 30 December 1915, Asquith/Henley papers, C542/2; Montagu to Grey, 30 December 1915, Montagu papers, A 56/10/28; Montagu to Asquith, 3 January 1916, ibid, AS 1/1/48.

73 Asquith to King George V, 1 January 1916, CAB 41/37/1; Asquith to Sylvia Henley, 1 January 1916, Asquith/Henley papers, C542/3; Lady Scott diary, 2 January 1916, Kennet papers.

74 Memorandum by Stamfordham, 31 December 1915, Royal Archives, GV K869/3.

75 Thomas C. Kennedy, *The Hound of Conscience: A History of the No-Conscription Fellowship, 1914–1918* (Fayetteville, AR, 1981), pp. 82–83; Adams and Poirier, *The Conscription Controversy*, pp. 138–41.

76 Parliamentary Debates, *House of Commons*, 5 January 1916, vol. 77, cols 949–58.

77 Ibid., cols 962–78.

78 Asquith's nickname for Simon.

79 Asquith to Sylvia Henley, 5 January 1916, Asquith/Henley papers, C542/3.

80 G. D. H. Cole, *A History of the Labour Party from 1914* (London, 1948), pp. 26–27; Henderson, Organized Labour and the Military Service Bill, 10 January 1916, CAB 37/140/17.

81 Henderson to Asquith, 10 January 1916, Asquith papers, vol. 16.

82 Asquith to King George V, 10 January 1916, CAB 41/37/3.

83 Minutes of the meeting, 12 January 1916, Asquith papers, vol. 90.

84 John Rae, *Conscience and Politics* (London, 1970), p. 39; *Annual Report of the Labour Party Conference*, 1916, p. 24.

85 R. J. Q. Adams, 'Asquith's Choice: The May Coalition and the Coming of Conscription, 1915–1916', *Journal of British Studies*, 25 (1986), p. 260.

86 As a sop to McKenna and Runciman, Asquith had set up the committee at the close of 1915 to adjudicate whether the country should supply more soldiers or money to the Alliance. For its conclusions see 'Report of the Cabinet Committee on the Co-ordination of Military and Financial Effort', 4 February 1916, CAB 37/142/11.

87 'Memorandum by the Chief of the Imperial General Staff Regarding the Supply of Personnel', 21 March 1916, CAB 42/11/8; Proceedings of the Army Council, 6 April 1916, Robertson papers, 1/11; Cassar, *Kitchener*, pp. 453–54; Viscount Oliver Esher, ed., *Journals and Letters of Reginald Viscount Esher* (London, 1938), iv, p. 17.

88 'Second Report of the Cabinet Committee on the Co-ordination of the Military and Financial Effort', 13 April 1916, CAB 37/145/35.

89 The purpose of the Army Council was to discuss and determine all questions of military policy. It was composed of the Secretary for War, the Financial Secretary, the Parliamentary Under-Secretary and the heads of the four military departments – the Adjutant-General, the Quartermaster-General, the Master-General of the Ordnance and the Chief of the Imperial General Staff.

90 Haig diary, 15 April 1916, Haig papers; Hankey diary, 15 April 1916, Hankey papers.

91 Proceedings of the Army Council, 15 April 1916, Robertson papers, 1/11.

92 Memorandum by Stamfordham, 16 April 1916, Royal Archives, GV K951/2, 3 and 4; Addison diary, 17 April 1916, Addison papers; Taylor, ed., *A Diary by Frances Stevenson*, pp. 105–06.

93 Memorandum by Stamfordham, 16 April 1916, Royal Archives, GV K951/2, 3.

94 Bonar Law to Asquith, 17 April 1916, Asquith papers, vol. 16.

95 Addison diary, 20 April 1916, Addison papers; Asquith to Stamfordham, 18 April 1916, Royal Archives, GV K951/6; memorandum by Stamfordham, 19 April 1916, ibid, GV K951/7; 'Proceedings of the Cabinet Committee on the Size of the Army', 18

April 1916, CAB 27/3; Wilson, ed., *Political Diaries*, pp. 199–200; Adams and Poirier, *The Conscription Controversy*, pp. 162–63.

96 Asquith to Stamfordham, 18 April 1916, Royal Archives, GV K951/6.

97 Asquith to Lady Scott, 19 April 1916, Kennet papers, 109/3.

98 Lady Scott diary, 18 April 1916, Kennet papers; memorandum by Stamfordham, 19 April 1916, Royal Archives, GV K951/7.

99 Parliamentary Debates, *House of Commons*, 19 April 1916, vol. 81, col. 2351.

100 Addison diary, 20 April 1916, Addison papers.

101 A copy of the resolution can be found in the Asquith papers, vol. 30.

102 Asquith to Stamfordham, 20 April 1916, Royal Archives, GV K951/9; Taylor, ed., *A Diary by Frances Stevenson*, pp. 107–8; proposal by Asquith at the secret session of the House of Commons, 25 April 1916, Asquith papers, vol. 30; Esher, ed., *Journals and Letters*, iv, pp. 18–19.

103 Asquith to Sylvia Henley, 20 April 1916, Asquith/Henley papers, C542/3.

104 Asquith to Sylvia Henley, 26 April 1916, ibid, C542/3.

105 Cecil to Asquith, 28 April 1916, Asquith papers, vol. 30.

106 Asquith to King George V, 29 April 1916, CAB 41/37/18.

107 Hankey diary, 2 May 1916, Hankey papers.

Notes to Chapter 10

1 'Military Conference of the Allies Held at the French Headquarters, 6–8 December 1915', CAB 28/1; Minutes of the War Committee, 28 December 1915, and 'Note for the War Committee by the Chief of the Imperial General Staff with Reference to the General Staff Paper Dated 16 December 1915', 23 December 1915, CAB 42/6/14.

2 'Views of the First Lord of the Admiralty on the Conduct of the War', 27 December 1915 and Minutes of the War Committee, 13 January 1916, CAB 42/7/5; D. Woodward, *Lloyd George*, p. 83.

3 Robertson, 'The Question of Offensive Operations on the Western Front', 1 January 1916, CAB 42/7/1.

4 Minutes of the War Committee, 13 January 1916, CAB 42/7/5; memorandum by Grey, 14 January 1916, and Chamberlain, 'Military Policy', 17 January 1916, CAB 42/7/8.

5 Wilson, *Myriad Faces*, p. 312.

6 Haig diary, 12 March 1916, Haig papers; Robertson, *Soldiers and Statesmen*, i, p. 258.

7 Minutes of the War Committee, 21 March 1916, CAB 42/11/6.

8 Arthur S. Link, *Wilson: The Struggle for Neutrality, 1914–1915* (Princeton, NJ, 1960), pp. 191–217; Patrick Devlin, *Too Proud to Fight: Woodrow Wilson's Neutrality* (New York, 1975), ch. 8.

9 C. M. Mason, 'Anglo-American Relations: Mediation and 'Permanent Peace'', in Hinsley, ed., *British Foreign Policy*, pp. 466–67.

10 On Anglo-American finance and supply, see Kathleen Burk, *Britain, America and the Sinews of War, 1914–1918* (London, 1985).

11 Charles Seymour, ed., *The Intimate Papers of Colonel House* (Boston, 1926), i, p. 378.

12 Devlin, *Too Proud to Fight*, p. 209; Link, *The Struggle for Neutrality*, pp. 221–23.

13 Arthur S. Link, *Wilson: Confusion and Crises, 1915–1916* (Princeton, NJ, 1964), p. 114.

14 Hankey, *The Supreme Command*, ii, p. 478.

15 The division of Ottoman spoils was formally embodied in the Sykes-Picot Agreement of May 1916. Russian influence would be extended to include Armenia, part of Kurdistan and adjacent territories in north-eastern Anatolia. France was to obtain outright the coastal strip of Syria north of the city of Tyre, the vilayet of Adana and a large slice of Cilicia. The rest of Syria and northern Mesopotamia would become an independent Arab zone under French protection. Britain was to receive southern Mesopotamia and an enclave around Haifa and Acre on the Mediterranean. Arabia, including the Muslim holy places, would be placed under Arab rule. Jerusalem and much of the rest of Palestine, at the insistence of the Russians, was to have an international administration, the details of which were to be settled later.

16 Seymour, ed., *Colonel House*, ii, pp. 179–82; Lloyd George, *War Memoirs*, i, p. 411.

17 Grey, *Twenty-Five Years*, ii, pp. 127–28.

18 Minutes of the War Committee, 22 Februrary 1916, CAB 42/9/3.

19 Seymour, ed., *Colonel House*, ii, p. 202.

20 Grey to the War Committee, 15 March 1916, Asquith papers, vol. 29.

21 Hankey diary, 16 March 1916, Hankey papers.

22 Montagu to Asquith, 18 March 1916, Asquith papers, vol. 16.

23 The minutes, and a memorandum by Grey, of the special meeting were appended to the minutes of the regular War Committee meeting, 21 March 1916, CAB 42/11/6.

24 Wilson, ed., *Political Diaries*, pp. 188–89.

25 Asquith to Sylvia Henley, 8 March 1916, Asquith/Henley papers, C542/3.

26 Ibid.; Lady Bonham Carter, *Winston Churchill*, pp. 365–66.

27 Parliamentary Debates, *House of Commons*, 7 March 1916, vol. 80, cols 1420–30.

28 Ibid., 8 March 1916, cols 1563–75.

29 Wilson, ed., *Political Diaries*, p. 191.

30 Gilbert, *Churchill*, iii, p. 730.

31 Asquith to Sylvia Henley, 9 March 1916, Asquith/Henley papers, C542/3. Asquith misdated the letter.

32 Lady Bonham Carter, *Winston Churchill*, p. 373.

33 Asquith to Sylvia Henley, 11 March 1916, Asquith/Henley papers, C542/3.

34 Gilbert, *Churchill*, iii, pp. 735–36.

35 Asquith to Sylvia Henley, 12 March 1916, Asquith/Henley papers, C542/3.

36 Asquith to Lady Scott, 15 March 1915, Kennet papers, 109/3.

37 'Extracts from Proceedings of a Conference Held at Paris, 27 March 1916'. Appended to the minutes of the War Committee, 7 April 1916, CAB 42/12/5; 'Process-Verbaux of Allied Conference, Paris, 26–28 March 1916', CAB 28/1; Hankey diary, 27 and 28 March 1916, Hankey papers; memorandum by Bertie, 27 March 1916, Bertie papers, FO 800/175.

38 Riddell, *War Diary*, p. 168.

39 Asquith to Lady Scott, 30 March 1916, Kennet papers, 109/3; Spender and Asquith, *Life of Herbert Henry Asquith*, ii, pp. 175–76.

40 Hankey diary, 2 April 1916, Hankey papers.

41 Asquith, *Memories*, ii, p. 121; Hankey to his wife, 1 April 1916, Hankey papers, 3/21.

42 Sir James Rennell Rodd, *Social and Diplomatic Memoirs, 1902–1919* (London, 1925), pp. 290–92; Hankey diary, 3 and 4 April 1916, Hankey papers.

43 Rodd to Grey (copy), 8 April 1916, Asquith papers, vol. 30.

44 Hankey diary, 5 April 1916, Hankey papers; Minutes of the War Committee, 7 April 1916, CAB 42/12/5.

45 French, *British Strategy*, pp. 181–2; Haig to Robertson, 4 April 1916; Robertson, 'Future Military Operations', 31 March 1916; and Minutes of the War Committee, 7 April 1916, CAB 42/12/5.

46 Robertson, *Soldiers and Statesmen*, ii, pp. 104–14; Tanenbaum, *General Maurice Sarrail*, pp. 90–94; Neilson, *Strategy and Supply*, pp. 146–49; Robertson, 'Note … on Co-ordination of Arrangements for Supplying and Equipping Serbian Army', 25 January 1916, CAB 42/7/13; Minutes of the War Committee, 23 March 1916 and 'Note by the CIGS on the Situation at Salonika', 22 March 1916, CAB 42/11/9; Robertson, 'Offensive Operations in the Balkans', 29 April 1916 and Minutes of the War Committee, 3 May 1916, CAB 42/13/2.

47 Asquith to Curzon, 21 March 1916, Curzon papers, EUR F112/116.

48 Good explanations of this strange episode can be found in Moberly, *Campaign in Mesopotamia*, ii, pp. 452–58; Margaret FitzHerbert, *The Man who was Greenmantle: A Biography of Aubrey Herbert* (London, 1983), pp. 178–81; Aubrey Herbert, *Mons, Anzac and Kut* (London, 1919), pp. 221ff. Captain Aubrey Herbert, a Conservative MP, was one of three Englishmen who negotiated the final details of the surrender.

49 Parliamentary Debates, *House of Lords*, 4 May 1916, vol. 21, cols 902–3; *House of Commons*, 2 May 1916, vol. 81, col. 2615.

50 The most recent book on the 1916 Irish uprising is Peter De Rosa, *Rebels: The Irish Rising of 1916* (London, 1990).

51 Jenkins, *Asquith*, pp. 396–98.

52 Grigg, *Lloyd George*, pp. 349–52.

53 Wilson, *Downfall*, pp. 70, 87.

54 Hankey diary, 31 May–3 June 1916, Hankey papers.

55 There are many accounts of the battle of Jutland but the best, in my view, is Marder, *From the Dreadnought*, iii.

56 Hankey, *The Supreme Command*, ii, p. 506.
57 Pease, 'War Reminiscences', p. 78, Gainford papers, vol. 42.
58 Lady Bonham Carter, *Winston Churchill*, p. 378.
59 Pease, 'War Reminiscences', p. 78, Gainford papers, vol. 42.
60 Asquith to Stamfordham, 8 June 1916, Royal Archives, GV K951/13.
61 D. Woodward, *Lloyd George*, p. 98.
62 Hankey diary, 6 June 1916, Hankey papers.
63 Balfour to Salisbury, 17 June 1916, Balfour papers, Add. 49758.
64 Wilson, ed., *Political Diaries*, pp. 216–17.
65 Beaverbrook, *Politicians and the War*, pp. 207–8.
66 Ibid., p. 209.
67 Memorandum by Stamfordham, 17 June 1916, Royal Archives, GV K951/17; Lady Scott diary, 16 June 1916, Kennet papers; Lloyd George to Asquith, 17 June 1915, Asquith papers, vol. 30; Wilson, ed., *Political Diaries*, pp. 218–19.
68 Jenkins, *Asquith*, pp. 406–7.
69 Memorandum by Stamfordham, 17 June 1916, Royal Archives, GV K951/17; Montagu to Asquith, 20 June 1916, Lloyd George papers, D/17/16/5. Montagu inadvertently placed a copy of the letter among papers which he gave to J. T. Davies, Lloyd George's principal private secretary.
70 Arthur Lee to Lloyd George, 18 June 1916, Lloyd George papers, D/1/1/21.
71 Memorandum by Stamfordham, 17 June 1916, Royal Archives, GV K951/17; Long to Stamfordham, n.d., ibid., GV K951/15; Jenkins, *Asquith*, pp. 408–9; R. Churchill, *Lord Derby*, p. 211.
72 Grigg, *Lloyd George*, pp. 356–57; D. Woodward, *Lloyd George*, p. 101; Lee to Lloyd George, 18 June 1916, Lloyd George papers, D/1/1/21.
73 Cooper, *Old Men Forget*, p. 54.
74 Cooper was then a junior clerk at the Foreign Office.
75 M. Bonham Carter, ed., *Autobiography of Margot Asquith*, p. 318.
76 V. Bonham-Carter, *Soldier True*, pp. 178–81.

Notes to Chapter 11

1 For a detailed description of the battle of the Somme see Edmonds, *1916* (London, 1932–38), i,ii; Lyn Macdonald, *Somme* (York, 1989); A. H. Farrar-Hockley, *The Somme* (London, 1964); Terry Norman, *The Hell they Called Highwood: The Somme 1916* (London, 1984). Gerald Gliddon, *When the Barrage Lifts* (Norwich, 1987) is based on the topography of the battlefield itself. See also the numerous biographies on Haig, the most recent one being Denis Winter, *Haig's Command: A Reassessment* (New York, 1991).

2 V. Bonham-Carter, *Soldier True*, p. 182.

3 Memorandum by Haig, 1 August 1916 in Blake, ed., *Douglas Haig* pp. 157–58.

4 Minutes of the War Committee, 5 August 1916, CAB 42/17/3.

5 Churchill, *The World Crisis*, iii, pp. 188–94.

6 Asquith to Sylvia Henley, 18 August 1916, Asquith/Henley papers, C542/4.

7 It can be found in the Asquith papers, vol. 129.

8 Minutes of the War Committee, 5 August 1916, CAB 42/17/3.

9 Parliamentary Debates, *House of Commons*, 11 October 1916, vol. 86, col. 103.

10 Paget and Tyrrell, 'Suggested Basis for a Territorial Settlement in Europe', 7 August 1916, FO CAB 42/17/4; Robertson to Lloyd George, 17 August 1916, WO 106/1510. These findings, and other similar investigations that followed, are examined and analyzed in Jaffe, *Decision to Disarm Germany*, pp. 27–35; Kenneth J. Calder, *Britain and the Origins of the New Europe, 1914–1918* (Cambridge, 1976), pp. 93–102; Rothwell, *British War Aims*, pp. 38–55; French, *British Strategy*, pp. 211ff.

11 French war aims remained undefined in the summer of 1916. See D. Stevenson, *French War Aims against Germany, 1914–1919* (Oxford, 1982), pp. 40–44.

12 Minutes of the War Committee, 30 August 1916, CAB 42/18/8.

13 Balfour, 'The Peace Settlement in Europe', 4 October 1916, CAB 37/157/7.

14 Six reconstituted Serbian divisions had joined the Anglo-French force in July. Early in August these were followed by an Italian division and a Russian brigade, bringing the total strength to 325,000 men.

15 Minutes of the War Committee, 5 September 1916, CAB 42/19/3; D. Woodward, *Lloyd George*, pp. 104–5.

16 Asquith to Sylvia Henley, 26 August 1916, Asquith/Henley papers, C542/4.

17 Asquith to Sylvia Henley, 31 August 1916, ibid., C542/4.

18 Hankey diary, 6 September 1916, Hankey papers; Asquith to Lady Scott, 13 September 1916, Kennet papers, 109/3.

19 Haig diary, 6 September 1916, Haig papers.

20 Asquith to Lady Scott, 13 September, Kennet papers, 109/3.

21 Hankey diary, 7 September 1916, Hankey papers; Roskill, *Hankey*, i, p. 297.

22 Minutes of the War Committee, 12 September 1916, CAB 42/19/6.

23 M. Bonham Carter, ed., *Autobiography of Margot Asquith*, pp. 316–17.

24 Jenkins, *Asquith*, p. 414.

25 Asquith to Sylvia Henley, 20 September 1916, Asquith/Henley papers, C542/4. Asquith wrote similarly to Lady Scott on the same day. That letter is quoted in Jenkins, *Asquith*, p. 415.

26 Koss, *Asquith*, p. 213.

27 Lloyd George to Asquith, 26 September 1916, Asquith papers, vol. 30; Hankey diary, 27 September 1916, Hankey papers; memorandum by Stamfordham, 12 October 1916, Royal Archives, GV Q1200/6; Lloyd George, *War Memoirs*, i, pp. 461–64; Grigg, *Lloyd George*, p. 389; R. Churchill, *Lord Derby*, p. 223.

28 Ministère de la Guerre, Etat-Major de l'Armeé, Service Historique. *Les armées françaises dans la Grande Guerre* (Paris, 1933), viii, annexes vol. 1, no. 522, p. 478.
29 Minutes of the War Committee, 12 October 1916, CAB 42/21/6.
30 D. Woodward, *Lloyd George*, p. 112.
31 Conference of Allied Ministers at Boulogne, 20 October 1916, CAB 28/1; Hankey diary, 20 October 1916, Hankey papers.
32 Minutes of the War Committee, 24 October 1916, CAB 42/22/5; Taylor, ed., *A Diary by Frances Stevenson*, p. 119.
33 Haig's tactics and style of command are perceptively assessed in Tim Travers, 'A Particular Style of Command: Haig and GHQ, 1916–1918', *Journal of Strategic Studies*, 10 (1987), pp. 363–76.
34 On this subject see Guy Hartcup, *The War of Invention: Scientific Developments, 1914–1918* (London, 1988).
35 Hankey to Asquith, 5 July 1916, CAB 63/6.
36 Parliamentary Debates, *House of Commons*, 18 July, vol. 84, cols 850–55.
37 Asquith to Sylvia Henley, 20 July 1916, Asquith/Henley papers, C542/3.
38 Hankey, *The Supreme Command*, ii, p. 521.
39 Hankey diary, 31 October 1916, Hankey papers.
40 Marder, *From the Dreadnought*, iii, p. 270.
41 A. Temple Patterson, ed., *The Jellicoe Papers* (London, 1968), ii, p. 89.
42 Note by Runciman, 9 November 1916, CAB 42/23/11. Appended to the Minutes of the War Committee, 9 November 1916.
43 For details of the Hindenburg programme and the Auxiliary Labour Law see Martin Kitchen, *The Silent Dictatorship: The Politics of the German High Command under Hindenburg and Ludendorff, 1916–1918* (London, 1976), ch. 3.
44 Minutes of the War Committee, 3 November 1916, CAB 42/23/4.
45 D. Woodward, *Lloyd George*, pp. 117–18.
46 French officers, profiting from their experience at Champagne and Verdun, had not followed the British example of sending slow plodding lines of heavily burdened men. Rather their troops dashed across No Man's Land and split into small loosely-spaced groups, giving each other cover as they advanced.
47 'Oc' was convinced that the Western Front could not be breached, saying that barbed-wire and a few machine guns could stop anything but tanks. See Hankey diary, 28 October 1916, Hankey papers.
48 Minutes of the War Committee, 3 November 1916, CAB 42/23/4; Hankey diary, 3 November 1916, Hankey papers.
49 Robertson to Asquith, 13 November 1916, Asquith papers, vol. 18.
50 Memorandum by Stamfordham, 10 November 1916, Royal Archives GV Q1200/17.
51 Hankey diary, 7, 9 and 10 November 1916, Hankey papers.
52 H. A. Taylor, *Robert Donald* (London, n.d.), p. 110.
53 'Statement Drafted by Mr Lloyd George as a Basis for the Prime Minister's Statement at the Paris Conference on November 15, 1916', CAB 28/1.
54 Hankey diary, 12 November 1916, Hankey papers.
55 'Copy of a Statement Read by the Prime Minister at a Conference Attended Only by Himself, Mr Lloyd George, M. Briand and Admiral Lacaze on the Morning of Wednesday, 15 November 1916', CAB 28/1.
56 Lloyd George, *War Memoirs*, i, pp. 555–56.
57 'Note by the Secretary of the War Committee on the Results of the Paris Conference, 15 and 16 November 1916', CAB 28/1; Hankey, *The Supreme Command*, ii, pp. 561–62; Lloyd George, *War Memoirs*, i, pp. 557–73; Haig diary, 15 and 16 November 1916, Haig diary.
58 Gollin, *Proconsul*, p. 353; Milner to Asquith, 1 December 1916, Asquith papers, vol. 17.
59 Marder, *From the Dreadnought*, iii, pp. 279–87.

60 Robertson, *Soldiers and Statesmen*, i, pp. 301–2; Robertson, 'Appreciation of the War Situation', 24 November 1916, CAB 37/160/15; 'Supply of Men for the Army: Memorandum by the Military Members of the Army Council to the Secretary of State for War', 28 November 1916. Appended to the Minutes of the War Committee, 30 November 1916, CAB 42/26/4.

61 Minutes of the War Committee, 21 and 30 November 1916, CAB 42/25/1, 42/26/4; Hankey diary, 30 November 1916, Hankey papers. By the time the committee completed its work, the government had ceased to exist. The next administration was worried about the political repercussions and the new policy was watered down. Although Lloyd George had encouraged the Army Council to draft a strongly-worded memorandum and had supported it enthusiastically in the War Committee on 30 November, he evidently changed his mind afer he became Prime Minister. It was not until the spring of 1918 that his government adopted compulsory national service.

62 McKenna, 'Our Financial Position in America', 18 October 1916, CAB 37/157/40.

63 Memorandum by Lansdowne, 13 November 1916, CAB 37/159/32.

64 Spender and Asquith, *The Life of Herbert Henry Asquith*, ii, pp. 241–42.

65 Robertson, 'Appreciation of the War Situation', 24 November 1916, CAB 37/160/15.

66 Minutes of the War Committee, 28 November 1916, CAB 42/26/2; Lloyd George, *War Memoirs*, i, p. 531.

67 Hankey, *The Supreme Command*, ii, p. 551.

68 Guinn, *British Politics*, p. 182.

69 Wilson, *Downfall*, pp. 37, 78–79.

70 Blake, *The Unknown Prime Minister*, pp. 298–99.

71 Hankey, *The Supreme Command*, ii, pp. 543–44.

72 Lady Scott diary, 1 November 1916, Kennet papers.

73 Hankey diary. See especially 11 May and 10 November 1916, Hankey papers.

74 Chamberlain to his wife, 26 April 1916, Chamberlain papers, AC 6/1/201.

75 John Vincent, ed., *The Crawford Papers* (Manchester, 1984), p. 356.

76 Ibid., p. 363.

Notes to Chapter 12

1 In the aftermath of the December crisis Robert Donald, editor of the *Daily Chronicle*, interviewed, among others, Asquith, Bonham Carter, Henderson, Bonar Law and Montagu (H. A. Taylor, *Robert Donald*, pp. 111–41). Bonar Law provided additional information in an unpublished account (Beaverbrook papers, G/8, fol. 12) as did Montagu (Montagu papers, AS 1/10/1). Others who gave the story from their side include Balfour (Balfour papers, Add. 49692), Lloyd George, *War Memoirs*, i, chs 34–35, Chamberlain (Chamberlain papers, AC 15/3/8) and Samuel (Samuel papers, A/56). Lord Errington (Assistant Private Secretary to George V) drew up a memorandum outlining the circumstances that led to Asquith's fall (Royal Archives, GV K1048A/2) and Crewe undertook a similar task which was published in its entirety in Asquith's *Memories*, ii, ch. 14.

2 Privy to much first-hand knowledge, Lord Beaverbrook produced the first comprehensive study in *Politicians and the War*, chs 26–41. Carson and Lloyd George were still alive when it was published and accepted it as basically accurate. Although not without flaws, it continues to dominate the field even today. Since Beaverbrook's book there have been other accounts that have challenged his interpretation of certain events or added to our knowledge of the history of this period. Among the most important are Blake, *The Unknown Prime Minister*, chs 19–21; Jenkins, *Asquith*, chs 26–27; Taylor, *Beaverbrook*, ch. 6; Wilson, *Downfall*, ch. 4 and its appendix, and *Myriad Faces*, pp. 418–23; Grigg, *Lloyd George*, ch. 17; B. Gilbert, *David Lloyd George*, ch. 10; John D. Fair, 'Politicians, Historians and the War: A Reassessment of the Political Crisis of December 1916', *Journal of Modern History*, 49 (1977) (Supplement), pp. 1329–43; J. M. McEwen, 'The Struggle for Mastery in Britain: Lloyd George versus Asquith, December 1916', *Journal of British Studies*', 18 (1978), pp. 131–56; idem, 'Lloyd George's Liberal Supporters in December 1916', *Bulletin of the Institute of Historical Research*, 53 (1980), pp. 265–72; idem, 'Lord Beaverbrook: Historian Extraordinary', *Dalhousie Review*, 59 (1979), pp. 129–43; Barry McGill, 'Asquith's Predicament, 1914–1918', *Journal of Modern History*, 39 (1967), pp. 292–97; Peter Fraser, 'Lord Beaverbrook's Fabrications in *Politicians and the War, 1914–1916*', *Historical Journal*, 25 (1982), pp. 147–66. The part the press played in the campaign to change the government is detailed in Stephen Koss, *The Rise and Fall of the Political Press in Britain* (Chapel Hill, NC, 1984), ii, pp. 298–306; J. M. McEwen, 'The Press and the Fall of Asquith', *Historical Journal*, 21 (1978), pp. 863–883; Stephen Inwood, 'The Role of the Press in English Politics during the First World War' (unpublished D.Phil. thesis, University of Oxford, 1971), ch. 13.

3 Lady Scott diary, 8 November 1916, Kennet papers.

4 Bonar Law, 'Statement on the Fall of the Government', 30 December 1916, Beaverbrook papers, G/8, fol. 12.

5 Beaverbrook, *Politicians and the War*, ch. 26; Blake, *The Unknown Prime Minister*, pp. 303–5; Bonar Law, 'Statement on the Fall of the Government', 30 December 1916, Beaverbrook papers, G/8, fol. 12.

6 Beaverbrook, *Politicians and the War*, p. 351; Bonar Law, 'Statement on the Fall of the Government', 30 December 1916, Beaverbrook papers, G/8, fol. 12.

7 McEwen, 'The Press and the Fall of Asquith', pp. 869–70.

8 The letter is published in its entirety in Blake, *The Unknown Prime Minister*, p. 307; Beaverbrook, *Politicians and the War*, pp. 355–57; Spender and Asquith, *The Life of Herbert Henry Asquith*, ii, pp. 250–51.

9 Bonar Law, 'Statement on the Fall of the Government', 30 December 1916, Beaverbrook papers, G/8, fol. 12.

10 Cecil, 'The War Situation: Need for Industrial Conscription and a Cabinet Committee on Civilian Organization', 27 November 1916, CAB 37/160/21; Crewe, 'The Break-Up of the Coalition Government', 20 December, 1916; Asquith to King George V, 30 November 1916, CAB 41/37/42; Vincent, ed., *Crawford Papers*, p. 368.

11 Asquith to Sylvia Henley, 29 November 1916, Asquith/Henley papers, C542/4.

12 Beaverbrook, *Politicians and the War*, pp. 362–77; Chamberlain to Chelmsford (Viceroy of India), 8 December 1916, Chamberlain papers, AC 15/3/8; Taylor, *Beaverbrook*, p. 112.

13 Memorandum by Lloyd George, 1 December 1916, Asquith papers, vol. 31. All the correspondence exchanged between Lloyd George and Asquith during the first week of December 1916 can be found in Lloyd George, *War Memoirs*, i; Spender and Asquith, *The Life of Herbert Henry Asquith*, ii; and Beaverbrook, *Politicians and the War*.

14 Hankey, *The Supreme Command*, ii, p. 565.

15 Asquith to Lloyd George, 1 December 1916, Asquith papers, vol. 31.

16 Hankey diary, 2 December 1916, Hankey papers.

17 Lloyd George went to see Bonar Law to report the results of his interview with the Prime Minister. The Conservative leader objected to the latest set of proposals about which he had not been consulted. He was concerned about the extent to which Asquith would be eliminated from the control of affairs and disliked the idea of being a party to an intrigue designed to force Balfour's removal from the Admiralty. Bonar Law, 'Statement on the Fall of the Government', 30 December 1916, Beaverbrook papers, G/8, fol. 12; Donald interview with Bonar Law in H. A. Taylor, *Robert Donald*, p. 115.

18 Bonar Law, 'Statement on the Fall of the Government', 30 December 1916, Beaverbrook papers, G/8, fol. 12; Beaverbrook, *Politicians and the War*, pp. 391–95.

19 How the editors of these newspapers learned of the impending changes in the government is a matter of controversy. Beaverbrook wrote that he leaked the information in order to bring the issue into the open and undermine Asquith's position. Both Fraser and McEwen have disputed Beaverbrook's contention, saying he probably shaped the story to suit his own purpose. Beaverbrook, *Politicians and the War*, pp. 396–99; Fraser, 'Lord Beaverbrook's Fabrications in Politicians and the War, 1914–1916', pp. 158–162; McEwen, 'Lord Beaverbrook: Historian Extraordinary', pp. 135–36.

20 Blake, *The Unknown Prime Minister*, pp. 314–15.

21 There is some dispute whether Balfour, who was ill, was present, but Lansdowne was in the country and unable to be at the meeting.

22 On this issue see Beaverbrook, *Politicians and the War*, pp. 413–14, 417; Chamberlain to Chelmsford, 8 December 1916, Chamberlain papers, AC 15/3/8; Bonar Law, 'Statement on the Fall of the Government', 30 December 1916, Beaverbrook papers, G/8, fol. 12; Curzon to Lansdowne, 3 December 1916, in Lord Newton, *Lord Lansdowne* (London, 1929), pp. 452–53; Vincent, ed., *Crawford Papers*, pp. 369–70.

23 McEwen, 'The Struggle for Mastery in Britain', p. 143.

24 Montagu, 'Account of the Political Crisis of December 1916', 9 December 1916, Montagu papers, AS 1/10/1; Donald interview with Montagu in H. A. Taylor, *Robert Donald*, pp. 138–39.

25 Jenkins, *Asquith*, pp. 439–40.

26 Crewe, 'The Break-Up of the Coalition Government', 20 December 1916.

27 Some Unionists had suggested at the earlier meeting that Lloyd George might be able to come to terms with Asquith by offering him a cabinet post.

28 Vincent, ed., *Crawford Papers*, p. 371.

29 Montagu, 'Account of the Political Crisis of December 1916', 9 December 1916,

Montagu papers, AS 1/10/1; Crewe, 'The Break-Up of the Coalition Government', 20 December 1916.

30 Beaverbrook, *Politicians and the War*, pp. 429–30; Blake, *The Unknown Prime Minister*, p. 326.

31 Asquith to Lloyd George, 4 December 1916, Asquith papers, vol. 31; Lord Errington, 'Memorandum on the Circumstances Relating to the Fall of Mr Asquith's Administration', December 1916, Royal Archives, GV K1048A/2.

32 Crewe to Asquith, 4 and 5 December 1916, Asquith papers, vol. 17.

33 Wilson, *Downfall*, p. 91.

34 Bonar Law, 'Statement on the Fall of the Government', 30 December 1916, Beaverbrook papers, G/8, fol. 12.

35 Marder, *From the Dreadnought*, ii, pp. 297–98; v, p. 342.

36 Ibid., ii, p. 298; Lloyd George, *War Memoirs*, i, pp. 597, 607.

37 Hankey diary, 3 December 1916, Hankey papers.

38 Lord Errington, 'Memorandum Relating to the Fall of Mr Asquith's Administration', December 1916, Royal Archives, GV K1048A/2.

39 Cited in Jenkins, *Asquith*, p. 443.

40 Asquith to Lloyd George, 4 December 1916, Asquith papers, vol. 31. Asquith used the term 'suggested arrangement' to indicate that no formal understanding had been reached. He made that point during his interview with Donald (H. A. Taylor, *Robert Donald*, pp. 119–20.) and his speech before a full party meeting at the National Liberal Club on 8 December 1916.

41 Clark, ed., *A Good Innings*, p. 161; Lloyd George to Asquith, 4 December 1916, Asquith papers, vol. 31.

42 Montagu, 'Account of the Political Crisis of December 1916', 9 December 1916, Montagu papers, AS 1/10/1.

43 Grigg, *Lloyd George*, pp. 457–58.

44 Crewe, 'The Break-Up of the Coalition Government', 20 December 1916.

45 Beaverbrook, *Politicians and the War*, p. 434.

46 Montagu, 'Account of the Political Crisis of December 1916', 9 December 1916, AS 1/10/1, Montagu papers.

47 Grigg, *Lloyd George*, p. 458.

48 Gollin, *Proconsul*, pp. 363–64; Hyde, *Carson*, p. 410; Grigg, *Lloyd George*, pp. 459–60; John Evelyn Wrench, *Geoffrey Dawson and our Times* (London, 1955), pp. 139–42; Beaverbrook, *Politicians and the War*, p. 428.

49 McEwen, 'The Press and the Fall of Asquith', pp. 880–82; *The Times*, 4 December 1916.

50 Montagu, 'Account of the Political Crisis of December 1916', 9 December 1916, Montagu papers, AS 1/10/1.

51 Wrench, *Geoffrey Dawson*, pp. 140–41; *The History of The Times* (London, 1952), iv, pt 1, p. 297.

52 Asquith to Lloyd George, 4 December 1916, Asquith papers, vol. 31.

53 Hankey diary, 4 December 1916, Hankey papers.

54 Lloyd George to Asquith, 4 December 1916, Asquith papers, vol. 31.

55 Beaverbrook, *Politicians and the War*, pp. 439–40; Addison diary, 4 December 1916, Addison papers.

56 Curzon to Asquith, 4 December 1916, Asquith papers, vol. 31; Beaverbrook, *Politicians and the War*, pp. 440–42; Newton, *Lord Lansdowne*, p. 454.

57 On 3 December 1916 Curzon, in explaining the reason behind the Unionist resolution, told Lansdowne: 'Had one felt that reconstitution by and under the present Prime Minister was possible, we should all have preferred to try it. But we know that with him as Chairman, either of the Cabinet or War Committee, it is absolutely impossible to win the War ...' Newton, *Lord Lansdowne*, p. 453. The following day Curzon pledged his

loyalty to Asquith in a letter and shortly after during an interview. Curzon to Asquith, 4 December 1916, Asquith papers vol. 31; Beaverbrook, *Politicians and the War*, pp. 442, 458; Beaverbrook to Chamberlain, 16 June 1916, Chamberlain papers, AC 15/3/41.

58 King George V diary, 4 December 1916, Royal Archives.
59 Bonar Law, 'Statement on the Fall of the Government', 30 December 1916, Beaverbrook papers, G/8, fol. 12.
60 Lloyd George, *War Memoirs*, i, p. 591; Grigg, *Lloyd George*, p. 462.
61 Samuel, 'Memorandum on Asquith's Resignation', 4 December 1916, Samuel papers, A/56; Addison diary, 4 December 1916, Addison papers.
62 Hankey diary, 4 December 1916, Hankey papers.
63 Asquith to Lloyd George, 4 December 1916, Asquith papers, vol. 31.
64 Montagu, 'Account of the Political Crisis of December 1916', 9 December 1916, Montagu papers, AS 1/10/1.
65 Bonar Law, 'Statement on the Fall of the Government', 30 December 1916, Beaverbrook papers, G/8. fol. 12.
66 Lloyd George to Asquith, 5 December 1916, Asquith papers, vol. 31.
67 Balfour to Asquith, 5 December 1916, Asquith papers, vol. 31.
68 Crewe, 'The Break-Up of the Coalition Government', 20 December 1916.
69 Montagu, 'Account of the Political Crisis of December 1916', 9 December 1916, Montagu papers, AS 1/10/1.
70 Asquith to Lloyd George, 5 December 1916, Asquith papers, vol. 31.
71 Chamberlain to Chelmsford, 8 December 1916, Chamberlain papers, AC 15/3/8; Chamberlain to Spender, 23 June 1931, ibid., AC 15/3/25; Chamberlain to Cecil, 30 June 1931, ibid., AC 15/3/31; Cecil to Chamberlain, 9 July 1931, ibid., AC 15/3/38.
72 The letter is cited in Balfour, 'Memorandum of the Government Crisis', 7 December 1914, Balfour papers, Add. 49692.
73 Samuel, 'Memorandum on Asquith's Resignation', 5 December 1916, Samuel papers, A/56.
74 Bonar Law to Asquith, 5 December 1916, Asquith papers, vol. 31.
75 Beaverbrook, *Politicians and the War*, p. 472.
76 King George V diary, 5 December 1916, Royal Archives.
77 J. H. Thomas, *My Story* (London, 1937), p. 43.
78 C. Asquith, *Diaries*, p. 242.
79 Asquith to Sylvia Henley, 6 December 1916, Asquith/Henley papers, C542/4.
80 Blake, *The Unknown Prime Minister*, pp. 334–35.
81 Bonar Law, 'Statement on the Fall of the Government', 30 December 1916, Beaverbrook papers, G/8, fol. 12.
82 Memorandum by Stamfordham, 6 December 1916, Royal Archives, GV K1048A/1; Balfour, 'Memorandum of the Government Crisis', 7 December 1916, Balfour papers, Add. 49692.
83 Murray diary, 6 December 1916, Elibank papers.
84 Crewe, 'The Break-Up of the Coalition Government', 20 December 1916; Montagu, 'Account of the Political Crisis of December 1916', 9 December 1916, Montagu papers, AS 1/10/1; Samuel, 'Memorandum on Asquith's Resignation', 6 December 1916, Samuel papers, A/56.
85 Crewe, 'The Break-Up of the Coalition Government', 20 December 1916; Montagu, 'Account of the Political Crisis of December 1916', 9 December 1916, Montagu papers, AS 1/10/1; Samuel, 'Memorandum on Asquith's Resignation', 6 December 1916, Samuel papers, A/56; Asquith, speech delivered to the Liberal Party meeting at the Reform Club, 8 December 1916. The speech can be found in any number of London dailies as well as the *Liberal Magazine*, 24 (1916).
86 Asquith to Bonar Law, 6 December 1916, Bonar Law papers, 81/1/1.
87 Taylor, ed., *A Diary by Frances Stevenson*, p. 133.

88 McEwen, 'Lloyd George's Liberal Supporters in December 1916', pp. 266–67.
89 Keith Middlemas, *Politics in Industrial Society* (London, 1979), p. 97; Wilson, *Myriad Faces*, pp. 422–23; Grigg, *Lloyd George*, pp. 478–80; Cole, *History of the Labour Party*, pp. 30–31; Wrigley, *David Lloyd George*, p. 177.
90 Beaverbrook, *Politicians and the War*, pp. 515–28.
91 Churchill, *Great Contemporaries*, p. 214; Bonar Law, 'Statement on the Fall of the Government', 30 December 1916, Beaverbrook papers, G/8, fol. 12; Balfour, 'Memorandum of the Government Crisis', 7 December 1916, Balfour papers, Add. 49692; Beaverbrook, *Politicians and the War*, pp. 502–3.
92 Blake, *The Unknown Prime Minister*, p. 340.
93 Ibid., p. 339.
94 Murray diary, 8 December 1916, Elibank papers; MacCallum diary, 8 December 1916, MacCallum papers; *Liberal Magazine*, 24 (1916), pp. 620–29.

Notes to Chapter 13

1 Asquith had not kept a journal of his daily activities so that when he compiled his material for *Memories and Reflections* he was forced to rely heavily on letters he had written to female friends, particularly Venetia Stanley. See Brocks, ed., HHA, appendix 1.

2 H. H. Asquith, 'Two Years of British Achievement', *Current History*, 5 (1917), pp. 842–46.

Bibliography

MANUSCRIPT SOURCES

Departmental Records, Public Record Office, London

Cabinet (CAB)
Foreign Office (FO)
Ministry of Munitions (MUN)
War Office (WO)

Private Collections

Addison papers, Bodleian Library, Oxford.
Asquith papers, Bodleian Library, Oxford.
Asquith/Sylvia Henley papers, Bodleian Library, Oxford.
Violet Asquith papers, private possession.
Balfour papers, British Library, London.
Beaverbrook papers, House of Lords Record Office, London.
Bertie papers, Public Record Office, London.
Bonar Law papers, House of Lords Record Office, London.
Burns papers, British Library, London.
Carnock (A. Nicolson) papers, Public Record Office, London.
Cecil papers, British Library, London.
Chamberlain papers, Birmingham University Library.
Crewe papers, Cambridge University Library.
Curzon papers, India Office Library, London.
D'Abernon papers, British Library, London.
Dawson papers, Bodleian Library, Oxford.
Derby papers, Liverpool Central Library.
Elibank papers, National Library of Scotland, Edinburgh. These consist of the correspondence of Lord Murray of Elibank and his brother, Lt-Col. A. C. Murray.
Esher papers, Churchill College, Cambridge.
Emmott papers, Nuffield College, Oxford.
Fisher papers, Churchill College, Cambridge.
Fitzgerald papers, Imperial War Museum, London.
Fitzroy papers, British Library, London.
French papers, Imperial War Museum, London.
Gainford (J. A. Pease) papers, Nuffield College, Oxford.

Gardiner papers, British Library of Political and Economic Science, London.
George V papers, Royal Achives, Windsor.
Grey papers, Public Record Office, London.
Gwynne papers, Bodleian Library, Oxford.
Haig papers, National Library of Scotland, Edinburgh.
Haldane papers, National Library of Scotland, Edinburgh.
Hankey papers, Churchill College, Cambridge.
Harcourt papers, Bodleian Library, Oxford.
Hardinge papers, Cambridge University Library.
Holt papers, Liverpool Central Library.
Kennet (Kathleen Scott) papers, Cambridge University Library.
Kitchener papers, Public Record Office, London.
Lloyd George papers, House of Lords Record Office, London.
Long papers, British Library, London.
McKenna papers, Churchill College, Cambridge.
Masterman papers, Birmingham University Library.
Maxse papers, County Record Office, Chichester.
Melville papers, House of Lords Record Office, London.
Montagu papers, Trinity College, Cambridge.
Murray papers. There are several files at the Public Record Office but the main collection is at the Imperial War Museum, London.
Reading papers, India Office Library, London.
Robertson papers, Liddell Hart Centre for Military Archives, King's College, London.
Runciman papers, University of Newcastle upon Tyne Library.
St Loe Strachey papers, House of Lords Records Office, London.
Scott papers, University College Library, Buckingham, Scotland.
Selborne papers, Bodleian Library, Oxford.
Simon papers, Bodleian Library, Oxford.
Spears papers, Liddell Hart Centre for Military Archives, King's College, London.
Spender papers, British Library, London.
Steel-Maitland papers, Scottish Record Office, Edinburgh.
Trevelyan papers, University of Newcastle upon Tyne Library.
Wilson papers, Imperial War Museum, London.
Wood papers, Bodleian Library, Oxford.

SERIAL PUBLICATIONS

Daily Chronicle   *Morning Post*
Daily Express   *Nation*
Daily Mail   *New Statesman*
Daily News   *Observer*
Daily Telegraph   *Pall Mall Gazette*
Evening Standard   *Spectator*
Globe   *The Times*
Manchester Guardian   *Westminister Gazette*

OFFICIAL PUBLICATIONS

Aspinall-Oglander, Brig.-Gen. C. F., *Military Operations: Gallipoli*, 2 vols (London, 1929–32).

Corbett, Sir Julian S., *Naval Operations*, vols i–iii (London, 1920–23).

Dardanelles Commission, *First Report* and *Final Report* (London 1917–19).

Edmonds, Brig.-Gen. Sir James E., *Military Operations: France and Belgium*, vols for 1914 to 1916 (London, 1922–38).

Falls, Cyril, *Military Operations: Macedonia*, i (London, 1933).

France, Ministère de la Guerre, Etat Major de l'Armée. Service Historique. *Les armées françaises dans la Grande Guerre*, annexes (Paris, 1924–26) for vol. 3.

Gooch, G. P., and Temperley, Harold, *British Documents on the Origins of the War, 1898–1914*, xi (London, 1926).

Great Britain, *History of the Ministry of Munitions*, i (London, 1920).

Mesopotamia Commission, *Report* (London, 1917).

Moberly, Brig.-Gen. F. J., *The Campaign in Mesopotamia, 1914–1918*, vols i–ii (London, 1923–24).

Parliamentary Debates, *House of Commons* and *House of Lords*, 1914–16.

War Office, *Statistics of the British Empire during the Great War, 1914–1920* (London, 1922).

MEMOIRS, SPEECHES AND COLLECTIONS OF DOCUMENTS

Addison, Christopher, *Four and a Half Years*, i (London, 1934).

Amery, Leo, *My Political Life*, ii (London, 1953).

Ashmead-Bartlett, E., *The Uncensored Dardanelles* (London, 1928).

Asquith, Lady Cynthia, *Diaries, 1915–1918* (London, 1968).

Asquith, Herbert, *Moments of Memory* (New York, 1938).

Asquith, Herbert Henry, *A Free Future for the World* (London, 1916).

—, *The Genesis of the War* (London, 1923).

—, *The Justice of Our Case* and *The Duty of Every Man* (London, 1914).

—, *Memories and Reflection*, 2 vols (London, 1928).

—, 'Mr Asquith's Reply to Lord French', *Living Age*, 302 (1919), pp. 65–73.

—, The War: Its Causes and Its Message (London, 1914).

—, *What Britain is Fighting For* (London, 1916).

—, 'Two Years of British Achievement', *Current History*, 5 (1917), pp. 842–46.

Beckett, Ian F. W., ed., *The Army and the Curragh Incident, 1914* (London, 1986).

Birkenhead, Earl of, *Contemporary Personalities* (London, 1924).

Blake, Robert, ed., *The Private Papers of Douglas Haig, 1914–1919* (London, 1952).

Bonham Carter, Mark, ed., *Autobiography of Margot Asquith* (London, 1962).

Bonham Carter, Lady Violet, *Winston Churchill: An Intimate Portrait* (New York, 1965).

Boyd, Francis, ed., *The Glory of Parliament* (London, 1960).

Brock, Michael and Eleanor, ed., *H. H. Asquith: Letters to Venetia Stanley* (Oxford, 1982).

Brown, Ivor, *The Ways of My World* (London, 1954).

Callwell, Maj.-Gen. Sir C. E., *Experiences of a Dug-Out, 1914–1918* (London, 1920).

Cecil of Chelwood, Viscount, *All the Way* (London, 1949).

Charteris, Brig.-Gen. John Charteris, *At GHQ* (London, 1931).

Churchill, Winston, *The World Crisis*, i–iii (New York, 1951–55).

Clark, Alan, ed., *A Good Innings: The Private Papers of Viscount Lee of Fareham* (London, 1974).

Conwell-Evans, T. P., *Foreign Policy from a Back Bench, 1904–1918* (London, 1932).

Cooper, Duff, *Old Men Forget* (London, 1953).

D'Abernon, Viscount, *An Ambassador of Peace*, ii (London, 1929).

David, Edward, ed., *Inside Asquith's Cabinet: From the Diaries of Charles Hobhouse* (New York, 1977).

Esher, Oliver Viscount, ed., *Journals and Letters of Reginald Viscount Esher*, iv (London, 1938).

Fisher, Lord, *Memories and Records* (New York, 1920).

Fitzroy, Sir Almeric, *Memoirs*, ii (New York, 1925).

French of Ypres, Viscount, *1914* (London, 1919).

Gathorne-Hardy, Robert, ed., *The Memoirs of Lady Ottoline Morrell, 1873–1915* (New York, 1964).

Gilbert, Martin, ed., *Companion* volumes (London, 1972) to *Winston S. Churchill: The Challenge of War, 1914–1916*, iii.

Grey of Fallodon, Viscount, *Twenty-Five Years*, 2 vols (New York, 1925).

Guillemard, Sir Lawrence, *Trivial Fond Records* (London, 1937).

Haldane, Richard B., *An Autobiography* (New York, 1929).

Hankey, Lord, *The Supreme Command, 1914–1918*, 2 vols (London, 1961).

Harris, Percy, *Forty Years In and Out of Parliament* (London, 1947).

Herbert, Aubrey, *Mons, Anzac and Kut* (London, 1919).

Herbert, Basil, ed. and comp., *Speeches by the Earl of Oxford and Asquith* (London, 1927).

Hewins, W. A. S., *The Apologia of an Imperialist*, ii (London, 1929).

Johnston, James, *Westminister Voices: Studies in Parliamentary Speech* (London, 1928).

Lloyd George, David, *War Memoirs*, 2 vols (London, 1938).

Lubbock, Adelaide, *People in Glass Houses* (London, 1977).

MacCarthy, Desmond, ed., *H. H. A.: Letters of the Earl of Asquith to a Friend, 1915–1922* (London, 1933).

McEwen, J. M. ed., *The Riddell Diaries, 1908–1923* (London, 1986).

Mackintosh, Sir Alexander, *Echoes of Big Ben: A Journalist's Parliamentary Diary, 1881–1940* (London, 1945).

Marder, Arthur J., *Fear God and Dreadnought: The Correspondence of Admiral of the Fleet Lord Fisher of Kilverstone*, iii (London, 1959).

Morgan, Kenneth O., *Lloyd George Family Letters* (Cardiff and London, 1973).

Morley, John Viscount, *Memorandum on Resignation, August 1914* (London, 1928).

Murray, Arthur C., *Master and Brother* (London, 1945).

Nevinson, Henry W., *Last Changes, Last Chances* (New York, 1929).

Patterson, A. Temple, ed., *The Jellicoe Papers*, ii (London, 1968).

Repington, Lt-Col. Court a Court, *The First World War, 1914–1918*, i (Boston, 1920).

Rhodes James, Robert, ed., *Memoirs of a Conservative: J. C. C. Davidson's Memoirs and Papers, 1910–1937* (New York, 1970).

Riddell, Lord, *War Diary, 1914–1918* (London, 1933).

Robertson, Field Marshal Sir William, *From Private to Field Marshal* (Boston, 1921).

—, *Soldiers and Statesmen, 1914–1918*, 2 vols (London, 1926).

Rodd, Sir James Rennell, *Social and Diplomatic Memoirs, 1902–1922* (London, 1925).

Samuel, Viscount Herbert, *Memoirs* (London, 1945).

Seymour, Charles, ed., *The Intimate Papers of Colonel House*, ii (Boston, 1926).

Simon, Viscount, *Retrospect* (London, 1952).

Spender, J. A., *Life, Journalism and Politics*, ii (London, 1927).

Taylor, A. J. P., ed., *Lloyd George: A Diary by Francis Stevenson* (New York, 1971).

Thomas, J. H., *My Story* (London, 1937).

Vincent, John, ed., *The Crawford Papers* (Manchester, 1984).

Wilson, Trevor, ed., *The Political Diaries of C. P. Scott, 1911–1928* (Ithaca, NY, 1970).

SECONDARY SOURCES

Adams, R. J. Q., *Arms and the Wizard: Lloyd George and the Ministry of Munitions, 1915–1916* (College Station, TX, 1978).
Adams, R. J. Q., and Poirier, Philip, P., *The Conscription Controversy in Great Britain, 1900–1918* (London, 1987).
Arthur, Sir George, *Life of Lord Kitchener*, iii (London, 1920).
Barker, A. J., *The Neglected War: Mesopotamia 1914–1918* (London, 1967).
Beaverbrook, Lord, *Politicians and the War, 1914–1916* (London, 1960).
Bell, G. K. A., *Randall Davidson: Archbishop of Canterbury*, ii (London, 1935).
Bennet, Daphne, *Margot* (London, 1984).
Blake, Robert, *The Unknown Prime Minister: The Life And Times of Andrew Bonar Law* (London, 1955).
Bolitho, Hector, *Alfred Mond, First Lord Melchett* (London, 1933).
Bonham-Carter, Victor, *Soldier True* (London, 1963).
Bosworth, R. J. B., *Italy and the Approach of the First World War* (London, 1983).
Bourne, J. M., *Britain and the Great War, 1914–1918* (London, 1989).
Burk, Kathleen, *Britain, America and the Sinews of War, 1914–1918* (London, 1985).
Calder, Kenneth J., *Britain and the Origins of the New Europe, 1914–1918* (Cambridge, 1976).
Cassar, George H., *The French and the Dardanelles: A Study of Failure in the Conduct of War* (London, 1971).
—, *Kitchener: Architect of Victory* (London, 1977).
—, *The Tragedy of Sir John French*, (Cranbury, NJ, 1985).
Churchill, Randolph S., *Churchill: Young Statesman, 1901–1914*, ii (London, 1967).
—, *Lord Derby: 'King Of Lancashire'* (London, 1959).
Churchill, Winston S., *Great Contemporaries* (Freeport, NY, 1971).
Cole, G. D. H., *A History of the Labour Party from 1914* (London, 1948).
—, *Labour in War Time* (London, 1915).
Crampton, R. J., *The Hollow Detente: Anglo-German Relations in the Balkans, 1911–1914* (London, 1979).
Crow, Duncan, *A Man of Push and Go: The Life of George Macaulay Booth* (London, 1965).
Dangerfield, George, *The Damnable Question: A Study in Anglo-Irish Relations* (Boston, 1976).
De Rosa, Peter, *Rebels: The Irish Rising of 1916* (London, 1990).
Devlin, Patrick, *Too Proud to Fight: Woodrow Wilson's Neutrality* (New York, 1975).
D'Ombrain, Nicholas J., *War Machinery and High Policy* (London, 1973).
Eade, Charles, ed., *Churchill: By His Contemporaries* (London, 1953).
Egerton, George W., *Great Britain and the Creation of the League of Nations* (Chapel Hill, NC, 1978).
Ehrman, John, *Cabinet Government and War, 1890–1940* (London, 1958).
Fergusson, Sir James, *The Curragh Incident* (London, 1964).
FitzHerbert, Margaret, *The Man who was Greenmantle: A Biography of Aubrey Herbert* (London, 1983).
French, David, *British Economic and Strategic Planning, 1905–1915* (London, 1982).
—, *British Strategy and War Aims, 1914–1916* (London, 1986).
Friedman, Isaiah, *The Question of Palestine, 1914–1918* (New York, 1973).
Fromkin, David, *A Peace to End All Peace* (New York, 1989).
Fry, Michael G., *Lloyd George and Foreign Policy*, i (Montreal, 1977).
Gardiner, A. G., *The Pillars of Society* (London, 1916).
—, *Prophets, Priests and Kings* (London, 1914).

Gilbert, Bentley B., *David Lloyd George: The Organizer of Victory, 1912–16* (London, 1990).
Gilbert, Martin, *Winston S. Churchill: The Challenge of War, 1914–1916*, iii (Boston, 1971).
Gollin, A. M., *The Impact of Air Power on the British People and their Government, 1909–1914* (Stanford, CA, 1989).
—, *No Longer an Island, Britain and the Wright Brothers, 1902–1909* (Stanford, CA, 1984).
—, *Proconsul in Politics* (New York, 1964).
Gooch, John, *The Plans of War* (New York, 1974).
Gordon, Donald C., *The Dominion Partnership in Imperial Defense, 1870–1914* (Baltimore, MD, 1965).
Grieves, Keith, *The Politics of Manpower, 1914–1918* (New York, 1988).
Grigg, John, *Lloyd George: From Peace to War, 1912–1916* (London, 1985).
Guinn, Paul, *British Strategy and Politics, 1914 to 1918* (Oxford, 1965).
Gwynn, Denis, *The Life of John Redmond* (London, 1932).
Halpern, Paul G., *The Mediterranean Naval Situation, 1908–1914* (Cambridge, MA, 1971).
—, *The Naval War in the Mediterranean, 1914–1918* (Annapolis, MD, 1987).
Hamilton, Ian B., *The Happy Warrior* (London, 1966).
Hamilton, K. A., *Bertie of Thame: Edwardian Ambassador* (London, 1990).
Hammond, J. L., *C. P. Scott of the Manchester Guardian* (London, 1934).
Hartcup, Guy, *The War of Invention: Scientific Developments, 1914–1918* (London, 1988).
Hayes, Denis, *Conscription Conflict* (London, 1949).
Hazlehurst, Cameron, *Politicians at War* (New York, 1971).
Hill, Sir Norman, *War and Insurance* (London, 1927).
Hough, Richard, *First Sea Lord: An Authorized Biography of Admiral Lord Fisher* (London, 1969).
Howard, Michael, *The Continental Commitment* (London, 1972).
Hurwitz, Samuel, *State Intervention in Great Britain* (New York, 1949).
Hyde, H. Montgomery, *Carson* (London, 1953).
Inwood, Stephen, 'The Role of the Press in English Politics during the First World War' (unpublished D.Phil. thesis, University of Oxford, 1971).
Jaffe, Lorna S., *The Decision to Disarm Germany* (Boston, 1985).
Jenkins, Roy, *Asquith* (London, 1978).
Johnson, Franklyn A., *Defence by Committee* (London, 1960).
Joll, James, *The Origins of the First World War* (London, 1984).
Jordan, Gerald H., 'The Politics of Conscription, 1905–1916' (unpublished Ph.D. thesis, University of California, Irvine, 1974).
Kennedy, Thomas C., *The Hound of Conscience: A History of the No-Conscription Fellowship, 1914–1919* (Fayetteville, AR, 1981).
Kitchen, Martin, *The Silent Dictatorship: The Politics of the Germand High Command under Hindenburg and Ludendorff* (London, 1976).
Koss, Stephen E., *Asquith* (London, 1976).
—, *Lord Haldane* (New York, 1969).
—, *The Rise and Fall of the Political Press in Britain*, ii (Chapel Hill, NC, 1984).
Laffin, John, *Damn the Dardanelles* (London, 1980).
Leon, George B., *Greece and the Great Powers, 1914–1917* (Thessaloniki, 1974).
Link, Arthur S., *Wilson: Confusion and Crises, 1915–1916* (Princeton, 1964).
—, *Wilson: The Struggle for Neutrality, 1914–1915* (Princeton, 1960).
Louis, W. Roger, *Great Britain and Germany's Lost Colonies, 1914–1919* (Oxford, 1967).
Mackay, Ruddock F., *Fisher of Kilverstone* (London, 1973).
McKenna, Stephen, *Reginald McKenna, 1863–1943* (London, 1948).
Marder, Arthur J., *From the Dreadnought to Scapa Flow*, 5 vols (London, 1961–70).
Marwick, Arthur, *The Deluge: British Society and the First World War* (Boston, 1965).
Masterman, Lucy, *C. F. G. Masterman* (London, 1968).
Maurice, Sir Frederick, *Haldane*, i (Westport, CT, 1970).

Middlemas, Keith, *Politics in Industrial Society* (London, 1979).

Morris, A. J. A., *Radicalism against War, 1906–1914* (Totowa, NJ, 1972).

Neilson, Keith, *Strategy and Supply: The Anglo-Russian Alliance, 1914–1917* (London, 1984).

Nevakivi, Jukka, *Britain, France and the Arab Middle East, 1914–1920* (London, 1969).

Newton, Lord, *Lord Lansdowne* (London, 1929).

Pound, Reginald, and Harmsworth, Geoffrey, *Northcliffe* (London, 1959).

Pratt, Edwin A., *British Railways and the Great War*, i (London, 1921).

Preston, Richard A., *Canada and 'Imperial Defense'* (Durham, NC, 1967).

Rae, John, *Conscience and Politics* (London, 1970).

Renzi, W. A., *In the Shadow of the Sword: Italy's Neutrality and Entrance into the Great War, 1914–1915* (New York, 1987).

Rhodes James, Robert, *Gallipoli* (London, 1965).

Robbins, Keith, *Sir Edward Grey* (London, 1971).

Roskill, Stephen, *Hankey: Man of Secrets*, i (London, 1970).

Rothwell, V. H., *British War Aims and Peace Diplomacy, 1914–1918* (Oxford, 1971).

Rowland, Peter, *David Lloyd George* (New York, 1976).

Ryan, A. P., *Mutiny at the Curragh* (London, 1956).

Searle, G. R., *The Quest for National Efficiency* (Berkeley and Los Angeles, 1971).

Simkins, Peter, *Kitchener's Army* (Manchester, 1988).

Spender, J. A., and Asquith, Cyril, *Life of Herbert Henry Asquith, Lord Oxford and Asquith*, 2 vols (London, 1932).

Spiers, Edward M., *Haldane: An Army Reformer* (Edinburgh, 1980).

Steiner, Zara, *Britain and the Origins of the First World War* (New York, 1977).

Stevenson, D., *French War Aims against Germany, 1914–1919* (Oxford, 1982).

Sumida, Jon T., *In Defence of Naval Supremacy: Finance, Technology and British Naval Policy, 1889–1914* (Boston, 1989).

Swartz, Marvin, *The Union of Democratic Control in British Politics during the First World War* (Oxford, 1971).

Tanenbaum, Jan K., *General Maurice Sarrail, 1856–1929* (Chapel Hill, NC, 1974).

Taylor, A. J. P., *Beaverbrook* (New York, 1972).

—, *Politics in Wartime* (New York, 1965).

Taylor, H. A., *Robert Donald* (London, n.d.).

The Times, *The History of The Times*, iv (London, 1952).

Trevelyan, G. M., *Grey of Fallodon* (Boston, 1937).

Turner, John, *British Politics and the Great War* (New Haven, CT, 1992).

Wasserstein, Bernard, *Herbert Samuel: A Political Life* (Oxford, 1992).

Williamson, Samuel R., *The Politics of Grand Strategy: Britain and France Prepare for War, 1904–1914* (Cambridge, MA, 1969).

Wilson, Sir Arnold T., *Loyalties: Mesopotamia, 1914–1917*, i (London, 1930).

Wilson, K. M., *The Policy of The Entente: Essays on the Determinants of British Foreign Policy, 1904–1914* (Cambridge, 1985).

Wilson, Trevor, *The Downfall of the Liberal Party, 1914–1935* (London, 1966).

—, *The Myriad Faces of War: Britain and the Great War, 1914–1918* (Cambridge, 1986).

Winter, Denis, *Haig's Command: A Reassessment* (New York, 1991).

Woodward, David R., *Lloyd George and the Generals* (Newark, NJ, 1983).

Woodward, Sir Llewellyn, *Great Britain and the War of 1914–1918* (London, 1967).

Wrench, John Evelyn, *Geoffrey Dawson and Our Times* (London, 1955).

Wrigley, Chris, *David Lloyd George and the British Labour Movement* (New York, 1976).

Ziegler, Philip, *Diana Cooper* (London, 1980).

ARTICLES

Adams, R. J. Q., 'Asquith's Choice: The May Coalition and the Coming of Conscription, 1915–1916', *Journal of British Studies*, 25 (1986), pp. 243–63.

Brailsford, H. N., 'The Last of the English Liberals', *Foreign Affairs*, 11 (1932–33), pp. 633–44.

Cohen, S. A., 'The Genesis of the British Campaign in Mesopotamia, 1914', *Middle Eastern Studies*, 12 (1976), pp. 119–32.

Coogan, John W. and Peter F., 'The British Cabinet and the Anglo-French Staff Talks, 1904–1914: Who Knew What and When Did He Know It?', *Journal of British Studies*, 24 (1985), pp. 110–31.

Cregier, Don M., 'The Last English Whig: Herbert Henry, Lord Oxford and Asquith', *Duquesne Review*, 11 (1966), pp. 1–14.

D'Ombrain, Nicholas J. 'The Imperial General Staff and the Military Policy of a "Continental Strategy" during the 1911 International Crisis', *Military Affairs*, 33–34 (1969–70), pp. 88–92.

Dutton, D. J. 'The Balkan Campaign and French War Aims in the Great War', *English Historical Review*, 94 (1979), pp. 97–114.

—, 'The Calais Conference of December 1915', *Historical Journal*, 21 (1978), pp. 143–56.

Ekstein, Michael, 'Russia, Constantinople and the Straits', in F. H. Hinsley, ed., *British Foreign Policy under Sir Edward Grey* (Cambridge, 1977).

—, 'Sir Edward Grey and Imperial Germany in 1914', *Journal of Contemporary History*, 6 (1971), pp. 121–31.

—, 'Some Notes on Sir Edward Grey's Policy in July 1914', *Historical Journal*, 15 (1972), pp. 321–24.

Ekstein, Michael, and Steiner, Zara, 'The Sarajevo Crisis', in F. H. Hinsley, ed., *British Foreign Policy under Sir Edward Grey* (Cambridge, 1977).

Fair, John D., 'Politicians, Historians and the War: A Reassessment of the Political Crisis of December 1916', *Journal of Modern History*, 49 (1977) (Supplement), pp. 1329–43.

Fraser, Peter, 'British War Policy and the Crisis of Liberalism in May 1915', *Journal of Modern History*, 52 (1982), pp. 1–22.

—, 'Lord Beaverbrook's Fabrications in *Politicians and the War*, 1914–1916', *Historical Journal*, 25 (1982), pp. 147–66.

French, David, 'The Military Background to the "Shells Crisis" of May 1915', *Journal of Strategic Studies*, 2 (1979), pp. 192–205.

—, 'The Meaning of Attrition, 1914–1916', *English Historical Review*, 103 (1988), pp. 385–405.

—, 'The Origins of the Dardanelles Campaign Reconsidered', *History*, 68 (1983), pp. 210–24.

—, 'The Rise and Fall of "Business as Usual"', in Kathleen Burk, *War and the State* (London, 1982).

Galbraith, John S., 'No Man's Child: The Campaign in Mesopotamia, 1914–1916', *International History Review*, 6 (1984), pp. 358–85.

Gardiner, A. G., 'Asquith', *Nineteenth Century*, 112 (1932), pp. 608–20.

—, 'Mr Asquith', *Spectator*, 149 (1932), pp. 527–28.

Gilbert, Bentley B., 'David Lloyd George and the Great Marconi Scandal', *Historical Research*, 62 (1989), pp. 395–417.

—, 'Pacifist to Interventionist: David Lloyd George in 1911 and 1914. Was Belgium an Issue?', *Historical Journal*, 28 (1985), pp. 863–85.

Gooch, John, 'The War Office and the Curragh Incident', *Bulletin of the Institute of Historical Research*, 46 (1973), pp. 202–7.

Goold, Douglas. 'Lord Hardinge and the Mesopotamia Expedition and Inquiry, 1914–1917', *Historical Journal*, 19 (1976), pp. 919–45.

Grant, Sheila Sokolov, 'The Origins of the War Book', *Journal of the Royal United Service Institute*, 117 (1972), pp. 65–69.

Haggie, P. 'The Royal Navy and War Planning in the Fisher Era', in Paul M. Kennedy, ed., *The War Plans of the Great Powers, 1880–1914* (London, 1979).

Hamilton, K. A., 'Great Britain and France, 1905–1911', in F. H. Hinsley, *British Foreign Policy under Sir Edward Grey* (Cambridge, 1977).

—, 'Great Britain and France, 1911–1914', in F. H. Hinsley, *British Foreign Policy under Sir Edward Grey* (Cambridge, 1977).

Hazlehurst, Cameron, 'Asquith as Prime Minister, 1908–1916', *English Historical Review*, 85 (1970), pp. 502–31.

Lammers, David, 'Arno Mayer and the British Decision for War, 1914', *Journal of British Studies*, 11–13 (1971–73), pp. 137–65.

Lowe, C. J., 'Britain and Italian Intervention, 1914–1915', *Historical Journal*, 12 (1969), pp. 533–48.

—, 'The Failure of British Diplomacy in the Balkans, 1914–1916', *Canadian Journal of History*, 4 (1969), pp. 71–100.

McEwen, J. M., 'Lloyd George's Liberal Supporters in December 1916', *Bulletin of the Institute of Historical Research*, 53 (1980), pp. 265–72.

—, 'The Press and the Fall of Asquith', *Historical Journal*, 21 (1978), pp. 863–83.

—, 'The Struggle for Mastery in Britain: Lloyd George versus Asquith, December 1916', *Journal of British Studies*, 18 (1978), pp. 131–56.

—, 'Lord Beaverbrook: Historian Extraordinary', *Dalhousie Review*, 59 (1979), pp. 129–43.

McGill, Barry, 'Asquith's Predicament, 1914–1918', *Journal of Modern History*, 39 (1967), pp. 283–303.

Mackintosh, John P., 'The Role of the Committee of Imperial Defence before 1914', *English Historical Review*, 77 (1962), pp. 490–503.

Neilson, Keith, 'Kitchener: A Reputation Refurbished?', *Canadian Journal of History*, 15 (1980), pp. 207–27.

Nevakivi, Jukka, 'Lord Kitchener and the Partition of the Ottoman Empire, 1915–1916', in K. Bourne and D. C. Watt, eds, *Studies in International History* (London, 1967).

Paget, Gregory, 'The November 1914 Straits Agreement and the Dardanelles-Gallipoli Campaign', *Australian Journal of Politics and History*, 33 (1987), pp. 253–60.

Prete, Roy A., 'French Strategic Planning and the Deployment of the BEF in France in 1914', *Canadian Journal of History*, 24 (1989), pp. 42–62.

Pugh, Martin D., 'Asquith, Bonar Law and the First Coalition', *Historical Journal*, 17 (1974), pp. 813–36.

Renzi, W. A., 'Great Britain, Russia and the Straits', *Journal of Modern History*, 42 (1970), pp. 1–20.

Robbins, Keith, 'British Diplomacy and Bulgaria, 1914–1915', *Slavonic and East European Studies Review*, 49 (1971), pp. 560–85.

Smith, C. Jay, 'Great Britain and the 1914–1915 Straits Agreement with Russia: The British Promise of November 1914', *American Historical Review*, 70 (1965), pp. 1015–34.

Spender, J. A., 'Lord Oxford and Asquith', *Contemporary Review*, 130 (1926), pp. 681–89.

Steed, H. Wickham, 'Asquith's Place in History', *Current History*, 28 (1928), pp. 42–46.

Steiner, Zara, 'The Foreign Office at War', in F. H. Hinsley, ed., *British Foreign Policy under Sir Edward Grey* (Cambridge, 1977).

Torrey, G. E., 'Rumania and the Belligerents 1914–1916', *Journal of Contemporary History*, 1 (1966), pp. 171–91.

—, 'The Rumanian Campaign of 1916: Its Impact on the Belligerents', *Slavic Review*, 39 (1980), pp. 27–43.

Weinroth, H. S., 'The British Radicals and the Balance of Power, 1902–1914', *Historical Journal*, 13 (1970), pp. 653–79.

Wilson, K. M., 'The British Cabinet's Decision for War, 2 August 1914', *British Journal of International Studies*, 1 (1975), pp. 148–59.

—, 'Grey', in K. M. Wilson, ed., *British Foreign Secretaries and Foreign Policy: From Crimean War to First World War* (London, 1987).

—, 'To the Western Front: British War Plans and the "Military Entente" with France before the First World War', *British Journal of International Studies*, 3 (1977), pp. 151–68.

Wilson, Trevor, 'Britain's 'Moral Commitment' to France in August 1914', *History*, 64 (1979), pp. 380–90.

Wrigley, Chris, 'The First World and State Intervention in Industrial Relations, 1914–1918', in Chris Wrigley, ed., *A History of British Industrial Relations*, 1914–1939 (Brighton, 1987).

—, 'The Ministry of Munitions: An Innovatory Department', in Kathleen Burk, ed., *War and the State* (London, 1982).

Index

(plate numbers in bold)